Gallipoli

Gallipoli
A ridge too far

EDITED BY ASHLEY EKINS

EXISLE
PUBLISHING

First published 2013
This paperback edition published 2015

Exisle Publishing Limited,
'Moonrising', 230 Narone Creek Road,
Wollombi, NSW 2325, Australia.
P.O. Box 60-490, Titirangi,
Auckland 0642, New Zealand.
www.exislepublishing.com

A CiP record for this book is available from the National Library of Australia

ISBN 978-1-921966-93-4

10 9 8 7 6 5 4 3 2 1

Text design and production by IslandBridge
Cover design by Christabella Designs
Printed in Shenzhen, China, by Ink Asia
This book uses paper sourced under ISO 14001 guidelines from
well-managed forests and other controlled sources.

Contents

Part 3 : Enemies and allies

Part 4 : Legacies

Gallipoli remains contested ground. 'No single military campaign of modern times has been the subject of such intense and prolonged attention and controversy as the Gallipoli Campaign of 1915,' observed British historian Robert Rhodes James. While writing his classic history, *Gallipoli*, first published in 1965, James found that many of the political, military and historical disputes generated by the campaign still continued to 'rumble sulphurously' half a century later.[1] As the centenary of the events of 1915 now approaches, interest in Gallipoli seems undiminished. Although the passionate invective of the earlier disputes has largely dissipated, controversy and debate continues over the campaign's origins and its strategic basis, its tactical shortcomings and outcomes, the supposed lost opportunities, and the responsibility for failure.

Criticism of the political and military mismanagement of the campaign first erupted in the British parliament in mid-1915 as allied operations stalled on the peninsula. By July 1916, six months after the evacuation from Gallipoli, the British government succumbed to pressure and announced an official commission of inquiry. Over the following twelve months, the Dardanelles Special Commission received evidence from some 200 witnesses, many of whom testified to the confused strategic planning, chaotic administrative arrangements, inadequate logistics support and bungled operations that had led to the futile expenditure of tens of thousands of lives. The commission's final report was not published until after the war; the evidence was to remain classified and closed to historians for decades.[2] Although the report avoided directly attributing blame to individuals or criticising the actual conduct of operations, its findings contained the restrained conclusion that: 'from the outset the risks of failure [of] the expedition outweighed its chances of success.'[3]

Over time, however, a romantic nostalgia pervaded the memory of the Gallipoli campaign. Many refused to accept the pragmatic verdict that it had been disastrously conceived and offered no realistic shortcut to victory. Proponents would claim that, with its failure, many larger opportunities had been lost. Typical was the conclusion of Australian war correspondent and author of an influential, popular history of the campaign, Alan Moorehead, who claimed Gallipoli was 'the most imaginative conception of the war and its potentialities were almost beyond reckoning.' The campaign had been vindicated by many former commanders, he believed, and 'although there was general criticism of the tactics, no serious student now questioned the wisdom of the Allies going to the Dardanelles.' To supporters, the campaign offered a viable alternative strategy to the trench warfare deadlock and terrible slaughter on the Western Front. It could have succeeded in defeating Turkey and drawing the neutral Balkan states into the war on the allied side to assist an allied advance on Austria-Hungary. An allied victory in the Dardanelles would also have opened a warm-water sea route to Russia to allow Britain to supply its decaying Entente partner with munitions and matériel and to transport Russian grain shipments to Britain. Some even claimed that this in turn may have averted the collapse of the Russian armies in 1917 and forestalled the Bolshevik Revolution.[4]

Later assessments, based on extensive research into the now available records, are more sober in their conclusions. Historians such as Robin Prior, for example, have argued that the Gallipoli campaign actually 'had no influence on the course of the war as a whole'. Even if the expedition had been successful, he concludes, 'it is doubtful if the war would have been shortened by a single day'. Notwithstanding the bravery of allied troops who fought on the peninsula, 'the campaign was fought in vain'. There is no evidence to suggest that Turkey would have surrendered under the pressure of a naval attack on Constantinople; an assault on Austria-Hungary from the south had little chance of success, with or without the unlikely assistance of the fractious Balkan states; Britain was proving unable to supply sufficient munitions to its own armies in the field in 1915 and could not have produced a surplus of arms and ammunition to send to Russia; in fact, Britain had neither the shipping nor the war matériel to assist Russia until at least 1917. In any event, the unavoidable reality was that the German army would still have to be defeated in northern France and Belgium before the war could possibly end.[5]

Given such widely diverging views over the significance and impact of the campaign, it seems hardly surprising that Gallipoli remains the subject of intense debate and scrutiny. Attention has generally focused on the overall strategy, the amphibious landings and the protracted occupation of the peninsula. Often overlooked are the largest and most sustained battles of the entire campaign, those of the August offensive that became the pivotal turning point of the struggle.

In early August 1915, after three long months of stalemate in the Gallipoli trenches, British, Australian, New Zealand and Indian troops launched a series of assaults in an all-out attempt to break the deadlock on the peninsula and force a decisive victory. The August offensive resulted in heartbreaking failure and costly losses on both sides. Many of the sites of the bloody struggle, places such as Lone Pine (Turkish: *Kanlisirt* or 'Bloody Ridge'), the Nek (*Cesaret Tepe* or 'Hill of Valour'), Chunuk Bair, Hill 60, Scimitar Hill and Suvla Bay, became sadly familiar names in Britain, Australia, New Zealand and Turkey.

Debate has continued to the present day over the strategy and planning of the August offensive, the conduct of its multiple operations, the real or illusory opportunities for success, and the causes of failure in what became the last throw of the dice for the allies. Some argue that these costly attacks were a lost opportunity; others maintain that the outcomes were simply inevitable. Many questions remain about the tactics employed, the capabilities, leadership and actions of allied commanders, the supporting role of allies, and the responses of Turkish commanders and troops. Among the many issues that compounded allied difficulties in the battles of August were the problems of supplying and maintaining forces through their long lines of communication, the limitations of available technology and weapons systems, and the use of combined arms.

In this volume, historians from Britain, Germany, Turkey, France, India, New Zealand and Australia, many of them renowned specialists in their fields, bring renewed multinational perspectives to these and related intriguing questions. They also explore the memory and enduring impact of Gallipoli. Each of the contributors originally presented their chapters at the international conference, *Gallipoli: a ridge too far*, convened at the Australian War Memorial in August 2010 to mark the 95th anniversary of the August offensive. It was a tremendous pleasure to welcome so many fine historians to the Memorial, and I thank them all for their generous participation in that outstandingly successful event and for kindly providing their chapters for this work.

Many people collaborated and assisted in the production of this book. A number of Australian War Memorial staff contributed their skills and energy. I thank my Military History Section colleagues, particularly editors Dr Robert Nichols and Andrew McDonald, who meticulously edited the diverse collection of papers to the highest standards. I also acknowledge Aaron Pegram and John Lafferty who assisted with photographs, and Ron Schroer who ably administered the publication arrangements. The Memorial's Multimedia team expertly produced the fine quality images to the publisher's specifications. Cartographers Keith Mitchell, Winifred Mumford and Sharon France provided the excellent maps; and Diane Lowther compiled the index.

I thank publisher Ian Watt and the team at Exisle Publishing for once again producing a high standard publication that the Australian War Memorial is proud to sponsor. The Australian War Memorial provided most of the photographs in the book, but I also thank the Alexander Turnbull Library in Wellington, New Zealand, for photographs. Every effort has been made to locate current holders of copyright for text and illustrations reproduced here, but we apologise for any omissions and would welcome information to enable amendments to be made to future editions.

I especially thank Steve Gower, former Director of the Australian War Memorial, for his constant support and encouragement of military history studies in the Memorial and for his efforts in striving to maintain the

Memorial's pre-eminence as one of the finest research facilities in the world. I must also gratefully acknowledge the support of the Australian Government's Department of Veterans' Affairs in sponsoring the Memorial's annual history conferences that serve to foster research and disseminate wider understanding of the service and sacrifice of Australians in conflicts.

Finally, I thank my partner Dr Debbie Lackerstein, whose unfailing support, patience and humour have been invaluable in helping me to complete this publication, as with so many others. My debt to her is immeasurable.

Ashley Ekins
Australian War Memorial
October 2012

Robin Prior is Visiting Professorial Fellow at the University of Adelaide. He was inaugural Head of the School of Humanities and Social Sciences at the University of New South Wales, Australian Defence Force Academy, where he taught for 22 years. A world authority on the history of the First World War, he specialises in the study of military operations, command, and technology. He is the author of numerous books and articles, including *Churchill's 'World Crisis' as History*, and (with Trevor Wilson), *Command on the Western Front: The Military Career of General Sir Henry Rawlinson 1914-1918* (1992), *Passchendaele: The Untold Story* (1996), *The First World War* (1999) and *The Somme* (2005). He is also a co-editor and contributor to *The Oxford Companion to Australian Military History* (1995, 2008) and has published chapters in numerous other books, including Hugh Cecil and Peter Liddle (eds), *Facing Armageddon: The First World War Experienced* (1996), journal articles, and entries in *The Oxford Illustrated History of the First World War*, the *Encyclopaedia of 20th Century Europe*, the new *Dictionary of National Biography*, and the *Encyclopaedia of Twentieth Century Britain*. Robin's most recent book is his acclaimed *Gallipoli: The End of the Myth* (published by Yale University Press and University of New South Wales Press, 2009). He is currently completing a book on Britain and the Second World War, titled *1940: The Year Britain Saved the West* (forthcoming, Yale University Press), as well as a book on the fighting on D-Day and in the Normandy campaign.

Stephen Badsey is Professor in Conflict Studies at the University of Wolverhampton, UK. Educated at Cambridge University, he has previously held positions at the Imperial War Museum, the BBC in London, and the Royal Military Academy Sandhurst. He is also an honorary Fellow of the Centre for War Studies at Birmingham University and a Senior Research Associate of the Centre for Defence Studies at King's College, London University. An internationally regarded specialist on the history of military–media issues and on military doctrine, he has written or contributed to over 80 books and articles on military matters, including several on the First World War and on amphibious warfare. These include *The Gulf War Assessed* (with John Pimlott, 1992), *The Crimean War: The War Correspondents* (with Andrew Lambert, 1994), and *The Media and International Security* (2000). Among his most recent books are *Doctrine and Reform in the British Cavalry*

1880–1918 (2008) and *The British Army in Battle and Its Image 1914–18* (2009); and he was also a contributor to *1918: Year of Victory* (edited by Ashley Ekins, 2010). He appears and advises frequently as a historian for television and other media. Further information may be found on his website: www.stephenbadsey.com.

Ashley Ekins is Head of the Military History Section at the Australian War Memorial. A graduate of the University of Adelaide, he specialises in the history of the First World War and the Vietnam War. He wrote the final two volumes of the Official History of Australian Involvement in Southeast Asian Conflicts 1948–1975, covering Australian Army ground operations in Vietnam: *On the Offensive: The Australian Army in the Vietnam War, 1967–1968* (co-authored with Ian McNeill, 2003), and *Fighting to the Finish: The Australian Army and the Vietnam War, 1968–1975* (2012). He has published widely on the role of Australian soldiers in the First World War and contributed chapters to a number of books. His most recent books include *1918 Year of Victory: The end of the Great War and the shaping of history* (edited, 2010); and *War Wounds: Medicine and the trauma of conflict* (co-edited with Elizabeth Stewart, 2011). He also compiled and wrote an introduction to the Memorial's third edition of *The Anzac Book* (2010). He has led the Memorial's annual battlefield tours to Gallipoli as historical guide and studied the Gallipoli campaign extensively, visiting Gallipoli on over twenty occasions to explore the battlefields with Turkish, Australian and British historians. He researched and wrote the popular pocket *Guide to the battlefields, cemeteries and memorials of the Gallipoli peninsula* (fifth revised edition, 2012).

Peter Burness is a senior historian at the Australian War Memorial where he has worked since 1973. Formerly Head of the Military Heraldry and Technology Section and a senior curator in the Exhibitions Section, he has been involved in numerous travelling, temporary, and permanent exhibitions. He has a special interest in the First World War and for almost 20 years has led the Memorial's annual battlefield tours to the Western Front. Peter has published numerous articles on Australians in the Great War, the colonial period and other conflicts, as well as entries for the *Oxford Companion to Australian History*, *The Oxford Companion to Australian Military History*, and more than 20 entries to the *Australian Dictionary of Biography*. More recently he wrote four of the volumes of the Department of Veterans' Affairs *Australians on the Western Front* series and writes regularly for the Memorial's journal *Wartime*. Peter is also the author of the *The Nek: the tragic charge of the Light Horse at Gallipoli* (1996, second revised edition 2012). He was curator of a series of First World War 90th anniversary exhibitions, and concept leader for *Over the Front: the Great War in the air*, and historical and curatorial adviser for the redevelopment of the Memorial's Hall of Valour. He is currently engaged in a range of projects culminating in the First World War centenary as Lambert Gallipoli Fellow.

Peter Pedersen is Head of the Research Centre at the Australian War Memorial. He has written eight books on the First World War and contributions to several others, as well as numerous articles on campaigns from the Second World War, the Vietnam War, and battlefields and military and aviation museums worldwide. He has guided many tours to the Western Front and other battlefields in Europe and Asia, which included leading and organising the first British tour to Dien Bien Phu in Vietnam. A graduate of the Royal Military College, Duntroon, the Australian Command and Staff College, and the University of New South Wales, he commanded the 5th/7th Battalion, the Royal Australian Regiment, and was a political/strategic analyst in the Australian Office of National Assessments. Peter's publications include *Monash as Military Commander* (1985), *Images of Gallipoli* (1988), *Hamel* (2003), *Fromelles* (2004), *Villers-Bretonneux* (2004), *The Anzacs: Gallipoli to the Western Front* (Penguin, 2007; paperback edition, 2010) and *Anzacs at War* (2010). His latest book is *Anzacs on the Western Front: The Australian War Memorial Battlefield Guide* (Wiley, 2012). He is currently writing a book on the Memorial's Gallipoli collections for publication in 2014.

John Tonkin-Covell is Senior Lecturer Strategic Studies at the New Zealand Command & Staff College, and previously the New Zealand Army's Military Studies Institute. He is a defence civilian in the New Zealand Defence Force (NZDF) and is also a Senior Teaching Fellow at Massey University's Centre for Defence Studies. He has been with the Military Studies Institute since 1994, and has been involved with the development of tertiary education within the NZ Army and NZDF. He teaches in the areas of strategic studies and military history. His doctoral thesis was on New Zealand's intelligence organisations during the Second World War. He is currently writing a book on the battle of Chunuk Bair; and a book on the Republic of Fiji Military Forces from its beginnings to 2014 (forthcoming 2015).

Kenan Çelik OAM is one of Turkey's leading experts on the Gallipoli campaign. For over 25 years he has worked as a professional guide to the battlefields of the Gallipoli Peninsula and has acquired an exhaustive knowledge of the significant historical sites of the region. After completing his education in Turkey, Kenan studied under a Fulbright scholarship at Oregon State University in the USA. He was awarded an MA degree in English literature for his work on British Edwardian poet Rupert Brooke, who famously died *en route* to Gallipoli in 1915. Since retiring in 2001 from his position as a lecturer in English language and literature at Onsekiz Mart (18th of March) University in Çanakkale, Kenan has devoted himself full-time to guiding visitors over the

Gallipoli battlefields and writing accounts of various aspects of the campaign. He has shared his knowledge of the battlefields and the events of 1915 with tens of thousands of people from all walks of life, guiding Australian and New Zealand back-packers and heads of state, prime ministers, presidents, and service chiefs from Britain, Commonwealth countries, and other nations. He has also been historical consultant to historians and researchers, and appeared in numerous documentary film and television programs. In 2000 Kenan was a visiting scholar at the Australian War Memorial. In that year he was also awarded an honorary Order of Australia, in recognition of his services to Australian history and Australian–Turkish relations.

Holger Afflerbach is Professor and Chair of Central European History at the University of Leeds. He was awarded his PhD by the Heinrich-Heine-Universität in Düsseldorf, Germany. Before coming to Leeds, he taught in Düsseldorf, was Alexander von Humboldt research fellow in Austria, and from 2002 to 2006 was DAAD Professor of Modern German History at Emory University in Atlanta, USA. Holger specialises in late nineteenth and twentieth century German history; international relations, especially from Bismarck to the First World War; military history, particularly both World Wars; and modern Austrian and Italian history. Among his publications are his biography of the Prussian War Minister and Chief of General Staff, *Falkenhayn* (Munich 1994, second edition 1996); his study of the Triple Alliance, entitled *Der Dreibund. Europäische Grossmacht und Allianzpolitik vor dem Ersten Weltkrieg* (Vienna 2002); and a history of the Atlantic Ocean, *Das Entfesselte Meer* (Munich, 2002). He also edited sources from the German Headquarters in the First World War: *Kaiser Wilhelm II als Oberster Kriegsherr Während des Ersten Weltkrieges—Quellen aus der Militärischen Umgebung des Kaisers* (Munich, 2005). His edited volume on the outbreak of the war, *An Improbable War? The outbreak of World War I and European political culture before 1914* (edited together with Professor David Stevenson of the London School of Economics), was published in 2007. His latest works are an edited volume, together with Professor Hew Strachan of Oxford University, on the history of surrender, *How fighting ends: a history of surrender* (2011); and his own book on the history of surrender (forthcoming). Holger has also published some 60 articles and essays and numerous reviews.

Harvey Broadbent is a Senior Research Fellow in Modern History at Macquarie University, directing a research project centred on the Turkish military archives and the Gallipoli campaign, in partnership with the Australian War Memorial. He is the author of two books on the Gallipoli campaign, *Gallipoli, The Fatal Shore*, an illustrated account (2005), and *The Boys Who Came Home: Recollections of Gallipoli* (ABC Books, 1990, 2nd edition 2000). Harvey was born and raised in Manchester, England, and graduated with Honours in Near Eastern Studies from the University of Manchester in 1974, where his major study was Turkish language, history and culture. He reads and speaks Turkish fluently, has lived in Turkey from time to time, and visits the country professionally every year. For 22 years he worked as a TV and radio producer and executive producer for the Australian Broadcasting Corporation, producing four documentaries about the Gallipoli campaign and specialising in historical documentaries, especially about the Mediterranean and Australasian regions. Harvey continues to produce regular programs as a freelance producer.

Elizabeth Greenhalgh is a QE II Research Fellow (Australian Research Council) in the School of Humanities and Social Sciences in the University of New South Wales at the Australian Defence Force Academy. She has published a number of articles on the 1916 Battle of the Somme, as well as on wider questions regarding the Franco–British coalition in such journals as *Historical Journal, International History Review, Journal of Contemporary History, Journal of Military History*, and *War in History*. She is the author of *Victory Through Coalition: Britain and France During the First World War* (2005); and *Foch in Command: The Forging of a First World War General* (2011). Currently she is working on two projects: a study of the French army during the Great War, and an analysis of how the allies won in 1918.

Frédéric Guelton is Chief of the Department of the Land Army at the French Military Archives, Vincennes, and editor in chief of *La revue historique des armées* (*The army historical review*). Colonel Guelton also teaches the history of international relations at *l'Institute d'etudes politiques* (Institute of Political Studies) in Paris; military history at the military academy at Saint-Cyr, where he is an associate professor; and he is a member of the advisory committee of the doctoral school of the University of Paris IV at the Sorbonne. He received his doctorate from the University of Paris I, with an honourable mention for his thesis on General Weygand in the inter-war period. Colonel Guelton has published eleven books as well as over 120 articles and individual chapters on many diverse aspects of military history, international relations and military command, especially during the First World War period.

Rana Chhina served in the Indian Air Force as a helicopter pilot. A qualified flying instructor, he saw active service in operations on the Siachen Glacier, with the Indian Peace Keeping Force (IPKF) in Sri Lanka, and in counter-insurgency operations in Mizoram and Nagaland. A recipient of the prestigious MacGregor Medal for best military reconnaissance in 1986, he had the distinction of carrying out the highest landing in the world by a medium-lift class of helicopter. A keen military historian, he was responsible for organising the Indian Air Force archives at Air Headquarters. He is currently

Secretary and Editor of the United Service Institution of India Centre for Armed Forces Historical Research, and Vice President of the Indian Military Historical Society in the UK. Squadron Leader Chhina's main field of interest is colonial Indian military history. He is the author of five books, the latest of which is *Medals and Decorations of Independent India*, a study of India's post-Independence military and civil honours and awards. His previous works include: *The Indian Air Force Memorial Book*, a consolidated account of battle casualties of the Indian Air Force from 1932–1996; a monograph on the pre-Independence gallantry award *The Indian Distinguished Service Medal*; *The Eagle Strikes: The Royal Indian Air Force at War 1932–1950*; and *The Indian Army: An Illustrated Overview*. In addition, he has edited a number of official war histories, the latest being *For the Honour of India: A History of Indian Peacekeeping*, by Lieutenant General Satish Nambiar.

Rhys Crawley is an historian with the Strategic and Defence Studies Centre at the Australian National University where he is currently working on aspects of Australia's security and intelligence history. He holds an honours (1st class) degree in history from the University of Wollongong, and a PhD from the University of New South Wales (University College, Australian Defence Force Academy). In 2007 he was selected as an annual summer scholar at the Australian War Memorial. His PhD thesis, "Our second great [mis]adventure": a critical re-evaluation of the August Offensive, Gallipoli, 1915', examined the plans, preparations, limitations and potential of the August offensive. A summary of his early findings was published as 'The myths of August at Gallipoli', in Craig Stockings (ed.), *Zombie Myths of Australian Military History* (2010). Rhys is currently writing three books about the Gallipoli campaign and the First World War, with specific focus on artillery, mobility, command, amphibious expeditionary operations, and logistics.

Janda Gooding is Head of the Photographs, Film, Sound and Multimedia section at the Australian War Memorial. She has previously been Senior Curator of Art at the Memorial, and from 1979–2005 was a curator at the Art Gallery of Western Australia. She is the author of eight books and winner of numerous awards, including the Gordon Darling Foundation Travel Grant 2007, a Yale Centre for British Art Visiting Fellowship 1998, and the Harold Wright and William Holmes Scholar at the British Museum 1991. Her most recent book, *Gallipoli Revisited: In the Footsteps of Charles Bean and the Australian Historical Mission* (2009) traces the work of the principal participants of the Australian Historical Mission to Gallipoli in 1919.

Robert O'Neill AO made the first of his several visits to the Gallipoli battlefields in 1963 and subsequently taught and analysed the Dardanelles campaign during the course of his distinguished career as an historian and strategic analyst. Among his many activities as Chichele Professor of the History of War at the University of Oxford, he taught a course on the Dardanelles campaign for fourteen years. Professor O'Neill is presently Chairman of the International Academic Advisory Committee for the US Studies Centre at the University of Sydney. He was the founding Head of the Strategic and Defence Studies Centre at the Australian National University, 1971–1982, and subsequently Director of the International Institute for Strategic Studies in London. From 1987 he was Chichele Professor of the History of War and a Fellow of All Souls College at the University of Oxford, until he retired in September 2001. He was also Chairman of the Council of the International Institute for Strategic Studies, London, 1996–2001; Chairman of Trustees of the Imperial War Museum 1997–2001; a director of the International Peace Academy, New York, 1990–2001; Chairman of the Council of the Australian Strategic Policy Institute (ASPI) in Canberra, 2001–2005; and Deputy Chair of the Council of the Graduate School of Government at the University of Sydney, 2002–2005. His long list of publications includes the official history of Australia's involvement in the Korean War, which was published in two volumes, *Strategy and Diplomacy* (1981) and *Combat Operations* (1985). He was also general editor of the re-issued twelve-volume series, *The Official History of Australia in the War of 1914–1918* (University of Queensland Press in association with the Australian War Memorial, 1981–1989).

Gallipoli strengths and casualties

The eight-month-long Gallipoli campaign involved a total of about one million men from both sides. Between one-third and one-half of them became casualties. Precise figures are unavailable for some nations and there are discrepancies between data from various statistical sources.

Approximately 469,000 British Empire soldiers served in the campaign (328,000 combatants and 141,000 non-combatants). About 120,000 became casualties, of whom over 34,000 died. The maximum British Empire strength at any time was 128,000 (85,000 combatants and 43,000 non-combatants). Approximately 79,000 French soldiers also served in the campaign.

About 500,000 Turkish soldiers are believed to have served on Gallipoli and their casualties are estimated at between 250,000 and 300,000, of whom (according to Turkish official sources) almost 87,000 died.

Between 50,000 and 60,000 Australians served on Gallipoli and a total of 8709 were killed in action or died of wounds or disease. In addition, a total of 19,441 Australians were wounded (including those wounded more than once) and 70 Australians were captured; 63,969 Australian cases of sickness were reported in the Gallipoli campaign. Of the 8556 New Zealanders who served in the campaign, 2721 died and 4752 were wounded (including those wounded more than once). Total Anzac casualties (Australian and New Zealand) amounted to 11,430 dead and 24,193 wounded.

A high proportion of those recorded as dead on both sides were missing: 3268 Australians and 456 New Zealanders have no known graves; and 960 Australians and 252 New Zealanders were buried at sea. Of the total of 9829 French dead, 6091 were listed as missing.

Gallipoli casualties (compiled from various official sources)

	Died	Wounded	Total
Australia	8,709	19,441	28,150
New Zealand	2,721	4,752	7,473
Britain	21,255	52,230	73,485
France	9,829	17,175	27,004
India	1,358	3,421	4,779
Newfoundland	49	93	142
Total *Allies*	43,921	97,112	141,033
Turkey	86,692	164,617	251,309

Measurements

The imperial system of measurements was generally used by British Empire forces during the First World War and is found in most documentary sources. The following conversions should be applied to convert to metric system equivalents:

1 inch	= 2.54 centimetres		1 centimetre	= 0.394 inches
1 foot	= 30.48 centimetres			
1 yard	= 0.91 metres		1 metre	= 3.28 feet / 1.09 yards
1 mile	= 1.61 kilometres		1 kilometre	= 0.62 miles
1 pound	= 0.45 kilograms		1 kilogram	= 2.2 pounds
1 ton	= 1.02 tonnes			
1 acre	= 0.40 hectares			
1 gallon	= 4.55 litres			

Turkish place names and personal names

Many of the topographical features and towns and villages on, and around, the Gallipoli Peninsula have acquired two or more names. In this volume, the names used generally follow the anglicised forms commonly used by British and dominion forces, and subsequently adopted in most English language histories of the campaign. Modern-day Turkish equivalents are sometimes also provided. Confusion occasionally arises because some of these anglicised names derived from Greek names used widely on the peninsula in 1915, including the name Gallipoli itself. Turkish names can be similar, as in *Gelibolu* for Gallipoli, or distinctively different, as in Turkish *Eceabat* for the Greek Maidos, or *Alçitepe* for the Greek Krithia. Under the reforms introduced by Turkey's first president, Mustafa Kemal, the Turkish republic adopted a modern Latin script alphabet from 1929. This effectively standardised most Turkish place names, although many old Turkish forms altered during transliteration from the ancient Arabic script: for example, the anglicised Sedd el Bahr became *Seddülhahir*, Chunuk Bair is *Conkbayiri*, and Kilid Bahr is *Kilitbahir*.[1] Some spelling variations persist in the romanised Turkish place names.

The names of many Turkish military commanders and political leaders also changed after the Gallipoli campaign when, from 1934, all Turkish citizens were compelled to adopt surnames. Mustafa Kemal, who introduced this modernising reform, assumed the surname Atatürk (literally 'father Turk' or father of the Turks). Some Turkish generals chose names recalling places marking their battle honours, while others adopted approved pure Turkish names reflecting masculine qualities, such as *Yilmaz* (uncowed), *Demir* (iron) and *Çelik* (steel).[2]

---

1   The variations in Turkish place names on Gallipoli (with English equivalents and translations) are listed in the following glossaries: C.E.W. Bean, *Gallipoli Mission*, ABC Enterprises in association with the Australian War Memorial, Sydney, 1990 (first published 1948), Appendix IV, pp. 373–8; Selahattin Osman Tansel, *Çanakkale Muharabe Alani Yer Adlari Sözlügü: Türkçe Ingilizce – Fransizca* ('A Dictionary of Gallipoli Battlefield Place names: Turkish English – French'), Bursa, 2010.

2   Andrew Mango, *Atatürk*, John Murray, London, 2004, pp. 464–7 (on alphabet reforms), 498–9 (on surname reforms).

1914

August

2 Ottoman ruler signs a secret alliance with Germany.

4 Following the German invasion of Belgium, Britain declares war.

5 Australia and other dominions join Britain in declaring war.

September

27 Turkey closes the Dardanelles, denying Russia access to the Mediterranean via the Black Sea.

October

31 Turkey enters the war on the German side; Turkish fleet bombards Russian cities of Odessa and Sebastopol in the Black Sea.

November

1 Britain and France declare war on the Ottoman Empire (Turkey).

2 Russia declares war on the Ottoman Empire.

3 Allied warships bombard Turkish coastal defences at the entrance to Dardanelles.

11 Ottoman Empire declares war on Britain, France and Russia; Ottoman ruler issues proclamation of a *Cihat* (*jihad* or Holy War) on 14 Nov.

1915

January

2 Russia appeals to Britain for assistance against Turkish pressure in the Caucasus.

3–13 Allies plan naval expedition to force the Dardanelles and capture Constantinople.

February

19 Allied fleet commences operations with bombardment of Turkish outer defences at the entrance to the Dardanelles.

Feb 25–Mar Allied naval assault proves unable to clear the minefields in the Dardanelles straits or to reduce Turkish artillery batteries and forts.

March

12 General Sir Ian Hamilton appointed commander-in-chief of the Mediterranean Expeditionary Force (MEF).

18 Major assault by combined allied fleet fails to force the Dardanelles and withdraws after incurring heavy losses.

April

Early Mediterranean Expeditionary Force (MEF) assembles at Lemnos.

25 Allied landings at Cape Helles, Kum Kale and Ari Burnu (later named Anzac Cove). *AE2* submarine slips through the Dardanelles.

April 25–May Heavy continuous fighting at Anzac and Helles.

28 First battle of Krithia as Allied forces at Helles attempt to advance on Achi Baba.

29 Turkish torpedo boat *Sultan Hissar* damages *AE2* which is scuttled in the Sea of Marmara and crew is captured. British submarine *E14* (which penetrated Dardanelles on 27 April) continues to disrupt Turkish shipping in the Sea of Marmara for three weeks.

May

2–3 Unsuccessful allied attempt to break out at Anzac with attacks on Baby 700.

4 Anzac attack on Gaba Tepe beaten off by Turkish defenders.

6–8 Second battle of Krithia at Helles.

13 Turkish destroyer sinks battleship *Goliath* at Cape Helles.

19 Turkish mass attacks at Anzac fail with heavy losses.

20 Unofficial truce to bury dead at Anzac.

24 Formal truce for recovery of dead and rifles at Anzac. Some brief fraternisation between Turkish and Australian soldiers.

25 German submarine *U21* sinks battleship *Triumph* offshore from Anzac; *U21* then sinks battleship *Majestic* at Cape Helles on 27 May.

29 Anzacs beat off Turkish attack on Quinn's post.

June

4 Third battle of Krithia.

28–Jul 5 Battle of Gully Ravine at Helles.

August

6 Allied August Offensive begins. Diversionary attacks begin at Helles and major Australian diversionary attack on Lone Pine.

6–9 Battle to hold Lone Pine against Turkish counter-attacks.

6–7 Main Anzac offensive begins in order to capture Sari Bair range.

7 British forces land at Suvla Bay. Anzac attack at the Nek.

8 New Zealand forces capture Chunuk Bair.

9 Gurkha troops briefly capture Hill Q.

10 Turkish forces led by Mustafa Kemal recapture Chunuk Bair.

15 British attack on Kiretch Tepe ridge.

21–22 Suvla offensive fails at battle of Scimitar Hill. Anzac attempt to take Hill 60 fails.

27–29 Second attack on Hill 60; lower slopes captured. August Offensive ends in stalemate.

September

Early Arrival at Anzac of 2nd Australian Division.

October

15 General Hamilton recalled by Lord Kitchener, Secretary of State for War, to be replaced by General Sir Charles Monro.

27 General Monro takes command of MEF; by end of Oct recommends evacuation.

November

Oct and Nov Severe storms hit Anzac.

27–28 Blizzards at Anzac and Suvla; thousands of troops evacuated due to frostbite and exposure.

December

7 Evacuation of Anzac and Suvla ordered.

8–17 Preparations for withdrawal. Sick, wounded, surplus troops, stores and vehicles removed from Anzac nightly.

18–19 10,000 troops taken off Anzac and 10,000 off Suvla.

19–20 Last troops withdrawn from Anzac and Suvla: 10,000 from Anzac and 10,000 from Suvla with no loss of life.

23 Evacuation from Helles ordered.

1916

January

1 Last French infantry leave peninsula at Helles.

7 Turkish attack on Gully Spur, Helles.

8–9 British troops evacuate Helles; Gallipoli campaign ends.

'… the most ghastly and costly fiasco'

Ashley Ekins

In August 1915 the Gallipoli campaign entered its fourth month. The war on the Western Front continued to grind on relentlessly in France and Belgium. But throughout much of the British Empire, attention remained focused on the remote peninsula in western Turkey where soldiers of France, Britain and the dominions had landed in late April and established their tenuous beachheads. The enthusiasm that greeted the first triumphant press reports of the allied landings was fading, however, as the promise of a swift and decisive victory at the Dardanelles began to recede. Few could have suspected that the campaign that began with such high hopes was now approaching a series of climactic battles that would become the turning point of the struggle on Gallipoli.

After the failure of the third costly 'battle of Krithia' in mid-July, the repeated attempts by British and French troops to breach the Turkish defences in the Helles sector at the southern tip of the peninsula came to a halt. Over the preceding months, allied forces had pushed slowly forward towards Krithia village and the distant peak of Achi Baba but the front line still lay several kilometres short of the original objective of 25 April. Allied commanders decided to shift the focus of their offensive operations further north to the rugged terrain of the Anzac sector where Australian and New Zealand soldiers remained hemmed in by the Turkish positions on the heights that dominated their confined enclave.

On 6 August, with the arrival of five fresh British divisions, a series of co-ordinated assaults was launched in order to break the stalemate. Separate landings at Suvla Bay established a third beachhead and extended the allied front line, but despite slight Turkish opposition, the Suvla operations stalled through ineffectual leadership and inertia. Simultaneous attempts by British and dominion troops to break out to the north from the Anzac sector by night attacks on the Sari Bair heights to seize Chunuk Bair and Hill 971 failed with heavy losses. A diversionary attack at Lone Pine incurred over 2,000 Australian casualties in capturing a small section of heavily defended Turkish trenches that would then remain a liability, exposed to Turkish observation and fire, for the remainder of the campaign. Hundreds more soldiers were killed and wounded in further futile attacks at positions along the Anzac front line, culminating in the slaughter of over 200 Australian Light Horsemen in four reckless bayonet charges across open ground at the Nek. By 10 August all the allied attacks had effectively failed.

In the last major operations of the offensive, on 21 August British and Anzac troops captured part of Hill 60 in a vain attempt to link the Suvla and Anzac sectors. British troops also mounted repeated attempts to seize the pivotal feature of Scimitar Hill overlooking Suvla, resulting in some of the largest battles of the entire campaign. By the end of the month the August offensive had ground to a halt with both sides exhausted and incapable of further action. Of the 50,000 British troops engaged at Suvla and Anzac, the casualties in just four days' fighting from 7 to 10 August had amounted to at least 18,000; the casualty toll had increased to 40,000 by the end of August. Turkish casualties in the Anzac sector alone were estimated at 18,000.[1] Notwithstanding their losses, the Turkish defenders still retained their firm hold on virtually every strategically advantageous feature on the peninsula. In the northern sector, British commander-in-chief General Ian Hamilton recorded that he was left with 'only some 50,000 men . . . to hold a line from the right of Anzac to the sea North-east of Suvla, a distance of 23,000 yards', leaving his soldiers spread thinly along a tortuous landscape of ridges and valleys.[2]

One acute observer of the August offensive, British war correspondent Ellis Ashmead-Bartlett, reported in a letter intended for the British prime minister that this 'last great effort to achieve some definite success against the Turks was the most ghastly and costly fiasco in our history since the Battle of Bannockburn'.[3] Ashmead-Bartlett argued that the plans drawn up by GHQ 'never had the slightest chance of succeeding':

> The [HQ] Staff seem to have carefully searched for the most difficult points and then threw away thousands of lives in trying to take them by frontal attacks . . . The muddles and mismanagement beat anything that has ever occurred in our Military History . . . We do not hold a single commanding position on the Peninsula and at all three points, Helles, Anzac and Suvla Bay, we are everywhere commanded by the enemy's guns . . . In Gallipoli we are dissipating a large portion of our fortune and have not yet gained a single acre of ground of any strategical value.[4]

With the failure of the August offensive, the last chance of success on Gallipoli was gone, although it would take a further three months of deliberation by the War Council of the British Cabinet in London before that reality was accepted. After August, only minor offensive operations were mounted. Battle casualties were fewer but the wastage due to disease, death and wounds increased steadily. The lack of adequate shelter, as Australian official historian Charles Bean observed, meant that 'the energy of the force was already being largely expended in fighting the climate rather than the enemy'.[5] With the onset of autumn the deteriorating weather gave a foretaste of the difficulties of sustaining a winter campaign on the peninsula. In November storms and blizzards forced the evacuation of thousands of troops suffering from frostbite and exposure at Anzac and Suvla. Allied commanders were also concerned about signs of German intentions to move heavy artillery to the peninsula. Total evacuation of the force was eventually seen as the only remaining option. From early December the remnants of the Anzac and Suvla garrison, wasted by disease and malnutrition, were evacuated in a meticulously planned withdrawal operation. Some 90,000 men were evacuated from Anzac and Suvla over eleven nights from 8 to 20 December, with only a handful of casualties. The final evacuations from Helles were similarly successful on 8–9 January 1916.

The acclaimed masterstroke of the 'secret' Allied evacuation was an early attempt to restore some shred of success to the defeat on Gallipoli. But the humiliation of the allied withdrawal was a dismal outcome for a campaign that had begun with high hopes that it could bypass the stalemate on the Western Front and so shorten the war. The loss to British prestige was immense and widespread in the Empire.

To many at the time, the failure seemed inexplicable. The combined military and naval might of Britain and France and their dominion and colonial forces had failed to defeat 'the sick man of Europe', the decaying Ottoman Empire. Not for the last time in the twentieth century, supposed technological superiority had failed to be a decisive factor in achieving a military victory. The costly failure of the August offensive came to epitomise the entire Gallipoli campaign. The enormous scale of the ambitious venture and its heavy losses meant that many questions remained to be addressed.

The campaign had involved a total of over one million men from both sides;

Two unidentified soldiers at a supply depot on Anzac Cove, surrounded by boxes of corned beef, known as 'bully beef', the main source of protein in the soldier's monotonous and nutrient deficient diet on Gallipoli. The tins in the foreground were used to carry kerosene or water.

AWM H03951

half of them became casualties, either killed, wounded or ravaged by sickness and disease.[6] Survivors of the Gallipoli campaign shared a unique common experience which set them apart from other veterans of the First World War.[7] That experience embraced many distinctive memories: the rugged terrain and geographical isolation of the peninsula, together with its extremes of climate; the constricted beachheads and areas of operation at Helles, Suvla Bay and Anzac, dominated by Turkish positions so that virtually no allied area was safe from enemy fire; and the sustained intensity of the fighting and the close proximity of the Turkish trenches that lent Gallipoli a human dimension almost entirely lacking from the mass 'industrialised' warfare of the Western Front.

The Gallipoli campaign also possessed a uniquely multinational character. Men from many nations were drawn together on the peninsula by the forces of what was a global conflict by 1915. The Turkish military included soldiers from Anatolia (or Asia Minor as it was then termed) and the Balkan regions of the former Ottoman Empire, as well as Syria, Mesopotamia, and Arabia. French forces included colonial troops from Algeria, North Africa and Senegal in West Africa. The British army included soldiers from England, Scotland, Ireland, Wales and dominions such as Australia, New Zealand, and, towards the end of the campaign, Newfoundland, not yet part of the dominion of Canada. Indian troops included men from Sikh and Muslim cultures from what would become modern Pakistan, Gurkhas from Nepal, and even troops from Ceylon (modern Sri Lanka). Logistic support was provided by labour companies from Malta, Egypt and Greece; and Russian Jewish refugees from the pogroms and Sephardic Jews displaced from Palestine served together in the Zion Mule Corps raised in Alexandria. The uniquely international character of the campaign is reflected in the chapters of this volume.

The first section establishes the strategic context of the campaign. In his opening chapter, Robin Prior argues against the dominant and enduring perception that Gallipoli was the great missed opportunity of the First World War, the decisive masterstroke that might have ended the war in half the time and at half the cost. Historians as varied as C.E.W. Bean, Winston Churchill and Robert Rhodes James have all glimpsed in the August offensive at Gallipoli the prospect of victory and the opportunity to shorten the Great War. The supposed victory hung by small threads – Churchill's 'terrible ifs' – if only General Stopford had acted more decisively at Suvla Bay, if Chunuk Bair and Hill Q could have been reinforced, and so on. This chapter addresses these 'ifs' to see if they have substance, while at the same time looking at the prospects of the campaign overall to see what might have flowed from an unlikely victory.

Next, Stephen Badsey observes that many modern historians have viewed the events of the August offensive from the perspective of separate nationalities, and especially from the perspective of the common soldiers on both sides. However, these were not the perspectives and preoccupations of the time. The decisions and events which led to the August offensive only become clear, and to a degree inevitable, when viewed as part of a much wider picture. What happened on the Gallipoli ridges was first of all the product of a greater British Imperial identity, and strategic assumptions that stretched back for decades. It was also an integral part of global British (and indeed French) grand strategy, including above all a continuing attempt to avoid both a long, bloody war and a possible allied defeat. At the same time, what happened at Gallipoli in August was also the product of day-to-day political decisions and assumptions in London from April 1915 onwards, many of which were wrong in hindsight but appeared plausible or desirable at the time. The question that, with hindsight, needs to be considered, Badsey maintains, is 'why the British government chose not to evacuate Gallipoli between May and August 1915, but instead chose to authorise further reinforcements and the August offensive, in circumstances that most historians are now convinced could not possibly have led to victory.'

The costly failure of the August offensive has come to characterise the Gallipoli campaign. The poorly co-ordinated series of assaults failed to achieve the promised breakout from the northern allied positions and force a conclusive victory. All the attacking forces were halted with heavy losses, none of the vital objectives were seized, and the Turkish ground captured was negligible. Popular accounts lay the blame for these failures on the actions or inactions of particular British commanders and the lacklustre performance of British soldiers. But there were multiple causes: deficiencies in the preparation and planning, the allocation of insufficient resources of men and materiel, logistical and intelligence lapses, and an underestimation of Turkish military capabilities, all contributed. Above all, as I argue in the third chapter, allied commanders' misconceptions about the terrain of the Gallipoli Peninsula hamstrung their planning and the chances of success. Many of their misunderstandings about the strategic and tactical advantages of the chosen objectives, and the feasibility of allied plans to capture and hold them, have been perpetuated in historical accounts to the present day. This chapter questions whether the key objectives of the August offensive actually offered the opportunities for victory claimed by senior commanders and their staff; and whether the constraints imposed by the terrain, available forces, resources, and weapons systems negated any realistic opportunities for exploitation. These remain crucial questions for a proper understanding of the Gallipoli campaign.

The second part of the book deals with the Anzac breakout battles. Peter Burness examines the series of attacks from Lone Pine to the Nek, the futility of which epitomise the offensive at Anzac. The main thrust of the August offensive was the capture of Chunuk Bair and Hill 971, crowning the heights of the Sari Bair ridge. Little is remembered today of the Anzac battles, however, beyond the names of places such as Lone Pine and the Nek. Indeed, Lone Pine is celebrated as a victory. But these attacks, and the ones between them – at Pope's Hill, Quinn's Post, and German Officers' Trench – were only intended to provide a diversion or give support to the main efforts on the heights. Yet at each place men charged into heavy machine-gun and rifle fire and their heavy casualties were disastrous. Despite numerous brave efforts and terrible losses, the results were limited and brought no strategic advantage. Today the tragedy of the August fighting is perpetuated in the string of cemeteries from Lone Pine to Chunuk Bair.

In his chapter, Peter Pedersen explores the important role of command. General John Monash's performance as commander of the Australian Corps in 1918 has justly earned him the accolade of Australia's greatest general. His performance as commander of the 4th Brigade on Gallipoli in 1915 is often considered mediocre at best. At the very heart of that assessment is Monash's handling of his brigade's advance on Hill 971 during the breakout from Anzac on the night of 6 August. His alleged utterance, 'I thought I could command men', when his advancing column disintegrated, has been quoted time and again as evidence of a breakdown under the stress of close combat. Pedersen questions whether this was actually the case by examining the advance and its context. He also probes Monash's role in the less well known but even bigger debacle on 8 August, when the 4th Brigade again tried for Hill 971, and in the mismanaged attacks on Hill 60 a fortnight later. In conclusion, he suggests how these experiences may have shaped Monash's approach to the higher command that he exercised later in the war.

John Tonkin-Covell recounts the pivotal struggle by New Zealand and British troops to capture Chunuk Bair during the August offensive. He examines the battle as it was planned, the futility of that plan and its implications, the actual battle that developed, and its abrupt culmination. The operational command and control of the New Zealand forces inevitably comes under consideration, and while Colonel Malone features, the unsung role of Colonel Meldrum also comes into play. In seeking explanations for the outcome of this battle, the author contends that it was already lost before the first New Zealand soldier began to move out of the Anzac area.

The third part of this volume deals with the August offensive from the perspectives of both enemies and allies. Many senior allied commanders seriously underestimated the capabilities of the Turkish defenders on Gallipoli. Racialist assumptions drove many of their attitudes, as revealed in the writings of General Ian Hamilton:

> Let me bring my lads face to face with Turks in the open field, we *must* beat them every time because British volunteer soldiers are superior individuals to Anatolians, Syrians or Arabs and are animated with a superior ideal and an equal joy in battle.

Hamilton felt the technology of modern warfare, such as wire, machine-guns and artillery shells, handicapped his preference for 'hand to hand, or rifle to rifle, style of contest', allowing:

> a single dirty Turk at the Maxim [gun to] kill ten – twenty – fifty – of our fellows on the barbed wire . . . *each of whom is worth several dozen Turks.*[8]

Kenan Çelik, in his chapter, presents informed insights into the character and motivation of Turkish soldiers. In August 1915, Turkish soldiers on Gallipoli faced their toughest test of the entire campaign when British and allied forces, reinforced with five fresh divisions and reinforcements from the dominions, threw their combined strength into a massive series of assaults aimed at breaking the deadlock. The Turkish defenders eventually prevailed, but the course and outcome of the August offensives left many questions unanswered. How did the headquarters of the Turkish 5th Army on Gallipoli first learn of the plans for an allied attack before August? How much did Turkish commanders know or deduce about allied intentions? Did they anticipate the principal breakout operation from the north of Anzac? How did Turkish commanders, particularly Mustafa Kemal, react to the allied offensive? What were the Turkish senior commanders' overall impressions of the allied attacks and their impact on the Turkish forces? Was the Turkish victory in August decisive or merely another Pyrrhic victory which came at too great a cost for the defenders? Can we compare the relative leadership, bravery, and endurance of Turkish soldiers, especially their commanders, to the qualities of allied soldiers and commanders? These and other important questions are explored through an examination of Turkish commanders' accounts and Turkish operational sources. The answers illuminate many aspects of Turkish soldiers' experiences, which remained virtually unknown to allied troops on the other side of no man's land.

The relationship between Turkish soldiers and their German military advisers and commanders was poorly understood by allied commanders during the Gallipoli campaign and is still shrouded in misconceptions today. British commanders believed that large numbers of German officers underpinned the Turkish defence and that German troops provided the backbone of the Turkish forces: in fact the number of Germans is estimated at no more than 500 to 700. There was also a popular, stereotypical view of the supposed strains in German–Turkish relations on Gallipoli, as Charles Bean later commented:

> there is no doubt that the Germans and Turks constantly grated on one another in both higher and lower ranks; the casualness and backwardness of the Turks irritated the Germans, and all German soldiers in authority were not as wise as Liman von Sanders.[9]

Holger Afflerbach explores and corrects some of these assumptions in his chapter. He shows that although German army officers generally did not give much credit to their Turkish brothers in arms, those few who were serving as commanders and advisers in the Ottoman army occasionally had different views. The direct German involvement at the Dardanelles operations included General Otto Liman von Sanders, commander of the defences of the Straits, and some 100 advisers and commanders. This chapter examines whether the German leaders believed that the allied attack on the Dardanelles constituted a vital threat to Germany's interests, and also explores the military as well as political responses the Germans considered in reacting to this threat. Afflerbach evaluates the real importance of the German–Turkish alliance, and the significance of the defence of the Dardanelles within the overall German war strategy. He also reveals some of the structures of German–Turkish military and political co-operation, relating them to both strategic questions and attitudes between allies.

Harvey Broadbent argues in his chapter that the failure of the allied August offensive cannot be attributed solely to bad planning and poor execution. Using recently accessed Ottoman military archival documents and memoirs of Turkish commanders translated into English by a Macquarie University–Australian War Memorial research project, he discusses the manner of the Turkish defence of the Sari Bair heights, Turkish tactics and Turkish commanders' concerns and reactions. These records also help to illuminate such questions as how close to success Generals Godley and Birdwood actually came to victory in the offensive; whether Generals von Sanders and Esat Pasha had an overall plan of defence; how important successful operations from Suvla Bay might have been in achieving a break-out from Anzac; and whether control of the Sari Bair heights might actually have resulted in control of the Dardanelles Straits.

General Ian Hamilton recorded his high regard for the professional competence of the senior French commander on Gallipoli, General Gouraud. He was less complimentary, however, about the capabilities of French colonial soldiers. On 13 April 1915 he watched Senegalese (West African) troops conducting practice landings in Mudros Harbour at Lemnos:

> These niggy-wigs were as awkward as golly-wogs in the boats. Every extra hour's practice will save some lives by teaching them how to make short work of the ugliest bit of their jobs.

On 2 May, he recorded: 'the proportion of white men in the French Division is low; there are too many Senegalese.' He also commented that it was always the Senegalese and Zouaves who were the 'weak link' who fell back under Turkish attacks or retreated under shelling.[10] The remarks are revealing about British attitudes and may also indicate some strains in British–French relations. But most French officers, despite harbouring some racialist stereotypes, regarded their Senegalese troops as aggressive and dependable fighters, belonging to a group the military characterised as a 'warlike race'.[11]

In their chapter, Elizabeth Greenhalgh and Frédéric Guelton examine an aspect of British–French relations through the revealing reports of Major de Bertier, a French liaison officer attached to General Hamilton's headquarters staff. Between 11 April and 29 December 1915, in addition to his official reports, Major de Bertier sent 29 handwritten letters to Colonel Hamelin of the French General Staff. These letters provide a direct, unofficial and 'human' perception of events in the Gallipoli campaign, as Major Bertier covered a wide field of issues, ranging from diplomacy to tactics and individual military behaviour. He frankly described and interpreted allied forces and soldiers, from Hamilton to the youngest officer or soldier. He also described aspects of the harsh realities of the army, the multinational force, the high command, and war and death. During the August offensive, which was planned to the exclusion of the French, in an 'absolute silence, with which General Bailloud put up impatiently',

A French colonial soldier guards 9.2-inch howitzer shells packed for transport in light rail cars, Helles, 1915.

G00480

Major de Bertier, in his personal opinions written between 9 and 10 August, at first spoke highly of the soldiers and was very severe in his judgement of the British high command; he finally provided his own assessment of the capabilities of GHQ, as a former student at the *École de guerre* (War College).

Units of the Indian army were an integral part of British Empire forces engaged throughout the Gallipoli campaign, yet the role of Indian troops on Gallipoli remains largely unknown to most general readers. Indian mountain gun batteries served in the Anzac area from the landing on 25 April and Australian official historian Charles Bean recorded their fine fighting qualities. During the August offensive, Indian soldiers were involved in operations with Australian, British and New Zealand units, notably during the multi-pronged assault on the Sari Bair ridge when troops of the Gurkha Rifles captured and briefly held Hill Q, the highest point attained by allied forces. Notwithstanding their significant military contribution, India was still agitating for Dominion status when the war ended. Their lack of a political identity tended to rob Indian soldiers not just of acknowledgement of their role or of a commemoration of their sacrifice, but also of their place in history. Rana Chhina examines who these soldiers were, what they did on Gallipoli, and how this stood in the context of the larger backdrop of global events connected with the Great War, as well as political developments and their social impact in India. Drawing on official records, regimental war diaries, and private papers, he provides a belated acknowledgement of a forgotten legion, those Indian soldiers who contributed an extensive footnote to a major historical event that became the cornerstone of the formation of an Australian national consciousness.

Logistics is a crucial component of war. While logistic supremacy does not necessarily lead to success, it is clear that supply of essential food, water and munitions can and often does have a direct impact on the success or failure of a battle. The potential of an offensive to succeed, especially a prolonged one like the August offensive, therefore rests upon the logistical and administrative systems that support it. Rhys Crawley provides a broad understanding of the complexities associated with supplying the Mediterranean Expeditionary Force during August 1915, as well as an understanding of the problems faced, and an assessment of the successes and limitations of the allied logistic system, and he questions whether the August offensive was a logistically viable operation of war.

The fourth and final section of the book explores the enduring legacies of Gallipoli. Charles Bean, Australia's official war correspondent, accompanied Australian troops throughout the First World War, from the landing on Gallipoli in 1915 to the armistice in Europe in November 1918. Central to his reporting of events was his commitment to create as 'truthful' a record of Australia's involvement in the war as possible. For Bean, the truth would be found in detailed research of military events. But it might also be revealed through photographic images that recorded all aspects of the battlefield landscapes, and works of art that conveyed something of the drama and emotional intensity of the events that had become so familiar to Australians. In early 1919, Bean had a unique opportunity to revisit Gallipoli and take with him a talented Australian artist, George Lambert, and a highly experienced photographer, Hubert Wilkins, to make a visual record of the battlefields that would assist Australians to understand the course and outcome of the campaign. Janda Gooding outlines the group's work on Gallipoli in 1919 with particular reference to the historical, photographic and artistic material associated with the tragic charge of Australian Light Horse units at the Nek in August 1915.

The Gallipoli campaign continues to cast a long shadow, conveying lessons and warnings about parallel conflicts, almost a century on. Robert O'Neill, in his chapter, shows how the Dardanelles and Gallipoli campaigns of 1914–1915 foreshadowed later conflicts in several significant ways. The campaigns pitted forces of the Christian West against those of the Muslim East; Western operations were founded on the illusion that the East would prove weak and crumble, allowing resolute invaders from afar to assert their will; and it was assumed that because Western sea power was militarily stronger, coastal bombardment and amphibious operations would be swiftly and economically effective. The British Government underestimated the calibre of its enemy at the Dardanelles. It overestimated the effectiveness of its battle fleet and it failed to develop a coherent concept of operations once troops were landed on Turkish shores. It also failed to pay heed to the strategic consequences of its recent policies in that region in strengthening the very Turkish defences that it proceeded to attack. Hasty action led it to make enemies unnecessarily, and thereby weaken its position in the Middle East as a whole. Nonetheless some important lessons were learned from the Dardanelles debacle, especially in the demanding techniques of amphibious warfare, that were to prove valuable in the Second World War. But other military undertakings more recently have shown all too little regard for the strength of determined indigenous defenders in the face of foreign attacks. O'Neill argues that it is time to re-examine our own military experience more rigorously, so that resources, when they have to be applied, can be used more effectively.

Clearly, the history of the Gallipoli campaign which has been a seminal event in the national histories of three nations, Australia, New Zealand and Turkey, is still being explored and expanded through a variety of approaches and new sources. The event and its history continues to resonate almost a century on.

A Turkish soldier's handmade leather identity tag, apparently cut from a boot, and a small page of Arabic text verses from the Koran, originally folded into postage-stamp size to allow the soldier to wear it close to his body as a form of amulet. Both items were souvenired by Colonel C.B.B. White, Chief of Staff, 1st Australian Division, at Anzac, 1915.

AWM REL29694

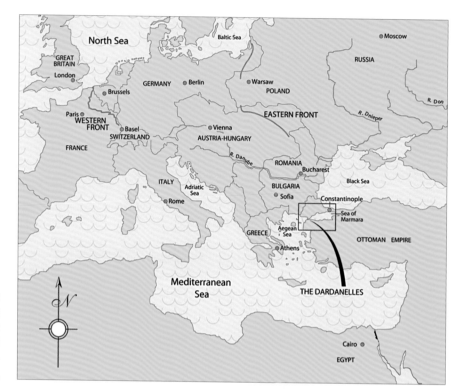

The main theatres of the First World War, showing the Eastern and Western Fronts in relation to the Dardanelles.

Cartographer: Sharon France

The Dardanelles and the Gallipoli Peninsula.

Cartographer: Sharon France

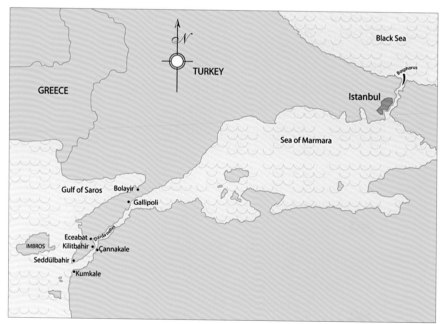

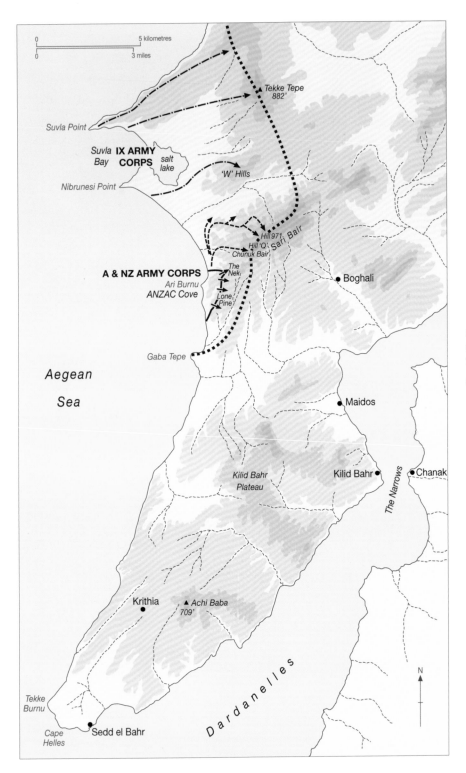

0   5 kilometres

0   3 miles

Suvla Point

Suvla Bay   **IX ARMY CORPS**   *salt lake*

▲ *Tekke Tepe 882'*

Nibrunesi Point

'W' Hills

Hill 971
Hill 'Q'   *Sari Bair*
Chunuk Bair

A & NZ ARMY CORPS
Ari Burnu
ANZAC Cove
The Nek
Lone Pine

● *Boghali*

Gaba Tepe

Aegean Sea

● Maidos

Kilid Bahr Plateau

Kilid Bahr ●   ● Chanak

The Narrows

● *Krithia*   ▲ *Achi Baba 709'*

N

Tekke Burnu

Cape Helles   ● Sedd el Bahr

Dardanelles

Allied principal lines of assault and objectives in the August offensive.

Cartographer: Keith Mitchell

Part 1

Strategies and plans

Chapter 1

The hand of history

Robin Prior

In 1936, the influential British economist John Maynard Keynes wrote: 'The ideas of economists and political philosophers, both when they are right and when they are wrong, are more powerful than is commonly understood.'[1] The same is true of historians, and the Gallipoli campaign is a shining example of this. The key phrase to note is 'both when they are right and when they are wrong'.

A popular view of the Gallipoli campaign is that it played a vital role in forging Australia's national identity. I believe this view is mistaken and that other forces played greater roles than Gallipoli, but that aside, there is no denying the force or the persistence of this view and the impact it has had on Australian society. In this chapter I aim to explore a second and even more surprising legacy of the Gallipoli campaign. It derives from the view that Gallipoli was the great missed opportunity of the First World War – that it was the decisive masterstroke that could have ended the war in half the time with half the cost. And this view of missed opportunities derives directly in turn from the August offensive at Anzac.

There are two episodes in the campaign that have been persistently held to be turning points, but where the campaign, through bad luck or incompetence or lack of perseverance, failed to turn. The first relates to the naval attack and is based on the view that by the evening of 18 March the Turkish forts were so short of shells that a renewed attack by the British fleet would have succeeded. The second and most important relates to the August offensive where – so the story goes – three opportunities for success went begging. First, the Sari Bair ridge could have been seized and great things accomplished, but for a

Two weeks before the August offensive begins, Captain C.E.W. Bean, Australia's official war correspondent, and later official historian, views the distant heights of Walker's Ridge, the Sphinx and Plugge's Plateau from a deep communication trench above North Beach, 26 July 1915. Bean was wounded by a rifle bullet on 7 August during the Australian and New Zealand assaults on the Sari Bair ridge.

AWM PS1581

lack of drive at Suvla Bay. Second, at Anzac those who reached the summit of Hill Q on 9 August were shelled off it by their own navy. Third, those who had reached the summit of Chunuk Bair lost a significant opportunity because they chose to dig in on the reverse slope instead of the forward slope.

I propose to examine the works of a number of historians who wrote about Gallipoli in the interwar period and, in particular, to examine what they thought of the overall strategic worth of the campaign and what role they saw the August offensive playing in the operation. It will become obvious that *even when those historians who wrote about the August offensive got it wrong*, they had effects on later historical events that they could hardly imagine.

I begin by looking at how some of the historians in the period between the two world wars, 1919 to 1939, dealt with the August offensive, starting with the Australian official historian C.E.W. Bean. Writing in 1924 of the appalling consequences of the failure to capture the major objectives on the Sari Bair ridge, Bean said:

> The vital objective, the actual crest of Chunuk Bair, was for several days within Birdwood's reach, and for a few hours actually in his hands. By fighting which was never surpassed ... an opportunity was made for securing results perhaps unattainable in any other land-battles of the war. After several brave failures ... that opportunity passed, never to return.[2]

And in his concluding remarks to this volume, he wrote: 'The failure of the Dardanelles Expedition made it evident that the war must be longer and more difficult than had been generally imagined.'[3] In other words, the failure in August ruined an enterprise that had the ability to shorten the war to a considerable degree – a good plan botched in execution.

Principal instigator of the Gallipoli campaign, British parliamentarian Winston Churchill, with Field Marshals Sir William Robertson, Commander-in-Chief, British Army of the Rhine (right), and Sir Henry Wilson, Chief of the Imperial General Staff (left), during an Army Council visit to British occupation forces on the Rhine, c. 1920. Churchill advocated generous terms for Germany after the Great War but he soon warned of German rearmament and became a staunch opponent of appeasement.

AWM H12243

This assessment is not different in essence from that given by Winston Churchill. In his history, *The World Crisis*, Churchill concentrated on the lost opportunities at Suvla Bay rather than at Anzac, but he arrived at a similar conclusion to Bean. He states:

> At every phase in the battle, down even to the last action ... the issue between victory and defeat hung trembling in the balance. The slightest change in the fell sequence of events would have been sufficient to turn the scale. But for the forty-eight hours lost by the IX Corps at Suvla, positions must have been won from which decisive operations were possible.[4]

Thus he concluded that:

> the opportunity was lost of confining the conflagration within limits which though enormous were not uncontrolled. Thereafter the fire roared on till it burnt itself out. Thereafter events passed very largely outside the scope of conscious choice. Governments and individuals conformed to the rhythm of the tragedy, and swayed and staggered forward in helpless violence, slaughtering and squandering on ever-increasing scales ... But in 1915, the terrific affair was still not unmanageable. It could have been grasped in human hands and brought to rest in righteous and fruitful victory before the world was exhausted.[5]

Next to Churchill's account of Gallipoli, one of the most influential accounts on the campaign was found in the war memoirs of former prime minister David Lloyd George. He deals with the operation in broad, but as part of his account he included the following:

> I shall not attempt even to summarise the story of the Dardanelles Campaign with its incomprehensible blunders and its tragic failure ... A small force of a few thousands landed in time would easily have overwhelmed the wretched garrisons to whom the defence of Gallipoli had been entrusted by the careless Turks. When we sent an army numbering tens of thousands to attack in April, Turkish reinforcements had arrived which were strong enough to prevent us from capturing one of our objectives. We were always too late. We ran race after race with the sluggish Turk and each time he invariably won, and arrived first at the winning post. He delayed and procrastinated according to his wont, but we beat him at the dawdling game. He gave us many chances and we never took one.[6]

Cecil Aspinall-Oglander, the British official historian, is also at one with Bean and Churchill on the value of the campaign and on the lost opportunities in August. He wrote in 1932 that:

> There is little doubt to-day that the idea of forcing the Straits with a view to helping Russia, eliminating Turkey from the war and rallying the Balkan States to the side of the Entente, was one of the few great strategical conceptions of the War.[7]

Of the August offensive at Anzac he stated:

> On a gaunt Ridge overlooking Kilia Bay, about three miles north of Chanak [present day Çanakkale], a massive stone obelisk can now be seen by all who make the passage of the Dardanelles. This monument is on the summit of Chunuk Bair ... Looking up at that shining memorial the traveler needs little military knowledge to recognize the vital importance of Chunuk Bair in August 1915, or the measure of the Turkish peril while that dominating height remained in British keeping.[8]

For the Suvla offensive, Aspinall-Oglander could find no better source than the official Turkish account, which he quoted at length. In part, this reads:

> Had this sound plan [the Suvla operation] been executed with resolution and energy it would have affected very far-reaching results. From the Suvla sector, which was for the most part undefended, and only watched by a very weak detachment, it would have been possible to capture Anafarta Sagir and Boghali. This objective once attained, the mastery of the Straits would have been definitely won, and the land communication of the greater part of the [Turkish] Fifth Army would have been cut.[9]

In other words, if sufficient energy had been shown by the British commanders at Suvla, the path to Constantinople would have been open and the Turkish army on the Peninsula would have withered on the vine. There would have been nothing to stop the large conceptions sketched out by Aspinall-Oglander in the first quotation from being fulfilled.

One the most influential writers in the interwar period on all aspects of the First World War was Basil Liddell Hart. In many books, *The Real War, The First World War* and others, he propagated the view that concentration on the Western Front was folly and that the most promising strategic idea was that of the Gallipoli campaign and that the most crucial point in that campaign was reached in August. He railed against the delay in mounting that attack and claimed that if troops had been sent earlier, great results could have been achieved. His views on Churchill are particularly interesting:

> Almost the only statesman who comes out well from the Gallipoli history is Mr Churchill, and he was one, significantly, who had made a study of war. He knew war – and he knew his own mind. He foresaw what the enemy leaders feared – as the history shows. It was owing to him that Sir Ian Hamilton was sent the force [for the August offensive] that would have fulfilled those fears. But it was in disregard of Churchill's insistence on the time factor that the force was sent too late.

General Sir Ian Hamilton, Commander-in-Chief of the Mediterranean Expeditionary Force (MEF), with other senior officers on board the Royal Navy warship, HMS *Triad*, after being recalled to London following the failure of military operations on Gallipoli, 17 October 1915. From left: Commodore Roger Keyes, Chief of Staff to Vice Admiral de Robeck; Vice Admiral John de Robeck, commander of naval forces at the Dardanelles; Ian Hamilton; and General Walter Braithwaite, Chief of the General Staff, MEF.

AWM H10350

'Too late' is the verdict not only on the Gallipoli campaign as a whole but on every step in it.[10] On the failure of the August offensive, Liddell Hart was particularly scathing:

> In August he [Hamilton] achieved a real tactical surprise ... Success was within reach and only had to be grasped ... But the incredible happened – his subordinates succeeded in bungling . It was an amazing chain of 'irresolution's' by which Stopford, Hammersley, Sitwell and Johnston, and lesser fry forfeited the chances and frittered away the hours while opportunity yawned wide on an enemy-deserted shore ... The chances then lost were never redeemed.[11]

Another influential book of the interwar period was John North's, *Gallipoli: The fading vision*, published in 1936.[12] North, who fought on Gallipoli, had no doubt of the worth of the campaign or who was responsible for it:

> The responsibility for the inauguration of the Dardanelles campaign rests upon Mr Winston Churchill. It is a responsibility which, at this time of day, he can be proud to bear ... today it is no longer in doubt that the campaign was brilliantly conceived.[13]

He went on to identify the August attack at Anzac as *the* crucial point in the campaign. In a chapter titled 'The men who saw the Narrows', he dwelt at length on the events at Chunuk Bair and Hill Q on 8–9 August. He identified these days as 'the climax' of the whole campaign and wrote that 'a peculiar fascination must always attach to the stories of these few parties of men that reached these heights and thus came within sight of the goal of the whole campaign'.[14] North ascribed the loss of 'one of the most momentous battles in the world's history' to the failure of the New Zealanders properly to consolidate their positions on Chunuk Bair and to the casting away of the 4th Brigade in an unnecessary attempt to capture Hill 971 – a peak that in his view was not vital to the success of the operation. Even so, North was of the opinion that the offensive came within an ace of success and that the entire war could have been shortened if it had succeeded.[15]

What we have, then, in the period from 1919 to 1939 is the emergence of a remarkable consensus about the Gallipoli operation: it was a daring strategic concept for which Churchill must be given most of the credit, even if, owing to his subordinate position, he lacked the authority to drive it through to a successful conclusion.

All of the authors mentioned (and I could have added many more) were of the view that the ruination of the August episode was one of the turning points, if not *the* turning point, in the entire campaign. They differed over how this ruination came about. Some held that the events at Anzac were crucial, others that the events at Suvla Bay wrecked the campaign. Most agreed that both operations offered opportunities that were thrown away. Liddell Hart and Churchill had no doubt that if the operations had taken place in July instead of August, success would have been ensured because the Turks would have had fewer reserves with which to oppose them.

In my view, almost all of the above opinions are wrong – both in the grand consequences they ascribe to a victory on Gallipoli and in the details concerning the August offensive. If the entire operation had succeeded, and Turkey had been knocked out of the war, there would still have been the considerable inconvenience of the German army intact on the Eastern and Western Fronts. In that sense, Gallipoli was not tackling the main problem of the war – namely, how to defeat the Germans. The adherence of the weak, fractious Balkan states to the side of the allies was the diplomatic equivalent of cavalry forces and might well have detracted from the strength of the British and French. As for aiding Russia, this idea was chimerical. At the time of Gallipoli the allies were suffering from a shortage of shells on the Western Front, and so they would have had no munitions to spare for Russia. Nor would they have had any spare shipping to transport Russian wheat from the Black Sea ports to pay for the non-existent munitions.

Turning to portrayals of the details of the August offensive, and to the alleged missed opportunities, these are the most speculative counterfactuals. Churchill and others have argued that if the attack had been made earlier, say in July, it would have succeeded because the Turkish force to be faced would have been weaker than it was in August. But surely the preparations for a July offensive would have been as obvious to the Turks then as they were a month later. In that case they could have brought up additional men to oppose the offensive. In any case, the Turkish troops available in July, with the advantage of firm possession of the heights and a steady flow of reinforcements, might well have proved sufficient to stop an August-style assault.

As for almost attaining the ridge, the Anzac and British forces did not have the entire Sari Bair ridge in their grasp even for a minute. For a short period of time, troops precariously occupied two points along the ridge: Hill Q and Chunuk Bair. The former position was held in particularly small numbers, and these men were about to withdraw when the position was hit by shells – almost certainly fired, not by the navy, but by friendly artillery desperately trying in impossible conditions to support the troops on the summit. In any case even in the absence of shells – whoever fired them – a small-scale Turkish counter-attack must have seen the demise of the position.

As for Chunuk Bair, its position was enfiladed from both flanks (hence the withdrawal of the force to the reverse slope), there were few reinforcements on hand, there was the difficult matter of supplying it with food, water and ammunition, and it too was bound to be overwhelmed by the large (if temporarily disorganised) Turkish forces.

Nor were there any opportunities at Suvla. That operation has been much misunderstood by historians. It was never intended as the prelude for a major advance across the peninsula, but rather merely to establish a base for all the northern forces in that area. Certainly the security of the base would have been greater if the ridge overlooking it had been secured. But an advance from the Anafarta Ridge was never going to assist the Anzac force or help any advance on the Narrows. A glance at a map will reveal that the line of advance from the ridge would have taken the non-existent reserves that would be required to make it *away* from the Anzac perimeter and *away* from the Straits. No strategic possibilities whatsoever were on offer from Suvla.

Let us 'fast-forward' 25 years to April 1940 and the situation in another world war. The British have attempted another amphibious operation across seas where they hold overwhelming naval predominance. This time the country in question is Norway and they are responding to a German invasion. The result is that they are worsted by a much smaller German force, which in the teeth of British naval supremacy has occupied an entire country in a matter of a few weeks. One of the prominent persons in relation to this enterprise is Winston Churchill, once more First Lord of the Admiralty, just as he had been in 1915. Once more we find Churchill in a subordinate position. Once more he is surrounded by politicians not noted for their daring. The prime minister, Neville Chamberlain, declared war on Germany on 3 September 1939. He has declared war but so far he has not waged it. His armies and those of the French have sat immobile along the Western Front while Poland (the ostensible reason Britain and France went to war in the first place) was overrun. The British air force has flown over Germany and dropped not bombs but leaflets urging the Germans to overthrow Hitler and give up. The Germans have not yet responded positively, but Chamberlain is sure that they will. The war, he confidently predicts, will be won in a few months by uprisings among the German population and by the steady pressure of the British blockade. Such is the way the war is being conducted.

After the invasion of Norway, a humiliating retreat has been forced upon the British. They are required under German pressure to draw their forces back from around Trondheim in central Norway and evacuate them back to Britain. There is outrage in the country and in the House of Commons that Britain's first military operation of the Second World War should be an evacuation. So great is the outrage that members of Parliament call for a debate on the whole situation of the war. It is widely held by the Labour Party and a growing section of the Conservative Party that the appeasers still in charge of Britain – Chamberlain; Halifax, the Foreign Secretary; and Sam Hoare, the Minister of Air – are not up to the job of running a modern war.

But the Conservative rebels and the Labour Party are by no means in a majority. Unease is growing, but the enormous preponderance of the Conservatives in the House of Commons, a Tory majority of just over 210 members, will have to be severely reduced to effect a change in war leadership and the way the war is to be waged. It is by no means certain that the rebels and the opposition have the numbers to install Churchill. If Chamberlain is to be deposed there is every chance that Halifax – another appeaser – would take his place. He was certainly Chamberlain's preferred successor and also the King's.

Churchill's position in all this is an anomalous one. As First Lord of the Admiralty he is a member of Chamberlain's War Cabinet. In addition, he presides over the Military Co-ordination Committee, which comprises the military chiefs of the three armed services. Yet this committee has no real power. It can only make recommendations to the War Cabinet. And more often than not these recommendations are turned down in favour of masterly inactivity.

Here, then, we have Churchill in a similar position to that of 1915. He is widely regarded as the only minister with any ideas and initiative in military matters. At the same time he is seen to be hobbled by Chamberlain and his company. In the coming debate he will be obliged to defend a government he does not believe worth defending and which, if it is defeated by a vote in the House, he might have some prospect of leading.

At the same time Churchill bears no little responsibility for the Norway affair. Without going into the decision-making concerning that campaign in detail, it does bear some resemblance to Gallipoli. Once more, Churchill has overestimated what British sea power can accomplish. At Gallipoli he overestimated its ability to overcome land-based guns and mines. In Norway he has overestimated what ships unaccompanied by air cover can do. Just as with Gallipoli, he has again tried to interfere with the actual naval operations – sending telegrams direct to the local commanders without clearing them with the naval staff. Like Gallipoli, others in the government bear at least as heavy a responsibility for the fiasco as Churchill, but there is no doubt that he should share some of the blame for the lamentable result.

The Norway debate commences in the House of Commons on the afternoon of 7 May 1940. Over the next two days, 28 speakers participate in the debate. By a remarkable coincidence no fewer than five of them had served on Gallipoli. If these five have come to view Gallipoli in a negative light and hold Churchill responsible for the fiasco, and if they have also gone on to draw parallels with Norway, then they alone may sink any chance Churchill has of succeeding Chamberlain as prime minister. But they do not think that way.

Earl Winterton, who had been an infantryman on Gallipoli, expresses very strong views about the operation to this effect:

> Speaking as a Gallipoli-ite, like the right hon. and gallant Member[s] … [Colonel Wedgewood, who had manned a machine-gun on the bows of the *River Clyde* to try and suppress Turkish fire from the Seddülbahir

fort] and the Leader of the Opposition [Clement Attlee, who was a major in the infantry on Gallipoli], I can say that those who were in Gallipoli greatly regret to this day that some Minister or Ministers were not impeached and some high generals not court-martialled for what occurred in that place.

This is looking ominous for Churchill, but Winterton goes on to conclude: 'In saying that I wish expressly to exclude from my condemnation the First Lord of the Admiralty.'[16]

In short, Winterton is making the familiar case that Churchill's brilliant conception at Gallipoli had been ruined by procrastinating politicians at home and dud generals at the front. Churchill emerges from Winterton's speech with his reputation enhanced.

One of the most dramatic speeches made during the debate comes from the Member for Portsmouth, Admiral Sir Roger Keyes, who appears for the occasion in the full dress uniform of an Admiral of the Fleet, complete with six rows of ribbons. Keyes had commanded the destroyer flotilla at the Dardanelles and is quick to get to Gallipoli in his speech:

> The Gallipoli tragedy has been followed step by step [in Norway] ... [The Gallipoli campaign] was a brilliant conception of the First Lord of the Admiralty to circumvent the deadlock in France and Belgium. It was defeated first by his Principal Naval Adviser of those days [Lord Fisher, First Sea Lord] who succeeded in eliminating him; and later by those who could see no further than the barbed wire of No Man's Land on the Western Front; and finally and decisively by the exaggerated fears in Whitehall of dangers which men on the spot were ready to face and overcome. A great friend of the First Lord of the Admiralty remarked to me that the iron of Gallipoli had entered into the soul of my right hon. Friend after he was submerged in the political upheaval, which followed his difference of opinion with his Principal Naval Adviser. Sir, the iron of Gallipoli entered into my soul too, for it was torture to watch the sufferings of men on Gallipoli Peninsula and their daily losses, when I knew it could all be put an end to by bold action ... My right hon. Friend has not had his opportunity [in this war] yet. [In 1915] he had many enemies, who discredited his judgment and welcomed his downfall. Now, however he has the confidence of ... the whole country.[17]

What Keyes is saying is in line with all the authorities quoted earlier, namely, that Gallipoli was a brilliant concept ruined by timid politicians and misguided advisers. He is enjoining Churchill not to despair – his time to seize the top job will soon come and this time the country will be behind him.

It must be noted that Wedgewood and Keyes are speaking against the government and therefore might be expected to make the best case they could for Churchill. If they thought that mention of the Gallipoli campaign would have damaged the reputation of the First Lord of the Admiralty, they would surely have omitted all reference to it. In fact, so confident were they that this was not the case that they made mention of the Gallipoli operation because they thought it would enhance Churchill's reputation by being associated with it.

There is another matter which confirms this view. Of the 28 speakers in the Norway debate, we can identify about 14 who speak in favour of Chamberlain and therefore implicitly against Churchill. It is a remarkable fact that not one of these speakers mentions the Gallipoli operation – confirmation that mentioning it will do Churchill nothing but good, something they are desperately trying to avoid.

What this all demonstrates is that by 1940 the way the Gallipoli operation was perceived had undergone a transformation since 1915 when Churchill was dismissed largely because of it. Then it had been a millstone around his neck. Then his public speeches were often interrupted by cries of 'What about the Dardanelles?' Now the Gallipoli operation was a badge of honour to be used to defend the strategic insight of the First Lord. The parallels with the Norway operation are so obvious they hardly need to be spelled out. Once again, here was a brilliant strategist being held back by 'older and slower' brains, both within the Admiralty and within the government. All that was needed for the war to be prosecuted with vigour was for Chamberlain to be thrown out of power and for Churchill to be installed as prime minister, where he would finally have responsibility to direct the armed forces and to choose members of the government who were in line with his thinking.

This is in effect what happened. When the vote on the Norway debate was taken on 8 May 1940, the government's majority had fallen from around 222 to 81. Forty of 50 Conservatives had voted against their own government and about 60 more had abstained. The position for Chamberlain was in fact much worse than these figures indicate. Many of the pro-government votes were loyalty votes by members such as Churchill. Others voted for Chamberlain only on the assumption that he would prosecute the war more vigorously, something that was never going to happen – so they were in effect casting a final vote for the prime minister. If these votes are added to the anti-government votes, Chamberlain's majority all but vanishes. In two days Churchill was prime minister. Was this important? Yes, it was. Churchill was the only leading Conservative not tainted with appeasing Hitler or Mussolini, or both. He was the only leading conservative willing to fight Germany to the bitter end. When he said his only aim was 'victory in spite of all terror', he meant it literally.[18] No one else in high Conservative circles thought like this in May 1940. Later that month the Foreign Minister, Halifax, would pressure

Churchill to approach Hitler via Mussolini for peace terms. Any such terms must have meant the end of Britain as an independent power.

The consequences of Churchill's resolute stand need to be spelled out. In 1940 Britain was the only power fighting Nazi Germany. Stalin was helping rather than hindering Hitler by supplying Germany with huge quantities of raw materials. Roosevelt was timidly trying to help the Allies but had no intention of entering the war – indeed he was only forced into the European war when Hitler declared war on the United States after Pearl Harbor. If Britain had chosen another path, the United States and the Soviet Union would have faced a Nazified Europe with immense economic potential. Whether Stalin could have survived a German attack in such circumstances is highly doubtful. Without the use of Britain as a base, it is difficult to see how the United States could have liberated Europe at all, had that been its intention. In other words, in 1940 the stakes could not have been higher.

My argument has strayed some way from the ridges of Sari Bair, but I believe I have demonstrated that the way historians at the time perceived the Gallipoli operation – and such key episodes within it as the August offensive – played a crucial role in the outcome of the Norway debate and the installation of Churchill as prime minister and, as a consequence, in the continuation of the war against Hitler.

'The adieu was a melancholy affair,' General Sir Ian Hamilton later wrote in his published *Gallipoli Diary*. Hamilton jokes with senior staff at GHQ on Imbros Island on the morning of his departure for England, 17 October 1915.

AWM G00529

Where does this leave us as historians? Hardly any historians writing about Gallipoli today would hold the views of the interwar historians. A brief glace at the historiography of the campaign since Robert Rhodes James wrote his *Gallipoli* in 1965 reveals that a much more sombre view of the campaign holds sway. Rhodes James, Nigel Steel and Peter Hart, Tim Travers, Trevor Wilson, and I myself are united in thinking that no great issues were at stake on the peninsula. Even if the Ottoman Empire had been overthrown, the impact on the German army would have been minimal. The war would have gone on. No doubt battles such as the Somme and Passchendaele would still have been fought. These days attention has shifted to how those battles and others on the Western Front were fought. We all have differing views on what could have been accomplished by Haig, Joffre or Falkenhayn, or on whether such prodigious loss of life was an unavoidable part of fighting on the Western Front, but few would now say that Gallipoli was any substitute.

Nor would we let Winston Churchill off as lightly as that previous generation of historians did. We would concentrate on the fact that the First Lord did not take his naval advisers fully into his confidence. We would stress his seemingly contradictory stance in pushing forward the naval attack and at the same time calling for troops – the result of which was a half-hearted naval effort followed by a military landing with an interval sufficient to thoroughly alert the Turkish command. We would question the whole rationale of the 'indirect approach' as a method of waging war.

Let me return to the August offensive. Those glimpses of the Dardanelles Straits by the Chunuk Bair contingent, the dash of Allanson's men up the steep slopes of Hill Q, the opportunities that *must* have gone begging at Suvla because the command was indeed incompetent – these are the events that convinced the interwar historians that in August the Gallipoli operation had come to within an inch of success. This enabled Gallipoli to be depicted as a great strategic idea. And this played its part in Churchill becoming prime minister in an hour of desperate need, not just for Britain but also for the West as a whole.

Those columns of tired and weary men struggling up the tortuous ravines and gullies towards Sari Bair, the indifferently led troops of the New Armies attempting to advance across the stifling Suvla Plain to the Anafarta Ridge, perhaps they wrought better than they knew. In terms of the campaign in which they were engaged, their efforts were entirely futile. They were too few to occupy Sari Bair; Anafarta had no relevance to future operations; and there were no reserves to exploit any advances that had been made. But to use a phrase that would not have won the approval of Keynes, but which nevertheless seems appropriate here, in the long run the efforts of these men to seize the Sari Bair heights had an effect that reached out over the ensuing 25 years to affect the course of the Second World War.

Chapter 2

The August offensives in British Imperial Grand Strategy

Stephen Badsey

By early May 1915, the great British mistakes of the Dardanelles campaign had already been made. With hindsight, the largest of these errors was the failure of British diplomacy before the war that led to the Ottoman Empire's decision to join the Central Powers in November 1914, thus creating the grand strategic problems that eventually led to the Gallipoli landings. Before 1914 neither side attached much importance to this issue, largely because both London and Berlin assumed that the Ottoman Empire was on the verge of disintegration, and that the Ottoman Army was of negligible fighting value.[1] The major errors of the campaign itself were the decision to launch a purely naval attack in February 1915, clearly signalling allied intentions to the Turks, followed by the lack of security surrounding the initial landings on 25 April. Once these landings had failed to achieve their objectives, the only remaining issue was whether the British should continue on Gallipoli, or simply cut their losses and evacuate the peninsula. The orders issued by Secretary of State for War Lord Kitchener to General Sir Ian Hamilton, commanding the Mediterranean Expeditionary Force (MEF), had been ambiguous on this very point, stating that '[h]aving entered on the project of forcing the Straits, there can be no idea of abandoning the scheme', but still that 'it seems undesirable to land any permanent garrison or hold any lines on the Gallipoli Peninsula'.[2]

On 5 May the first British reinforcements for the MEF began to arrive, from 42nd (East Lancashire) Division, but on the same day, Major General Sir Stanley von Donop, Master General of the Ordnance at the War Office, cabled Hamilton to warn him that a continuing campaign was only one option, and perhaps not the most likely:

> The ammunition supply for your force, however, was never calculated on the basis of a prolonged occupation of the Gallipoli peninsula. We will have to reconsider the position if, after the arrival of the reinforcements now on their way to you, the enemy cannot be driven back and, in conjunction with the Fleet, the Forts barring the passage of the Dardanelles cannot be reduced.[3]

At its final meeting on 14 May, the War Council of the Liberal government under Prime Minister Herbert Asquith considered the possible evacuation of Gallipoli; and the same question was discussed at the first meeting on 7 June of its successor, the Dardanelles Committee of the new Asquith coalition government, held in response to a memorandum written by Kitchener on 28 May setting out the future options at Gallipoli.[4] The question that, with hindsight, needs to be answered is why the British government chose not to evacuate Gallipoli between May and August 1915, but instead chose to

British Secretary of State for War Lord Kitchener greeted by Anzac and British troops during his visit to Gallipoli, 13 November 1915. After inspecting the positions at Helles, Anzac and Suvla, Kitchener recommended evacuation of the peninsula.

AWM H10354

authorise further reinforcements and the August offensives, in circumstances that most historians are now convinced could not possibly have led to victory.

We may be sure that a complete answer to this question is beyond reach, and probably always has been. The evidence required for such certainty simply does not exist. Maurice Hankey, secretary to both the War Council and the Dardanelles Committee, pointed out in 1916 that, contrary to later practice, his handwritten notes of meetings recorded only the general trend of the discussion, were not circulated to members for verification, and were 'not of much value' in depicting individual views or statements. The record of the critical first meeting of the Dardanelles Committee, for which Hankey was not present, is also particularly inadequate.[5] Several of those involved in the decision-making process made efforts to distort the historical record as it was still forming, one notable case being Hamilton's *Gallipoli Diary*, published in 1920 ostensibly as a contemporary record of his experience, but in fact written in 1916, although Hamilton did include selective quotations from official cables, and possibly drew on some day-to-day notes.[6] Even in this partly-fabricated version, Hamilton wrote more than once of his need to read between the lines of the cables he received, including those from Kitchener marked as 'private and personal'. Hamilton was also deliberately secretive or ambiguous in the cables that he sent back to London: 'Least said to a Cabinet,' his ostensible diary entry for 3 June reads, 'least leakage.'[7]

There was also much about the decision-making process in London that was never officially recorded, including the role played by wives, mistresses, salons and soirées. The diary of Hamilton's vivacious and gossipy wife, Jean, records her frequent visits to senior politicians and generals in order to lobby on behalf of her husband, with whom she was in frequent contact. On 30 June she learned first of the attack on Gully Ravine, which had taken place two days previously, from another lady who had been shown two of Hamilton's secret telegrams by the newly appointed First Lord of the Admiralty, Arthur Balfour; Lady Hamilton was indignant, not at the security breach but because she had not already been informed by her husband.[8] Also, part of the expected duties of Hamilton's staff was to exchange information informally with friends and contacts at the War Office and with the British Expeditionary Force (BEF) on the Western Front.[9] In addition to important visitors, Hamilton noted the arrival on 5 July of 'a sort of professional gossip' from BEF General Headquarters (GHQ), followed on 15 July by an officer, Captain Glyn, whom Hamilton and his chief of staff were certain was 'a sort of emissary', although they could not decide whether he came from Kitchener, from War Office Intelligence or from the Admiralty; and of course they could not ask.[10]

On 14 May Hamilton gave a notoriously ambiguous reply to a War Council enquiry as to exactly what forces he required for victory on Gallipoli: for this, he has drawn criticism from historians who believe that a general should have been more decisive. But this reply was only one example of how only careful reading between the lines, at the highest political and strategic levels, provides evidence for the British decision-making process. What was (or may have been) at stake between May and August 1915 was not simply the future of the Gallipoli campaign, but nothing less than whether the Middle East should take precedence over the Western Front as the British Empire's main war effort.

In 1915 Great Britain and its Empire were part of a grand alliance that had lost the strategic initiative at the war's start, and would not wrest that initiative back from the Central Powers until early 1917. This strategic problem was greatly exacerbated by the tactical deadlock imposed on many, but not all, of the First World War's battlefields by new and unprecedented levels of firepower and troop densities. The expert solution offered by generals on all sides to this deadlock in 1915 was artillery and shells in previously unimaginable quantities, requiring levels of production that were not achieved by the French and British (with assistance from the United States) until 1917, and never by the other belligerents. The rest of the answer to the trench deadlock came from new military doctrines and tactics that were well understood by later 1917, and remained essentially unchanged in land warfare for the rest of the twentieth century. As the only major, opposed amphibious operation mounted by the allies, the Gallipoli campaign was unique in the war. But otherwise, it fits very well into the pattern of all British offensives between early 1915 and early 1917: attacks made and continued by undertrained and underequipped forces under unfavourable tactical circumstances, driven by wider political and strategic considerations. The British decision-making process that led to the August offensives was determined first by a grand strategy that had been accepted for centuries, then by the need to solve military strategic problems barely a decade old, and finally by a set of political imperatives which changed weekly and almost daily from early May 1915 onwards.[11]

Historically, the British had for centuries fought any power that sought to establish hegemonic domination in Western Europe, in order to avoid a future war against a European super-state with the resources to defeat the Royal Navy in British waters, and hence to invade or starve the country into submission. Habitually, the British did this as part of an alliance, supplying finance, munitions and soldiers to the main European theatre of war in a Continental strategy, and also to one or more peripheral theatres. The only major British defeat since the late seventeenth century had occurred when they had not followed this strategy: the American Revolution of 1775–83, in which they were defeated chiefly by the French and Dutch in a peripheral campaign. In this sense the British entry into the war in 1914 was a strategy that was both predictable and traditionally correct, although at the time objections and even cabinet resignations showed that it was not universally accepted or understood. The greatest strategic consequence of this British participation in the war was that the blockade imposed by the Royal Navy, in conjunction with the British Empire's immense resources and military potential, meant that the Central Powers knew by September 1914 that they could not win a long war, while the British largely expected to fight a long war with enough time to develop and train their volunteer New Army, relying on their French and Russian allies to provide land forces in the interval.

A critical part of this centuries-old British grand strategy was to hold the costs of their armed forces to very low levels in peacetime, and then expand them in war as needed. In the decade up to 1910, total expenditure on the army and the navy was only 2.5 per cent of net national product.[12] It was recognised that the all-volunteer regular British Army could never be large enough to carry out its diverse wartime roles and to police the British Empire as well. The idea that the colonies, and later the dominions, should provide soldiers not only for their own defence but for Imperial campaigns under British command, was first advanced by the Carnarvon Commission in the 1870s, and achieved fruition in the Boer War of 1899–1902. The British use of the Indian Army for overseas wars also became common from the 1860s onwards, and in 1914 four of the best Indian divisions (two infantry and two cavalry) were sent to the Western Front, where they were still serving at the time of Gallipoli.

In this sense the British strategic position in 1915 was nothing new. The army that the British sent to Gallipoli in April was an improvised collection of regulars, volunteers and colonial or dominion troops of the kind that had successfully fought wars across the globe for over half a century. But in the First World War this traditional British strategy was distorted by two large differences from all their previous wars. One was the impact on land warfare of decades of industrialisation, meaning that each battle on the Western Front in 1914–15 represented an immense British loss of life and matériel. Increasingly, the costs of a long war strategy looked too great, leading to frustration with the Asquith Liberal government, and the belief that Britain might no longer have the luxury of years in which to build up its land forces and to allow its economic blockade to take effect.

In March 1915 Lord Esher, the *éminence grise* of British defence diplomacy, railed against government complacency over a war costing 'two millions a day' in economic terms; while by August Field Marshal Sir John French, commanding the BEF, was showing immense emotional strain in coping with the deaths under his command, and may have been suffering from clinical depression.[13] In keeping with traditional British force structures, the original MEF should have included a core of trained regular British troops, but the demands of the Western Front made this almost impossible. Although Hamilton's 29th Division is often described as a regular formation, this is misleading: all but one of its infantry battalions had a pre-war regular existence, but it was otherwise an improvised wartime formation. Also, by August the 29th Division was, like all front-line units on Gallipoli, seriously

under-strength. Kitchener did not send Hamilton a single fully trained or veteran division, and the improvised divisions that were sent to Gallipoli were deficient, particularly in artillery. It was not a case of allowing green troops to gain experience on a quiet sector before making a major attack (as on the Western Front), but of exposing them at once to the risk of debilitating diseases and serious casualties: at least five brigade commanders would be killed or wounded in the August offensives.[14] Hamilton's chief reason for rejecting Lieutenant General Sir John Ewart as commander of the expected IX Corps in June was that in health terms he would not 'last out here for one fortnight' (not, as is often claimed, because he was too fat to walk down the trenches). Hamilton himself contracted a virulent form of the prevalent dysentery, from which he did not completely recover for almost a decade.[15] The problems of disease and the difficulties in replacing casualties on Gallipoli also highlight the inappropriateness of the 'nibbling' attacks undertaken by Lieutenant General Sir Aylmer Hunter-Weston's VIII Corps in June and July; whatever the validity of such tactics in other theatres, on Gallipoli they wore out fighting formations for no meaningful gains.

One strategic preoccupation in considering whether to stay after April 1915 was the British belief that, given the relatively small size of their forces across the Empire, failure on Gallipoli would have repercussions throughout the Islamic world, including Egypt and Persia, and among the Muslim troops of the Indian Army. A fortnight after the entry of the Ottoman Empire into the war on the German side, on 14 November 1914, a *Cihad Ekber* (*jihad* or 'holy war') had been proclaimed in Constantinople, and Gallipoli was to be the only battle for which the Ottoman government organised an accompanying propaganda campaign.[16] Although British anxieties proved unfounded while the war continued, in the long term Gallipoli played an important part in undermining the ideological basis for Imperial rule, including a belief in inherent British superiority.

Hamilton's *Gallipoli Diary* for 15 June reads, 'Let me bring my lads face to face with Turks in the open field, we *must* beat them every time because British volunteer soldiers are superior individuals to Anatolians, Syrians or Arabs and are animated by a superior ideal and an equal joy in battle.'[17] Presumably this was written after the event to set the scene for the later failure. Indeed, one of the most startling features of the August offensives, given the British officer ethos of the period, is that generals from Hamilton downward, and even observers like Charles Bean, were quite prepared to blame the volunteer New Army troops and their commanders for the defeat.[18] On 30 August Hankey reported to the Dardanelles Committee that 'the newly arrived British troops have varied much in quality', concluding startlingly that 'the super-excellence of the Turkish soldier in defence, his superior staying power in this climate, and his local knowledge, bring the forces man for man to about equal'.[19] Mustafa Kemal (later Atatürk) also claimed later in the war that at Tekke

Tepe on 9 August, 'when the Ottoman soldiers attacked ferociously, supported by accurate shrapnel fire from mountain batteries, the "English" soldiers could only think of escaping towards the sea'.[20]

The other major difference in British grand strategy from previous centuries was that Great Britain's main enemies were no longer France and Russia, both countries whose strategic geography the British had studied intimately. As part of the culmination of the diplomatic revolution of 1902–7 that led to the Triple Entente, the Royal Navy drew up in 1907 its first ever written war plan, for a possible war against Germany.[21] In consequence, the British also had to consider war with the Ottoman Empire, including naval or amphibious operations in the Dardanelles, in the face of the rapidly emerging new technology of sea mines and torpedoes, as well as the traditional debate on the superiority of coastal artillery and fortresses when compared with ship-to-shore bombardment. Despite claims to the contrary, like all pre-war arguments about firepower this issue was far from clear-cut, with British naval views swinging from about 1910 onwards towards warships having the advantage over shore batteries, opinions that were reinforced by the unexpected effectiveness of German heavy artillery against the forts of Liège in 1914.[22]

British soldiers of the Royal Irish Fusiliers in trenches at Cape Helles.

AWM G00425

Rather than pursuing any significant amphibious capability, the main British defence priorities for the navy and the army before the war had been the creation of a new high seas battleship fleet with the launch of HMS *Dreadnought* in 1906 and of the BEF and the Territorial Force in the Haldane Reforms 1906–08. Nevertheless, in 1904, Sir Henry Rawlinson as Commandant of the Army Staff College Camberley introduced the practical study of opposed amphibious landings, and next year a joint army–navy committee reported on the need for a common amphibious doctrine. In 1907 the new army post of General Officer Commanding Mediterranean was created, based at Malta where Sir Leslie Rundle was Governor General. Kitchener declined this new post when it fell vacant in 1909, but Ian Hamilton took it a year later, combining it with the post of Inspector General of Overseas Forces. In 1911 the War Office issued its first *Manual of Combined Naval and Military Operations*, and part of Hamilton's job was to develop and translate this manual's concepts into practice. In 1912 his itinerary for the training season started in Egypt, where Kitchener as Consul General shared his residence with Major General the Honourable Julian Byng, commander of the British garrison. This was followed by test mobilisations at Malta and Gibraltar, and in May by a conference at Malta led by Asquith, Kitchener and Winston Churchill, First Lord of the Admiralty. After a summer of army–navy exercises, Hamilton spent the rest of the year travelling around the world, returning to Egypt in December. In early 1913 further army–navy exercises took place under Hamilton at Malta, including a practice amphibious landing by three battalions, linked to a revised 1913 version of the *Manual*. This was followed by more globe-trotting, including visits to Canada in 1913, and in early 1914 to New Zealand and Australia.[23] By 1915, Hamilton could reasonably claim to be Great Britain's expert on the theory of amphibious warfare under modern conditions.

Despite this, and a close professional relationship which went back to the Boer War, Hamilton was not Kitchener's first choice to command the MEF; Kitchener wanted Sir Leslie Rundle, suggesting that he saw the chief problems of the campaign as political and administrative. Intriguingly, Admiral Sir John Fisher as First Sea Lord favoured General Sir William Robertson, at that time Quartermaster General of the BEF, and perhaps the best organiser and administrator in the army.[24] Like all senior British generals, Hamilton had long experience of both army politics and national politics, although he was unusual in being a Liberal supporter rather than a Conservative, and in the British constitutional crisis of 1911 he had been marked by the Liberal government for a possible peerage in order to help break the House of Lords logjam.[25] Hamilton would have preferred Lord Haldane to Kitchener as Secretary of State for War, seeing Haldane as one of his two closest political allies, the other being Winston Churchill, whose younger brother Jack he brought with him to Gallipoli as a staff officer.

Lord Kitchener (left) and Lieutenant General William Birdwood, commander of the ANZAC Corps, making their way down the steep slope of Walker's Ridge to North Beach after an inspection tour of the trenches at Anzac, November 1915. Kitchener was one of the key proponents of the Gallipoli campaign, but his visit convinced him the campaign had failed and that withdrawal was the only option.

AWM G00574

In August 1914, Kitchener took the cabinet minister appointment of Secretary of State for War only with the greatest reluctance. In addition to his call for a mass volunteer army of some 60 divisions, which could not be properly trained until late 1916 at the earliest, he insisted on retaining his position as Consul General in Egypt, giving this position up only in January 1915 while continuing to exercise indirect authority over British policy in Egypt, and repeatedly threatening to abandon politics for a field command.[26] Kitchener's relationship with Sir John French, commander of the BEF, was also far from straightforward. The army's General Staff, tasked to carry out war planning, had been established in 1904 following a long evolution, and had committed itself to a Continental strategy. In 1914 in imitation of German practice, almost all the senior officers had deployed under French as the GHQ of the BEF, and been replaced in Whitehall by other officers, a decision only reversed in December 1915. Of the two Chiefs of the Imperial General Staff under Kitchener, Sir Charles Douglas died from overwork in October 1914, and his successor, as a mere lieutenant general, Sir James Wolfe Murray, was overshadowed by both Kitchener and French. Kitchener belonged to no political party and held his cabinet position through being a peer of the realm, but as a field marshal he was senior to French, and habitually wore uniform in office (British field marshals remained on the active list until death). French felt that Kitchener had unwarrantably 'assumed the air of a Commander-in-Chief', the position of professional head of the army that had been abolished in 1904.[27]

The ambiguities of this relationship between Kitchener and French were to become a key factor in the Dardanelles campaign. By January 1915 the view, shared by Kitchener and other senior members of the government, that the Western Front might be irrecoverably deadlocked naturally drew British attention to the Middle East.[28] Studies of a possible attack on the Dardanelles, made for the Committee of Imperial Defence (CID) from July 1906 onwards, had envisaged that any such operation should be mounted only as part of a much wider war against the Ottoman Empire, including the involvement of British Empire troops on other fronts, and preferably troops from other countries in a traditional British alliance strategy.[29] As soon as the Ottoman Empire declared war on 5 November 1914, Indian troops were ready to move from Bahrain to Basra and into Mesopotamia, while the British also offered support to a nascent Arab revolt in Syria.[30] An Ottoman assault on the Suez Canal on 2 February 1915 was repulsed with heavy losses, apparently confirming pre-war views of Ottoman military weakness.

On 8 January Kitchener suggested to the War Council an amphibious assault to capture Alexandretta (modern Iskenderun) in Turkish Syria, following this with proposals to use the town as a base to link up with offensives mounted from Egypt and Mesopotamia, aimed at the heart of the Ottoman Empire.[31] While Kitchener had to balance the competing demands of the Western Front and the Middle East throughout 1915, he never abandoned this strategic plan, of which Gallipoli was seen as only one part. Indeed, immediately after the failure of the August offensives Hankey suggested to the Dardanelles Committee that 'an attractive alternative would be to make a dash into Syria', following which 'the capture of Damascus should be a comparatively easy business', and coupled with an expected capture of Baghdad should more than offset any loss of prestige from evacuating Gallipoli.[32] Even in November 1915, Sir Douglas Haig, as French's presumptive successor to command the BEF, was insistent that Kitchener should remain at the War Office rather than take a command in Egypt because by his 'masterful action he will give that sphere of the operations an undue prominence in the strategical picture'.[33] In the same month, *The Times*'s military correspondent, Lieutenant Colonel Charles à Court Repington, warned Andrew Bonar Law (leader of the Conservatives within the Asquith coalition government) that 'I hear of mad schemes for [Kitchener] joining [General Sir John] Nixon via Damascus and for plunging into the centre of Asia Minor'.[34]

While the British trained their New Armies, including dominion troops, they remained largely reliant for the first two years of the war on the French and Russians, both of whom had by May 1915 shown themselves to be generally tactically inferior to their German enemies. In pre-war negotiations, notably the Wilson–Dubail Memorandum of 1911, the French had seen the BEF's contribution to the Entente entirely in political rather than military terms, disregarding its fighting value.[35] After the First Battle of Ypres in October–November 1914, the French General Headquarters (*Grand Quartier Général* or GQG) under General Joseph Joffre accepted that British troops could be trusted for line-holding purposes. The French became convinced that the BEF might have some real fighting value following, first, the British attack at the small Battle of Neuve Chapelle on 10 March 1915, then their contribution to the defence in the Second Battle of Ypres on 22 April (coinciding with the first landings at Anzac and Cape Helles on 25 April). But Field Marshal French had to lobby hard to obtain artillery and reinforcements for a further British offensive, and on 31 March he recorded that Kitchener had told him:

> Joffre and I were 'on our trial' – that if we showed within the next month or 5 weeks that we really could make 'substantial advances' and 'break the German Line' then he would – so far as we were concerned – always back us up with all the troops that he could send. But if we failed it would be essential that the government should look for some other theatre of operations.[36]

In support of the next major French offensive on the Western Front, the Second Battle of Artois, scheduled to begin on 19 May, the British renewed their attacks in the Battle of Aubers Ridge on 9 May, followed by its continuation, the Battle of Festubert, on 15 May, both of which were heavy defeats marking the temporary exhaustion of the BEF.[37] The Second Battle of Artois also ended inconclusively, on 16 June, with heavy French casualties. The French Army's numerical and matériel strength was set to peak in autumn 1915, for which Joffre envisaged another major offensive, including a British contribution.[38] Coinciding with the end of the Battle of Festubert, on 27 May the French War Minister, Alexandre Millerand, was severely criticised both by President Raymond Poincaré and by the Senate for the French Army's failure to make better progress against the German defences. On 16 June the British learned of 'a cabal in Paris against General Joffre', concluding that Joffre and Millerand badly needed a victory on the Western Front to restore their own prestige, and possibly to avoid a French government coming to power that would seek a separate peace on German terms.[39]

Meanwhile, both the Entente's biggest problems and its biggest opportunities lay in the East. Part of the impetus for the Gallipoli campaign came from a Russian appeal on 2 January 1915 for a British 'demonstration' against the Ottoman Empire, to relieve pressure on the Caucasus Front.[40] Even so, Kitchener told the War Council only a day earlier of the critical importance to Russia of the British presence on the Western Front, and said that '[o]ur role on the continent was to contain as large a German army as possible in order to prevent them transferring sufficient troops to beat the Russians'.[41] Before the war, Russian military planning had been based on the belief that their own industry was incapable of producing artillery and shells to a required standard, and that in the event of war they would instead depend on British matériel, paid for in part by exports of Russian wheat. But in 1915 the British could not produce enough munitions even to supply themselves, and without access through the Black Sea, any Russian supply lines were irredeemably choked. Facing a shell crisis, throughout the year Russian officials accused the British of bad faith for failing to do the impossible.[42] If Russia collapsed or made a separate peace, then Germany could concentrate its armies in occupied Belgium and France, where there was every reason to believe that they could hold indefinitely against any allied attacks.

As information both from the Russian government and from allied military attachés fluctuated between confident predictions of victory and pessimistic demands for help, it was hard for the British to reach any assessment of the Russian Army's fighting qualities. The British took heart from the crushing Russian defeat of Ottoman forces in the Caucasus in January 1915 in the Battle of Sarikamis, their capture of the fortress city of Przemysl from the Austro-Hungarians on 22 March, and further Russian victories over the Ottomans in the Caucasus, including the capture of Van on 13 May. Unknown to the allies at the time, after the loss of Przemysl, Austria-Hungary had threatened to make a separate peace unless it received immediate German support. The response was the Battle of Gorlice-Tarnow, a German and Austro-Hungarian counter-offensive launched in Galicia on 2 May, leading to the fall of Lwów on 22 June. Hankey later attributed Kitchener's reluctance to transfer good British divisions from the Western Front to Gallipoli to his fear that 'the Germans would soon be in a position to come Westward again' if Russia collapsed.[43] The loss of Warsaw to the Germans on 5 August (one day before the Suvla landings), announced to the world ten days later, clarified for the British the extent of the Russian defeat, which was followed by the fall of Brest-Litovsk on 26 August, just as the Gallipoli offensives were ending.

In September 1914, even before the Ottoman Empire had entered the war, Winston Churchill had suggested that a Russian corps of 50,000 soldiers could be transported to the Dardanelles by way of Archangel or Vladivostok.[44]

The place of Gallipoli in the broader British grand strategy was confirmed by the Constantinople Agreement on 18 March, whereby the British and French promised the city to Russia after an allied victory – a remarkable concession, and a reflection of just how much they needed or expected Russian military support. It was also an attempt to ensure that Russia would not make a separate peace.[45] Another part of this grand strategy fell into place when Italy (which had annexed Libya and the Dodecanese from the Ottoman Empire in 1911–12) entered the war against the Central Powers on 23 May, in accordance with the Treaty of London signed four weeks earlier. Although Italian troops almost immediately became bogged down in the First Battle of the Isonzo, there was no way at the time for the British to predict that a further eleven unsuccessful battles would follow before the end of the war.

Similarly, British hopes that Greece or Romania might join the war against the Ottomans were not unrealistic, and although Bulgaria (which had done well against Ottoman forces in the First Balkan War of 1912–13) was a more remote possibility, at least a neutral Bulgaria meant that Germany remained without a land route through which to reinforce the Ottoman Empire with troops or matériel. The problem Britain faced in attempting to assemble this alliance was that the Balkan countries being approached needed convincing that they were not joining the losing side, and would not be simply overwhelmed by enemy forces, as was already threatening to happen to beleaguered Serbia. Although the Italian coastline could be protected with help from the Royal Navy, Bulgaria in particular could only be protected by Russia.[46]

According to Hamilton, one of the wider British motives for the original April landings on Gallipoli had been to galvanise all these countries into playing an active role in the war against the Ottoman Empire. His *Gallipoli Diary* for 17 May reads: 'The landing has been made but the Balkans fold their arms, the Italians show no interest, the Russians do not move an inch to get across the Black Sea.'[47] Although this was hindsight, it was on the same day that Hamilton sent a long cable to Kitchener asking for more British troops and shells or better diplomatic progress, or as he later put it, 'two corps or an Ally'. Meanwhile, the message that Hamilton gave to his wife to spread around London was that even an extra brigade on 25 April would have brought him decisive results.[48] On 19 May, the same day that a massive Turkish counter-attack against the ANZAC-held positions on Gallipoli failed with heavy losses, Hamilton received Kitchener's private reply to his demand: 'The question whether we can long support two fields of operation draining on our resources requires grave consideration.'[49] Two days later, Hamilton learned of the resignations of both Fisher and Churchill from the Admiralty, with a heavy hint from Kitchener that he might also be stepping down, as the Asquith government began to unravel. The implication of all this was clear enough. With minor exceptions, the Ottoman Army had no offensive capability against British and dominion troops, although their artillery could force a British retreat from critical ground; conversely, the British had so far stood a good chance of holding whatever ground they gained in their attacks on Gallipoli. But Hamilton needed a large and successful offensive both to justify the campaign's continuation and quite possibly Kitchener's position in the War Office.

On 30 July Hamilton ordered a *feu de joie* fired in the trenches in celebration of the Anglo-Indian victory at the Battle of Nasiriyeh in Mesopotamia three days earlier.[50] At the time it seemed that even Baghdad might be within British reach, not that the advance would lead to the disastrous surrender at Kut-el-Amara in April 1916. Hamilton also later claimed that throughout May he continued to expect the Russians either to send a corps to reinforce him or to renew their attacks elsewhere against the Ottoman Empire, only finding out unofficially on 2 June that he could expect no Russian help at all. He at once cabled Kitchener that equivalent military support must be found either from Bulgaria or Greece, or substantial British reinforcements sent out, or both. Hamilton also continued to hope confidently for further success in Mesopotamia, and for Italian or Greek support. In mid-June he wrote to Field Marshal French that the initial landings in April had prompted Italian entry into the war (a view that appears to have originated with his wife after a misunderstood conversation with Lord Haldane). In fact, the Greek general election in June provoked a crisis between King Constantine I and his government that was not resolved until August, too late for Hamilton even if the wrong side (from the allied viewpoint) had not won.[51]

Nevertheless, the need for allied action in coordination with the Gallipoli campaign remained a cornerstone of British strategy. In late May Britain made Bulgaria a promise of greater territory in return for entering the war, but to no avail.[52] On 16 June one of the first papers presented by Hankey to the new Dardanelles Committee identified the critical need to prevent further Ottoman reinforcements from reaching the Gallipoli peninsula, but he was unable to suggest a way for the British to do this for themselves.[53] On 3 August another effort was made with a renewed Anglo-French diplomatic offer to Bulgaria, followed on 13 August by a further British appeal to Serbia, Greece and Bulgaria to combine their forces for an offensive; but after the news of the fall of Warsaw this understandably came to nothing.[54]

Meanwhile, on 10 May, with awful timing (it was the day after the start of the Battle of Aubers Ridge), Field Marshal French received a War Office order to send substantial amounts of shells to Gallipoli; he responded by protesting about the shortage of shells to *The Times* correspondent Colonel Repington, whose sensational 'shell scandal' article duly appeared on 14 May. Coinciding with Fisher's resignation as First Sea Lord, this helped precipitate the Asquith government's collapse, leading to the formation of the new coalition government on 26 May. French's real target in complaining to

Repington may have been Kitchener rather than Asquith, and historians have generally given him less credit for the fall of the last British Liberal government than he gave himself; by law, a new government had to be formed by the end of 1915 anyway, either through a general election or by some other method.[55] But at the time it certainly looked as if French had just helped bring down the government, and had weakened Kitchener's authority. The inclusion of Conservatives in the government was also a victory for the army's views and a Continental strategy against a Liberal Party that traditionally favoured the navy. Kitchener's authority was further weakened by the appointment of David Lloyd George as Minister of Munitions, while Hamilton lost his two strongest political supporters, Churchill from the Admiralty and Haldane from the government altogether. Churchill, still a member of the Dardanelles Committee as Chancellor of the Duchy of Lancaster, continued to press hard for a renewed attack at Gallipoli.[56]

With the British failure to provide another ally for Hamilton, the remaining alternative – if the Gallipoli campaign was to continue – was to send him the equivalent of a second corps to join the existing VIII Corps. Kitchener's temporary weakness in relation to French was highlighted by his rejection of Hamilton's request for either Rawlinson or Byng to command the new IX Corps for the Suvla landing, an episode usually but inaccurately portrayed as a farcical squabble over military seniority. Kitchener's response to Hamilton's request on 15 June gave first of all the real reason for refusal, 'I am afraid that Sir John French would not spare the services of the two Generals you mention,' meaning that he was not prepared to ask, followed by the excuse that both were junior to Sir Bryan Mahon commanding 10th (Irish) Division, whom Hamilton had already rejected as a corps commander, possibly not realising that Mahon also had some political influence.[57] Hamilton's final and much criticised choice of Sir Frederick Stopford to command IX Corps should be seen in this context. At no point in the Dardanelles Committee's deliberations was the idea mentioned of sending Hamilton one or more veteran divisions from the Western Front. At its first meeting on 7 June the Committee instead authorised his reinforcement by three green New Army divisions.[58] One of the arguments used by Kitchener at this meeting was that the losses already suffered by Australian and New Zealand troops might provoke dominion criticism of any evacuation; otherwise the views of the dominions hardly figured in British considerations.[59]

The Conservatives in the new coalition were at first prepared to support a strategy of defence on the Western Front while reinforcing Gallipoli.[60] But the British in summer 1915 did not have control over their own strategy. In early June, along with Hamilton's numerous complaints, Kitchener also had to deal with a French delegation at the War Office making their argument for the proposed major offensive on the Western Front that autumn.[61] Although naturally Field Marshal French still wanted priority for the BEF and the

Western Front, he vacillated on whether to recommend the accompanying British offensive that the French were demanding. In consequence, from mid-June onwards French was visibly losing the confidence of both King George V and the Dardanelles Committee, which began to consider his replacement by Haig, then commanding First Army.

One of the arguments later used repeatedly by Churchill and Hamilton was that the government's failure to respond rapidly to Hamilton's request for reinforcements in mid-May played a major part in the eventual British failure at Gallipoli. This argument ignored the wider strategic context in which the decision to send reinforcements was made. In February, Germany had declared that any British merchant ships might be sunk without warning, and began a major submarine offensive. On 7 May, the liner SS *Lusitania* was sunk in the Atlantic, signalling a serious threat to British maritime communications, but also opening the possibility that the United States might enter the war on the allied side. On 5 June, partly in response to the severe American reaction to the *Lusitania* episode, the Germans secretly forbad their submarines from attacking large ocean liners; but the British did not know this, and the number of their ships being sunk continued to rise until the end of September.[62] At the time, this might have been the prelude to a completely unrestricted submarine campaign, or to much larger German naval operations such as a sortie by the High Seas Fleet into the North Sea. On 7 June Churchill proposed reinforcing the three New Army divisions already allocated to Hamilton with two further Territorial Force divisions, but with merchant ships and their destroyer escorts overstretched in the face of the submarine threat the only way to get five divisions to Gallipoli before October was to employ three large liners as troop transports: the SS *Aquitania*, SS *Olympic*, and SS *Mauritania* (the *Lusitania*'s sister ship). This decision had very large political and strategic implications, including the risk of losing another liner. It took until 5 July for the Dardanelles Committee to reach its final decision to proceed with the deployment, following which all five divisions joined Hamilton by the end of the month without mishap, although the *Aquitania* did report a near-miss from a German torpedo in the English Channel.[63]

The British were very well aware of the strategic dilemma they were now facing. In late June, Rawlinson, serving as a corps commander on the Western Front, gave a very clear summary of the situation in his diary, probably in response to Hamilton's request for him to command IX Corps. Agreeing that the deadlock on the Western Front was presently unbreakable, and regretting that there was no way for the British to attack Austria-Hungary directly, Rawlinson conceded that Germany held the initiative and could either attack in the West, or more likely overrun Serbia, thereby at the very least intimidating the other Balkan states into continuing neutrality. Without Balkan allies the Dardanelles campaign would fail, with a major impact on Islamic opinion. Rawlinson had no solution to the underlying problem that 'we began the attack on the Dardanelles before we were safe in the West'. He concluded that the only viable strategy remaining was to attempt the capture of Constantinople by a renewed offensive at Gallipoli, before Serbia was overrun.[64] This was also the inevitable conclusion reached by the British government.

Even so, any British decisions about Gallipoli had important consequences for the Western Front and the alliance with France. On 24 June, Joffre and French met at Chantilly and agreed between themselves that an allied defensive posture on the Western Front would be fatal to Russia, Serbia and Italy; Joffre's plan remained that the French Army would make a major attack in early autumn 1915, now set to take place in the Champagne region, with a secondary attack in Artois, to which the BEF must make a significant contribution at Loos.[65] This entire strategy was contradicted two days later by Kitchener, who proposed instead that the allies should make their main effort in the Dardanelles, while re-

TAKE UP THE SWORD OF JUSTICE

maining on the defensive in the West. On 3 July, after conferring with Field Marshal French, Asquith's coalition government decided to send the bulk of the trained New Army and Territorial Force divisions to France before the end of the year in order to hold more line, but also to reinforce Hamilton with two further divisions, a decision that (as already described) was confirmed by the Dardanelles Committee two days later.[66]

In consequence of this strategic dispute, the first ever conference of the war held between the British and French governments to coordinate their strategy was convened at Calais on 6 July (the day after the Dardanelles Committee had agreed to send Hamilton his reinforcements by using the three ocean liners). At this conference, Kitchener repeated his case for a renewed offensive on Gallipoli and a defensive posture on the Western Front. No official record was kept of what was said or decided, but most of those who attended believed that Kitchener's strategy had prevailed. Hankey, who attended the conference but not its critical meetings, described its conclusions as 'unformulated', but as including an agreement that the British would launch 'no great offensive' on the Western Front.[67] Lady Hamilton got her information next day from Colonel Repington's wife, writing gleefully that 'there is an idea of making

Poster published by the British Parliamentary Recruiting Committee in response to the sinking of the ocean liner, *Lusitania*, torpedoed by the German submarine U-20 on 7 May 1915, urging Britons to avenge the drowning of innocent civilians. John Bernard Partridge, *Take up the sword of justice*, 1915, chromolithograph on paper on canvas backing, 101.5 x 63.6 cm.

AWM ARTV03925

the Dardanelles the principal centre of the war now – how mad that would make General [*sic*] French! And how splendid that would be.'[68] On the same day, Lord Esher wrote to the King urging him to strengthen Kitchener's authority, including possibly reviving for him the old post of Commander-in-Chief of the Army.[69] On 12 July, Lady Hamilton had it confirmed for her by family friend Lord Dalhousie that Kitchener wanted to give the Dardanelles precedence over the Western Front.

This apparently firm decision was followed by a very puzzling episode. On 7 July, as Hankey, Lady Hamilton and Lord Esher were writing down their impressions, an inter-allied planning conference headed by Joffre met at Chantilly. To all appearances, it reversed the strategy that the British and French governments had agreed at Calais on the previous day. At this meeting, Joffre announced that his offensive in Champagne would definitely take place, and French undertook to plan the British attack at Loos in support. While definite evidence is lacking, the most probable explanation for this behaviour is that some unrecorded compromise had been reached by the British and the French, whereby Joffre would not oppose the August offensive on Gallipoli in return for more British troops in France and for a broad British promise to make preparations for Loos.[70] Hamilton later reflected on the strategic issue in his *Gallipoli Diary*:

> 'Stopping all operations in France' is the very kernel of the question. If half the things we hear about the Bosche [*sic*] forces and our own are half true, we have no prospect of dealing a decisive blow in the West until next spring. And an indecisive blow is worse than no blow. But we can *hold on* there till all's blue. Now H[igh] E[xplosive] is offensive and shrapnel is defensive. I ought to attack at once; French mustn't. Therefore, we should be given, *now*, dollops of H.E.[71]

Much more than a simple battlefield victory was now riding on the August offensive on Gallipoli. In mid-July Hankey arrived at Hamilton's headquarters as an observer reporting back directly to Asquith (possibly as the 'emissary' of Hamilton's cryptic note). Churchill also planned to accompany Hankey, a decision approved by Asquith, Kitchener and even Balfour, but blocked by strong opposition from Conservative members of the Cabinet.[72] On 28 July, Kitchener cabled Hamilton that 'in the short time available before the bad weather intervenes the Dardanelles operations are now of the highest importance'.[73]

What this amounted to in strategic terms was that Hamilton was required to attack with the troops that he had been sent, and that he might be reinforced with more and better troops if he succeeded, in which case Kitchener's wider scheme for a campaign against the Ottoman Empire in preference to the Western Front might come into play. Lady Hamilton wrote in her diary on 12 August that 'I hope Gallipoli's fate was not decided when the Government took the fatal decision of making the push at Loos' (a battle about which she already knew some weeks before it was due to start) 'and sent the reinforcements there that my poor Ian was clamouring for at Gallipoli'.[74] On the same day Hamilton wrote to her, informing her of how close he believed that he had come to victory and that the fighting at Gallipoli must continue, information that she immediately used to lobby against calls for a British evacuation from the peninsula.

In the event, the August offensives failed to achieve any of the larger objectives hoped or expected of them. On 14 August Hankey cabled Asquith and Kitchener that 'the surprise attack has definitely failed', and that the campaign would probably continue into 1916; once back in London, on 30 August he submitted a paper to the Dardanelles Committee advising that 'it seems unlikely that an early and complete success can be looked for' and that the only realistic choices were between either a long campaign involving major reinforcements, or evacuation.[75] It was not just a matter of ground not gained on Gallipoli, but of whether the Dardanelles Committee was prepared to call off the forthcoming Battle of Loos as the British contribution to Joffre's offensive on the Western Front, with all the political consequences of that decision. After a further meeting between Kitchener and Joffre, on 20 August, the Dardanelles Committee, followed by a meeting of the entire Cabinet, rejected Hamilton's request for further reinforcements and approved the Battle of Loos, with Kitchener's famous observation: 'Unfortunately we had to make war as we must and not as we would like to.'[76] Like Hamilton, French would be allowed his chance, and with some reluctance he launched his attack on 25 September.

The Battle of Loos was a predictable British defeat, leading by the end of 1915 to French's dismissal and replacement by Haig, and to the further curtailing of Kitchener's authority by the appointment of Robertson as the new Chief of the Imperial General Staff with increased powers.[77] In January 1916 the last of the British forces at Cape Helles evacuated Gallipoli, and Haig with Robertson's support began plans for a major offensive on the Western Front that would become the Battle of the Somme. By the end of that year the Gallipoli campaign would pale almost into insignificance against the scale of the massive British military effort and mounting human losses on the Western Front.

Chapter 3

A ridge too far
The obstacles to allied victory

Ashley Ekins

On the morning of 8 August 1915 the allied offensive on Gallipoli reached its climax. For the first time since the landings in April, New Zealand troops reached the summit of Chunuk Bair and viewed the distant prize of the Dardanelles straits. This 'brief moment of triumph' would later be regarded as a lost opportunity, but at the time, as Private Cecil Malthus of the Canterbury Battalion recalled:

> The position was untenable and had no future . . . It was found almost impossible to supply even this handful of men. They got little food, less water, little ammunition and no bombs.[1]

To secure the summit would have required an infantry force of several fresh divisions to simultaneously capture the higher peak of Hill 971 to the north while sweeping down the Sari Bair ridgeline to link up with the 'old Anzac' sector. Yet even if such numbers had been available, it was soon obvious that they could not be supplied through the steep and tortuous terrain. British Commander-in-Chief General Sir Ian Hamilton recorded drily in his diary on the day after the summit was captured that it was not possible to send reinforcements to support the Anzac assault on Sari Bair because, 'the effort to carry food, water and cartridges to the firing lines is already overtaxing the Corps'.[2]

In retrospect, it seems extraordinary that Hamilton and his senior staff had failed to anticipate this situation during their detailed planning for the August offensive. The difficulties involved in holding, reinforcing and supplying Chunuk Bair were symptomatic of those confronting allied soldiers at virtually every major objective of the offensive. The New Zealanders, reinforced by British troops, clung tenaciously to their exposed positions on Chunuk Bair for two days under heavy Turkish fire. On 9 August, British and Gurkha skirmishers crested the adjacent peak of Hill Q only to be driven off by artillery fire. Later that same day, when the shattered survivors of the Wellington Battalion were withdrawn from Chunuk Bair, just 70 men remained from the 760 who had briefly held the summit. The fighting there had left the earth stained the 'dull browny red ... [of] dried blood', one soldier recalled.[3] In the early hours of the following day, their British replacements were overwhelmed by a massive Turkish counter-attack which effectively terminated the August offensive and left the Turks in possession of all the crucial high ground. For the Turks it was a costly victory; for the allies, an even more costly defeat. To some, the terrain itself would be considered the only true victor.

Questions remained about the allied commanders' apparent underestimation of the limits imposed by the terrain, particularly given the physical condition of their exhausted troops. From the beginning of the Gallipoli campaign, commanders had repeatedly squandered large numbers of troops in fruitless and costly assaults on features of no real tactical or strategic value. Now, in the August offensive the same mistakes had been repeated on an even larger scale and with even more catastrophic results.[4]

The mastery of terrain

'Geography is the bones of strategy', observed American military historian Theodore Ropp. British military historian John Keegan similarly emphasised the influence of terrain in military operations, arguing that the American Civil War was in many ways 'a story of the struggle of man against geography, in which those who had a feel for the country eventually succeeded because they knew how to work with the landscape instead of ignoring or defying it.'[5] That judgement could equally be made of the Gallipoli campaign.

The campaign's enduring fascination and romantic appeal derives in large part from its dramatic natural setting. The remote and rugged Gallipoli peninsula of western Turkey that was the site of the eight-month-long military struggle in 1915 continues to inspire historical conjecture and 'retrospective sentimentality' in ample measure, often at the expense of rational analysis.[6] The Gallipoli landscape, with its distinctive topographical features and forbidding terrain, draws increasing numbers of visitors to explore the former battlefields; but few realise the degree to which that landscape was a powerful influence on the campaign, shaping its course and outcome in significant ways.

At the level of planning and command of operations, the Gallipoli terrain compounded the difficulties confronting allied commanders, already struggling with their limited forces, munitions and matériel, and their long and inconstant lines of communication and supply. At virtually every stage of the campaign, the advantages and limitations imposed by the peninsula's challenging terrain dominated the battlefield and on several occasions they were pivotal in determining the outcome.[7] The allied leaders' misjudgements and misconceptions about the terrain hamstrung their planning, frustrated their troops' efforts and reduced their chances of success. Misunderstandings about the strategic and tactical advantages of their chosen objectives, and the feasibility of allied plans to capture and hold them, have been perpetuated in many historical accounts to the present day.

Most of the peninsula presented hazardous country for offensive operations, particularly for amphibious assaults. The southern coastline consisted largely of rugged cliffs with few wide beaches suitable for the allies to land and assemble large forces. In the hinterland, the Turkish defenders had the added advantage of the steep and confusing terrain which lent itself readily to defence, providing the Turks with a strong 'force multiplier', in modern military jargon. The influence of the terrain on the objectives and outcomes was crucial at two decisive phases: firstly, during the initial amphibious landings in April and their immediate aftermath; second and most significantly, during the co-ordinated series of major offensives in August, directed at breaking out of the Turkish encirclement and containment at Helles and Anzac.

The landings in April and the operations in August were directed at three principal allied objectives, all of them conspicuous features on the high ground of the peninsula. Firstly, Achi Baba in the southern Helles sector. At 218 metres high, this hill supposedly dominated the centre of the southern end of the peninsula. Second, in the central Anzac sector, the Sari Bair ('Yellow ridge') and its highest peak, Kocaçimentepe ('Hill of the great pasture') known to the allies as Hill 971 (971 feet high) and marked on naval charts as Hill 305 (305 metres or 1,000 feet).[8] Third, in the northern or Suvla sector, the Anafarta ridge with its peak of Tekketepe (270 metres) and the adjacent Kireçtepe ridge (200 metres).

Almost a century later, a critical reassessment of the strategic and tactical advantages − both real and supposed − of these main objectives, and their impact on the course of the campaign, might be considered long overdue.

'That gigantic fraud' – the objective of Achi Baba

The August offensive stemmed directly from the failure of British and French forces at Helles to capture their primary objective of Achi Baba following the landings of 25 April. Two weeks after the landings, General Hamilton had declared that 'the only sound procedure is to hammer away . . . until we get Achi Baba'. As a result, for three months allied commanders had launched repeated attacks, attempting to advance towards the low hump that dominated the allied area of operations.[9] The attacks often involved costly frontal assaults

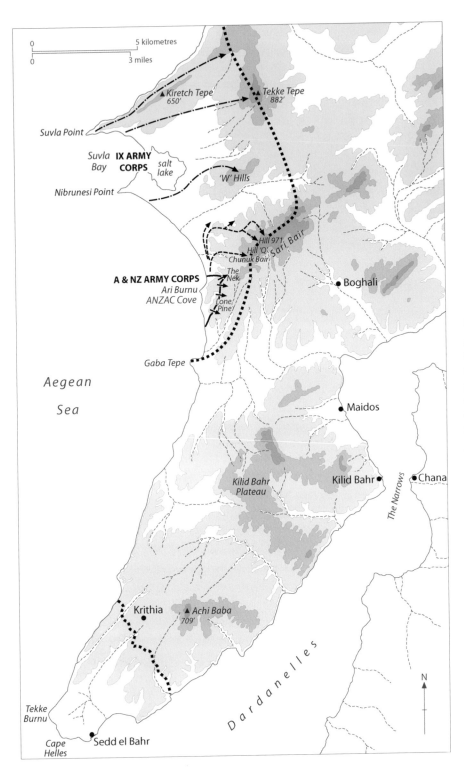

Map 3.1

Allied objectives for the August offensive, showing the lines proposed to be occupied at the end of the main offensive operations.

Cartographer: Keith Mitchell

across open ground and in broad daylight. Allied casualties rose relentlessly, but by the end of July the allied front line was still three kilometres short of Achi Baba which remained firmly in Turkish hands.

Faced with this deadlock, Hamilton was persuaded by the ANZAC Corps commander Lieutenant General William Birdwood to shift the focus of offensive operations north of the Anzac area. New Zealand scouts had discovered that Turkish positions on the heights were apparently lightly held and presented an 'open flank' for a large-scale breakout push from Anzac. Birdwood's proposal became the genesis of plans for the August offensive.

The months of protracted, futile and costly assaults against Achi Baba should have served as a clear warning of the folly of misjudging the terrain features. By the time the August offensive was launched, however, it had become accepted doctrine that once Achi Baba was captured, it would allow attacking forces to break through into open country as well as to dominate the Turkish defensive positions in the Dardanelles straits. First Lord of the Admiralty Winston Churchill, the resolute political proponent of the Gallipoli campaign, was one who remained convinced. Even after the failure of the entire campaign, Churchill argued that the capture of 'the vital observation-point' of Achi Baba would have enabled 'indirect naval fire to be directed with the utmost accuracy upon the forts at the Narrows', in order to destroy those coastal defences and allow the fleet to sail through to Constantinople.[10]

Churchill's conviction was based on a misreading of the terrain. The concentrations of Turkish forts and coastal artillery batteries on both sides of the Narrows were the ultimate target of both the naval assault and land attacks. But the forts and gun emplacements were *not actually visible* from the Achi Baba summit due to the high spurs of intervening ridges and the shoulder of the Kilid Bahr plateau, the large, horseshoe-shaped massif at the centre of the peninsula (see Maps 3.2 and 3.3).[11]

The Kilid Bahr plateau was in fact the principal objective of the landings, *not* the intermediate objective of Achi Baba. As stipulated in Hamilton's original operation order for the landing, the role of the landing forces was 'to assist the fleet to force the Dardanelles by capturing the Kilid Bahr plateau, and dominating the forts at the Narrows'.[12] Secretary of State for War Lord Kitchener had emphasised in his instructions to Hamilton that the plateau was 'the key' to controlling the western or peninsula side of the Narrows, a view reiterated by the British official historian who described the plateau as 'the key of the Dardanelles'.[13] Once astride the Kilid Bahr Plateau, British artillery could subdue the Turkish batteries on the Asiatic side of the Dardanelles as well as the Turkish defences on the peninsula.[14]

The Kilid Bahr plateau presented a formidable natural obstacle, however. Rising sharply to over 200 metres high with very steep, in places precipitous, escarpments on the north, northwest and west sides, the feature comprised a natural fortress. On the southwest side, facing Achi Baba, the plateau was

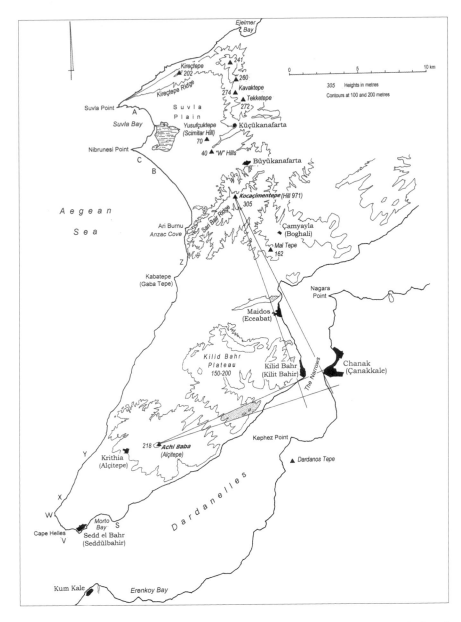

Map 3.2

Topography of the
Gallipoli Peninsula,
showing the 'line of
sight' observation
possible from the two
principal objectives of
Achi Baba (*Alçitepe*) and
Hill 971 (*Kocaçimentepe*).
Shading indicates
the features which
obscured a clear view
of the Narrows and forts
on both sides of the
Dardanelles from direct
observation.

Cartographer: Winifred Mumford

slightly less steep but the approaches were cut across by the steep-sided and rocky ravine of the Soghanli Dere and covered with dense scrub which would prove extremely difficult for troops to penetrate.[15]

Achi Baba was in reality nothing more than a stepping stone for the advance to the Kilid Bahr plateau, and 'second in importance' to the plateau.[16] Achi Baba offered no opportunity for dominating the Narrows defences, although this misconception was to be perpetuated for decades.[17] Most historians and veterans of the campaign who studied the ground after the war shared no such illusions.[18] Australian official historian Charles Bean reconnoitred the summit

Map 3.3

Topography of the
Gallipoli Peninsula
(detail), showing the
'line of sight' observation
possible from the two
principal objectives of
Achi Baba (Alçitepe) and
Hill 971 (Kocaçimentepe).
Shading indicates the
features of the Kilid Bahr
(Kilitbahir) plateau which
obscured the forts and
shore batteries on both
sides of the Dardanelles
from direct observation.

Cartographer: Winifred Mumford

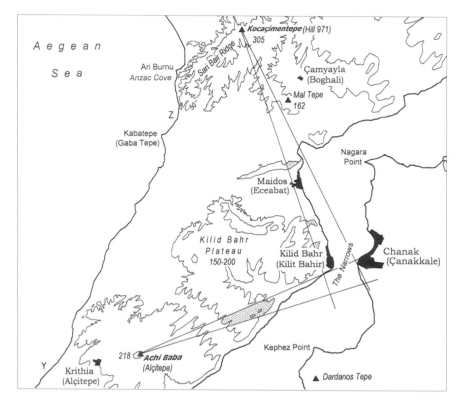

of Achi Baba in February 1919. Although the hill 'commanded the whole foot of the Peninsula', he observed, 'not the slightest observation over Chanak (Çanakkale) or the Narrows could be had from there – only a featureless little triangle of the Narrows'.[19] In Bean's view:

> even had Achi Baba been reached, few who served with the M.E.F. [Mediterranean Expeditionary Force], or who have seen the ground since, will believe that Hamilton's force could ever have forced from the south the defences of the Kilid Bahr Plateau.[20]

Bean's judgement was supported by the independent conclusions of a British artillery officer, Major W.R.E. Harrison, who served on Gallipoli during the campaign and visited the former battlefields in the early 1930s. With an experienced gunner's eye for ground, Harrison noted that the prospect from Achi Baba looking north was 'very disappointing'. Far from dominating the Dardanelles and the Narrows, he found that Achi Baba is confronted by 'four miles [over six kilometres] of very broken ground . . . by no means dominated by Achi Baba'. Beyond this, the Kilid Bahr Plateau rises 'like a rampart across the Peninsula'. Harrison concluded that the possession of Achi Baba was 'infinitely more valuable' to the Turkish defenders and its capture by the allies 'could not have produced decisive results'.[21]

Another who examined the terrain was Commodore Roger Keyes, chief of staff to the three successive admirals who commanded the British fleet during the campaign. Keyes later visited the peninsula and climbed Achi Baba together with Hamilton and his former GHQ staff officer, Lieutenant Colonel Cecil Aspinall (subsequently author of the British official history of the campaign). It was 'an unpleasant shock to us', Keyes later wrote, 'to find that the forts we had hoped to destroy, with the assistance of observation from Achi Baba, were not even visible from *that gigantic fraud*'.[22] However, Keyes's commander, Admiral Wemyss, who assumed command of the Dardanelles fleet in November, remained convinced to the end of the campaign that possession of Achi Baba 'was the real key of the situation' and could provide sufficient observation to assist the fleet in forcing the straits.[23]

Such speculation remained academic as the prospects for capturing Achi Baba rapidly faded. Hamilton continued to support the strategy of his chief of staff, Major General Walter Braithwaite and Major General Aylmer Hunter-Weston, commander of the British 29th Division, of 'hammering away' at Achi Baba, striving vainly to reach it 'by stages', employing ever heavier bombardments, short night advances, and digging in to withstand Turkish counter-attacks.[24] As the cost in casualties and munitions mounted in the prolonged effort to reach 'that unattainable goal' of Achi Baba, wrote Bean, it 'never came near complete success, and, even if it had done so, would have entailed no result approaching a decision'.[25]

Meanwhile, there was a gradual displacement of the main objective, the Kilid Bahr Plateau. Although 'Achi Baba itself commanded no vital position', Bean noted, 'this peak came naturally to be regarded as the crucial objective of the expedition'. Even Hamilton seemed 'to have persuaded himself that, when once its summit was reached, his army would break through into open country'.[26] The transfer of objectives became embedded in further planning: as the main August offensive operations got under way further north in the Anzac sector, the attacks at Helles, which were by then purely diversionary, still had as their stated aim: 'the capture of Krithia and Achi Baba [as] the first steps towards the final victory'.[27] This substitution of the main objective with a valueless secondary aim was a serious lapse by both the commander-in-chief and his staff. It was to be repeated on a larger scale and at even greater consequences during the August offensive.

'The keys to the Narrows'?
The objectives of Chunuk Bair and Hill 971

In the Anzac sector, 20 kilometres to the north of Helles, the allied assault around Ari Burnu had stalled within days of the landing of 25 April. As at Helles, none of the assaulting troops managed to secure their initial objectives on the first day. The attacking forces fell back into hastily dug defensive positions and soon became mired in the same form of static siege warfare on the Western Front that the Gallipoli campaign had been intended to circumvent. Desperately short of the ordnance and equipment needed for trench fighting, lacking sufficient reinforcements and exposed to continual enemy fire, the Anzacs clung to their tenuous beachheads, unable either to break out of the Turkish encirclement or safely break off the engagement. By 1 May, 27,000 troops had been landed at Anzac and the front line was more secure. But further advance proved impossible.

From early May, a stalemate set in at Anzac with the opposing front lines closely interlocked. Neither side had the numbers, heavy artillery or tactical means to end the deadlock. The tortuous terrain in the Anzac area soon made the entrenched positions virtually impregnable to either side. A Turkish staff officer noted in his diary, five weeks after the Anzac landing:

> The situation in the battlefields is not improving. The British [meaning Anzacs] in their strong trenches, we are in ours. We can only kick the British with self-sacrificing attacks. The field is narrow, there is no place to manoeuvre. Our attacks don't bring the final success. The attacks result in heavy losses.[28]

Clinging to a confined area less than one kilometre deep and three kilometres from north to south, the Anzac positions were overlooked from all sides by Turkish positions on higher ground. American artillery specialist Major Sherman Miles, who studied the campaign extensively in the early 1920s, noted that the terrain at Helles and Anzac 'lent itself to artillery defense, and

A section of the Anzac front line, looking from Wellington Gully, below Russell's Top, across Shrapnel Valley towards the rear of Quinn's Post (partly concealed on left skyline) and Courtney's and Steele's Posts (right), showing the terraces and steps cut into the steep slopes by soldiers in constructing their support and reserve lines.

AWM A02750

throughout the campaign the Turks possessed admirable observation posts dominating most of the Allied lines'.[29] As the senior artillery commander at Anzac later recounted:

> The Turks had three great advantages over us. They had all the commanding ground, both at the top and sides, and they could see all our movements and look into our lines, and see every single thing we did. They could see what we were doing, but we could not see what they were doing. We were also enfiladed from both flanks and could be shelled anywhere from the front.[30]

Similarly, the British artillery commander at Helles recalled that Turkish observers on Achi Baba could see the British gun positions clearly, and as a result, his batteries 'suffered severely'. In just two months, June and July, one 6-inch howitzer, twenty-five 18-pounders (over one-third of the British total of 72 at Helles), and one or two 60-pounders were 'put out of action by direct hits' from Turkish artillery.[31]

In this situation, possession of the heights was considered essential for victory. Birdwood convinced Hamilton that with an additional fresh division he could seize and hold the high crest line to the north of the Anzac area and enfilade the Turkish trench lines. In approving the plans for the August offensive, Hamilton emphasised that the Sari Bair ridge was 'the "keep" to the Narrows' and Chunuk Bair and Hill 971 were 'its keys'.[32] Allied troops holding the summit of Hill 971 would be able to control Turkish sea and land communications with their forces holding Kilid Bahr and the Achi Baba position, argued the British official naval historian. The naval staff believed the capture of Hill 971 would also secure a spotting station for effective bombardment of the forts guarding the Narrows.[33]

This assumption amounted to another serious misreading of the terrain. The Sari Bair range from Chunuk Bair to Hill 971, while arguably 'the key' to Turkish defences securing the Anzac area, could not provide allied control of the peninsula, the Kilid Bahr plateau or the Narrows. Major Harrison, the British artillery officer who assessed the terrain at Helles in the 1930s, also reconnoitred the Sari Bair heights. He concluded that, although the Dardanelles straits are visible from the summit of Hill 971 and Chunuk Bair, the ridge peak 'in no way "commands" the Straits, still less the Asian shore beyond'. The capture of the peaks would not enable accurate observed fire to be brought to bear on the Turkish defences of the Narrows, nor would it command the Turkish line of communications between Maidos and Helles. Lying between the Sari Bair ridge, Harrison observed:

> is a tumbled mass of hills, little less in height than the mountain itself; this stretch of country is almost indescribably difficult for

military operations; it consists of a tangled mass of deep ravines with precipitous sides and choked with scrub. Had we taken Sari Bair we should still have been faced with an advance of some six miles across this type of country before we could have secured positions dominating the Straits.[34]

Harrison argued that the Sari Bair peaks were 'in no way a "key" to the Peninsula' and that only the allied capture of the Kilid Bahr plateau could have decided the campaign. Few observers since have noted that from both Hill 971 and Chunuk Bair, the Kilid Bahr plateau obscured the major Turkish defensive positions at the Narrows, including the fort at Kilitbahir and the adjacent gun batteries (see Map 3.3). Few have also considered the tremendous distances involved: from Hill 971 to Kilid Bahr is almost 14,000 metres; and to Çanakkale on the opposite side of the Narrows is over 15,000 metres.[35] No guns of the allied artillery available on Gallipoli and few naval guns could fire shells with consistent accuracy to such extreme ranges, even if the problems of spotting and correcting the fire could have been solved.

The Dardanelles viewed from Hill 971 (*Kocaçimentepe*), looking southeast towards Chanak (*Çanakkale*) on the far side of the Narrows. Fort Çimenlik at Çanakkale is faintly visible across the Dardanelles at a distance of 16,500 yards (15,088 metres). Obscured by the northern scarp of the Kilid Bahr Plateau (the dark promontory at the right centre) are the crucial Turkish defensive positions on the peninsula, the fortress at Kilit Bahir and the adjacent gun emplacements at a distance of 15,160 yards (13,862 metres). One of a series of photographs taken by the Australian Historical Mission in early 1919.

AWM G01825

Furthermore, as became obvious in the August assaults, the difficulties of supplying ammunition and water through the ravines and gullies to troops holding the heights would have demanded virtually the entire strength of the Anzac force.[36]

In yet another example of displacement of the main aim, the capture of Hill 971 became GHQ's primary objective in the northern sector, just as the objective of Achi Baba had in the south. Following the failure of allied forces to capture Hill 971, the ever-optimistic Hamilton simply substituted the secondary peak of Chunuk Bair as his principal objective: 'Koja Chemen Tepe (Hill 971) not yet', he wrote on 8 August, 'but Chunuk Bair will do: with that, we win!'[37] Typically sanguine, despite the heavy casualties his troops were suffering, the commander-in-chief displayed little appreciation of the realities of the terrain.

The limitations of artillery

By early 1915, the deadlocked trench warfare on the Western Front had clearly demonstrated the crucial role of artillery in both defending ground and supporting infantry advances against defended positions. The objectives of Achi Baba at Helles, and Chunuk Bair and Hill 971 on the Sari Bair ridge north of Anzac, became the primary focus of operations because of the advantages they appeared to offer to allied artillery. But the battles to capture those high features actually exposed the limitations of British and dominion artillery on Gallipoli.

The First World War was a powerful accelerator of technological development, particularly in military aviation, weapons and artillery. The state of military technology in the latter years of the war, however, should not be confused with that actually available during the Gallipoli campaign in 1915. By 1918, advances in design and manufacture would greatly improve the accuracy and reliability of British artillery, but at the time of the Gallipoli campaign guns wore out quickly in use, shell fuses were temperamental and sometimes dangerous to both guns and crews, and the accuracy of artillery fire was often haphazard.[38] In 1915 British industry had not yet begun its massive expansion of munitions production and the British simply did not have enough guns and ammunition of any quality on Gallipoli. In the Anzac sector by the middle of May, for example, the Australians and New Zealanders had just 40 field guns and six howitzers and the shortage of ammunition limited the field guns to firing two rounds daily per gun.[39] By the end of July, the total had increased to merely 124 guns at Helles and 70 guns at Anzac, the latter often poorly sited due to lack of space in the confined Anzac enclave.[40]

The science of gunnery advanced dramatically during the war from its relatively primitive state in 1915. Innovative techniques of flash spotting, sound ranging, accurate aerial spotting, and accurately registering artillery fire from map grid references, would transform the effectiveness of artillery and help drive the British army to victory on the Western Front. But such techniques simply did not exist at the time of the Gallipoli campaign. The fundamental artillery problem that remained unsolved in 1915 was how to control indirect fire. At that time, according to one authority, 'The only reliable means of ensuring accuracy of fire continued to be for an [artillery] FOO [Forward Observation Officer] on the ground or in the air to observe the fall of shot and indicate corrections'. Where direct observation was not possible, the British army in 1915 resorted to the comparatively primitive techniques of 'shooting from the map' or the use of aerial spotting from aircraft or kite balloons. However, on Gallipoli neither accurate ordnance survey maps nor reliable aircraft and wireless sets were available to make these techniques effective. The end result was that in 1915 'the artillery was not likely to hit, with any certainty or regularity, a target that could not be seen'.[41] Effective artillery fire required high observation positions with unrestricted views of selected targets.

A further factor also limited British artillery capabilities. Presuming that observation positions could be attained, most of the available guns lacked the range, accuracy and explosive power to effectively engage and destroy the most distant Turkish gun sites and defensive positions at the Dardanelles (see comparative data in Table 1).

Most of the available guns were 18-pounder field guns and not howitzers, particularly heavy howitzers, which were most desperately needed for the fighting conditions on the peninsula. The mountainous nature of the Anzac area, in particular, made the terrain unsuitable for field guns with their relatively flat trajectory shells.[42] The former commander of artillery at Anzac, Brigadier General C. Cunliffe Owen described the problem:

> Owing to the shape of the ground, 18-pounders had to be practically in the front line and always under heavy shelling or they could not clear the crest at short range or shoot at the Turkish trenches which were generally only 20 yards from our own. The only solution was to shoot from the flanks.[43]

In addition, the available ammunition consisted mainly of shrapnel rounds which had little effect against Turkish trench systems. What was desperately required was high-explosive (HE) ammunition in large quantities to destroy enemy defensive works, but throughout the campaign there were severe shortages of such rounds. At Helles the British had a battery each of 4.5-inch and 6-inch howitzers, but HE ammunition for howitzers was in such short supply that the artillery commander ordered that no howitzer at Helles was ever to fire HE rounds without his authority, as they were reserved exclusively for bombarding Turkish trenches in support of British attacks.[44]

Table 3.1   Data on British artillery employed in the Gallipoli campaign, 1915

Field guns and howitzers

Gun	Calibre	Projectile weight	Muzzle velocity	Maximum range
18-pr Mk I field gun (*weight in action: 1 ton 6 cwt; 1321 kg*)	3.3 in (84 mm)	18 lb (8.2 kg)	1655 f/s (504 m/s)	6,500 yds (5,940 m)
4.5-in howitzer (*weight in action: 1.44 ton; 1462 kg*)	4.5 in (114 mm)	35 lb (16.3 kg)	1010 f/s (308 m/s)	7,300 yds (6,675 m)
4.7-in field gun (*weight in action: 3 ton 16 cwt; 3870 kg*)	4.724 in (120 mm)	46 lb (20.9 kg)	2500 f/s (762 m/s)	10,900 yds (9,970 m)
5-in howitzer (*weight in action: 1 ton 3 cwt; 1054 kg*)	5 in (127 mm)	50 lb (22.7 kg)	788 f/s (240 m/s)	4,800 yds (4,389 m)
60-pr Mk I field gun (*weight in action: 4.5 tons; 4572 kg*)	5 in (127 mm)	60 lb (27.2 kg)	2080 f/s (634 m/s)	12,300 yds (11,247 m)
6-in howitzer (*weight in action: 3 ton 9 cwt; 3508 kg*)	6 in (152 mm)	122 lb (55.3 kg)	777 f/s (237 m/s)	5,200 yds (4,750 m) / 7,000 yds (6,400 m) Increased elevation with siege carriage

Data compiled from: Brigadier General C. Cunliffe Owen, 'Artillery at Anzac in the Gallipoli Campaign, April to December 1915', *The Journal of the Royal Artillery*, Vol. XLVI, No. 12, 1920, pp. 535–55, table p. 555; I.V. Hogg and L.F. Thurston, *British Artillery Weapons and Ammunition 1914–1918*, Ian Allen, London, 1972; S.N. Gower, *Guns of the Regiment*, Australian War Memorial, Canberra ACT, 1981.

The commander later catalogued the deficiencies in guns and ammunition in that sector, especially the shortages of howitzers and high-explosive ammunition. He recorded just fifty-six 18-pounders at Helles at the end of May, which increased to 72 at the end of July; ammunition was always in short supply and had to be fired according to a daily ration and stockpiled for use in attacks. Through the large offensives of June, July and August there were never more than 88 to 95 operating guns and howitzers. Many of these were old, badly worn and consequently inaccurate: some had even been in continual use since the battle of Omdurman, seventeen years earlier.

Ammunition supplies were wholly insufficient to support the four British divisions at Helles. Supplies never exceeded 25,000 rounds of 18-pounder ammunition, of which no more than 12,000 rounds could be expended in support of a British attack. By 22 August, as the main August offensive ended, the daily ration was reduced to two rounds per gun at Helles; shortly afterwards, the same restriction was re-imposed on the Anzac and Suvla fronts.[45] Such shortages led the French forces at Helles, who were much better provided with both guns and ammunition, to jokingly disparage the British artillery, and its commander, with the epithet 'un coup par pièce' (one shot per gun). British attacks at Helles were dependent upon the support of guns, howitzers and ammunition loaned by the French, and on occasion French batteries under British command provided all the artillery preparation and support.[46]

There was clearly a pressing need for heavy artillery on Gallipoli, but heavy siege howitzers were not produced in substantial numbers in Britain until 1916. The most useful heavy artillery available at the time of the campaign was the 60-pounder field gun, a 5-inch (127 mm) calibre gun firing a 27.2 kilogram shell for a maximum range of approximately 11,000 metres. However, by late July only two batteries, each of four 60-pounders had reached Helles. When the major offensive commenced in early August, all except for one gun were unserviceable due to mechanical breakdowns and lack of spare parts. Consequently, recalled the British artillery commander,

> we had no heavy guns capable of replying to the Turkish heavy guns which enveloped us on three sides, and from whose fire our infantry and artillery suffered severely.[47]

Although prototypes already existed of improved, heavier artillery pieces which would later dominate the battlefields on the Western Front, it would be several years before these weapons were produced in large numbers.[48] Moreover, given the weights of these massive guns it is most unlikely that they could have been managed in the difficult terrain on Gallipoli. The 9.2-inch Siege Howitzer provides a typical example. This formidable weapon was introduced in 1914 and although prototypes reached France in 1915 it was

A British 9.2-inch howitzer battery in action near Morlancourt on the Somme, France, May 1918. Heavy earth-filled steel boxes attached to the front of the guns stabilised their recoil when firing.

AWM E04836

not produced in large numbers for the Western Front until the end of 1916. Firing a 290-pound (131 kilogram) shell to a maximum range of 10,060 yds (9,198 metres), the 9.2-inch (233 mm) howitzer had tremendous power and could have effectively destroyed Turkish trenches and strong points.

However, the 9.2-inch howitzer's 'all-up' weight in action was over 16 tons (16,460 kg). Movement of the gun required a 36-hour operation to dismantle and transport it using three purpose-built carriages hauled by horses or traction engines which would have been virtually impossible to manage in the terrain around Anzac. In preparation for firing, the gun needed to be securely anchored with 9 tons (9144 kilograms) of soil as ballast.[49] This was scarcely a practical weapon for use on Gallipoli, especially in the steep terrain at Anzac where the artillery commander described the difficulties involved in positioning a much lighter, 4.7-inch gun on the hills at Anzac in the summer heat:

> We got a 4.7 gun landed from a lighter with much difficulty, and sleighs were built, and the Australian gunners dragged it half a mile through sand and up the hill where they had built a really good roofed emplacement. It was a great feat to get a 4.7 weighing five tons, up to the top of these hills. But the Australian gunners did wonders.[50]

A small number of the heavy 9.2-inch howitzers were deployed in the more open country at Helles by July, but shell shortages meant the available stocks were used sparingly.[51]

An additional limiting factor was the effective range of even the most powerful of these guns. The distance from Achi Baba to Kilid Bahr was over 12,000 yards (11,000 metres) and from Achi Baba to Çanakkale was over 14,000 yards (almost 13,000 metres). Such distances were at the extreme limit of even the 9.2-inch howitzer's maximum range of 12,740 metres and considerably in excess of the effective range.[52] The distances from Hill 971 were even greater: over 15,000 metres to Çanakkale across the Dardanelles and almost 14,000 metres to Kilitbahir and its crucial gun emplacements. This was well beyond the range of the heaviest land artillery pieces, assuming that it was even possible to haul them up to the peaks and safely install them there.

Most allied infantry attacks during the August offensive received paltry artillery support by the standards of the Western Front. Where possible, additional naval gunfire support was provided by warships and from heavy guns mounted on monitors. But the comparative ineffectiveness of the Royal Navy's gunnery against an enemy entrenched in defensive positions had already been amply demonstrated during the failed naval assault of February and March.[53] The 200 large guns of the 18 warships had tremendous range and destructive power, but their flat trajectory shells had already proved inadequate for the reduction of land fortifications.[54] An exhaustive study by the British Admiralty in 1919 identified serious technical deficiencies in the naval operations at the Dardanelles. Among many problems, the naval shells were unsuitable, as were their fuses, and the low elevation of the naval guns was unable to provide accurate plunging fire.[55]

Soldiers haul the barrel of a 6-inch gun up Walker's Ridge at Anzac in April 1915, using an improvised sled on wooden rollers. One hundred men took 48 hours to complete the task.

AWM P01531.001

The Royal Navy was still developing its primary weapon system, the dreadnought battleship, which had been introduced less than ten years earlier. Range finding and centralised fire control systems for accurate long-range fire were still in the developmental stage and the problem of indirect fire on unobserved targets was not yet solved. Even at anchor, which proved difficult in the currents and under harassing fire from the shore batteries, the warships were capable of hitting a Turkish gun with only one or two rounds of every 100 fired. Turkish gunnery, in contrast, proved much more effective than anticipated. During the naval assault on 18 March, Turkish heavy batteries fired a total of 1600 rounds and scored direct hits on the ships 139 times (one hit for every 11.5 rounds fired).[56] Given the limited ammunition supplies of the fleet and the damage inflicted on the ships, this equation could clearly have only one outcome if the naval assault persisted.

The Royal Navy's newly commissioned super-dreadnought, *Queen Elizabeth*, with its eight powerful 15-inch guns, was the most modern vessel in the fleet. Sent to the Dardanelles mainly to calibrate its armament, the warship fired a total of only eighty-six 15-inch shells and seventy-one 6-inch shells at Turkish forts and other targets. Despite the difficulties of aerial spotting with kite balloons, its heavy guns were rated among the most accurate in the fleet. The ship achieved some spectacular successes, firing shrapnel shells against Turkish troops in the open, and even sank a Turkish transport in the Dardanelles, firing across the peninsula at the extremely long range of 18,000 yards. But the 15-inch shells caused only superficial damage to the

Royal Navy sailors handling the massive shells, each weighing over 1900 pounds (862 kilograms) for the 15-inch guns of the super-dreadnought *Queen Elizabeth*, preparing to fire on the Gallipoli peninsula, May 1915.

AWM G00195

Table 3.2 Data on British naval gunnery employed in the Gallipoli campaign, 1915

Naval guns (battleship main armament and monitors)

Gun	Ship	Projectile weight	Muzzle velocity	Maximum effective range	
12-in Mk VII	Majestic, Ocean, Goliath, Prince George,				
(30.5 cm)	Canopus, Vengeance	850 lb	2350 f/s	14,860 yds	(13,588 m)
12-in Mk IX	Cornwallis, Irresistible, Prince of Wales,				
	Queen	850 lb	2525 f/s	16,650 yds	(15,225 m)
12-in Mk X	Agamemnon, Inflexible, Lord Nelson	850 lb	2700 f/s	18,630 yds	(17,035 m)
14-in (U.S.)	Monitors: Abercrombie, Raglan,				
(35.5 cm)	Havelock, Roberts	1,400 lb	2600 f/s	21,000 yds	(19,202 m)
15-in Mk I	Queen Elizabeth	1,920 lb	2400 f/s	23,387 yds	(21,385 m)
(38 cm)					

(Note: By the end of the First World War improvements in fire control enabled battleships to engage targets at much greater ranges. In the 1930s mounting modifications to the Queen Elizabeth class increased the maximum gun elevation from 20 to 30 degrees, thereby increasing the maximum effective range to approximately 30,000 yards.)

Data compiled from: Sir Julian S. Corbett, Naval Operations, Vols II, III, Longmans, Green and Co, London, 1921, 1923; C.F. Aspinall-Oglander, Military Operations: Gallipoli, 2 vols, William Heinemann, London, 1929, 1932, Maps and Appendices, Vol. I, Appendix 8, 'Composition of squadrons showing principal armaments'; Maps and Appendices, Vol. II, Appendix 6, 'Composition and principal armaments of naval squadrons for August operations'; Peter Hodges, The Big Gun: Battleship Main Armament 1860–1945, Conway Maritime Press, Greenwich, 1981, Appendices, pp. 122–7.

medieval forts guarding the Narrows.[57] In May the *Queen Elizabeth* was recalled due to the threat of German submarines and was not available for the August offensive.

Overall, the guns of the warship were of limited effectiveness in supporting infantry operations. An early Turkish General Staff history of the campaign concluded that the naval guns, 'owing to their flat trajectory, and the unsuitability of their shells for use against land targets, could not effectively support the infantry advance, and had very little effect on the artillery of the [Turkish] defence'.[58] Moreover, the naval guns were dependent upon unreliable aerial spotting techniques. Accurate fire control of the warships guns required the use of ship-borne balloons or the available aircraft, generally utilising primitive wireless sets mounted in underpowered, low-flying and slow seaplanes which required suitable winds for take-off and calm seas for landing, and which were consequently vulnerable to Turkish ground fire.[59]

Even when accurately directed onto enemy targets the naval gunfire support was generally unable to destroy the earthwork defences of gun installations or eliminate dispersed groups of Turkish troops in broken cover.[60] A senior Turkish staff officer later recalled, 'The effect of the British naval artillery was moral without being material'.[61] Major Zeki Bey, commander of a Turkish battalion at Anzac during the campaign, told Charles Bean, 'We found that the ships' fire was not so terrible as at first we had thought that it would be', adding that the howitzers which the allies later deployed on land 'were very much worse'.[62]

The problem of maps

The inaccuracy of the available maps of the Gallipoli peninsula compounded the difficulties of both the allied artillery and the naval guns. As the commander of Anzac artillery recalled:

> The chief difficulty was the absence of a reliable map. The map we had was one that had been done in 1840, I think. It was divided into 2-mile squares, with smaller squares marked by letters, and each subdivided by nine numbers. These maps did not agree with the ground, and what was most important for ships' fire, the compass bearing was two degrees out.[63]

The first accurate map of the Anzac area was obtained almost one month after the landing from the body of a Turkish officer killed during the Turkish attack of 19 May. Charles Bean recorded that this was used together with others captured at Helles to compile 'an excellent map' that was issued to all allied forces.[64] But it is doubtful that any allied maps approached the accuracy and detail of those available to Turkish officers and senior commanders.[65]

No significant ground reconnaissance had been carried out on the peninsula prior to the landings of April, but British officers had conducted sporadic visual reconnaissance of the peninsula from destroyers and aeroplanes. Their observations were entered on detailed maps divided into squares for artillery use and purporting to show elevations with 100 feet wide contour interval lines. This 1:40,000 squared map, which was issued for the landings of 25 April, was an enlarged version of a British War Office one-inch (to the mile) map of 1908, which was in turn based on an old 1:50,000 French map dating from the Crimean War.[66]

When issued with these maps, Australian officers found them 'marvels of detail', according to Australian official historian Charles Bean.[67] But the detail was less valuable than it seemed. The vague topographical features and wide contour lines failed to convey to soldiers a realistic sense of the difficulties of the peninsula terrain, particularly in the Anzac sector.[68] The 'complete unreliability' of the maps, according to the British official history of air operations, was 'a serious handicap' to airmen called upon to conduct reconnaissance and to observe and direct naval and artillery fire.[69]

Much of the overprinted map information supplied by aerial observation was either misleading or incorrect.[70] In some areas, Turkish defensive lines, trenches, camps, gun batteries and emplacements marked on the map do not coincide with Turkish maps and records of troop dispositions and defensive installations; in other areas, the observers appear to have completely missed strong Turkish positions and significant topographical features.[71] The techniques of aerial photography were still in an experimental stage in 1915 and the tactical interpretation of aerial photographs could result in potentially dangerous errors. The Anzac troops who attacked at Lone Pine in August, for example, were issued with sketch maps of the Turkish trenches based on the interpretation of aerial photographs over the Turkish lines. But the maps missed important features, including the fact that the Turks had roofed over the southern half of their trenches at Lone Pine; further, that a deep depression behind the Turkish lines, terraced with bivouac positions and crammed with Turkish reserves and regimental headquarters, restricted any further advance to the east. The absence of accurate contours and natural features failed to show which enemy trenches were on higher or lower ground, and some Turkish communication tracks and terraces were incorrectly indicated as trenches.[72]

Unsurprisingly, many officers came to regard the maps issued by GHQ with some suspicion. Attempts were made before the landings to enhance the information on the issued 1:40,000 squared artillery map with the addition of tinted-colouring of presumed contours, annotations of Turkish defences and descriptions of the terrain. But many errors remained in the modified sheets, the terrain behind Anzac Cove being inadequately described as 'low scrub' and that facing North Beach as 'steep sand bluffs': few of the actual features, ridges or contours were accurately depicted.[73] Despite these efforts, the most current

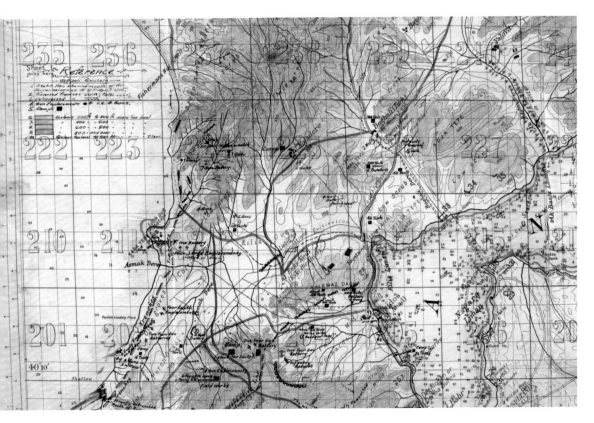

Map 3.4 Squared artillery map of Gallipoli, Sheet 2, 1:40,000 scale (detail) 'showing results of Air Reconnaissances to 18th April 1915', with colour-tinted contours and annotations depicting Turkish tents, camps, artillery batteries and gun emplacements, including Turkish trenches on the seaward side of Plugge's Plateau (square 224); concentrations of Turkish defences around Kaba Tepe (squares 211, 212) and the Kilid Bahr plateau (squares 203, 204); and Turkish 19th Division reserves at Boghali (square 226).

annotated maps, whether accurate or not, were apparently not even issued to many officers prior to the landing. Captain A.M. Ross, a staff captain on the headquarters of the 3rd Australian Brigade, the covering force at the Anzac landing on 25 April, was one of the first to land with the 9th Battalion. He later sent Charles Bean the map he used to write the brigade's landing order and which he carried in his map case at the landing (Map 3.5): this sheet was virtually 'blank', lacking all the details and annotations of Turkish defensive positions and gun emplacements identified by air reconnaissance up to 18 April.[74]

This oversight was to be repeated during the August offensive when a 'stultifying policy of excessive secrecy' by GHQ restricted the issuing of adequate maps and plans to commanders prior to the Suvla Bay landings. On the eve of the operation that would come to characterise failures throughout the Gallipoli campaign, many officers of the British 11th Division 'had never seen a map of the area in which they suddenly found themselves, and had little or no idea of what was required of them'.[75]

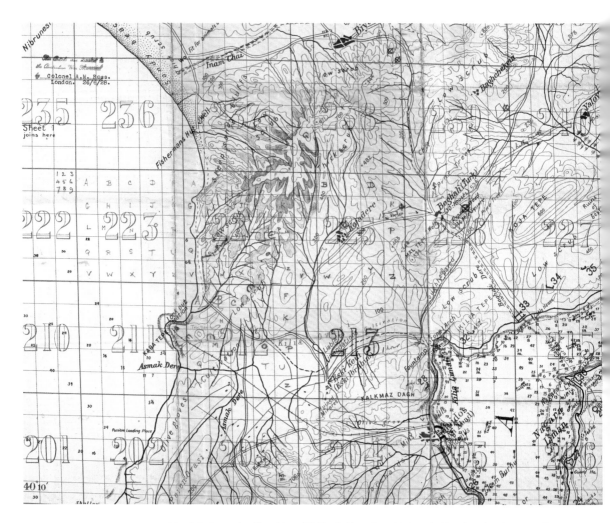

Map 3.5 Squared artillery Map of Gallipoli, Sheet 2, 1:40,000 scale (detail), with colour-tinted contours but minus annotations showing Turkish defences identified by aerial reconnaissance. Captain A.M. Ross of the 3rd Australian Brigade headquarters used this map to write the brigade landing order; he then carried it in his map case at the landing.

Mistakes repeated – Suvla Bay

On 6 August the major allied offensive began with the 1st Australian Brigade's attacks on the southern end of the Anzac position at Lone Pine. This was soon accompanied by attacks at several points along the Anzac front line. Then followed the series of co-ordinated night assaults against the heights of the Sari Bair ridge, while British troops carried out amphibious landings at Suvla Bay.

The primary aim of the British IX Corps under the command of Lieutenant General Stopford was to land and establish a base at Suvla which could be used to supply the northern sector through the winter. Stopford's secondary task was to secure the surrounding semicircle of hills and ridges which overlooked the proposed base areas on Suvla Plain. Only after these two objectives had been achieved was the landing force expected to assist the breakout assault at Anzac. In the event, the Suvla landing was the only objective achieved. As historian Robert Rhodes James commented, the Suvla landing remained 'an irrelevancy' unless all the attacking forces simultaneously captured the Anafarta ridge peaks of Kiretch Tepe and Tekke Tepe and the Sari Bair heights (see Map 3.1).[76]

The planning behind the Suvla operation was remarkable for its confusion of aims and the means available to pursue them. Hamilton's orders to Stopford were imprecise, sprinkled liberally with the phrases 'if possible' and 'it is hoped', while granting the corps commander 'an entirely free hand in the selection of [his] plan of operations'.[77] In the evolution of the plan, Stopford's objectives were progressively watered down from the original conception to the primary mission of merely securing Suvla Bay as a base.[78] Hamilton's ultimate objective, however, was for British forces 'to seize a position across the Peninsula from Gaba Tepe to Maidos, with a protected line of supply from Suvla Bay'.[79] Aside from the fact that this made no mention of the original aim of eliminating the Turkish forts and gun emplacements at the Narrows, the broad objective indicated an utterly unrealistic appreciation of the terrain and distances on the peninsula. The landing at Suvla would be ten kilometres further north of the axis of the Gaba Tepe to Maidos route that was to be followed after the Anzac landings in April; and the line of supply from Suvla Bay could only remain 'protected' if the entire Sari Bair ridgeline was seized as well as the Turkish positions on the Kilid Bahr plateau (see Map 3.1). Once again the principal strategic aim had apparently been displaced for a less significant tactical objective.

On the night of 6 August the IX Corps landed just south of Nibrunesi Point using armoured, motorised landing craft ('beetles'), originally built for aborted Baltic landing operations, but denied to Hamilton for the Gallipoli landings in April 1915. They were finally provided in time for the Suvla landings when they were no longer actually required, as the landings at Suvla were not heavily opposed.[80] By the morning of 7 August over 20,000 men were ashore and resistance was negligible; they were opposed initially by some 1500 Turks who harassed them with sniper fire. The British suffered more casualties on 7 August than the total numbers of the Turkish force opposing them. The landing force stalled on the beaches in confusion and disarray. The following day, 8 August, was truly 'a wasted day at Suvla' in the words of the British official historian. While Anzac and British troops were engaged in heavy fighting from Lone Pine to Chunuk Bair, all momentum was lost at Suvla. Hamilton's GHQ failed to intervene until the situation was beyond remedy.

The capture of the low-lying Chocolate Hills and W Hills which should have been a relatively simple task by direct assault from the beaches, became an unnecessarily elaborate manoeuvre around the dry salt lake due to a brigade commander's fear of non-existent Turkish forces in these positions.[81] The hills surrounding Suvla Bay form a natural amphitheatre which gave the Turks a commanding view of the British operations, especially the troops' painfully slow struggle to cross the salt lake and the rough ground of the Suvla Plain before climbing the low foothills some five kilometres inland.[82]

Most soldiers had little idea where they were heading and what their objectives were. Amid the obsession with security, one map compiled by GHQ in September provides some insights into the serious lack of intelligence about the terrain and the Turkish defences that confronted the British infantrymen (see Map 3.6).[83] Based on a captured Turkish 1:10,000 map, with details taken from aerial photographs, it shows the trench lines and main terrain features of the Suvla area of operations and carries the warning, 'Not to be carried into any attack', due to the detail shown of British lines. Most significant, however, is that the Anafarta ridge and its high features of Kavak Tepe and Tekke Tepe – the key British objectives of the Suvla landing operations in early August – are shown as still uncharted and unknown.

The scattered British troops who advanced inland towards the foothills suffered in the heat from shortages of water and faltered under Turkish fire. By the time an organised advance was attempted, the Turks had called up two divisions from Bulair in the north. On 9 August a single Turkish division of 6000 men counter-attacked from Tekke Tepe. They routed the advancing British force which fled back across the plain, their wounded becoming consumed in scrub fires started by intense machine-gun fire.

Apparently overlooked by the planners of the operation was a crucial potential weakness in the Turkish defences of the Suvla (Anafarta) area, the small harbour of Ejelmer Bay (Ece Limani). Although overshadowed by steep hills rising to the Kireçtepe ridge, this isolated bay on the northwestern side of the peninsula offered allied forces a protected harbour from which they might have outflanked the Turkish defences on the Anafarta and Kireçtepe ridges. The commander of the Turkish northern group, Colonel Mustafa Kemal, had identified this vulnerable region when he warned the local commander on 11 August that his essential duty was 'to prevent the Allies' disembarkation at Ece Harbour'.[84] Any opportunity this may have presented for a diversionary attack went unrecognised by Stopford and his staff.

A daring and effective example of covert ground reconnaissance in this area also went largely unnoticed by those planning the Suvla operation. On the night of 20 June, a New Zealander, Lieutenant Blackett of the Canterbury Mounted Rifles, was landed by trawler on the northern coast at Suvla, crossed the Kireçtepe ridge and scouted inland to locate the Turkish artillery battery in the W Hills that daily harassed the northern beaches at Anzac. He lay concealed, eating his sandwiches as he watched the Turkish gun crews at work, before returning to the coast to be collected the following night. Weeks

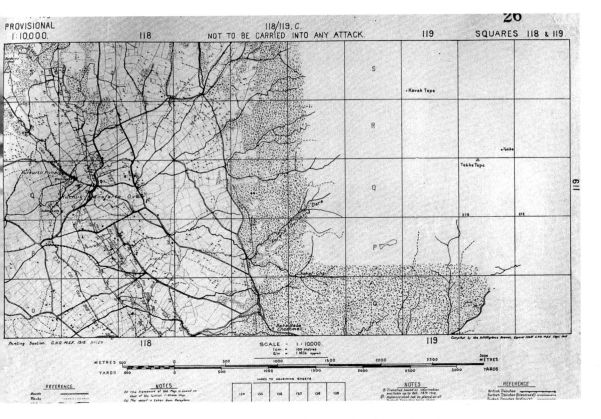

Map 3.6 1:10,000 map of the Suvla sector issued by GHQ, Mediterranean Expeditionary Force, in September 1915. Based on a captured Turkish 1:10,000 map, with details taken from aerial photographs, the map shows the trench lines and main terrain features of the Suvla area of operations and carries the warning, 'Not to be carried into any attack'. The Anafarta ridge area around the Kavak Tepe and Tekke Tepe features is depicted as uncharted.

AWM map collection, Sheet nos 118/119

later, during the planning of the Suvla offensive, Major General Braithwaite, Hamilton's chief of staff curtly dismissed an offer to GHQ by General Birdwood and his able chief of staff Lieutenant Colonel Skeen to provide assistance from Anzac in locating the W Hills guns and other defences at Suvla. The planning proceeded at GHQ in utter ignorance of this intelligence already gained.[85]

All the allied operations in August either stalled or were repulsed by the Turkish defenders at enormous cost to both sides in dead and wounded. By 10 August, in just three days' fighting, some 50,000 British troops at Suvla and Anzac had suffered at least 18,000 casualties. Turkish forces remained firmly in possession of every significant vantage point of the high ground, dominating the allied positions.[86] By the end of August, further futile allied assaults at Hill 60 and Scimitar Hill had failed, leaving the Turks holding two features overlooking the Suvla plain and the British base. Lieutenant Colonel Aubrey Herbert, a British officer assigned to the Anzacs for intelligence work, noted dispiritedly in his diary: 'It's on the same old lines: on the hills we are the eyebrows and the Turks are the forehead'.[87] The front-line positions of both sides settled into positions that would remain substantially unchanged until the allied evacuation four months later at the end of 1915.

General Hamilton denied that the Suvla operations amounted to a defeat. He wrote in his diary on 14 August that although the 'capture' of Suvla Bay and the linking up with Anzac was a 'cruel disappointment', two more similar operations, 'measured in mere acreage, will give us the Narrows'.[88] Hamilton seemed incapable of grasping the realities of the obstacles the terrain presented to his plans. He reported on 29 August: 'Knoll 60, now ours throughout, commands the Biyuk Anafarta valley with view and fire—a big tactical scoop.'[89] In fact, the allies had failed to capture the summit of Hill 60 which was still held firmly by the Turks, and it offered no significant tactical advantages.

Hamilton later wrote that 'as a result of the battles of August 1915, we had gained elbow-room and inflicted enormous losses on the enemy . . . but we had not succeeded in our main aim: to get command of the Narrows. The spirit of the Turks had, however, been broken, and they had been thrown entirely on the defensive.' As Robert Rhodes James noted, 'Self-deception could hardly go further'. Hamilton 'had lost over 40,000 men in under three weeks, and had gained little or nothing'.[90]

Many soldiers viewed the August offensive differently to the commander-in-chief. Sergeant Cyril Lawrence of the 2nd Field Company, Royal Australian Engineers, followed the course of the offensive from his position at Anzac, digging communication trenches through the terrible carnage at Lone Pine. He learnt that the push on the Sari Bair heights had failed and also witnessed the sorry aftermath, writing bitterly in his diary on 14 August:

> The men are in a bad state. Before the [Lone] Pine affair they were bad enough, but the last few days' exertions have completely broken them up. It is piteous, really, to see them. Great hulking fellows or at least the remains of them crawling about doubled up with internal pains due to dysentery, lying down exhausted every hundred yards they go, others, masses of septic sores and bandaged from head to foot, all utterly done up. Jingo, if only their folk at home could see them. I'll bet there would be such a Hell of an outcry that we would be spelled in a very short time.[91]

Conclusion

With the failure of both the Suvla operations and the attempt to seize the Sari Bair ridge went the last British hope of victory on Gallipoli. Distinguished Australian military historian Alec Hill later wrote that the August offensive, through its scale, complexity and the importance of its aims, was 'one of the great battles of the war'. Its failure was 'one of the great disasters'.[92] The scale

of that failure demands investigation and explanation. Why did the allies, with their apparently superior resources, strength and technological power, fail to achieve a resounding victory over the Turkish defenders?

The co-ordinated series of assaults had failed to achieve the promised breakout from the northern allied positions and force a conclusive victory. All the attacking forces were halted with heavy losses, none of the vital objectives were seized, and the Turkish ground captured was negligible. Popular accounts lay the blame for these failures on the actions or inactions of particular British commanders and the lacklustre performance of British soldiers. But there were multiple causes: deficiencies in the preparation and planning, the allocation of insufficient resources of men and matériel, logistical and intelligence lapses, and an underestimation of Turkish military capabilities, all contributed.

Explanations for the failure must take account of the factors of terrain. The limitations imposed by terrain meant that the key objectives of the Gallipoli landings and the August offensive operations never offered the opportunities for victory claimed by senior commanders and their staff (and many subsequent historians and commentators); the same point could be argued on a more general level for the entire Gallipoli enterprise. Moreover, the limitations imposed by the terrain, available forces, resources and weapons systems negated any realistic opportunities for exploitation of any successes that occurred.

British commanders continued to maintain that possession of the Sari Bair heights was the key to the entire campaign, yet the advantage of the ridges invariably favoured the Turkish defenders. Due to the nature of the terrain, the Turkish troops could always reach, reinforce and supply the heights quicker from their side. They also had the geographical advantages of plentiful fresh water supplies and ready access to villages and rear areas along relatively shorter lines of communication.

Terrain obstacles in the case of each major objective – Achi Baba, Hill 971, and the Anafarta ridge encircling Suvla Bay – gave the Turkish defenders the natural physical advantage; and even if these objectives could have been captured, the limitations of artillery technology in 1915, and the limited supplies of guns and shells combined with the difficulties of establishing and supplying them in such difficult terrain, would have most likely negated any tactical advantage or longer-term strategic aim.

We are left with the question of what led senior commanders to make such grave mistakes. Many were professional soldiers who were trained and experienced and might be expected to have mastered their profession of arms. It would be facile to make critical judgements based solely on hindsight: a balanced assessment should not underestimate the difficulties senior commanders confronted in an arduous campaign to which the necessary men, weapons, ammunition, supplies and matériel were committed piecemeal and rarely in the numbers and quantities required.

Part 2

The Anzac breakout battles

Chapter 4

By bomb and bayonet

The attacks from Lone Pine to the Nek

Peter Burness

From early in the war, Britain, as the world's mightiest naval power, pursued a naval solution to take Turkey out of the war by striking directly at Constantinople with warships; but initial attempts in 1915 failed. Following on, in April that year there were amphibious landings on the Gallipoli peninsula in support of this solution, but these only managed to provide toeholds at a few places ashore. Australians and New Zealanders (the 'Anzacs') were part of these landings, but they were only able to get a tenuous grip on the rim of ridges enclosing their tiny beachhead and repel Turkish efforts to drive them back into the sea.

In the weeks and months of fighting, dying and squalid living that followed the landings, there was no more progress. Still, the British did not abandon the campaign and soon sought to reinforce their efforts. More land troops were provided for a second strike at the elusive prize.

Among the schemes proposed for the revitalisation of the campaign, the most convincing came from the commander at Anzac, Sir William Birdwood, who wanted to see a fresh offensive from there rather than the British-held tip of the peninsula: Cape Helles.[1] He, like many others, believed that the heights of the Sari Bair range, stretching northwards from the entrenched positions, and rising to the hills known as Chunuk Bair and Hill 971, held the key to unlock the deadlocked land campaign. The problem was that the Anzac area was very cramped and difficult to supply, and hardly provided a firm position from which to make a concentrated breakout.

The Sari Bair heights could be attacked directly from ANZAC along the spine of the range as well as directly up the seaward slopes, but a proper base would be needed for any operations that might follow in the future. So, coinciding with Birdwood's plans to use both approaches, in particular a 'left-hook' advance up the northern valleys and gullies, to gain the heights, there would be further landings made still further north along the coast at Suvla. These landings would also protect the flank of the attacks upon the heights. While the Anzac and Suvla endeavours were linked, each was a distinct operation under separate command. Meanwhile, the main efforts extending from Anzac were to be supported by a series of secondary or diversionary attacks. All of this was set to commence on 6 August.

The series of supporting actions at Anzac, not just the main attacks on the heights, are worthy of study. They were all fought in sight of one another, and all have their own names; however, only one would ever be a separate battle honour: 'Lone Pine' would be remembered long after most of the other actions had been forgotten.

The tasks of the supporting attacks were split between the two divisions in which the Australians ashore were serving. Dismounted light horsemen were to assault at key points along the front line, at places called the Nek, Pope's Hill and Quinn's Post. These efforts could connect directly with the main attacks on the heights. The light horsemen were part of the New Zealand and Australian Division under Major General Sir Alexander Godley. Elsewhere, other brigades within this division had the main task of conducting the attacks on the heights. The Light Horse attacks would be preceded by Australian infantry assaults on Turkish positions at Lone Pine and at German Officers' Trench. These infantrymen were from the 1st Australian Division under the command of Major General Harold 'Hooky' Walker.

Walker, having only recently been given command of the division, had a point to prove. At the landing back in April, the major role had been given to the 1st Australian Division, then under Major General William Bridges, while Godley's division had been a smaller composite one. At that time Walker had only temporary command of just a brigade under Godley. Godley's command had now grown with the addition of mounted units (serving on foot) and with British and Indian reinforcements and had become a very large one, virtually the size of a corps. Walker did not want to be overshadowed or have his force wasted on secondary supporting attacks. He proposed other uses for his battalions, but Birdwood insisted on having his way.

Birdwood's plans for the August offensive were ambitious. The ground to be directly assailed, particularly the heights, was rugged and steep, and the men were mostly in a sad physical state. Poor diet, and disease spread by flies feeding on the exposed dead and waste over the past months had caused large-scale evacuations of the sick, and even those left were mostly in a weakened condition.

We also need to consider the weaponry used here. The title of this chapter – 'By bomb and bayonet' – recognises the limited range of weaponry available to ordinary soldiers, on both sides. At this stage of the war, in this far-off

Major General Sir Harold 'Hooky' Walker (standing, left, with stick), commander of the 1st Australian Division, conferring with ANZAC Corps commander Lieutenant General Sir William Riddell Birdwood (sitting) and other senior officers on the path from Anzac Cove to Plugge's Plateau, May 1915.

AWM P02648.023

campaign, the infantryman was still mostly reliant upon his rifle and bayonet, the most basic tools of the soldier. As a consequence, tactics too remained fairly simple. In attack, rifles were supplemented by grenades – 'bombs' – usually of the most primitive kind.

There were machine-guns on Gallipoli, but these were on a lower scale than used later on the Western Front. Each battalion initially had two Maxim guns and this was in the process of being increased to four.[2] There were no light machine-guns or other automatic weapons, or rifle-discharged grenades, and hardly anything that qualified to be truly called a modern mortar. Artillery was present on a small scale with guns and ammunition in limited supply. Sir Ian Hamilton, the overall British commander, complained that the 'super-brass hats' in London always denied his requests for more artillery in favour of the Western Front.[3]

The Turks had artillery, their own Maxim machine-guns, rifles and bayonets, all mostly of German origin, and bombs. They had shortages too, although the Anzacs felt they used their bombs most willingly and must have had an unlimited supply. The enemy's machine-guns, abetted by the folded landscape, were deadly in defence. So effective were they that their actual numbers were usually overestimated by the allies. Attacks with rifles and bayonets across open ground against well positioned machine-guns, often firing in enfilade, could be suicidal for either side.

Leading up to the new offensive, reinforcements had been landed at Anzac. With secrecy being maintained, the arrival of these fresh units was the first indication to the soldiers ashore that something big was about to

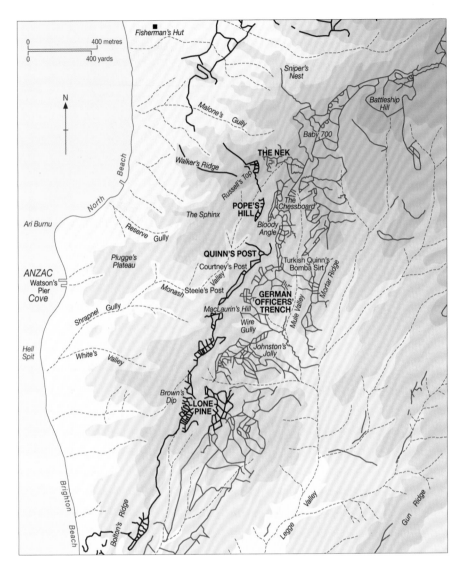

Map 4.1

The attacks along the Anzac front line during the August offensive, 6–10 August 1915.

Cartographer: Keith Mitchell

take place. But these troops – mostly British – lacked experience and most had never been under fire. Newly arrived Australians showed a similar lack of battle appreciation. Incredibly, a rifle-range had to be constructed at Anzac to further train men in shooting.

Lone Pine

Although the offensive due to commence on 6 August was focused around Anzac, the grand scheme also included an initial, and ultimately costly, limited role for the British troops at Helles. The idea was that they should make an attack at 3.50 pm on the first day. This was a feint to draw the Turks' attention away from what would shortly commence elsewhere. At ANZAC, the curtain-raiser to the series of battles about to be unleashed was the attack by the 1st Australian Brigade at Lone Pine. This was set for 5.30 pm.

While the main fighting was to be directed towards Chunuk Bair and the high ground, it was felt that a 'demonstration' blow at Lone Pine would draw in the Turks' reserves and prevent them from reinforcing those places from where the main attacks would come. Three hours after the Lone Pine assault began, columns of troops would begin their moves against the heights. Once the high ground was taken, troops there could link up with the light horsemen, who would make their attacks on the Nek, and nearby targets, early in the morning. This way the vital hills would be linked to the Anzac perimeter via Baby 700. According to optimistic forecasts, if success was absolute, the second ridge running from Lone Pine to Hill 971 would be in British hands and the allies would hold the dominant ground.

Sir Ian Hamilton was most anxious to secure Chunuk Bair. At the height of the fighting, when for a moment it seemed that the feature had indeed been captured, he said: 'Chunuk Bair will do; with that we win!'[4] But the hill was not held for long, and even if it had been it would not have guaranteed the campaign's overall success. Instead of saying 'with that we win', Hamilton might have said 'without that we lose'. For that is what ultimately happened.

Turkish soldiers in their trenches at Lone Pine or *Kanlisirt* ('Bloody Ridge') as they called the position. The Turkish trenches were deep and well-constructed, with heavy overhead cover and tunnels to provide protection from artillery shells.

AWM A02599

It may not have been the most important battle of the August offensive, but Lone Pine has become the best known of the Australian efforts. The fighting there went on for days and there were heavy casualties on both sides, with the Australians' killed and wounded amounting to over 2000. The Turks estimated their own losses at over 6000, including approximately 1520 killed.

Lone Pine took its name from a single tree that had stood there early in the campaign on the southern end of a broad, flat feature, named by the allies 400 Plateau. While held by the enemy, it gave the Turks observation and some tactical dominance of the area stretching to the south and also posed a threat to the northern part of the front line. The Turkish positions were a maze of support and communications trenches standing behind a front line that, unbeknown to most of the Australians, had mostly been covered over with stout logs and earth. In the Turks' trenches there were numerous narrow tunnels that provided some further shelter during artillery shelling.

The Australians opposed the Turks across a no man's land that was about 150 metres wide. The two lines were closer towards the centre. The enemy defences were thinnest on the barren north side of the line (their right); behind these, the ground fell away into a gully.

Weeks earlier, a British aircraft had flown over Lone Pine and obtained aerial photographs. However, interpretation of these was poor. Little notice was taken of the fact that the front trenches were roofed over. Other observations had revealed coverings, but as it was not unusual for the trenches at Anzac to be partially covered as protection against bombs, this was not considered remarkable.[5]

For 'Hooky' Walker and his division, the attack on Lone Pine was to be their main contribution to the big offensive while Godley would have the main show. Walker was a capable though 'old school' leader – he was 53 – who always demanded maximum effort both in purpose and execution. He did not like small, low-return 'eye-wash stunts'. It concerned him that here his troops would be used merely for a 'demonstration' action. There was uneasiness between Walker and Birdwood, who, while they may have respected each other, were not friends. Walker was always outspoken in his discussions with Birdwood, and at times the chief tired of it. Despite his protests, Walker accepted his orders, although he did manage to get a small delay in the proposed timing for the attack.

Months earlier, before the Gallipoli campaign, Walker had been Birdwood's chief staff officer. But he was a fighting soldier who, from the time of the Anzac landing, was happy to hand over this role to Brigadier General Andrew Skeen, another British staff officer much preferred by Birdwood. For a time Walker filled in, having temporary command of the New Zealand Brigade and then the 1st Australian Brigade. He eventually took command of the Australian division after Bridges was killed and his successor, James Legge, was sent to Egypt to command the 2nd Division.[6]

Having accepted his role, Walker confidently gave the task of attacking Lone Pine to Brigadier General Nevill Smyth VC, another British officer, and his 1st Australian Brigade. As Walker had commanded this brigade for a time, he knew the officers well. The brigade had four battalions and, of these, the 2nd, 3rd, and 4th Battalions (arranged left to right) would make the assault while its 1st Battalion was in reserve.

Initially, in the planning stage, Birdwood had also wanted an attack made at Johnston's Jolly, immediately to the north of Lone Pine, to support the Lone Pine assault. He was quite insistent. In response, Walker and his chief of staff, Lieutenant Colonel Brudenell White, an Australian, said they would need twice the number of troops if this was to happen. Walker wanted none of the idea. Birdwood did not give up, but agreed that 2nd Brigade's 7th Battalion would make an attack there should the opportunity arise. It did not.

Along the front line at Anzac, tunnels often extended underground towards the enemy positions; sometimes the most forward troops were those invisible below the ground. Sir Iven Mackay was a young company commander at Lone Pine. He later recalled: 'Those who served on Gallipoli will recall how cool these underground passages were and how they were used for rest and sleep or to escape the plague of flies.'[7] Before the attack, engineers burrowed further towards the enemy and had created an underground parallel front line which, once the soil (about 30 centimetres thick) from the roof was pulled down, would provide a fresh line to attack from.

At Lone Pine, the first attacking wave would come from the tunnels, the second would advance from the main fire-trench, while the third line, some of whose men would carry picks and shovels, followed swiftly behind. The plan was mostly devised by White and the staff from the 1st Brigade.

The attack was to be preceded by a slow three-day-long artillery bombardment which would intensify an hour before the assault. Ammunition was limited and the number of guns few. Smyth later wrote that the final shelling was 'dignified as "continuous and *heavy*" in one account', but, he added: 'After our subsequent experiences on the Western Front it would probably have been described as *light* shelling.'[8]

The shelling was not without purpose. It did substantial damage to the enemy trenches, forcing the Turks into tunnels and rattling their nerves. The overhead cover along the enemy's front line provided little protection against artillery fire. It was thick enough to detonate high-explosive rounds but so thin that the shells penetrated, bursting, and causing terrible casualties inside.

In further preparation, three mines were exploded underground in no man's land. These had been set at the end of other long tunnels. Besides their effect on morale, these created craters that provided some cover for the attackers and later gave the engineers a starting point for digging a communications trench to the captured trenches.

As the time of the battle approached on 6 August, Walker shifted his headquarters to the head of White's Gully to be closer to the action. He was going to exercise close control. Here, and elsewhere, the troops set to make assaults were given white cloth armbands and a patch to stitch to the backs of their jackets so they could be distinguished from Turkish soldiers in the fighting, which was expected to extend into the night-time and actually went on for almost four days. As the hour for the attack drew nearer there was an issue of rum with a promise that there would be more after the battle. Watches were synchronised through the day.[9] Along the firing line the sandbags lining the parapet were pulled down to enable easier exit from the trenches. Catholic soldiers attended a mass; the Anglicans had held a service the day before.

Then the moment arrived. The attack was launched with the blasts of a whistle blown by Major Dennis King, the brigade major.[10] The shrill was taken up along the line: everywhere whistles were blowing. The first wave burst forth and quickly went towards the enemy.

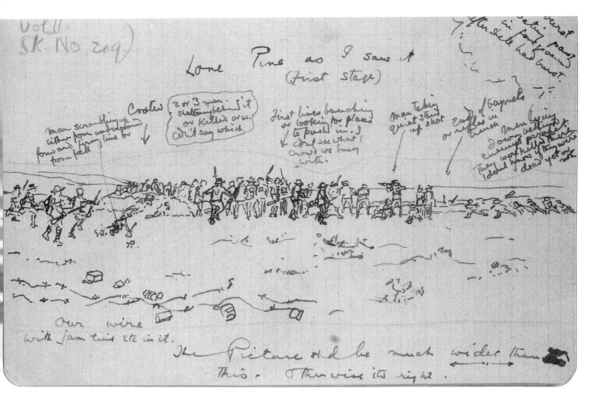

'Lone Pine as I saw it (first stage)', sketch drawn from memory by Australian official war correspondent Charles Bean, showing the 1st Australian Brigade's assault on the Turkish trenches at Lone Pine, as he witnessed it from the Australian front-line trenches on the afternoon of 6 August 1915. Part of the sketch was reproduced in Volume 2 of Bean's official history, *The Story of Anzac* (1924), p. 504.

C.E.W. Bean's diary, February 1916, AWM 38 3DRL606/37/1, pp. 50–51.

In a despatch for the newspapers at home, Charles Bean, the official correspondent, provided a real-time description of what he saw. He was alongside his brother, the 3rd Battalion's medical officer, waiting for the second line to go out. The first line went. Then, in Bean's words:

> 5.33. Word passed by the officer crouching with the men. 'Prepare to go over the parapet.' The officer placed a whistle between his teeth, and the next instant, when the whistle was blown, men were scrambling over sandbags in the dust.
>
> I can see through a periscope flocks of our men running forward from the trenches all along this part of the line, and all racing at a good running pace. I can see white-patched uniforms running forward thickly all over the space in front of me.
>
> 5.45. About 80 yards away, is the white heap of gravel forming the Turkish trench. As our men reach this, they did not jump in, but stood along the edge, looking down at something which I could not see.
>
> Turkish shells are beginning to burst fiercely, not so much over the

advancing men as over the trenches from which succeeding lines are continuously issuing. As each crowd bolts across ... a certain number fall here and there, but often get up and run on again. A few little bundles of khaki and white patches are lying in the scrub. Other crouching figures [of the wounded] are crawling slowly back.

5.48. Turkish shrapnel is now bursting thick and low over the space between the trenches. The 2nd, 3rd and 4th Battalions have made their rush. The 1st Battalion is now filing into the fire trench behind me.

6.30. Turkish shells have been simply lathering our trenches. The space before the trenches has been whipped up into a dust haze by a lather of shells, bullets and rushing feet, and through this still occasionally rushed white patched khaki uniforms, all bathed in the reddening light of evening.[11]

Upon reaching the enemy's trenches, the discovery of the roofed-over sections caused momentary disruption. But the initiative was not lost. Many of the enemy had been killed in the shelling, parts of the cover had been broken down, and some Turks were caught still sheltering in tunnels. For the Turks, the overhead cover had provided a bit of protection, but it also trapped them in their own trenches, limiting their ability to fire out or escape.

Above the trenches the Australians found that the timbers, covered in earth, were mostly too heavy to lift. About half the men went on past the front line, dropping into communications and support trenches, and attacking from there. Many of the officers led their men on towards objectives a little deeper back, ignoring the covered lines.

Map 4.2

The attack on Lone Pine, showing front-line trenches assaulted and held, 6–10 August 1915.

Cartographer: Keith Mitchell

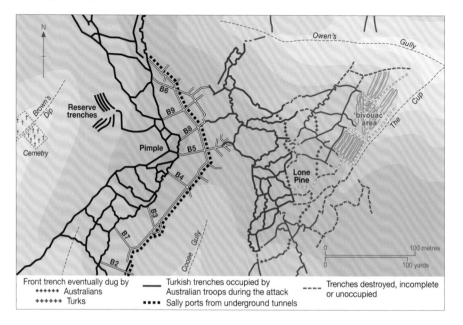

Turkish firing loopholes constructed in the overhead cover of the trenches at Lone Pine, as they confronted Australian soldiers charging the position on 6 August 1915. Photographed during Charles Bean's visit to Anzac with the Australian Historical Mission in February 1919.

AWM G01960

The fighting that followed, particularly in the dim cave-like covered trenches, was horrendous. A soldier of the 2nd Battalion later said: 'Lone Pine was a frightful hand-to-hand struggle like a battle of savage beasts at the bottom of a pit.'[12] Shots were exchanged at close range, bayonets were used, and bombs thrown. The bombs were effective, but the need for them was not met by the supply. It was a bloody and brutal affair. At places men lay dead in heaps.

Some attackers went beyond the objectives and stumbled into 'the Cup' – a depression at the rear of the enemy lines that held accommodation and headquarters. This feature had not been properly identified or appreciated during earlier aerial reconnaissance.[13] Back in the trenches, in many places men found they were in a maze of connecting alleys and, as they moved down one, they were shot from an intersecting one. Blockages, usually sandbags and timber, were set up in captured stretches of the lines. In places, troops of both sides held the same trench only separated by hastily set-up barricades.

Initial success came quickly. By 6 pm the Australians had established themselves in the captured trenches. A telephone line was rushed across no man's land and engineers extended the mine craters and set about making more linking trenches. The attack had worked, but within a short while the Turks could be seen reorganising. They were not going to give up this position without a further fight.

Fighting went on during the night, but the Australians had a firm grip. The 2nd Battalion's war diarist had already noted: 'Enemy's dead everywhere and we cannot avoid walking on them as they are so thick.'[14] Then dawn brought heavy enemy counter-attacks and it seemed these would never end. The Turks sent in reinforcements as expected, but the Australians had to throw in more men too. The Turks did not want to give up Lone Pine, believing the attack was a thrust directed at the next (that is, the third) ridge. Each side was caught in the trap of having to use more men.

Throughout the campaign, Birdwood's forces remained cramped along the coast while the Turks had room to manoeuvre and shift their forces. Hardy men, the enemy's reinforcements could be forced-marched overland at short notice. Lone Pine was not too far from the main attack on the heights, and Turkish troops sent there could also be employed nearby.

'As a feint [Lone Pine] was all too effective,' Charles Bean later wrote. He provided an assessment: 'It so impressed the Turkish commanders that not only were all their local reserves drawn to it but a division was immediately sent from Helles … and it arrived just in time to be hurried on farther to defeat the main effort on the summit north of Anzac next morning.'[15] This is something that Sir Ian Hamilton had not anticipated.[16]

German Officers' Trench

Six hours after the capture of the trenches at Lone Pine, the second part of the role Walker's division played in the offensive unfolded. After midnight, as 7 August broke, the Victorians of the depleted 6th Battalion (a part of the 2nd Brigade) were sent against German Officers' Trench. German officers had been seen there early in the campaign, giving the feature its name. Now it was a strong point from where enemy machine-guns could enfilade any Australian attempt to take the Turkish positions at Quinn's Post and the Nek. Since light horsemen were set to attack these places in just a few hours, it was vital that this threat be removed.

An audacious and ill-conceived plan to take German Officers' Trench was prepared. At Lone Pine some troops attacked from tunnels; here they would all do so – and in darkness. Three main approach tunnels were driven towards the enemy's lines; each was deep enough to stand in and just wide enough for two armed and fully kitted men to pass. The three lines fed into a shallow tunnel running parallel to the front line from which crawl holes extended and where three or four men could emerge at a time. Just before the attack, the roofs of the tunnels would be brought down to open them up.

As at Lone Pine, the actual assault was to be preceded by the detonation of three underground mines at different times within a one-hour period. It was expected that these would blow up some part of the enemy's line, leaving only demoralised defenders to be dealt with. While waiting, the attackers were kept clear of the main tunnels in case the explosion of the mines caused some collapses. When the mines did go off, their impact was minimal and barely noticed by many of the Australians. The Turkish trenches remained intact.

Once the explosions had been set off, the element of surprise was lost. Worse still, the Turks responded to the muffled bursts by calling down artillery fire that smashed some of the Australians' tunnels and trenches. Earth and debris soon hampered any forward movement. One main tunnel was blocked, causing a crush and confusion in the underground darkness. The start time was held up. Meanwhile divisional headquarters impatiently demanded the attack get moving.

The assault at German Officers' Trench was a disaster. When the whistle finally sounded, half an hour late, men scrambled from the line of open forward saps and broken tunnels and went out into no man's land. But the Turks were ready and quickly shot them down. Some men fell back into the holes, while others who had been wounded tried to crawl back, blocking the way of those coming along behind.

The 6th Battalion was under Lieutenant Colonel Gordon Bennett, who in the next world war would command the 8th Australian Division in Malaya and arouse great controversy with his decision to leave the troops when Singapore fell. But for the moment he was a young and bold commander who reported to his brigade headquarters the folly of continuing the attack in the face of such devastating firepower. However, the order came back that he should try again as soon as possible. The message was sent by phone from White to the brigadier, who passed it on.[17] Meanwhile, it took a long time to clear the tunnels of debris and dead and dying soldiers.

With the brigade major, Major Carl Jess, standing close by, Bennett ordered a second attack. But it was now after 3.00 am.[18] The result was the same. Machine-gun and rifle fire immediately tore through the men as they emerged. As before, the tunnels became choked with casualties.

Again headquarters was advised of the futility of continuing, yet once more Bennett was ordered to get ready for another attempt. Divisional headquarters told the brigade's recently appointed commander, Brigadier General John 'Dad' Forsyth, a 48-year-old long-serving soldier, to go forward and take personal control. When he got there what he found, besides a furious Bennett, was a shattered battalion. It was almost impossible to reorganise the men, who were now noticeably rattled, to shift the dead and wounded, and clear passages.[19]

Those on the spot, including Jess, wanted the attacked stopped. Next, Major Duncan Glasford, a regular staff officer from Walker's headquarters, was sent across, but he too recognised the impossible task facing the remnants of the battalion.[20] Hours passed and it was now fully daylight, but the instructions remained: reorganise, get ready to charge, and wait for further orders. It was almost 8.30 am before the attack was finally called off, after Birdwood was consulted, and those left in the 6th Battalion were told to rest.[21]

Walker and White had been preoccupied by the major events at Lone Pine while they tried to deal with the unfolding debacle at German Officers'

Trench. They both added insult to injury in believing that the 2nd Brigade's planning must have been defective and that the 6th Battalion had not shown enough vigour in its attack. In later years White expressed regret over having continued the charge when there had been no change to the conditions in which the earlier waves had failed.[22] This was a strong admission, although how much of the blame should go to Walker and how much to White is not clear. What is interesting is that White accepted the blame at divisional level, and there is no suggestion that the battalion or the brigade commanders had the authority to stop the attacks.

Hooky Walker, and White too, had a reputation within the AIF of being leaders who did not waste men's lives. However, this reputation seems to overlook their performance at German Officers' Trench. Not only had they sent the two waves of men out, but they continued to hold the third wave in the expectation of an attack well after the time that the other battles they were supposed to have been supporting had been abandoned.

The night of 6–7 August had been one of heavy fighting. Now the dawn brought on the main attacks; this was to be the campaign's day of destiny. The light horsemen of Godley's division were to make their assaults along the main Anzac front line at the crucial points of the Nek, Quinn's Post and Pope's Hill. Although the dismounted Light Horse regiments had been on Anzac for many weeks, they had not fought major battles, and now these men, supposedly Australia's élite, would have to prove themselves alongside the infantrymen.

The three Light Horse attacks were to connect with other elements of the division against the heights to the north on the Sari Bair range. However, further up on the hills and in the craggy ridges and gullies below the summit, things had not gone well through the night. Timings had been thrown out, and there was no longer a chance of the attacks converging. Despite not being able to link up, the attacks along the ANZAC perimeter were allowed to proceed in the hope that they would take the pressure off the New Zealanders still bravely trying to take Chunuk Bair. Before it even began, the attack at the Nek had ceased to be a pincer movement and had been reduced to another feint.

The Nek

The attack across a narrow bridge of land called 'the Nek' would be undertaken by the 3rd Light Horse Brigade's 8th and 10th Regiments. It was to be synchronised with the 1st Light Horse from New South Wales attacking at Pope's Hill and the Queenslanders of the 2nd Light Horse assaulting at Quinn's Post. Here too the men wore white patches and armbands.

In the early morning the Turkish trenches at the Nek were shelled. Then after a seven-minute pause, at 4.30 am, according to the watch of Lieutenant

Colonel Alexander White of the 8th Light Horse, the 150 Victorians of the first wave leapt from their trenches and dashed into no man's land. Warned by artillery shelling and given ample time to prepare by the pause that followed, the Turks were waiting. Several machine-guns and concentrated rifle fire turned the narrow Nek into a killing zone through which the successive lines of light horsemen tried to pass. Only a few even reached the enemy's trenches and they were soon killed. Two minutes later, the second wave followed. Colonel White, leading his men, was among the first to fall.

The two waves of Victorians were to be followed by two lines of Western Australians from the 10th Light Horse. The 10th's Commanding Officer, Lieutenant Colonel Noel Brazier, pressed the brigade headquarters where Lieutenant Colonel Jack Antill, the brigade major, was in charge, to stop the attack. The two men had quarrelled before, and the antagonism between them was in no way reduced by the gravity of the situation. Antill was furious at the impertinence of Brazier who had left his post to query orders that had been firmly given. Brazier later claimed that Antill responded to his appeal by roaring, 'Push on'! He then returned to the front line where he gravely announced: 'I am sorry lads but the order is to go.'

The third line of light horsemen went over the top, and it too was swept away by machine-gun and rifle fire. Again Brazier tried to call for a halt, but in the confusion part of the final line charged, and it too was shot down. British troops were briefly thrown in on the flank but they were repulsed straight away.

At the Nek, Birdwood had devised a plan that had little chance of success and placed its conduct in the hands of a brigade commander, Brigadier General Frederic Hughes, in whom he had little confidence while knowing that Antill was mostly in control. The confusion of timings that created the fatal seven-minute pause, seemingly caused by a failure to synchronise watches, had only made the situation worse.[23]

Charles Bean later wrote: 'In the history of war there is no more signal example of reckless obedience than that given by the dismounted light horsemen at the Nek when, after seeing the whole first attacking line mown down within a few yards by the whirlwind of rifles and machine-gun fire, the second, third, and fourth lines each charged after its interval of time, at the signal of its leaders, to certain destruction.'[24]

Soldiers of the 9th Australian Light Horse man a machine-gun post at Turk's Point, to the left of Walker's Ridge and 120 metres from the Turkish positions facing the charge at the Nek. This machine-gun crew provided supporting fire across the Nek during the attack on 7 August 1915.

AWM J02704

Pope's Hill

A short distance away, the attack at Pope's Hill was made within sight of the Nek. The post commandant at Pope's, Major Thomas Glasgow, destined to become one of the great Australian leaders to emerge from the war, was given command of the two squadrons of the 1st Light Horse Regiment ordered to make the charge. These Australians were on a hill formed by a spur at the head of Monash Gully. The Turks were opposite on a slope across Waterfall Gully, which was now dry, and in front of the rows of trenches that formed the 'Chessboard' feature. The approach across the head of the gully was direct enough, but at the deep end the attacking squadron had to get on to the forward slope, crawling in single file under the cover of darkness, and attack from there.

The attack was launched, but again the Turks were waiting. They had spotted troops getting into position. Meanwhile on the left, the squadron under Major James Reid, with a shorter distance to cover, managed to fight its way into the enemy trenches. Here too the action was wild and bloody. Eyewitnesses saw Reid fighting gamely: after being hit in the right hand, he changed his revolver to the left and continued on. He was last seen amid the bomb smoke while the Australians fought to reach a third line of trenches. Reid's body was never recovered.[25] Dozens died around him.

Soldiers of the 1st Light Horse Regiment parade for roll call after their attack at Pope's Hill on 7 August 1915. Fewer than 50 men of 200 returned unwounded.

AWM H00356

The Turks counter-attacked at Pope's and the light horsemen had to hold on desperately. With ammunition, particularly bombs, running low, some brave individuals made the dash back for more. However, things quickly got worse and Glasgow, seeing that attacks were failing elsewhere, knew further resistance was futile. After holding on for two hours, the Australians withdrew under heavy fire, carrying as many of their wounded as they could. Their losses were appalling: of the 200 in the attack, 154 had been killed or wounded, including every officer except Glasgow – a casualty rate of 77 per cent.

Quinn's Post

Quinn's Post was the third of the Light Horse attacks and involved the 2nd Regiment. The attack at Quinn's was also set to coincide with the larger attack at the Nek. It was soon shown to be just as foolhardy, and drew the same tragic result as the others. The officer to lead this attack, Major George Bourne, later recalled:[26]

> We now found that the attack on German Officers' Trench had failed. There was no sign of the New Zealanders on Chunuk Bair and certainly no evidence of them threatening the Chess Board and Turkish's Quinn's. A few shrapnel burst over our objective – but nothing in the nature of a bombardment. Nevertheless our order to attack still stood.[26]

Almost an hour before the attack, the light horsemen had drawn heavy fire from the Turks at Quinn's while trying to find out whether the enemy was still there in strength. That was enough for Bourne to report to brigade headquarters that it was 'not possible for him to attack under existing conditions'. The brigade advised the divisional headquarters but was told that the attack must still proceed.[27]

The regiment was to storm across the ground between the opposing lines on a narrow frontage in four waves of 50 men in each. Here too some would attack from an opened tunnel. They were to begin in the dim light at 4.30 am, when a mine would be exploded. But when the time arrived, no big explosion was seen or heard, so Bourne gave the order to charge. The men could see their fate before them.

Once again the Turks were prepared and waiting. Here too the Australians rushed out into a hailstorm of rifle and machine-gun fire. The majority of those in the first wave were killed or wounded before they had gone five metres. This time, instead of the next waves being sent forward, Bourne, who had earlier judged the attack to be impossible, stopped it. Many lives were saved by his prompt act. The order was then confirmed by Lieutenant Colonel Robert Stodart, who was in local command. The ill-fated charge at Quinn's Post was over in a minute.

By mid-morning the supporting feints at the Nek, Pope's Hill and Quinn's Post were all over. Charles Bean concludes his chapter dealing with them:

> During the long hours of that day the summit ... could be seen crowded with their bodies. At first here and there a man raised his arm to the sky, or tried to drink from his water-bottle. But as the sun of that burning day climbed higher, such movement ceased. Over the whole summit the figures lay still in the quivering heat.[28]

Lone Pine continues

Throughout 7 August, and for days after, Lone Pine remained a crackling cauldron. Even after Chunuk Bair was seized and then lost, wild fighting went on. But what about the proposed adjoining attack by the 7th Battalion, ordered by Birdwood but never favoured by General Walker, at Johnston's Jolly? It did not take place. The decisive defeat of the sister battalion (the 6th) at German Officers' Trench doomed any attempt to take and hold Johnston's. Instead, the 7th joined in at Lone Pine and distinguished itself there; the 3rd Brigade's 12th Battalion, which had been in local reserve, was eventually thrown in too.

Lone Pine was under threat from the strong and relentless enemy counter-attacks, so the 7th Battalion was badly needed. At first teams of bombers were provided, and by the afternoon of 8 August almost all the battalion had moved into the bloody trenches to support the exhausted 1st Battalion, which had gone into the fight after the first assaulting waves. The enemy would persist in their efforts until finally abandoning them on 9 August. The ground, remaining under enemy observation and fire and always a dangerous spot to be, would stay in Australian hands until the end of the campaign.

Lone Pine had been captured on the evening of the 6th, but it was in furious fighting over the following days that some of the most remarkable single actions were recorded; in that period seven Australians won the Victoria Cross there. Four of the Victoria Crosses went to the 7th Battalion in just 24 hours. It was something almost unprecedented in the history of the award. The 1st Battalion would also receive two Victoria Crosses, while another went to the 3rd Battalion. The taking of enemy ground at Lone Pine, together with the cluster of high awards, ensured the name of this battle would survive long after the others fought nearby were forgotten.

The August offensive failed. Chunuk Bair was briefly captured on 8 August by New Zealanders of the Wellington Battalion but was lost to massed enemy counter-attacks within 48 hours; Lone Pine fell to the 1st Australian Division, and British troops did get ashore at Suvla. But none of this delivered any great strategic advantage. What had begun as a planned series of interlinking actions had collapsed into a shambles of disconnected attacks as the Turks

shot most of them to pieces and held their positions on the high ground. Headquarters at different levels had to deal with a stream of disasters. In places local commanders took control, and at others they could not. With its eyes on the ultimate objective, senior command kept urging the attacks on, even when there was no hope left.

Birdwood had asked too much of the troops, many of whom were already in a weakened condition and in depleted units. He and Skeen, his optimistic chief of staff, had shown too little concern for the nature of the wild, hilly country over which the battles were to be fought, and they relied too much on impossible timetables. Too often they underestimated the enemy. Birdwood should have ensured his troops had the conditions and resources to provide a resounding success rather than rely on a sporting chance.

Over the vital days of the offensive, the possibility of surprise had been lost; often artillery support was ineffectual; the Turks had the opportunity to use reserves and manoeuvre; machine-gun and shrapnel fire was deadly against men in the open; and where close fighting descended into bayonet and bomb fighting, progress virtually ceased.

By the night of 10 August, the attempt to break out from the Turkish encirclement at Anzac was over. On 21 August, the last 'push' of the August offensive failed as British, Australian and New Zealand troops launched repeated assaults to capture the isolated knoll of Hill 60, in a vain attempt to link the Anzac and Suvla sectors. Losses amounted to over 1100 casualties. Simultaneous British attacks against Scimitar Hill, which dominated the Suvla plain, produced some of the largest battles of the entire campaign but also failed at a heavy cost in casualties.

In the end there could be no celebration of victory, for there was none. The objectives of the landing had remained out of reach, the August offensive gained only some more useless coastal real estate, and the fighting went into stalemate, finally ending with the troops evacuating the peninsula in the following December and January.

The 7th Battalion's Commanding Officer, Lieutenant Colonel Pompey Elliott, recalled: 'trenches two and sometimes three deep with bodies ... mangled and torn beyond description by the bombs, and bloated and blackened by decay and crawling with maggots. Live amongst this for days ... This is war and such is glory.'[29]

No one studying the Gallipoli battles can help but wonder how men could have fought such savage and heroic actions. We find expressions of the unimaginable bravery and the savagery in descriptions of the battle of Lone Pine. The 3rd Battalion's historian noted the heavy losses at the end of three days. He says that the battalion had boasted a fine brass band, but it was now left with too few men. He tells of a stretcher-bearer who did 'superhuman' work and when finally hit, said: 'Leave me. Leave me. I'm done.' At some places badly wounded men pleaded with their mates to shoot them to put

them out of agony. Charles Bean writes of men throwing the Turks' bombs back, adding: 'one by one the men who were catching bombs were mutilated'.

The 2nd Battalion's historian recorded 430 casualties from an attacking force of 580. He estimated only five percent of these were from shellfire; they were mostly from close hand-to-hand fighting with rifle and bayonet and bombs. The loss rate was as high as in France the following year where Pozières remains generally regarded, due to the high casualty rate from artillery fire, as the worst place Australians fought. Lone Pine should not be remembered in isolation from the other battles of the August offensive; each held its own horror. But it is not hard to understand why soldiers never forgot the experience of Lone Pine.

Australian soldiers, wounded in the attack at Lone Pine on 6 August, make their way along the beach at Anzac Cove, past barges and piles of stores towards the Red Cross flag of a dressing station. The men are still wearing their white patches and armbands, attached for identification in the fighting.

AWM A01937

Chapter 5

'I thought I could command men'

Monash and the assault on Hill 971

Peter Pedersen

At 7 am on 7 August 1915, two men met in the Aghyl Dere, a valley three kilometres north of the foothold that the Anzacs had captured in their landing on the Gallipoli Peninsula on 25 April and had only just broken out of. One was Brigadier General John Monash, commander of the 4th Australian Infantry Brigade, which had played a leading role in the breakout but was now stalled. The other was Major Cecil Allanson of the 1/6th Gurkhas. There was nothing Livingstonian about this meeting, no 'General Monash, I presume!' On the contrary: 'Monash seemed to have temporarily lost his head, he was running about saying, "I thought I could command men",' Allanson later claimed. He tried to explain that his battalion had been put at Monash's disposal but Monash snarled, 'What a hopeless mess has been made of this, you are of no use to me at all.' Allanson left, 'as quickly as I could, as I felt thoroughly upset by what I had seen.'[1] This chapter examines the encounter, the planning and execution of the operation in the August offensive at Anzac that led to it, and the aftermath.

The operational concept for the offensive was a rehash of the one for the original landing in April, beginning with the capture of the three peaks of the Sari Bair range: Chunuk Bair and Hills Q and 971, of which 971, at 330 metres, was the highest. New Zealand scouts under Major Percy Overton had found the peaks' approaches almost undefended, probably on account of their steepness. With the peaks secured, the Turkish siege of the Anzac position might be broken and the Narrows on the far side of the peninsula directly threatened. Little thought had been given to where the troops and logistics for these later phases would come from. This was the operational art as Mr Micawber would have practised it, a belief that 'something will turn up'. But the alternative, continuing the costly frontal assaults at Cape Helles on the toe of the peninsula, which had gained little over the preceding months, was worse.

At Anzac the offensive would begin at 5.30 pm on 6 August with a feint on the southern flank at Lone Pine. By 10.30 pm the New Zealand Mounted Rifle Brigade (NZMR) should have seized Old No. 3 Post, Table Top and Bauchop's Hill, the Turkish security positions in the foothills on the northern flank, clearing the way for the New Zealand Infantry Brigade to swing via Rhododendron Ridge up onto Chunuk Bair. Meanwhile the British 40th Brigade was to secure the Damakjelik Bair, opposite Bauchop's Hill at the mouth of the Aghyl Dere, which the 4th Brigade and the 29th Indian Brigade could then enter. At the Aghyl Dere's most inland fork, the 4th Brigade, having detached two of its four battalions for picquet duties, was to veer left together with half the 29th Brigade, onto a long spur, the Abdul Rahman Bair, which led to Hill 971. The rest of the 29th was to head directly to Hill Q. All three peaks were to have fallen by dawn on 7 August. The British would land at Suvla to establish a base and prevent the Turks concentrating against Anzac.[2]

The 4th Brigade was grouped in column with the 29th Brigade under its commander, Brigadier General H. Vaughan Cox, whom Monash described as 'one of those crotchety, peppery, livery old Indian officers whom the climate

The planned night advance on Sari Bair, 7–8 August 1915: a contour map model made by Mr Justice Ferguson (c. 1920), showing the three main peaks and the proposed lines of assault: (1) 4th Australian Infantry Brigade and 29th Indian Brigade routes to Hill 971 and Hill Q; (2) and (2) the New Zealand infantry routes to Chunuk Bair.

(Source: Bean, *The Story of Anzac*, Vol. 2, facing page 462)

has dried and shrivelled up into a bag of nerves'.[3] He grumbled post-war that 'Cox hampered me greatly, as I had constantly to refer to him and defer to his views.'[4] Monash had apparently forgotten that Cox, as the column commander, was entitled to have his views deferred to and that Cox, too, was constrained by higher authority.

Cox's column would advance within what was, given the scale of the operation, a corps setting. His plan therefore had to conform to the corps plan, which set the tasks for all the columns and ensured co-ordination between them. So Lieutenant General Sir William Birdwood, the Anzac commander, and Major General Alexander Godley (commander of the New Zealand and Australian Division) the breakout commander, prescribed the Aghyl Dere for Cox because it was the most direct route to Hill 971 and passed well clear of Rhododendron Ridge, the New Zealanders' axis to Chunuk Bair.[5] Monash's brigade at the head of the column faced dreadful terrain as a result. 'Confused … mad looking country', Cox called it.[6] No one who has walked the area would disagree.[7]

Winding inland, the Aghyl Dere scattered fanwise into five branches that issued from 'a wild tangle of at least thirty steep scrub-covered gullies and ravines'.[8] Not only would the column be moving at night along the Aghyl Dere for 2.3 kilometres; it also had to cross the precipitous Asma Dere to reach Abdul Rahman Bair after another 900 metres, and then go a further kilometre to Hill 971. By contrast, the New Zealanders' route was half as long and got to Rhododendron Ridge very early on. Charles Bean, the Australian official correspondent and, later, Australian official historian, concluded: 'The task of reaching Chunuk Bair was child's play compared to the extraordinary difficulty of making those right and left hand turns into gully after gully across the foothills before Abdul Rahman Bair was reached.'[9]

Cox also had to consider the corps plans as regards timings. His advance could not commence until after the NZMR had begun clearing the foothills along the foreshore. It would start that task at 8.30 pm and, joined by the 40th Brigade, complete it two hours later. Cox's column would step off at 9.45 pm, when the nearer foothills should be secure. By the time it reached the Aghyl Dere, all of the foothills should have fallen. Cox expected to get to Abdul Rahman Spur by 2 am. He had another two hours to complete his mission because dawn broke at 4 am, by which time Hills 971 and Q were to be captured.[10]

The march timetable that Monash worked out had the 4th Brigade reaching Abdul Rahman at 1.40 am, having taken almost two and a half hours to complete the 3.2-kilometre trek via the Aghyl and Asma Deres, 'assuming no halts or checks'.[11] Godley's headquarters had advised that 1.5 kilometres per hour was the best pace attainable for a column in broken country at night, half the pace for good nocturnal going given in *Field Service Regulations: Part 1, Operations*, the British Army's doctrinal bible.[12] By Godley's standard, the trek would have taken about two hours, so Monash's two and a half hours appeared a generous estimate.

So much for appearances. Based on a brigade 3400-strong, marching in column of fours, Monash figured that the 4th Brigade would stretch 1.4 kilometres.[13] As two battalions from the 29th Indian Brigade would replace the two 4th Brigade battalions picquetting the Aghyl Dere, the column would still arrive on Abdul Rahman with four battalions and stretch over the same distance. Using Godley's yardstick for pace, it would take almost an hour to pass a given point, which meant that the end of the column would not crest Abdul Rahman until around 2.40 am rather than 2 am. If the column had to switch to single file, as it probably would in the Aghyl Dere, it would not be complete on Abdul Rahman until much later. Assuming that Monash considered time past a point, and his records suggest otherwise, his march timetable was highly optimistic.[14] In practice, there would be a lot less than two hours to take Hill 971, especially after the preliminaries to the attack were carried out.

Cox's operation order specified a halt at Abdul Rahman 'until a report has been received from the line of scouts who will examine the spur'.[15] This was an essential precaution to ensure a secure forming-up place and line of departure for the assault, and to pinpoint any Turkish positions. Orders for Hill 971's capture would then be issued. As Cox should be credited with some grasp of battle procedure, these would probably have taken the form of a brief 'fragmentary' order outlining any changes necessitated by the scouts' report to the detailed orders that had been given before the march. But disseminating even this order down to platoons and sections in the era before tactical radio communications was a lengthy process. Add the time taken for the scouts' reconnaissance, and Cox could not have started for Hill 971 much before 4 am, let alone have seized it by then. To use modern soldiers' slang, he had no 'fudge factor' to accommodate the frictions arising from enemy action or terrain.

Neither of these frictions was anticipated on the foreshore leg of the march. With easy going and the adjacent foothills secure, it amounted in the eyes of both Cox and Monash to an administrative move. Proof of this fact is that Cox instructed Monash, who did not protest, to stay behind the two leading battalions.[16] Were contact likely, the *Field Service Regulations* guidance that commanders must be well forward, where they can react quickly should the need arise, would have applied.[17] Once the column had entered the Aghyl Dere and the two leading battalions peeled off to their picquet positions, Monash would be up front, as *Field Service Regulations* recommended.

By then frictions were inevitable owing to a manifest consequence of the corps scheme. The Turks dislodged from the foothills would retreat northeast, either inland and around to their line at Anzac, or towards Suvla. Either way, they would bump into Monash's right flank in the Aghyl Dere, creating confusion in the darkness out of all proportion to their numbers.[18] Godley wanted those in contact with the Turks to deal with them while the rest moved on.[19] Only skilled troops can do this at night, and even they risk losing cohesion. Cox, on the other hand, directed that 'all troops other than those engaged will lie down'.[20] Time would be lost while the Turks were overcome, but his column would remain intact. Given the state of the 4th Brigade, he had little option.

The 4th Brigade had held the head of Monash Valley, the most critical sector at Anzac, for the first five weeks after the landing. Bean rated that effort one of the four finest feats of the AIF.[21] About 1400 of the brigade's original personnel, well under half its strength, survived to go into rest in Reserve Gully.[22] Like the other Anzac formations, it was topped up by poorly trained reinforcements from Egypt. Some could not even load their rifles properly.[23] 'Rest' was a euphemism for fatigues that precluded recuperation. By mid-July, Monash was supplying 1706 men daily for labouring tasks.[24] The combination of exhausting work in the burning summer heat, an enervating diet and a fly plague on a biblical scale spread dysentery like wildfire. By the end of July, the 'Gallipoli trots' were out of control in the 4th Brigade, as they were throughout Anzac. 'Most of us have forgotten what solid motion means and when it happens we'll think we are in the family way,' one officer gibed.[25] Monash admitted that his men's health was rotten but gambled that 'any change from the present conditions would be welcome, and that the stimulus of active operations would call out their reserve powers'.[26]

Though gastrically sound himself, Monash was handicapped in other ways. He was a 50-year-old whose weight of 100 kilograms and his girth of 112 centimetres had made him look shorter than his 170 centimetres height when he left Australia in 1914.[27] His figure was still eye-catching at Anzac but had not been an impediment in the sedentary war there, where his superb organisation of the defence of the valley named after him was crucial to its retention. But Monash's age and amplitude hardly augured well for a night advance on foot through atrocious terrain. Nor did he have any experience of this type of operation. The 'advances-to-contact' practised in the desert around Cairo before Gallipoli were no preparation for it. Cox was five years older than Monash and only arrived at Anzac on 1 August, having just recovered from a nervous breakdown at Helles. But he was a tried leader of mountain troops, which gave him the edge when it came to selecting the column commander.

Constrained by the corps scheme and Cox's planning for the column, Monash's preparations were limited to his own brigade. The march timetable typified his meticulousness, wrote Bean.[28] So did the longitudinal section he drew of the ground between Abdul Rahman and the coast, which showed the gradients throughout the march.[29] He chose the 13th Battalion to lead it, followed by the 14th, because they could then constitute the picquet line, a relatively easy task for their new commanders. The 15th and 16th Battalions,

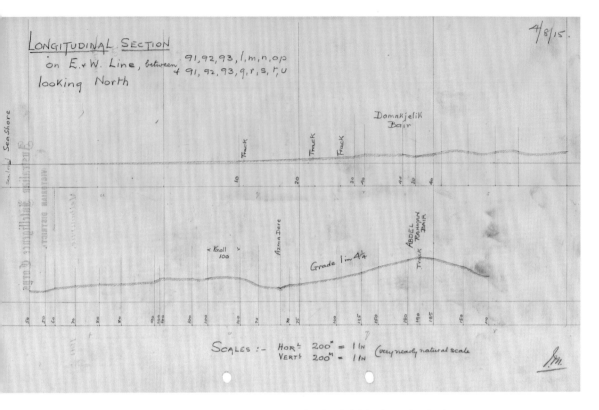

Longitudinal section of the gradients from the sea shore to the height of Abdul Rahman Bair (spelt 'Abdel Rahman Bair'), drawn by Monash on 4 August 1915 with characteristic thoroughness in preparation for the 4th Brigade's night assault on Hill 971. Due to shortages of paper at Anzac, drawn on the reverse of Australian Intelligence Corps memorandum stationery.

Monash papers, AWM Folder 20, Series 3, 3DRL/2316.028

led by their proven original commanders, Lieutenant Colonels James Cannan and Harold Pope, would assault Hill 971.[30] Monash thrashed out every detail with all four battalion commanders at a long conference on 5 August, and next evening briefed all leaders down to lance corporal in Reserve Gully.[31] The 4th Brigade set off a few hours later. All things considered, it had as little chance of taking Hill 971 as the 2nd Brigade had in the initial landing operations almost four months earlier.

Writing in 1932, the British official historian, Brigadier General Cecil Aspinall-Oglander, put it differently, remarking that 'Even as a peacetime manoeuvre ... the task of reaching the top of Hill 971 by night in the allotted time would have tried the mettle of troops in perfect health, and left little margin for any mistakes in direction.'[32] In 1990 a party of battle-experienced Australian infantry commanders concluded that attempting it in peacetime would be foolhardy.[33] Bean simply said in his official history that 'the attainment of Hill 971 ... was never within the range of human possibility.'[34]

As it happened, things went awry almost straight away. The NZMR's clearance of the foothills, while tactically brilliant, had fallen behind the clock, delaying the British 40th Brigade behind it at No. 3 Post. Monash's brigade in turn ran into the back of the 40th Brigade there. Monash could not leave No. 3 Post until 11 pm, half an hour later than his timetable required. From there the march quickly degenerated into 'a shuffle, slower than a funeral, with innumerable halts'.[35] Men threw themselves into the scrub, imitating those in front without knowing the cause of the alarm. *Field Service Regulations* prosaically remarks that when a march becomes a 'concertina affair' with alternate checking and hurrying as this one had, it is 'most exhausting to the troops'.[36]

Friction increased as further mishaps followed. Instead of following the planned route around Walden Point into the Aghyl Dere, Major Overton, who was guiding the column, heeded the advice of a local Greek villager that a narrow defile separating Walden's from Bauchop's, later named Taylor's Gap, was a shortcut into the Aghyl Dere. He led the column into it. His decision was catastrophic. As the NZMR had not completed the capture of Walden's and Bauchop's, the column was engaged by Turks on both slopes of Taylor's Gap. Using only bayonets, in order to avoid casualties through friendly fire, companies from the 13th Battalion charged off to deal with them. Overton kept the rest of the column moving instead of lying down, but progress slowed to a crawl in single file before stopping altogether as they reached a part of the defile overgrown with scrub so dense that the 13th's pioneers had to hack a path. The passage of the 550-metre-long defile by the head of the column took three hours, until 2 am. By then it was already due on Abdul Rahman Bair.[37]

Stuck at the centre of his brigade, Monash despatched some staff officers to hurry matters along. Nothing happened, so he finally went forward himself after asking Cox's permission. Monash recalled that he forced his way through Taylor's Gap, which was 'choked with troops', to the Aghyl Dere, and 'found that the column was halted because one (or two) platoons of the 13th had been sent forward . . . and had not reported back!!' Overton and the 13th's commander were 'conferring and arguing, and apparently unable to decide what to do. I vividly remember saying, "What damned nonsense! Get a move on, quick."'[38]

Leading the column into the Aghyl Dere himself, Monash ordered another company of the 13th Battalion to silence persistent Turkish fire and then reorganised the 14th Battalion and the remnants of the 13th at the foot of a wide tributary valley almost opposite Taylor's Gap. Later called Australia Valley, it was a gaping void, for the night was black as pitch with visibility down to nine metres. Overton's diversion had destroyed the navigational plan, which was based on paces and compass bearings, but the prominent features needed for a location check could not be seen in the darkness. Monash was unsure how far along the Aghyl Dere they were. When the moon rose at 2.30 am, Monash, and the officers with him, estimated that Australia Valley was where the 13th and 14th Battalions should leave to assume their picquet line. He ordered them to break off. In reality, they should have gone another 650 metres.[39]

Hurrying back to Taylor's Gap, Monash bustled the 15th and 16th Battalions past Australia Valley, where he set up his headquarters. Overton, who was killed soon afterwards, had said the two battalions should 'march two fingers S. of moon'.[40] Constantly bumping into Turks retreating from the foothills (the predictable outcome of the corps plan), and also overrunning a Turkish camp, they covered about 1.5 kilometres by dawn. The 15th linked on the left with the picquets, while Pope reckoned that the 16th on the right was on Abdul Rahman. At 5 am, he and Cannan reported their men 'absolutely done and lying panting instead of digging'.[41] They fell asleep at every halt, and rousing them to move again was difficult.

Visiting both battalions, Monash saw that they were exhausted and badly scattered. They would still not be complete that afternoon. Cox had wanted him to attack at 11 am, and sent the 6th Gurkhas up to help. Monash was now convinced that a further advance was impossible, especially since the 16th Battalion appeared not to be on Abdul Rahman after all but overlooking the Asma Dere, 500 metres short of the spur. He returned to his headquarters to find Allanson there. Allanson's stay was brief. Cox turned up slightly wounded soon after. Following a heated argument, he allowed Monash to entrench on his present line.

The New Zealanders and the Gurkhas had failed to take Chunuk Bair and Hill Q but got a lot closer to those peaks than the 4th Brigade did to Hill 971. Savage fighting continued at Lone Pine and the Light Horse had been slaughtered at the Nek. By comparison, Monash met only light opposition. Aspersions were cast upon him and his brigade. Birdwood, Cox and Godley weighed in.[42] Bean, who had never been impressed with Monash in their previous dealings, and whose brother's battalion at Lone Pine had alone lost more than the 4th Brigade's 300 casualties, charged Monash with wrecking the whole scheme of operations north of Anzac. He stopped 'without being stopped . . . a decision which many weak commanders would make but utterly unjustifiable,' Bean recorded in his diary.[43] But Allanson's remarks, which did not see the light of day until the publication in 1965 of *Gallipoli*, a magisterial study by British author-politician, Robert Rhodes James, remain 'the most damning evidence against Monash in all his military career'.[44]

Monash was definitely shaken early on 7 August. Company Sergeant Major Les Bain of the 14th Battalion had noticed him in the Aghyl Dere at 2.30 am looking 'rather worried'.[45] Seeing the parlous state of the 15th and 16th Battalions would have been another shock. So Allanson's account of what Monash said to him is credible. He had made a similar outburst after the 4th Brigade's disastrous attack on Baby 700 on 2 May, which Monash had argued strongly against, and there would be another in 1918 when his attack on the Hindenburg Line was almost derailed by the American failure to get on at the start.[46] Allanson's description of Monash as having 'temporarily lost his head' is problematic however.

To start with, Allanson apparently did not put pen to paper about the encounter for 20 years. He had been incensed to read in Monash's *War Letters* (published in 1934 but originally intended for home consumption), the condescending line that 'the Indian Brigade came up on our right, but did not do nearly so well'.[47] As Allanson harboured a self-confessed dislike of Australians, his disparagement of Monash was not just understandable but perhaps also inevitable.[48] Whether it reflected fact is questionable. Field Marshal Lord Slim, who fought with Allanson on Sari Bair and knew him well, remarked that he was an unreliable witness, who 'tended to embroider badly' with the passing of time.[49]

Allanson's reliability aside, it is strange that not even a scintilla of corroborative evidence for Monash's alleged breakdown has survived. As his biographer Geoffrey Serle says, 'if true, it probably would quickly have become notorious'.[50] Many people saw Monash as he trudged to and from the 15th and 16th Battalion locations shortly before he met Allanson, but none thought his demeanour warranted comment.[51] Far from corroborative evidence, Allanson contradicted his own evidence when he told the Dardanelles Commission in 1917 that the 4th Brigade 'meant to co-operate' with his battalion but was

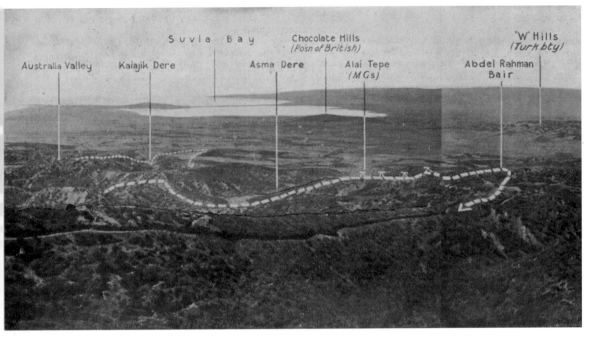

View from Hill 971, looking north towards Suvla Bay over the country through which the 4th Australian Infantry Brigade attempted to assault the Turkish-held heights on 8 August 1915. The long ridge in the foreground is Abdul Rahman Bair (or Spur). The thick white line indicates the intended route; the thin white line shows the route actually followed. Photograph taken by Australian Historical Mission in 1919, AWM G01845a-b.

(Source: Bean, *The Story of Anzac*, Vol. 2, facing page 654)

The same view from Hill 971, looking north to Suvla Bay in 1990.

Author's photograph, courtesy Peter Pedersen

'tied up in impossible country'.[52] Even more remarkable, he did not mention Monash while discussing incompetent commanders with Bean at the end of the August offensive.[53] Had he done so, Bean would have recorded it. Bean might also have gone further than merely comparing Monash unfavourably with Stonewall Jackson or J.E.B. Stuart in the official history.[54]

With one exception, Jackson and Stuart would have struggled to do better than Monash on 6–7 August. He had personally deployed his battalions to revive an advance that had little hope of succeeding in the first place. He went forward after daylight to gauge the situation for himself. As the 15th and 16th Battalions were hardly in a position to carry on to Hill 971, his decision to halt was probably correct. Monash's one indubitable error was not to have moved to the head of his brigade as soon as it stalled at Taylor's Gap. He would almost certainly have told Overton to stick to the original route, but his failure to take that action was as much Cox's mistake for insisting that Monash stay back. Monash's seeking permission to go up, even when it was clear that the brigade was stuck, shows how strong that insistence was. Stonewall Jackson and J.E.B. Stuart would have gone up immediately; in fact, they probably would have ignored Cox's order.

At 7 pm on 7 August, Cox informed Monash that the attack on all three peaks was to be renewed next morning. The 4th Brigade would assault Hill 971 at 4.15 am, when a pre-arranged naval bombardment lifted. The brigade's advance would begin at 3 am.[55] Monash's protests that his men were too exhausted were overruled. Godley wanted them to attack 'with loud cheering'.[56] As the 13th Battalion would hold the line, Monash briefed the commanders of the 14th, 15th and 16th Battalions at about 8.30 pm.[57] No written confirmatory orders survive – the urgency probably precluded any – so determining the command arrangements is impossible. That Monash remained at his headquarters in Australia Valley, and was linked by telephone to Pope, the senior battalion commander, is certain. The letters of some of the officers involved refer to Pope as 'acting in the capacity of forward brigadier' and as practically being in charge.[58] If that were the case, Pope commanded the brigade and his battalion but Monash did not augment his headquarters for the extra task.

This attack had less than no chance of taking Hill 971. The reason was not obvious at the time. Though Monash reconnoitred for an hour and a half after getting his orders from Cox, neither he nor anyone else picked up the navigational error made the previous evening. The 4th Brigade was not on the Asma Dere opposite Abdul Rahman Bair but on the spur, 650 metres west, that overlooked the Kaiajik Dere. Both deres had to be crossed before reaching Abdul Rahman for the final leg to Hill 971. That could not be done in the 75 minutes between the start of the advance and the lifting of the bombardment.[59]

Making matters worse, the 15th Battalion in the lead found the planned

exit from the Kaiajik Dere all but unclimbable. Not until 4.15 am did the battalion emerge onto a spur of what was thought to be Abdul Rahman. As it entered an oatfield, grazing fire of 'tornado-like intensity' erupted from the real Abdul Rahman, 550 metres away, across the Asma Dere.[60] The 15th 'seemed to wilt away from in front of us', recalled Major Charles Dare of the 14th Battalion.[61] Then the Turks streamed across the Asma Dere. The 14th, which had escaped the fusillade by taking to the reverse slope of the spur, narrowly escaped envelopment.

As shells from a Turkish field gun near Hill 971 had cut the telephone wire at the very start, Monash was unable to maintain effective command of the situation until it was repaired at 7.05 am. Pope urged withdrawal; Monash asked Cox, who agreed.[62] But an orderly retirement was impossible. 'Everyone seemed scattered,' Private Charles Smith wrote. 'Wherever one looked, there were troops, yet no-one seemed to have any fixed objective.'[63] The supporting field ambulance had not been informed of the attack, with the result that Australian soldiers abandoned their own wounded for the first time in the war. Spirits in the 4th Brigade plummeted.

One wonders what Monash thought as he surveyed the wreckage of his formation. His decision to remain in Australia Valley was deeply flawed. A commander must position himself where he can exercise command effectively. On 8 August, Monash was commanding a mobile operation at the tactical level. As the night march had shown, and *Field Service Regulations* required, he had to be well forward in these conditions. Worse yet, Monash must have known that telephone communications were bound to be tenuous and, after his reconnaissance, that the terrain precluded the use of runners. He also knew from the increasingly heavy fire from the direction of Abdul Rahman

The left of the Anzac position as extended after the August offensive. British troops are moving from Australia Valley, where Monash established his headquarters, towards Cheshire Ridge. The line reached by the 4th Australian and 29th Indian Brigades lay along the hills on the extreme left and in the middle distance.

AWM G01170

and Hill 971 on 7 August that the Turks had reinforced both, making strong resistance likely.

Why, then, did Monash not accompany his brigade? Perhaps due to his physical condition: the Kaiajik Dere was a daunting obstacle to a man of his bulk. Certainly he was tired: he had had just four hours' sleep and endured the exertions of the night march in the 48 hours before the attack. The disastrous oversight concerning the medical arrangements, which was so atypical of Monash, is explicable if he were close to total exhaustion. Monash also held a strong conviction that he could best operate from a headquarters well to the rear, into which all communications flowed, giving him a complete picture of the action.[64]

Certainly, Monash's presence would not have altered the outcome. But it might well have resulted in a much earlier order to pull out. His authority would certainly have quelled the reluctance of the 14th and 15th Battalions to co-operate during the withdrawal, the result of tensions that had simmered between them ever since a friendly fire incident after the landing. It is very difficult to avoid the conclusion that, for whatever reason, Monash displayed a temporary lapse in command of his brigade on 8 August 1915. His sin has largely gone unnoticed, thanks to the undue focus placed on the night march by everyone since Bean.

Hill 971 was not attacked again. Chunuk Bair and Hill Q were taken and

War diary of the General Staff Headquarters, Australian and New Zealand Army Corps (ANZAC), 8 August 1915, describing positions held following the series of attacks from Lone Pine to the Nek at Anzac, and preparations for the assaults on Chunuk Bair by the 'right column' and on Hill 971 by the 'left column'.

AWM 4, 1/25/5 Part 1

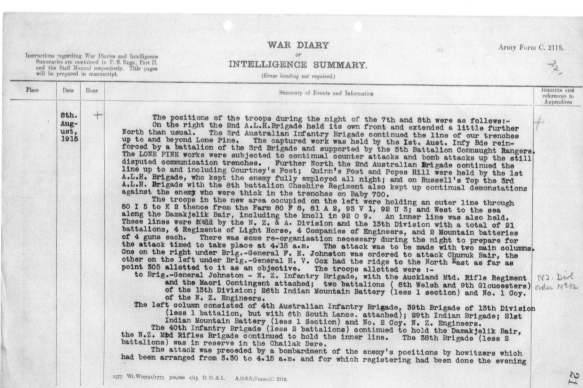

lost. The offensive fizzled out with three attempts to secure the junction between Anzac and Suvla by capturing Hill 60, the minor knoll at the end of the spur on which the 4th Brigade had been held up under heavy Turkish fire on 8 August. Monash had little to do with the planning of the two attacks in which the remnants of his brigade participated. They were the 4th Brigade's last battles on Gallipoli. At the end of August, when those attacks were over, it was just 968 strong.[65]

As everyone knows, Monash went on to earn a reputation as one of the war's foremost generals, as commander of the Australian Corps on the Western Front. One of his greatest successes occurred on 8 August 1918, the famous black day of the German army. Three years earlier, it had been the black day of the 4th Brigade. But it was not so black as to change Monash's thinking on a commander's location. Only once after it did he go forward – in May 1917 – for a reconnaissance before the attack at Messines. In Monash's defence, though, the fighting in France and Belgium was unimaginably different to that on the ridges and valleys below Hill 971, and he did enjoy almost uninterrupted success.

Yet the Hill 971 actions left their mark. They let Monash experience the infantryman's war, filling a yawning gap in the education of a commander who had spent the two pre-war decades in the coastal artillery and in intelligence. The grim results of Overton's departure from orders at Taylor's Gap helped steer him towards Napoleon's aphorism, 'Order, Counter-order, Disorder'. Once issued, Monash insisted from August 1915 onwards, orders must not be modified unless success depended on it.[66] As his enfeebled brigade answered call after call, he saw the limits to which men could be pushed, and applied this knowledge, despite those who criticised him for allegedly ignoring the exhaustion of the Australian Corps towards the end of 1918. Compared with the 4th Brigade in August 1915, his corps was a healthy formation. Monash too was a comparatively fit commander by 1918, his weight reduced to 80 kilograms.[67] In this respect, he may not have conquered Hill 971 but he did conquer himself, and was better able to withstand the rigours of war because of it.

Major General John Monash, commanding, 3rd Australian Division, at his headquarters in the Villers-Bretonneux sector, 25 May 1918.

AWM E02350

Chapter 6

'From the uttermost ends of the earth'

The New Zealand battle
for Chunuk Bair

John Tonkin-Covell

The capture of the ridgeline of Chunuk Bair, and then holding it for 36 hours under unrelenting pressure, was the most significant battle for New Zealand troops on Gallipoli.[1] It was a struggle against adversity and the culmination of 16 weeks of hard times on the peninsula. In conception, it promised to be the hinge point of the planned August breakout from the Anzac area, but the ridgeline struggle degenerated into a grinding battle – and ultimately failed. That result was perhaps inevitable, but the battle remains a symbol of unbroken defiance in the battle honours of the New Zealand army. The New Zealand experience is the focus of this chapter, though that focus cannot overlook the role of Australian, British and Indian army units which also contributed to the struggle for the ridge.

It was unfortunate for the New Zealand troops on Gallipoli that they were under the command of Major General Alexander Godley, in charge of the main Anzac offensive. Godley was an accomplished administrator, a British officer who had been engaged before the First World War to raise the standard of the New Zealand army. A man with a 'can do' attitude, during the August offensive he proved less able in operational command of the many formations under him, including those of the New Zealand & Australian Division. Indeed, his 'can do' approach was to be his own undoing and would cost the New Zealand units dearly as well as influencing the varying fortunes of other units under his overall command during the August operations.

In conference at Anzac, Major General Alexander Godley (centre), commander of the New Zealand & Australian Division, pressing his views on Colonel Harry Chauvel (left), commander of the 1st Australian Light Horse Brigade and ANZAC Corps commander Lieutenant General William Birdwood (right).

AWM H15753

The August offensive failed due to misconceptions in its planning. It involved expensive feints along the Anzac front line and movement north from Anzac, up and onto the Sari Bair range. The tactical complexity of the geography, the distances to be covered under the timetable, the logistical problems and the operational intentions would have presented problems even for fresh, experienced troops.

The Suvla landing was tactically irrelevant to the operations mounted from the Anzac area against the Sari Bair range, and this irrelevance was compounded by the subsequent operational lethargy of the British IX Corps. Distance, as well as the merely advisory nature of Hamilton's supposed 'orders', served substantially to exacerbate this irrelevance with regard to the Anzac operations.

There was also an illusion that affected control of allied ground forces in action. It was the optical illusion, created through the telescopes and binoculars of officers on warships offshore, that they were close to the action. While of great practical assistance in certain respects, these observations tended to underestimate the complexity of the ground in the Sari Bair range. Observing from a distance through binoculars did not give commanders sufficient information about developing tactical situations, such as would emerge on Chunuk Bair in the days ahead. Yet the illusion of visual proximity provided by binoculars bolstered notions that one could see what was going on and therefore knew what was going on. Nevertheless, numbers of officers went aboard ships to observe the terrain prior to the offensive operations. As the commander of the Wellington Battalion, Lieutenant Colonel William Malone, noted in his diary on 3 August, 'Went for a reconnaissance trip on HM Destroyer *Colne*. General Godley and General Shaw, 13th Division, came too.'[2]

The aim for the New Zealand Infantry Brigade was to capture the summit of Chunuk Bair, turn right and attack along and down the Sari Bair ridgeline through Baby 700 into the rear of the Turkish positions, while the Australian Light Horse simultaneously attacked at the Nek, in effect fracturing and 'rolling up' a substantial portion of the enemy line. The right turn of the New Zealand attacking force, after cresting Chunuk Bair, involved exposing their left flank and rear to any enemy forces on the peaks, including those that might be present to the northeast on Hill Q and Hill 971. This deficiency was supposed to be countered by the Australian 4th Brigade previously seizing Hill 971 and by British units taking Hill Q. When the timetable for the task of assaulting Chunuk Bair fell apart, this supposition evaporated. Nevertheless, the idea that the Nek attack should now be a feint that would somehow assist the New Zealand attack up onto the Sari Bair range recalled the earlier intention. It

Allied soldiers, believed to be men of the Wellington Mounted Rifles, occupy a trench on Table Top which they captured on the night of 6 August 1915, in preparation for the assault on Chunuk Bair.

J.C. Read Collection, Alexander Turnbull Library 1/4-058131-F

gives the lie to any suggestion that the New Zealand infantry taking Chunuk Bair could become a potential springboard for offensive operations over the ridge and down in the general direction of the Narrows of the Dardanelles.

This account will not dwell on the start of operations and the seizing of the lower hill positions by the New Zealand Mounted Rifles Brigade. The capture of features such as Bauchop's Hill and No. 3 Outpost, were prerequisites for movement by the New Zealand infantry battalions up onto the Sari Bair range. Certain problems were evident from the start: the tasks were more difficult than had been thought, with regard to their timings; and the gullies and the confusion their terrain created led to delays which made it impossible for the infantry to be ready to attack Chunuk Bair before first light. The steepness of the feature Table Top is illustrative of the physical difficulties in taking the hill positions, although Major James Elmslie's Wellington Mounted Rifles experienced fewer problems in taking Table Top by night assault than other units had in capturing other enemy positions.

The planned progress of the New Zealand infantry units on 7 August fell out of sequence on the way up, and the Wellington Battalion had to move through the dispersed Otago Battalion, which was busy dealing with Turkish resistance to the advance. The Canterbury Battalion had become lost in a parallel valley and returned to the start line, which put an end to any notion of concentrating the infantry brigade in the early hours on Rhododendron Ridge. At first light, the Australian attack at the Nek began, notionally to support the New Zealanders' progress by putting pressure on the Turkish positions.[3]

The lead infantry unit to climb up Rhododendron Ridge was the Wellington Battalion. By this time it was strung out in a long line and moving slowly and carefully up onto the ridge.[4] Lieutenant Colonel Malone sent a report with a sketch map back to the commander of the New Zealand Infantry Brigade, Brigadier General Francis Johnston, although it is unclear when Johnston received this report:

> I am occupying a position at head of gully. As it is day and I am not sure of my position I am lining the crest of surrounding ridges, so as to ensure reasonable safety. I am reconnoitering further and will act on further knowledge [and] report.[5]

As the lead elements came cautiously up over the top of the ridge within sight of Chunuk Bair, they came under fire and went to ground on an area known as the Apex. Just before they emerged on the other side of the ridge, a German senior officer and two staff officers had ridden up to the Turkish artillery battery near the crest of Chunuk Bair. Having given a rude awakening to the artillerymen there, Colonel Hans Kannengiesser went to the ridge top. To his consternation he saw Suvla Bay crowded with ships and troops being landed.

He then noticed enemy infantry slowly emerging several hundred yards away. He ordered the covering platoon of infantry to open fire, which initially they refused to do unless ordered by their own commander. After Kannengiesser jumped into the shallow trench and urged them to fire, they opened up and the enemy infantry dropped and took cover.[6] It was after 6 am and now quite light. Kannengiesser sent off immediately for reinforcements, and within two hours two companies of the Turkish 72nd Regiment had arrived.[7] An hour later the Turkish position had strengthened to a full battalion with the arrival of the first battalion of Kannengiesser's Turkish 9 Division.[8]

A question arises as to whether, had the Wellingtons attacked at this point, the Turkish defenders might have been overrun.[9] The probability is high. However, it is also clear that the enemy would have been galvanised into counter-attacking, and what was to occur on the following two days would have been initiated earlier. But the probing forward by the lead elements in daylight was now well behind schedule, and any reluctance to attack may have been due to Malone's concerns about both the state of his men and the command abilities of Brigadier General Johnston. Three days earlier, Malone had recorded in his diary:

> The men are run down and the reinforcement men are in a big majority so I am not too sanguine about what we can do. General Birdwood, it is reported, said the NZ Inf Bde [Infantry Brigade] had had so much hard work and been so knocked around that it should not go out in the present move but our Brigadier wouldn't listen to that and insisted that we be given one of the toughest pieces of the job. He is too airy for me and does not know the weakness of his Brigade. It really ought to have a long spell of rest … My Battalion too has done extra work, has had no spell at Imbros as did the Canterbury and Otago Battalions and will go straight out of the trenches again to fight again, climbing great hills … I wouldn't be surprised if the Wellington Battalion gets up alone 1st and has to dig in and stick it out … I do feel that the preparation as regards our Brigade anyway is not thorough. The Brigadier will not get down to bed rock. He seems to think that a night attack and the taking of entrenched positions without artillery preparation is like 'kissing one's hand'. Yesterday he burst forth 'If there's any hitch I shall go right up and take the place myself'. As it where [sic] in a minute and on his own! He says 'there's to be no delay'… If it were not so serious it would be laughable. So far as I am concerned the men, my brave gallant men, shall have the best fighting chance I can give them or that can be got. No airy plunging and disregard of the rules and chances.[10]

The Wellingtons were joined by the Auckland Battalion in occupying Rhododendron Ridge up to the Apex, along with Brigadier Johnston, who

Opposite

Troops descending the steep slopes of Table Top to Sazli Bait Dere following the route New Zealand soldiers used in climbing Rhododendron Ridge to Chunuk Bair in early August 1915. Table Top and the connecting ridges were formidable obstacles to the New Zealand assault.

AWM C03606

arrived at around 8 am.[11] According to Major Arthur Temperley, the brigade major, Malone had been most forceful in urging caution at this point.[12] Nevertheless, it was agreed at a conference between Johnston, Malone and Lieutenant Colonel R. Young (the commanding officer of the Auckland Battalion) that a pause and period of consolidation should take place, and a message was sent back to that effect to General Godley, who answered at 9.30 by ordering Johnston to mount an attack at once.[13]

The brigade major, no friend of Malone's, urged Johnston not to obey this order, but Johnston would have had none of it. Lieutenant Colonel Young personally went to look over the ground and found that any movement forward of the Apex produced heavy fire.[14] Johnston was adamant that they attack, and the 2/10 Ghurkas were attached to the Auckland Battalion in support. Major Jesse Wallingford, in command of the brigade's machine-guns, wanted half an hour to get all the machine-guns up to support the attack, but Johnston refused to delay, and the attack went in at 11 am.[15] Led by the 6th Haurakis and the 15th North Auckland companies, the Auckland Battalion attacked in echelon, owing to the narrowness of the saddle. Losing men quickly, a small group of the Auckland Battalion made it to the Pinnacle only a short distance further on, and well short of Chunuk Bair.[16] Here they occupied a shallow old trench, which they attempted to improve under fire for the rest of the day. Only 111 of the battalion had made it that far.[17] The Ghurkas had gone to the left under fire and went down into the Aghyl Dere. The attack had failed with heavy casualties. During this attack, Johnston had 'stood on the crest of Rhododendron Ridge cheering his men on. [He] had to be removed almost by force by his staff.'[18]

Johnston now ordered the Wellington Battalion to attack, along with half of Lieutenant Colonel Hughes's Canterbury Battalion in support. On the crowded Apex among the troops an argument took place involving Brigadier Johnston, Lieutenant Colonel Malone and Major Temperley. According to Lance Corporal Charlie Clark:

> So the Wellington Battalion was called to go up … So these two colonels [sic] and Colonel Malone had a big row … Malone said … 'My men are not going over in daylight – but they'll go over at night time and they'll take that hill.' So he said, 'Wellington Battalion come away from the ridge,' and so we did. Colonel Malone said, 'I will take the risk and any punishment. These men are not going until I order them to go. I'm not going to send them over to commit suicide.'[19]

This effectively stopped the attack, but the matter was not over. Instead of trickling his half battalion in small parties up onto Rhododendron Ridge, Lieutenant Colonel Hughes had his men form up in the open. They were immediately bracketed with artillery fire from Hill Q and suffered considerable

casualties, and just 53 men were available to support the Wellington's projected attack.[20] In addition, the Otago Battalion suffered casualties while digging in on Rhododendron Ridge during the day and required reorganisation. Three of the four New Zealand infantry battalions had been mauled, and only the Wellingtons remained intact. Johnston, having reported the failure of the Auckland Battalion's attack, now received permission from Godley not to attempt any further assault until after dark.[21]

An interesting question arises here. Given the strict application of military justice of the day, would Lieutenant Colonel Malone have been court-martialled if he had come out of this battle alive? Given both Johnston's and Temperley's hostility towards Malone, it would not have been surprising if such action were taken.

As part of a renewed plan of attack issued by Godley, the New Zealand Infantry Brigade was to take Chunuk Bair, while Monash's 4th Australian Brigade was to continue to try to seize Hill 971, and the 29th Indian Division was to take Hill Q.[22] Two British units, the 7th Gloucesters and the 8th Welch Regiment Pioneers, were to support the Wellington Battalion at Chunuk Bair, while the Auckland Mounted Rifles and the Maori contingent were to be the New Zealand reserves.[23]

Orders from Godley were received by New Zealand Infantry Brigade headquarters at 9.45 pm, and Malone was not given his orders until

A section of the steep and confusing terrain soldiers climbed to the Sari Bair ridge: Rhododendron Spur viewed from No. 1 Outpost with Chunuk Bair on the right and Sniper's Nest at right centre below Chunuk Bair. Photographed by the Australian Historical Mission in early 1919.

AWM G01810B

somewhere between midnight and 1 am on 8 August.[24] He and his second-in-command, Major William Cunningham, discussed the orders and prepared the company commanders' orders. Malone went to brigade headquarters to ask for additional supplies of water and ammunition to be brought up. After a short sleep, Malone woke his batman Private Ben Smart at 3 am, told him about the attack and gave him his wife's address. Smart recalled, 'I thought he would pass out as he shook hands with me before he went over and said "goodbye".'[25]

Wallingford's 12 machine-guns were lined up across the crest of the Apex and down Cheshire Ridge.[26] A very heavy bombardment of Chunuk Bair ridge opened up from the Anzac artillery and naval guns. Under weak moonlight, the Wellington Battalion lined up in their shirtsleeves, the two leading companies, a solid mass 16 men across, with the Wellington West Coast on the left and the Hawke's Bay company on the right, and behind them the Ruahine and Taranaki companies in support.[27] The bombardment ceased at 4.15 am and the battalion moved off with fixed bayonets, at the double for the first couple of hundred yards, then slowed down to a walk. The Wellingtons fanned out as they approached the ridge. There was no return fire: the enemy had largely gone, leaving just a machine-gun section which was quickly captured, and other small parties who quickly withdrew. By 4.40 am they were on top of the position. First light had come up at 4.30.[28]

Behind the Wellingtons, the 7th Gloucesters waited at the Apex for room to move after the New Zealand infantry, there being insufficient room for them to go together. The forward companies of the Wellington Battalion moved over the crestline on Chunuk Bair to occupy the shallow trench, and pushed out small parties further down the forward slope. The rear companies were to dig in some 30 yards to the rear of the crestline trench.[29] The ground on the crest was extremely hard clay and it was impossible to improve the trench depth rapidly. As the companies dug in, around 20 minutes after the

The view that met New Zealand soldiers who crested the summit of Chunuk Bair early on the morning of 8 August. The Dardanelles from Chunuk Bair (*Conkbayiri*), looking southeast towards Chanak (*Çanakkale*) on the far side of the Narrows in the top right. This photograph was taken by the Australian Historical Mission in early 1919 from the position furthest inland reached by New Zealanders on 8 August 1915.

AWM G01801

Wellingtons arrived, the morning haze lifted sufficiently for the enemy on Hill Q to notice activity on top of Chunuk Bair. So the Wellingtons had between 20 minutes and half an hour at best of undisturbed occupation of the ridgeline. The Gloucesters' leading companies got in unscathed, but the rear companies and the following 8th Welch Pioneers came under heavy fire; not many of the latter made it through, perhaps 60 to 80 getting into the right of the line.[30]

While the forward companies came under pressure, Malone had distributed his forces along the top and behind the ridgeline. Major Cunningham, the Wellingtons' second-in-command, recounted:

> the Colonel immediately divided up the frontage between our four companies allotting two companies of the Gloucesters to the left of the line and a little later when the Welch Pioneers reported he ordered them to extend the line to the right.

The Wellingtons' companies held the centre and, as Cunningham went on:

> We had only got fairly started with our digging when the enemy appeared right in front of the Wellington Battalion and opened fire. This was the signal for the Gloucesters and Welch on our right to get off the crest and they came right back behind us nearly causing a panic among our own men.[31]

An adjustment had to be made immediately. The Gloucesters and Welch on the right were now on the reverse slope and part of the right-hand company of the Wellingtons moved to keep the line intact. As Cunningham related:

> In consequence our battalion had to bend back on the right to try and cover as best it could the now exposed right flank. During the day the men who had come back did not dig in but lay down behind several steep parts of the hill and stood up and fired volleys from the shoulder, standing whenever the enemy came unpleasantly close to them. The whole brunt of the fighting was borne by our boys and it is disappointing to find so little credit given them.[32]

The ridgeline position on Chunuk Bair quickly proved to be open to enfilade fire from Hill Q to the left, Battleship Hill from the right, and fire from the more distant Hill 971 to the northeast. Chunuk Bair being a long narrow position from the allied perspective meant that the 'unders' from the guns of the British warships and the Anzac artillery also provided additional hazards.

The Turkish forces were galvanised by the presence of the enemy in possession of the Chunuk Bair ridgeline, and they mounted repeated counter-attacks during the day, often preceded by showers of grenades along with shelling and rifle and machine-gun fire. Malone directed his operations from a small headquarters trench in the rear of the centre part of the Wellingtons' line. The two Wellington machine-guns were put out of action.[33] Several times the Wellingtons were compelled to mount bayonet charges to clear the enemy out, and Malone himself led at least two of these, rifle in hand.[34]

Later in the morning there were attempts to lay a telephone line between the Apex and Chunuk Bair. Two parties of signallers were engaged in this task, which involved not only laying line, but also repairing repeated breaks in the line. The signallers were running about in the open, and a wounded man observing Corporal Cyril Bassett, who was commanding one of the signaller parties, remarked that he hated it when Bassett came close as the enemy fire followed Bassett around. The adjutant of the Wellingtons, Captain Ernest Harston, found a signaller, probably Bassett, forward of the Pinnacle with a phone. Harston then told brigade headquarters about the situation on the ridgeline. He asked for reinforcements and also requested that naval gunfire not be directed onto them but over the hill. He had a hard job persuading headquarters that the troops on the ridge had sustained heavy casualties.[35] Bassett would later receive a Victoria Cross for his work: his comment was that all his mates ever got were wooden crosses.[36]

Casualties were mounting on the Apex too, among the Otago Battalion and what was left of the Auckland Battalion. It was decided to send reinforcements onto Chunuk Bair in the form of parties of Auckland Mounted Rifles. These made their perilous way across the slopes and understandably took a long time to get there. Those who got through were placed on the right of the Wellington line.

It is worth commenting here on the 'reverse slope controversy' that later arose. Temperley believed Malone had stubbornly persisted with his defence arrangements, despite previous instructions, by using the reverse slope; but it is abundantly clear that had Malone not done so, the Wellington Battalion would have been destroyed faster and *in toto* during the day. The problem on Chunuk Bair was less where the rear trenches lay, and more that most of the position was exposed to fire from some quarter or other. Had the reverse slope not been used, the defence could not have held out that day.

On the afternoon of 8 August, Godley called for a conference at Johnston's headquarters on the Apex. He had decided that the attempt to take Hill 971 was to be abandoned, and instead Brigadier General A.H. Baldwin with the 38th Brigade would be brought forward, move through Chunuk Bair, and attack to the left along the crest in the northerly direction towards Hill Q. General Cox was also to renew his attack on Hill Q. Godley said that he would come forward to the Apex and confirm, once he had seen the ground, that Baldwin's force should proceed via the tortuous path up Rhododendron Ridge to Chunuk Bair that night.[37] Technology intervened. Godley failed to come to the meeting, as he was held up speaking to Cox on the phone, and he did not bother to send a staff officer to represent his views.[38] Johnston chaired the conference. He ignored the suggestion from Temperley that Baldwin should go across the saddle of Rhododendron Ridge, and instead determined that the British troops should travel through unreconnoitred steep gullies and ridges, then ascend the cleared slope of a former sheepfold, termed 'the Farm', towards Hill Q. As historian Christopher Pugsley has rightly observed, this made it impossible for Baldwin's brigade to move against Hill Q before daylight on 9 August.[39]

By the end of the day, the Wellingtons, the Gloucesters, the Welch and the Auckland Mounted Rifles were holding Chunuk Bair by the narrowest of margins. Of more than 750 infantry who assaulted the peak, only 70 Wellingtons remained, the rest now being dead, missing or wounded. Malone stood up at around 5 pm to look at the position just as a shrapnel shell burst overhead and he was killed. Colonel R.P. Jordan, CO of the 7th Gloucesters, was also severely wounded.[40]

As darkness fell, the Otago Infantry Battalion, just 400 strong, and the Wellington Mounted Rifles moved in and a relief took place, though this was not what brigade headquarters intended. But the first day's troops on Chunuk Bair had reached the end of their endurance. A smaller force now occupied the position, consisting of just 583 men. Lieutenant Colonel Moore of the Otago Battalion took command briefly, as Lieutenant Colonel William Meldrum recounted:

> Colonel Moore was wounded almost immediately and retired leaving me in charge of the post. There was a lot to be done. The trenches were

The cleared plateau known as 'the Farm', viewed from Turkish positions on the crest of Chunuk Bair. The Farm area was briefly occupied by British troops on 9 August before massed Turkish attacks overran their positions on 10 August. One of a series of photographs taken by the Australian Historical Mission in early 1919.

AWM G02003

narrow and shallow and we were all soon at work – Otago on the right and left flanks and Wellington [Mounted Rifles] in the centre. We dug in until daylight.[41]

Meldrum would soon earn his nickname of 'Fix Bayonets Bill'. Only a small number of the Auckland Mounted Rifles remained, and Meldrum sent them back to the Apex around dawn. Meldrum's hold on the Chunuk Bair ridgeline came under attack as early as 4 am on 9 August.[42] As the light came up, so things got worse. Unbeknown to Meldrum, to his north the 1/6th Gurkhas led by Major Cecil Allanson had crested Hill Q at 5.23 am, only to be driven off by either naval gunfire or Anzac artillery. The bombardment also landed on the left of Meldrum's line, killing Major Frank Statham and several other men. Part of the line fell back, and in Meldrum's words:

> It was a very critical moment for the Turks were very close up. Major Elmslie was close by me at the time in the centre and while Captain Kelsall and I ran out to turn back the men who were retiring, he called on one of his troops to follow him and led them up to the trench that had been vacated. He fell just as he reached the trench, but picked himself up, quickly dived over the parapet, the men following. As he got up so quickly I thought that he had only stumbled and it was not until the Turkish attack had been broken … that I heard that he had been fatally wounded.[43]

Elmslie's last words were 'I'm afraid I can't help you much further boys, but you're doing well – keep on.'[44]

By early morning the defenders on Chunuk Bair had lost half their strength. The trenches were packed with the dead and wounded and another line was scratched behind and men lay behind bodies for cover. Twice Meldrum asked for reinforcements but got no reply.[45] Then around midday 50 men from the 6th Loyal North Lancashires made it onto Chunuk Bair, the remainder of a full company that had set out to help. More Turkish counter-attacks came in. Meldrum observed:

> The bombs did us the most harm. The Turks swung them in long woollen socks and they came hurtling through the air for some 30 or 40 yards, rolling into our trenches and exploding there. Many men were wounded. Some jumped behind the trench and lay or knelt behind the parapet … we fought them all along the trench line.[46]

The Wellington Mounted Rifles and the Otago Battalion hung on grimly. Harry Browne noted:

If only Abdul had known how few were left in that gap, but there he didn't and possibly he was as exhausted as ourselves for New Zealanders had not died there for nothing. In the little neighbouring trench over which no Turk had come alive, the only sign of life among the many there, was the stump of an arm which now and then waved feebly for help and a voice which called 'New Zealand' to four listeners, who could give or get no aid for him. On the parapet above lay a hand. That hand had been throwing back Turkish bombs.[47]

By last light on 9 August, the Apex was itself a shambles, full of men, wounded and scattered equipment. Meldrum had sent back to say that the ridgeline troops could hold out no longer than the end of the day, and that two battalions would be needed to hold the position. The Otago Battalion and the Wellington Mounted Rifles were each down to just over 70 officers and men.[48]

Godley decided that the exhausted New Zealanders should be pulled out. The British commander of the 13th (Western) Division, Major General F.C. Shaw, would take over defences south of the Farm, which included the Apex and Chunuk Bair. The 6th North Lancashires would move into Meldrum's defensive position. The 6th Leinsters, already present on Rhododendron Ridge, could be the second battalion, but this was overruled by Godley, who did not want his only fresh, reserve battalion committed. Instead, the 5th Wiltshires, part of Baldwin's column, would have to suffice.[49]

A last patrol by Lieutenant J.E. Cuthill of the Otago Battalion had reported that the Turks appeared to be massing for an attack behind the top of the ridge, and Meldrum briefed the incoming battalion commander.[50] One of Meldrum's subalterns, Lieutenant Bishop, as he left gave some unsolicited, if insubordinate, advice to the British commanding officer:

> 'You are making a great mistake.' They piled arms, and men laid down to go to sleep. I said, 'You have got to dig, the only chance to save your lives is to dig.' He said, 'No, my men are too tired.' 'Well,' I said, 'we have been fighting for several days now and we can hardly move and you are making a big mistake.' So he said, 'I know what I am doing, I am commanding this battalion.' 'Well,' I said, 'you will be wiped out in the morning' and as I turned round I said, 'You are not fit to command pigs, let alone men, if that is the way you are going to treat them', and with that I went back to Brigade Headquarters.[51]

The 5th Wiltshires were not to arrive before 2 am on 10 August. Meantime, the Turks had indeed been preparing several thousand troops – a force of three or four regiments – for a massive counter-attack to begin at first light. At 4.45 am the Turkish assault rolled in, deliberately without artillery preparation, so as not to alert their enemy. Waves of Turkish soldiers swept over the crest *en masse*.[52] Wallingford's machine-guns were on the Apex. Sergeant Dan Curham was just test-firing his gun in the direction of Hill Q:

> until I knew the gun was in good order and I was still fingering it and looking at the hill and I saw a most amazing sight. A great mass of Turks coming over the hill … I had my gun trained on the very spot and all I had to do was press the trigger and, of course, they fell all over the place.[53]

The Turkish attack was seen by allied warships and ANZAC artillery which joined in the slaughter. However, it was too late for the Lancashires and the Wiltshires who were swept away, and too late for the soldiers of Baldwin's brigade at the Farm. The British trenches were 'overwhelmed by sheer weight of numbers', notes the British official history, 'and very few of its garrison escaped'. Casualties were enormous and some units were 'killed almost to a man': in the 6th Loyal North Lancashires, for example, the commanding officer, nine other officers and almost 500 men were reported missing.[54] The New Zealand machine-gunners and the Leinsters and some Auckland infantry had a desperate fight to hold on to the Apex, while the Pinnacle position was overrun by the enemy. But the Apex held.

Two decades later, General Godley reflected that the objectives of August 1915 were too ambitious and that they should have concentrated on Chunuk Bair and Hill Q. Doing it again, he would have used the New Zealand and Australian Light Horse, he wrote, and gained the ridge on the first night. Then New Zealand, Australian and Indian infantry brigades could have relieved the Light Horse units and established themselves on Chunuk Bair and Hill Q.[55] However, it might have been instructive to ask Godley why, and to what purpose?

Encrusted with dried mud, a brass shoulder title of the 5th Wiltshire Regiment attached to a scrap of khaki shoulder-strap from a British tunic: a relic of the heavy British losses in the fighting for Sari Bair. Most soldiers killed during the four days of fighting for the heights were left unburied. In 1919 the remains of hundreds who died in August 1915 were found by the Australian Historical Mission around the ridges where they fell, together with fragments of uniforms, equipment and personal possessions. The Historical Mission found this item on 3 March 1919 near the Farm, on the seaward approaches to the northern shoulder of Chunuk Bair.

RELAWM00382.006

An aerial photograph (see overleaf) taken of this part of the line in September 1915 gives a clue to the vulnerability of the Chunuk Bair ridgeline[56]. It should be noted that the 'old NZ line' marked on the accompanying sketch was not the section subsequently well dug-in by the Turks. The enemy's well fortified redoubts were on slightly higher ground to the north. The reality was that a force on the Chunuk Bair crest at the old New Zealand line was open to assault from a variety of directions. The trench line on Chunuk Bair ridge could not be held without inviting destruction. Dominated by higher ground, it was open to enfilade fire by rifles, machine-guns and artillery, both friendly and enemy, and allied naval gunfire.

The idea of an August breakout through Chunuk Bair was utterly impracticable. There were simply not enough allied troops. No matter which way allied troops turned, if they were successful and proceeded to move inland, their flanks and rear would be exposed. Even if Hill Q was also seized, the higher Hill 971 still remained in Turkish hands; and there was a ravine in front of Hill 971 so any attempt to advance along the narrow saddle from Chunuk Bair would have invited slaughter. The gullies leading to the heights, especially when jammed with wounded being evacuated, were too narrow for the transit of large numbers of troops and supplies of water, food and

Weary New Zealand soldiers sheltering in trenches dug in new positions on Rhododendron Spur several weeks after the failure of the assault on Sari Bair, September 1915.

AWM G01217

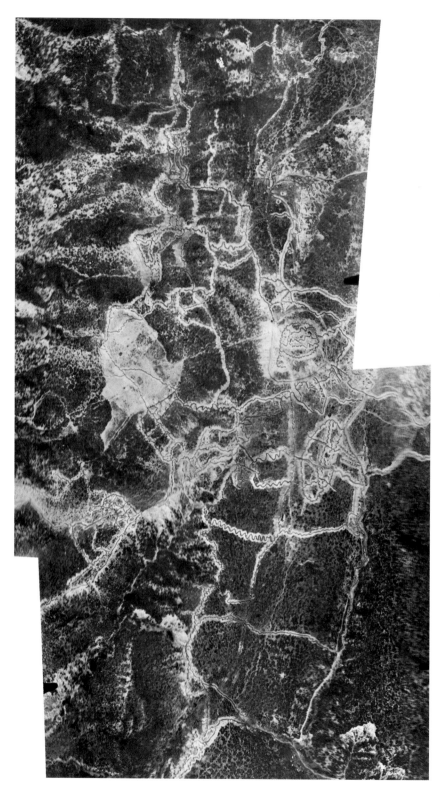

An aerial photograph taken in September 1915 showing the New Zealand positions occupied on the summit and main ridge at Chunuk Bair on 8–9 August, and the redoubts subsequently constructed by the Turks. See features noted on the map opposite.

AWM G01534ai-ak (reproduced in Bean, *The Story of Anzac*, Vol. 2, p. 719 and facing page)

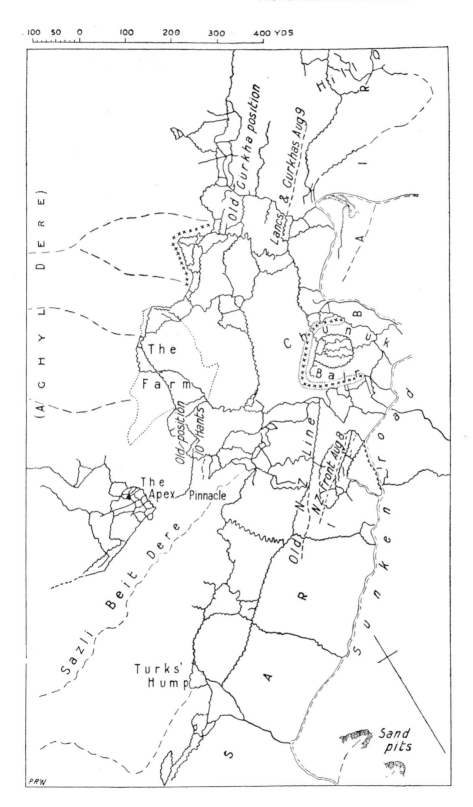

ammunition – and those gullies were impassable to heavy guns. Moreover, with each step forward from Chunuk Bair, the logistics line would lengthen. If sufficient water, men, food and ammunition could not be delivered to the top of Chunuk Bair from 7–9 August, the chances were even slighter of doing so and proceeding down the forward slopes successfully once the Turks were actively defending the area. The offensive operations were doomed even before the onset of any advance.

So what are we left to conclude about Chunuk Bair? It remains a crux of the August offensive that in itself had no chance of success with tired troops and poor logistics. It required, in any event, the capture of Hill Q and Hill 971 to succeed. There were displays of tactical command incompetence by Godley and Johnston. On the other hand there were examples of fighting tenacity by Malone and Meldrum: a bloody demonstration of what can be done in adverse tactical circumstances defending an enfiladed position over two long days: the determination to stick *in situ*, on improbable ground, despite impossible odds and simply hang on. There was also the grim inevitability of running out of New Zealand troops. There is no doubt that had the remnants of Meldrum's command still been on Chunuk Bair ridge on the morning of 10 August, they would have been virtually wiped out to a man. As it happened, the New

Some of the principal ANZAC commanders during the August offensive await Lord Kitchener's visit to Anzac on 13 November 1915. From left: Colonel G.N. Johnston, commander New Zealand Field Artillery Brigade; Brigadier General Andrew Russell, commander New Zealand Mounted Rifles Brigade; Brigadier General John Monash, commander 4th Australian Infantry Brigade; Brigadier General F.E. Johnston, commander New Zealand Infantry Brigade; Major General Alexander Godley, commander New Zealand & Australian Division; Brigadier J.M. Antill, commander, 3rd Australian Light Horse Brigade.

AWM G01325

Zealanders were exhausted by the end of the Chunuk Bair ordeal, and it took the subsequent folly of Hill 60 on 21 August to finish off the remnants of the New Zealand Mounted Rifles as a fighting force on Gallipoli.

Chunuk Bair became a soldiers' battle, proving futile in the end, but displaying the New Zealanders' tenacity against terrible odds. Grit and obedience to orders led them to capture and hold the exposed crest in sight of the Narrows under heavy fire for 36 hours. If Chunuk Bair evinced little in the way of operational skill, it did establish the reputation of New Zealand soldiers to endure under fire. Paradoxically, although seven Australians were awarded Victoria Crosses (VCs) for their actions in the battle of Lone Pine, only one New Zealander won that highest decoration for valour under enemy fire, because Godley and Russell coldly decreed that soldiers should not receive VCs merely for doing their job.

In the remote cemetery below the summit of Chunuk Bair, facing the Dardanelles, there are only ten identified graves amid the remains of 620 unidentified soldiers, most of them buried by the Turks after the August offensive. The ten graves are those of eight New Zealanders, an Indian sergeant of the 10th Gurkha Rifles and a British soldier of the Loyal North Lancashire Regiment. The nearby New Zealand Memorial to the Missing, with its poignant epitaph, 'From the uttermost ends of the earth', commemorates the 850 New Zealanders who died in the August offensive and subsequent battles and operations, and who have no known graves. Their names are incised on the white stone wall between the memorial and the cemetery, as an enduring record of their valour and sacrifice – and the tragedy of the conflict on Gallipoli.

The view from the cemetery below the summit of Chunuk Bair looking southeast towards the Dardanelles and Çanakkale on the far side of the Straits. Headstones on the lower slope of the cemetery mark the only known graves of just eight of the approximately 850 New Zealanders who died in the August offensive.

Photograph courtesy of John Lafferty.

Part 3

Enemies and allies

Chapter 7

'There will be no retreating'

Turkish soldiers' reactions to the August offensive

Kenan Çelik

Following the prolonged battles for Kereves Dere and Gully Ravine in the Helles sector from early June to mid-July 1915, the question facing Turkish commanders was whether the allies would continue their bloody attacks or abandon the Gallipoli campaign. One thing was certain: little was happening on the peninsula. The stalemate was like the silence before a thunderstorm. In the Turkish headquarters, commanders considered several options, until reports of Winston Churchill's speech in Dundee settled the matter: the British would continue the campaign, no matter at what cost and sacrifice in order to pursue their wider aim of opening a naval passage through the Dardanelles and ending the Ottoman Empire's involvement in the war.[1] Meanwhile the commanders on Gallipoli and Enver Pasha, Minister for War in Istanbul, made plans to counter any new offensives.

Many questions remain about the Turkish commanders' preparations and their responses to the major allied offensive that began in early August. This chapter will examine, from the Turkish perspective and using Turkish sources,[2] a number of important issues that are central to an understanding of why the allies failed in their last and largest military effort to capture the Gallipoli peninsula. Some of the questions to be addressed here include the following: How much, and by what means, did the headquarters of the Turkish 5th Army learn of the allied plans before the offensive began in August? In their preparations, did Turkish commanders anticipate the precise locations and objectives of the August breakout push from the north of Anzac? Did the diversionary attack at Lone Pine confuse the Turkish group headquarters at Anzac? How effectively were Turkish commanders able to assert their control over the various battles fought in widely dispersed sectors and against allied formations of substantially increased strength and numbers?

More broadly, what were Turkish commanders' and historians' assessments of the allied offensive plan in August? How did they evaluate the allies' aims and objectives and what they tried to achieve with their plans in August? Could Hamilton's plan have succeeded if Mustafa Kemal had not taken control of the events developing in the north of Anzac and around Suvla in early August? Is it possible to compare the actions and capabilities of Turkish commanders with those of allied commanders? And finally, was the Turkish repulse of the allied offensive in August inevitable, or was this yet another pyrrhic victory for the Turks, won at too great a cost to have been worthwhile?

Planning and intelligence

In the middle of July, the 5th Turkish Army on Gallipoli was reorganised.[3] The Asian Group, consisting of three divisions supported by the Çanakkale Gendarme Battalion, was positioned on the eastern side of the Dardanelles. Six divisions were positioned on the south of the Gallipoli peninsula in the Helles sector. Four divisions – the 5th, 9th, 16th and 19th – were stationed in the Anzac sector. At Suvla, some eight kilometres north of Anzac, there were only four battalions, two of infantry and two of gendarmes. Further north, the 4th Cavalry Brigade defended the Tayfur region. The Saros Group covering Bolayir, Enez and Kavak consisted of the 6th, 7th and 12th divisions of the 16th Army Corps.

Meanwhile a new Turkish commander of the Southern Group in the Helles sector, Brigadier Vehip Pasha, applied a new tactical plan.[4] Previously, many Turkish soldiers under German command had been squandered in costly counter-attacks, causing friction between the German commander, General Otto Liman von Sanders, and Vehip Pasha. The issue was referred to Istanbul and Enver Pasha, who visited Cape Helles to assess the situation. He and Vehip climbed to the top of Alçitepe, which dominated the region. Vehip ordered his artillery to fire on British positions, and the British artillery responded with a much heavier and more destructive barrage of their own. Having demonstrated his point, Vehip asked Enver to imagine the effect on Turkish soldiers if they attacked under this fire. Enver agreed: 'You are right. Stay in the trenches. No more bloody counter-attacks.' Vehip later said that von Sanders continued to order the Turkish forces to 'push the enemy into the sea', but everyone knew it was impossible. The Turks at Cape Helles generally stayed in their defensive positions and mounted no further counter-attacks.

Day by day, rumours of a new landing gained momentum. On 17 July 1915, Enver sent a telegram to Gallipoli, warning the 5th Army headquarters of the possibility of further allied landings. He was particularly worried about Bolayir (Bulair) and the Gulf of Saros, and, claiming he had conclusive intelligence about proposed British landings in Saros Bay, he directed von Sanders to reinforce the region with all available Turkish reinforcements.[5] Von Sanders disagreed and, although he put the troops there on high alert, he did not deploy such large formations at Saros. If he had done so, he would not have had reserves available to redeploy rapidly back to meet the allied thrusts at Anzac and Suvla in August.

Von Sanders wrote to III Corps headquarters, asking for their assessment of possible allied offensives. Vehip, the commander in the south, responded that he did not expect an attack on his lines at Helles. He thought a breakout at Anzac, combined with a landing either north or south of Anzac, more likely. The III Corps commander, Brigadier General Esad Pasha, Vehip's brother, expected a breakout towards Gaba Tepe, south of Anzac; he did not expect a breakout north, towards Chunuk Bair and Hill 971 (Kocacimen Tepe). Both thought a new landing, supported by a strong offensive from forces at Anzac or Cape Helles, the most likely. However, Cape Helles was surrounded on three sides by sea, so an offensive east or west was impossible. Anzac, on the other hand, could support a landing to either the north or the south.

At the same time, Lieutenant Colonel Mustafa Kemal, commander of the 19th Division at Anzac, was worrying about the vulnerability of the Sari Bair heights to the north of Anzac. He apparently read the intentions of allied commander-in-chief, General Ian Hamilton, and ANZAC commander, General William Birdwood. Two months before the allied August offensive, he had warned the 5th Army's chief of staff, Kazim Bey, that north of Anzac, Turkish defences were weak. Kazim agreed and said measures would be taken to shore up the area – but nothing had been done. Mustafa Kemal continued to write to the III Corps headquarters about the problem.

Finally, Esad Pasha and his chief of staff, Lieutenant Colonel Fahrettin Bey, visited the 19th Division's headquarters to discuss the matter. On 1 June 1915 Mustafa Kemal took them to the crest of Battleship Hill. From there he pointed out Sazli Dere, Agil Dere and Suvla (Anafartalar). Here he explained his conclusions about the area north of Anzac and Suvla. The panoramic view from Battleship Hill revealed a tortuous landscape, laced with gullies stretching towards Suvla. It was like a maze, and very confusing. Seeing this, the chief of staff said, 'Only bandits can walk in these gullies.' Esad, commander of the III Corps, asked,

Colonel Mustafa Kemal, commander of the Anafartalar Northern Group on Gallipoli, 1915. In 1923 Mustafa Kemal became the first president of the Turkish republic and held this position until his death in 1938. He dedicated himself to modernising the nation, assuming the surname Atatürk ('father of the Turks') in 1934.

AWM J00288

'From which direction will the enemy come?' Kemal pointed toward Anzac and Suvla. 'There,' he said. 'Very well', responded Esad, 'suppose they came through there. How could they move?' Kemal drew a half-circle from Anzac towards Chunuk Bair (Conk Bayiri). 'Like that, sir,' he replied. The corps commander smiled and patted Kemal on the shoulder. 'You need not worry, because they won't do it.' Defeated, Kemal conceded, 'God willing, may it happen the way you think, sir.'[6]

But in early August the allied offensive proceeded just as Mustafa Kemal had forecast. 'I do not know,' he later wrote, 'how the Corps Commander and the others reacted to the warnings I had given them.' In the end, Esad had placed only one battalion of the 14th Regiment to the north of Anzac. In Kemal's words, the area was 'the most important point in our defences and the most inadequately manned'.[7] Meantime, von Sanders moved the 4th and 8th Divisions from the eastern shore of the Dardanelles to the hills near Cape Helles and formed the II Corps under Brigadier Faik Pasha.

On 4 August, the Turks at Anzac noticed activity between Lone Pine and Gaba Tepe. The Australians were digging new trenches parallel to their lines and new advance lines. The same process was reported at Cape Helles: British troops were building new piers on the beaches there. Meanwhile, the Turkish build-up on the peninsula continued, reaching its highest figure of almost 150 000 men.

General Hamilton too received 50,000 reinforcements, almost half of them assigned to ANZAC formations, increasing their number to 37,000 men. A breakout was planned from Anzac towards Sari Bair, to capture the key peaks of Hill 971, Chunuk Bair and Hill Q, combined with a simultaneous landing in Suvla. To confuse the Turkish defenders, Hamilton ordered several diversions. A British naval squadron commanded by Admiral Nicholson bombarded Sigacik Koyu (Cove) near Izmir (Smyrna). Troops were landed on Greek islands near Turkey. Orders were issued to print maps of the whole of Turkey. And 300 Greek pioneers, commanded by Lieutenant Gruparis, landed between Karacali and Sazlidere near Enez.

The British diversion at Cape Helles

On 6 August, British artillery and naval guns opened fire on Turkish positions at 2.30 pm, a bombardment lasting two and a half hours. The British 88th Brigade attacked Turkish lines and captured some trenches, which the Turkish 30th Regiment regained in counter-attacks. Having lost the trenches, the British artillery and navy again bombarded them and followed with another attack. The British briefly reoccupied the Turkish trenches, but then were driven back again by counter-attacks. On the following day, the British 42nd Division attacked after a preliminary bombardment at 9.40 am. Attack and counter-attack continued until 13 August. The Turks lost approximately

7000 men wounded and killed at Cape Helles. However, Vehip Pasha deduced that these were merely diversionary attacks on his lines. He dispatched two available regiments, the 28th and 41st, to his brother Esad, commanding the III Corps at Anzac, where they were urgently needed. Later, on 10 August, the 28th Regiment would be invaluable to Mustafa Kemal when he made his successful recapture of Chunuk Bair at a critical time.

The attack at Lone Pine

Two Turkish divisions were holding Ariburnu (Anzac): Mustafa Kemal's 19th Division, consisting of the 72nd, 18th, 27th and 57th Regiments; and the 16th Division, consisting of the 125th, 47th, 48th and 77th Regiments. On 6 August at 5.30 am, five transports were seen on the beaches of Anzac, and Turkish artillery opened fire on them immediately. Ammunition boxes were being carried to the front line and the reserves were moving up. The Turkish trenches at Lone Pine were being bombarded. These were observed by the Turks the day before the attack at Pine Ridge. At 4.30 pm the rate of fire at Lone Pine increased. Although relatively light by comparison with artillery on the Western Front, the artillery fire directed onto Lone Pine was the heaviest yet seen on Anzac. The Turkish trenches at Lone Pine had heavy overhead cover of pine logs to protect the men underneath, and loopholes through which they could shoot across no man's land. They believed that their trenches were strong and secure, but in the howitzer fire coming from Russell's Top, many of the roofs collapsed, blocking the Turkish trenches and communication lines underneath. Two battalions from the 47th Regiment were holding these covered trenches; most of the men holding them were either killed or wounded in the bombardment, and many of those who survived were unnerved by shells detonating in the tunnels.

Esad Pasha, watching this bombardment, moved the 13th Regiment forward as reinforcements and also ordered the 15th Regiment to Lone Pine. Moreover, the 64th Regiment was ordered up closer to the Turkish lines at Anzac. All available guns were ordered to fire on Lone Pine if the Australians attacked. Even a Turkish mortar, which had only 21 rounds, was ordered to fire on Lone Pine. At 5.30 pm, the British barrage lifted to concentrate on the Turkish communication trenches behind the front lines. Simultaneously, the Australians came out of their lines in two waves, immediately followed by a third wave. The Australians fought aggressively and soon occupied two lines of the Turkish front-line trenches. The fighting in the dark tunnels and trenches was savage and intense, a hand-to-hand struggle at close quarters using bombs (hand grenades) and bayonets. When the Turks regained some trenches in bloody counter-attacks, they found dead Turks and Anzacs heaped together, including even an instance of Australians and Turks who had bayoneted each other, still frozen in standing positions, holding their rifles.

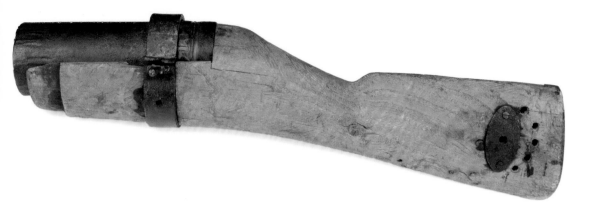

An improvised Turkish trench mortar captured by the 1st Australian Infantry Brigade at Lone Pine on 6 August 1915. The mortar barrel is made from a 75 mm shrapnel projectile clamped to a roughly carved wooden stock which has holes drilled into the rear to act as elevation points when the mortar was attached to a base plate and cradle arrangement. Both the allied and Turkish armies had a shortage of effective mortars and other trench weapons on Gallipoli.

RELAWM00302

Despite repeated counter-attacks, the Turks were unable to push the Australians back from the lines they had occupied. When the 15th Regiment got to Lone Pine, they counter-attacked at 11 pm and fighting lasted until the next day. But the Australians held the positions. The battle of Lone Pine (*Kanli Sirt* or 'Bloody Ridge') was fought mostly with bombs, and prodigious quantities of bombs were thrown by both sides. The Turkish commanders of the 15th Regiment, Lieutenant Colonel Ibrahim Sukru, and the 47th Regiment, Major Tevfik Bey, were both killed by bombs.

More Turkish reinforcements – the 10th, 11th, 25th and 64th Regiments – were thrown into the battle. But they did not attack at Lone Pine because there was another dangerous development at Chunuk Bair, to the north of Anzac, and these four regiments were dispatched there. The counter-attacks at Lone Pine continued until 10 August. Some sections of the second Turkish line were regained, but then the fighting ceased. The battle of Lone Pine had lasted three days and four nights. The five Turkish regiments involved lost 7114 men: 1520 killed, 4700 wounded, 760 missing and 134 captured.

Australian losses were 2000. From these comparative figures, it would appear that allied firepower was far superior. The battle of Lone Pine was clearly intended in the plans for the August offensive as a diversionary feint to draw Turkish reserves away from the main thrust northwards from Anzac.[8] But their costly experience led Mustafa Kemal and some Turkish commanders to the view that it was more than a diversion, and actually aimed at pushing the Anzac lines as far as the Third Ridge. The actual ground gained by the Australians, little more than 100 metres across a narrow front, was trivial measured against the losses on both sides.

When the battle of Lone Pine started, Mustafa Kemal was watching from his commanding position and immediately ordered his guns to fire on the ridge at Lone Pine. He also moved one battalion forward to reinforce the Turkish position. He could see Australian infantry moving across no man's land, almost unopposed by the Turkish infantry, and wondered what was wrong with the defences there. Later he learned that Tevfik Bey, commander of the 47th Regiment, had developed the habit of moving his men back to covered trenches so as not to suffer heavy losses during bombardments. This was a serious mistake, especially at Anzac, where the trenches were so close and there was insufficient time after bombardments for the Turkish infantry to return through the tunnels and to reoccupy the trenches they had abandoned.

The Director of Military Operations in Çanakkale (Gallipoli), Lieutenant Colonel Kemal Bey (not to be confused with Mustafa Kemal) reported that heavy howitzer fire was coming from Yuksek Sirt (Russell's Top) onto Lone Pine. On Russell's Top, the New Zealand artillery was camouflaged very well. The Turkish soldiers were unused to heavy artillery fire, which stunned them. The Turks believed their trenches at Lone Pine were strong and impregnable, but the enemy's artillery fire was concentrated, collapsing the roofs of the

The results of close-quarters trench fighting. The bodies of dead Turkish soldiers on the Chessboard feature at Anzac being gathered for burial during an armistice on 24 May 1915, following the massed Turkish attacks five days earlier. After the heavy fighting of the August offensive most allied and Turkish bodies lying in no man's land remained unburied.

AWM P02649.027

trenches and blocking the communication trenches with shell craters. The Turks estimated that 16,000 shells were fired on their trenches at Lone Pine: nearly every metre of the 220 metres of the Turkish lines received more than 80 shells, killing an estimated 500 Turkish soldiers. A comparison of Turkish losses suffered in the August offensive shows that the second highest losses, after Chunuk Bair, were at Lone Pine. In the August offensive the main allied objective was Chunuk Bair, where the Turks lost 9000 men.

The Turkish headquarters considered Lone Pine a strategically important position and moved almost all their reserves behind Third Ridge to Lone Pine, even moving one division from Kabatepe to Anzac. This further weakened Mustafa Kemal's 19th Division because he had to send a battalion to Lone Pine, in turn receiving one battalion of the 14th Regiment. This had been stationed near Hill 971, its departure creating a 'domino effect', with almost all the Turkish troops moving towards the south, even one unit stationed at Suvla.

The assaults to the north from Anzac

On the night of 6 August, the trenches held by Mustafa Kemal's 19th Division were bombarded by British artillery and naval guns. Kemal could also hear the crack of rifle-fire coming from the northern end of Anzac; he knew something serious was happening there. He concentrated on his line because he knew there would be a strong attack coming. At the same time, he could not help watching what was happening elsewhere. He took strong measures to repulse the expected attack, moving reserves closer to the lines, and issued orders for his troops to keep a vigilant watch through the night. He did not sleep either, watching the battlefield from his observation post. An officer and a few men from the 14th Regiment, deployed in the north, came to Mustafa Kemal's headquarters and reported that their whole regiment had been wiped out. Kemal's 19th Division now risked being outflanked.

On the morning of 7 August, just before 4 am, the Turkish trenches were again heavily bombarded, destroying trenches and dugouts. After 45 minutes of bombardment, the Anzacs charged the lines held by the 19th Division. The attack was repulsed, though a few Anzacs reached the Turkish trenches in the centre and on the right. Soon after, the Turks counter-attacked and wiped out the Anzacs in the Turkish trenches. From 4.30 am, repeated attacks at Cesarettepe (the Nek) also failed. Mustafa Kemal could see the Australian light horsemen trying to come out of their lines, but as soon as they emerged, Turkish fire wiped them out.

Lieutenant Colonel Sefik Bey, the commander of the 27th Regiment, holding the lines between the Nek and the Quinn's Post, wrote that about a month earlier he had received orders to put heavy cover over the trenches for safety. The order came to him through Mustafa Kemal, his divisional commander, and was a general order from army headquarters. Sefik thought covering the trenches would not be a good idea, as it could trap his men in their trenches after the bombardment. He took responsibility for not covering his trenches. His neighbouring commander, the 18th Regiment's Major Mustafa Bey, did not cover his trenches either. Sefik believed that the reason for the loss of the Lone Pine trenches was the covering put over them. If the trenches at Bomb Ridge and the Nek had been covered like the Turkish trenches at Lone Pine, he believed they could have faced the same disaster.

Mustafa Kemal, seeing crises developing behind him, dispatched one battalion from the 14th Regiment and two companies from the 72nd Regiment to Chunuk Bair. When the battalion arrived, it reported that the situation was critical; Mustafa Kemal ordered the battalion commander to hold the ground at all costs. Two companies, although weak, held the ridges from Chunuk Bair to Besim Tepe (Hill Q). Two other companies were able to hold the south of Chunuk Bair. These were the first units to block the advance of the New Zealanders. Finally, the 64th and 25th Regiments of the 9th Division arrived to reinforce them. The 25th Regiment reinforced the two companies from the 72nd Regiment, and the 64th Regiment reinforced the two companies from the 14th Regiment on the right. Soon after this, Colonel Hans Kannengiesser, commander of the 9th Division, was wounded and replaced by his chief of staff, Hulusi Bey. Chunuk Bair was heavily bombarded and then the New Zealanders attacked again. The Turkish 1/14th Battalion was hard pressed to repel the attack until the 25th Regiment arrived with new reinforcements. Meanwhile, Cemil Conk was appointed as the new area commander. In the evening, the 11th Battalion of 4th Division also arrived to reinforce them, and five machine-guns were brought to Chunuk Bair.

In the north of Anzac, the men of the 2nd Battalion, 14th Regiment, were surprised and scattered. Suffering many losses, they retreated to the slopes of Asma Dere, where the 1st Battalion, 32nd Regiment, reinforced them; there the Turks checked the Australian advance. In the fighting on Chunuk Bair, Lieutenant Colonel Kisiklili Nail, the commander of the 25th Regiment, and his battalion commander, Lieutenant Colonel Vidinli Mehmet Ali, were both shot.

On the night of 7–8 August, Cemil Conk, the 9th Division commander, was planning a counter-attack to regain Sahin Sirt (Rhododendron Ridge). He spent the night at the 64th Regiment headquarters, with heavy fire coming from naval and land artillery. The commander of the 64th Regiment advised against a counter-attack, which would be very costly under such heavy fire. This was advice that Cemil Bey agreed to follow.

We now know that this was a serious mistake. That night, the New Zealand soldiers of the Wellington Regiment occupied the Turkish trenches in a surprise attack, which succeeded despite there being 12 Turkish battalions in the area. However, when the New Zealanders occupied the trenches in

Primitive defensive measures. Wire entanglements from the trenches at Quinn's Post, fabricated from wooden branches bound together by barbed wire. The Turkish and allied trenches were less than five metres apart at some points, leading to intensive bombing fights across no man's land. This item was collected by the Australian Historical Mission from Quinn's Post in early 1919.

RELAWM00301

the attack, the Turks were confused and did not know if they were friend or enemy. One Turkish officer watching the action reported to Mustafa Kemal, 'Some men are moving from the shore along Sahin Sirti to Chunuk Bair and I do not know whether they are enemy or Turks.' Later, the same officer reported that they were digging in on Chunuk Bair. Mustafa Kemal thought they were enemy troops and was worried about the confusion there.

Mustafa Kemal could see the crisis at Chunuk Bair from his headquarters and felt compelled to act. He despatched his aide-de-camp to Chunuk Bair to report, but the aide was shot on the way. Next, Kemal sent his chief of staff, Major Izzettin, who reported that the situation was critical. By now, Kemal's headquarters was under fire from Chunuk Bair and some of his men were wounded. When the 10th Regiment arrived as reinforcements, Kemal immediately dispatched them to Chunuk Bair.

Major Nuri Bey, commanding the 24th Regiment, who was Mustafa Kemal's friend, telephoned and asked about Chunuk Bair. 'At the corps headquarters they told me to attack on Chunuk Bair, but I didn't know the ground and asked for details. When I asked, Esad Pasha and his chief of staff said angrily, "There is no point in talking, just go." Tell me, who is the commander there?' Mustafa Kemal replied, 'Go to Chunuk Bair immediately and the time and circumstances will decide who is the commander there.'

There was clearly a command crisis. At first, the German officer Kannengiesser was commander of the 9th Division, but he was wounded on 7 August.

A Turkish soldier's brass belt buckle with a white metal circular badge featuring a crescent moon and a five-pointed star in relief on a pebbled background. The belt buckle was collected by an Anzac soldier near the Nek on 24 May 1915 during the truce organised to allow both sides to bury their dead, following the disastrous Turkish casualties in their attack of 19 May.

REL/18154

His chief of staff, Major Hulusi, took command but he was killed. Cemil Bey was appointed as the new commander, but when the 8th Division arrived, Ali Riza Bey became the commander. Meanwhile, von Sanders appointed another German officer, Lieutenant Colonel Pötrih, as the commander of the 9th Division, making command and control even more confusing. Another decision shifted responsibility for Hill 971 to the Suvla Corps. Chunuk Bair was the responsibility of the III Corps headquarters which had sufficient men available on Chunuk Bair, but they lacked coordination and leadership.[9]

Once more Mustafa Kemal called the III Corps headquarters at Kemal Yeri (Scrubby Knoll) and warned them about the critical situation. He did not know whether the enemy had taken the strategic hill or not, but his officers reported that the enemy was filling sandbags to improve their lines, while Turkish soldiers of the 25th and 64th Regiments were just 25 to 30 metres away. Finally, on 8 August, Mustafa Kemal was contacted by von Sanders's chief of staff, Kazim Bey who asked, on behalf of von Sanders, for Mustafa Kemal's opinion on Chunuk Bair. Mustafa Kemal said, 'It is very critical and if you do not take the only remaining final option to correct it, there will be a disaster.' In his opinion the final option was to bring all the available men under one command. 'You should combine all the men under one leadership and make me their commander.' The chief of staff replied, 'Isn't that too much?' Mustafa Kemal responded, 'Even *that* is less than is needed, you will see.'

Mustafa Kemal takes command at Suvla

Meanwhile, when the XVI Corps arrived at Suvla (Anafartalar) under Brigadier Ahmet Fevzi, they were ordered to attack immediately, but Fevzi Bey declined: 'The men have covered 50 to 60 kilometres to get here from Bolayir,' he said. He wanted to delay the attack until the following day.

The 16th Army Corps commander, Fevzi Bey held a meeting with his divisional staff. Fevzi Bey had not slept for two nights to bring his men from Bolayır, almost 60 kilometres to the northeast of Suvla. Whole units had not arrived yet, and he did not want to make a piecemeal attack before being fully prepared. In the past, when such attacks had been carried out they incurred heavy losses. The time of day was also not favourable: it was late in the afternoon and the Turkish army would have to attack towards the sea, facing the sun behind the British army, and would not be able to see the British clearly. Turkish troops would make perfect targets for the British naval guns. The men were very tired because of their 20-hours' march, and they needed rest. If they failed in an attack, there would not be another force to replace them. Because of the hour, Turkish troops could not get closer to the British lines in the open country. The night would be better for getting closer to the enemy, to then prepare for an attack before dawn. Lastly, since there was no activity in the British lines, there seemed to be no urgency.

Those were the arguments Fevzi Bey and his staff put before General von Sanders on 8 August with plans for an attack for the next day. The 7th Division, weaker than 12th Division because it had only two regiments, would attack towards the north of Anzac to stem the allies' advance towards the Sari Bair heights. The 12th Division would advance towards the British army at Chocolate Hill, and Gelibolu Gendarmes would hold the Kireçtepe Hills. It was a sound plan but von Sanders dismissed Fevzi Bey summarily, some believe unfairly, and appointed Mustafa Kemal as commander of the corps. When Mustafa Kemal got the command, he applied the same plan without change. He left Ariburnu (Anzac) at 11.30 pm, and on the way to Suvla he found the 5th Division headquarters. He wondered what they were doing there when their 14th Regiment had been wiped out in the north of Anzac. Wondering who could have placed them there doing nothing, he ordered them to Suvla.

After walking through the gullies and ridges, he reached the Anafarta detachment headquarters. The German commander of the detachment, Major Wilhelm Willmer, was asleep. Kemal asked for directions to the headquarters of the XVI Corps. At 1.30 am, in the pitch dark, he finally found the corps headquarters and asked the commander what orders he had given to the men for the next day. An unsigned order was produced. Mustafa Kemal asked for a signature, but the commander declined. Seeing no point in further discussion, Kemal issued an order to the corps. The corps would attack at Suvla at 4.30 am, the 12th Division on the right and the 7th Division on the left. They would drive towards Damakcilik Spur to split Suvla from Anzac.

The Turkish attack in Suvla succeeded, checking the British, Indian and Australian advance towards the strategic heights of Hill 971, Teke Tepe and Kavak Tepe. But Kemal's mind was still on Chunuk Bair. Before leaving Suvla for Chunuk Bair, Mustafa Kemal visited the corps headquarters at Camli Tekke. He met von Sanders and they discussed what to do with two new regiments coming from Cape Helles as reinforcements. Von Sanders put forward two options: they were to attack either on Damakcilik Spur or on Chunuk Bair. Mustafa Kemal declined the attack on Damakcilik Spur because he felt it would not succeed: the position was not favourable as the Turks could be fired on from two sides. If they did not achieve their goal, they would not have the men to try another option. The two regiments were the last reserves available to be used on Chunuk Bair. In Mustafa Kemal's view, the best option would be an attack on Chunuk Bair. Von Sanders said, 'It is up to you. I just voiced my opinion on the matter.'

Kemal returns to Chunuk Bair and leads the counter-attack

Immediately afterwards, Mustafa Kemal returned to Chunuk Bair to direct the attack. When he came to Chunuk Bair, he saw that the highest ridges were in no man's land. Trenches were about 30 metres apart, with the Turks and New Zealanders facing each other. But the New Zealanders' fire was not able to hit or sweep the gullies behind the Turkish trenches. Kemal went to the 64th Regiment's headquarters in a gully just behind the ridge of Chunuk Bair. Soldiers from the 24th Regiment were in the trenches on the front line at Chunuk Bair. Just behind them were the men from the 23rd Regiment, the only regiment not in use. The 10th, 23rd, and 24th Regiments were from the 8th Division under Ali Riza Bey. The 9th Division was also there, under Pötrih, but they were scattered and mixed up with other units. Further to the right, men from the 4th Division were deployed on Abdurrahman Bayiri (Abdul Rahman Bair).

In fact, men from the 4th, 8th and 9th Divisions were mixed together; only the 23rd Regiment was in good order. Kemal decided to use this regiment in the attack on Chunuk Bair. Another regiment was coming from Cape Helles, but he could not be certain they would arrive in time. They might have become lost in the night, but fortunately they did arrive: this was the 28th Regiment, dispatched by Vehip Pasha to Anzac. He knew there would be no point in staying on Cape Helles when he was outflanked by the Anzacs and the British.

When Mustafa Kemal explained his intention to attack Chunuk Bair to Galip Bey, the 8th Division chief of staff, Galip warned against it. 'We have been attacking for two days but every attack has been futile and there may be another disaster.' Logically, Galip Bey was right, but Kemal had made his decision. He was confident that a surprise attack would succeed.

He ordered Ali Riza Bey to prepare the attack overnight. He put the 23rd Regiment on the right just in front of Chunuk Bair, the 28th Regiment he placed on the left, to attack towards Sahin Sirt, and the 28th Regiment squeezed in between the 24th and 10th Regiments, who were occupying the front-line trenches. The attack would be a bayonet charge, unsupported by any bombardment, for shock effect. This would be accomplished in one minute, and after that Kemal did not know what would happen. He later recalled:

> It was early in the morning, on the tenth of August, the dawn was about to break. I was standing just outside the tent, and I could see all the men. The time was 4.30 am. I was worried about my men waiting in densely packed infantry lines. If the enemy opened artillery fire on these lines, it would be a disaster. I immediately ran to the front to greet and inspect the men and said, 'Soldiers! I am sure that you will defeat the enemy. Do not hurry, let me go first: when you see my whip

Opposite

Map 7.1

General Otto Liman von Sanders's 1:25,000 map of the Suvla and Anzac areas, showing allied and Turkish positions after the August offensive in 1915. Allied front-line trenches were indicated in blue and Turkish positions in red. Some place names have been transliterated from Ottoman Turkish (Arabic) script into Latin script. Annotations in red depicted Turkish divisions, regiments and artillery batteries.

AWM G7432.G1 S65 VIII.27/34 (comprising two joined sheets)

go up, all go together.' Then they walked with the commanding officers. All the men were in attack position, one step forward, rifles with fixed bayonets, officers with revolvers or swords in hand, listening for my signal.

At Mustafa Kemal's signal, 5000 men in seven lines charged the New Zealanders and the British at Chunuk Bair. A second later there was only one sound, 'Allah … Allah … Allah.' The British did not have time to fire and all the men in the front-line trenches were bayoneted and overrun. The British troops scattered wildly. In four hours, the 23rd and 24th Regiments regained the lines at Chunuk Bair. The 28th Regiment regained the Pinnacle, the highest point on Rhododendron Ridge. Just after the Turks regained Chunuk Bair, the allied navy and artillery began firing. Iron rained from the skies over the Turks as men accepted their fate. All around, they were killed and wounded. While Mustafa Kemal watched the fighting, a piece of shrapnel hit his pocket watch. The watch was broken but it saved his life, leaving nothing worse than a bruise on his chest. He seemed destined to save the nation.

At 12.15 pm, he ordered Ali Riza Bey to stop the attack. They had been fighting for about eight hours. In the fighting around Chunuk Bair, 9000 Turks had been killed or wounded but they again held the highest ground. Although the allies had engaged with a force of 50,000 men, nothing had changed substantially on Gallipoli. It was a terrible waste of human life. For the allies, it seemed there was no way of gaining their objective. After the August fighting, Mustafa Kemal sent a report to 5th Army headquarters. 'I think they are finished and the British cannot launch another serious attack on Gallipoli.'

Evaluations of the August offensive – Fahri Belen's lessons learned

In 1915 as a young officer in the Turkish army, Fahri Belen was wounded north of Anzac during the August offensive; his brother was killed in the same area in the same offensive. After the war, Fahri was a teacher at the Turkish military academy and gave lectures on the Gallipoli campaign. The following extracts from his lectures present the perspective of an informed Turkish officer who was also a participant in the August offensive.[10]

1. The attacks made at Cape Helles at the end of June and the beginning of July weakened both armies. It was an unsound decision by the British commander, General Hamilton, and the French commander, General Gouraud, given that they were planning a surprise attack in the north of Anzac and Suvla. The men lost in these attacks could have been better used later in the August offensive.

2. The French plan was to land on the coast between Anzac and Cape Helles, but it was ill-advised because this area was strongly held by the Turkish army. Hamilton learned in April, with the Cape Helles landing, that it was very difficult to land on strongly held ground. After the war, Gouraud visited Gallipoli with the British military attaché. After seeing the terrain both north of Anzac and at Kabatepe, he said to the British military attaché, 'This is why I insisted on Kabatepe', and he criticised the British plan to assault Hill 971 and Chunuk Bair. Gouraud's successor, Bailloud, also proposed landing three new divisions on the Asian side of the Dardanelles, but this was in error because a force of three corps would have been needed to make a successful landing on the Asian side.[11]

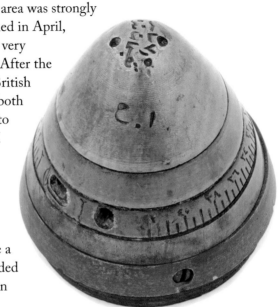

A time-percussion nose fuse from an artillery shell fired onto Anzac Cove by the Turkish artillery battery that the Anzacs nicknamed 'Beachy Bill'. The Turkish guns were sited in a well-concealed position known as the 'Olive Grove' near Kabatepe, and allied artillery and naval guns were unable to hit them. The brass fuse has a time-setting scale numbered in Turkish Arabic numerals from 2 to 42 with subdivisions of half a unit.

AWM RELAWM11469

3. Hamilton's plan to break out to the north from the Anzac enclave, targeting Hill 971 was good but in practice it failed because of a lack of strong leadership in the British army.

4. If Hamilton had been able to tie down six Turkish divisions in Cape Helles with strong attacks, his plan at Anzac (Ariburnu) and Suvla (Anafartalar) could have been brilliant. This was a lesson for the Turkish military: feint attacks which do not help the main plan should be avoided. Hamilton had already found it was impossible to break through at Cape Helles so he should have supported the five new divisions in the August offensive landing in Suvla by using the two experienced divisions at Cape Helles.

5. Premature demonstration attacks, made at Anzac and Cape Helles the day before (6–7 August), caused the Turkish headquarters to move reserve divisions to the area where Hamilton was planning a breakout and his main operations.

6. The landing at Suvla started too early in the night, alerting the Turkish reserves in time to move to meet the attack. Hamilton should have landed his force at Suvla just before dawn and advanced to the W Hills (İsmailoğlutepe) and Tekketepe by day.

7. Hamilton (and Birdwood) should also have considered that a night advance in difficult country is virtually impossible with inexperienced (and physically exhausted) men.

8. The change in the Suvla plan was wrong and Hamilton spread his force too much, as he had done in the April landings. The original plan was better.

9. Vague orders were disseminated to all leaders in Suvla and this almost rendered them ineffective.

10. Von Sanders firstly considered a landing at Kum Tepe (south of Kaba Tepe) and secondly at Suvla but his plan of defence took no account of this. We cannot know why he did not make strong precautions against a possible landing in Suvla. Von Sanders had a difficult time in August, but he should have kept three divisions around the Anzac and Suvla area, as he had in April. He was also worried about the north of Anzac, but again he did not take measures to deal with this problem.

11. After the August offensive the Turkish army learned how important leadership is, as encapsulated in Napoleon's saying: 'In war men are nothing; *a man* is everything.'

12. The British leaders could have corrected their mistakes on the second day, but they failed to grasp this opportunity. Their commander-in-chief did not appreciate this either and did not interfere. Even on the third day the British still had an opportunity, but did not take it.

13. Von Sanders gave orders six hours after the attacks on Suvla began. If the Turkish reserves had been moved earlier, the result could have been swifter. Mustafa Kemal used them in the correct place and at the right time. In this battle, technical shortages and heavy losses of men were compensated by the leadership of the Turkish army.

Conclusion

Mustafa Kemal had predicted the Anzac breakout two months before the allied offensive. His urgings for counter-measures were ignored by corps and army headquarters, but he still proved able to deal with the August crisis. He displayed vigorous and decisive leadership at a critical time and he placed himself in command, leading his troops from the front, just 30 metres from the enemy lines.

Some final judgements may be instructive – from America's most famous fighting general of the Second World War, General George S. Patton Jr. In 1936, two decades after the Gallipoli campaign, the then Lieutenant Colonel Patton undertook a thorough study of the Gallipoli campaign for his Staff College paper which aimed 'to examine the methods use in defense against landing operations as illustrated by the Turkish defense of Gallipoli'.[12] He included in his detailed assessment some trenchant observations about the comparative strengths and weaknesses of the British and Turkish forces, their leaders and their plans, and suggested reasons for their respective command failures and successes.

Patton agreed that the British objective of the main attack on the Sari Bair ridge 'was to capture Hill No. 971, the key to the peninsula'. But delays due to a Cabinet crisis in London, and German intelligence reports suggesting the movement of 50,000 fresh British troops to the theatre, gave the Turks six weeks to prepare. Patton believed the main objective of capturing the heights, combined with the subsidiary operations at Suvla, 'was an excellent conception, and failed because of bad leadership'.

Recounting the inertia, confusion of orders and counter-orders, and delays in the British operations at Suvla, Patton quoted the damning assessment of the British commanders from the final report of the Dardanelles Commission:

> None of the three Brigadier Generals concerned in the attack on Chocolate Hill accompanied the troops. They established their report centres about two miles distance from Chocolate Hill and remained there.

On 7 August:

> General Sitwell, who was in actual command, decided on a defensive attitude even after he found out that he was being reinforced by five additional battalions . . . at that time, Tekke Tepe Ridge was to be had for the asking and with it in British hands even General Stopford might have won a victory.

In comparing the qualities of commanders, Patton described the inaction of the British IX Corps on 8 August as 'a striking example of the fact that in war, it is not numbers but leadership which counts, for here we have three (Turkish) battalions and four batteries checking one and a half (British) divisions and a majority of the Corps troops.' Pointing to the lacklustre leadership at Suvla he observed, 'it was not the Turkish Army which defeated the British. It was von Sanders, Kemal Pasha, and Major Willmer who defeated Hamilton, Stopford, Hammersley and Sitwell. Had the two sets of commanders changed sides, it is believed that the landing would have been as great a success as it was a dismal failure.'

Patton's overriding conclusion from his study was that 'Leaders must still lead in person to win'; and he deplored 'the most pernicious teaching of the [First] World War . . . that a commander should be a pusher rather than a leader'. The defeat of the British on Gallipoli, he concluded, was 'a monumental example of the pre-eminence of leadership over planning'. This might be considered an appropriate epitaph on the August offensive.

Chapter 8

'Only 1 per cent of our own strength'

German military command in the Gallipoli campaign and the impact of the Ottoman alliance on German strategy

Holger Afflerbach

The Gallipoli campaign was not a German military campaign, despite the fact that a German general, Otto Liman von Sanders, was commanding Turkish troops defending the Gallipoli Peninsula. A few hundred German soldiers – estimates vary from around 500 to as many as 700[1] – were fighting at the Dardanelles in 1915, and a considerable number of them lost their lives. But in terms of sheer numbers they were a rarity on the battlefield: so much so that on one occasion German machine-gunners got arrested and barely escaped being executed by Turkish troops who mistook them for English.[2]

Hundreds of Germans, but hundreds of thousands of soldiers from other nations, fought and died on Gallipoli, which has become a *lieu de mémoire* (site of memory) especially for British, Australian, New Zealand and Turkish people – but not for Germans. Contemporary Germans outside the narrow circle of military historians do not recall many battles of the Great War, not even the major ones. Therefore, it is not surprising that non-specialist German audiences link Mel Gibson and Australia with Gallipoli, but not Liman von Sanders and Germany.

This chapter will deal with the various aspects of German involvement in the campaign. The general topic of this volume is the major allied offensive operation of 6–10 August 1915, involving four British army corps totalling some 14 divisions, diverse military operations across a broad theatre of several widely separated fronts, and a series of amphibious landings. This was – at least from the perspective of German headquarters – completely overshadowed by the conquest of Warsaw by the Central Powers on 5 August. Nevertheless, Germany was far from uninterested in the Turkish defence of the Dardanelles Straits and its involvement in the campaign was of crucial importance for its outcome. I will demonstrate this by highlighting some central aspects of the German alliance with Turkey and of the assistance Germany provided its ally during the Gallipoli campaign. For obvious reasons, I will not limit myself to August 1915, but show events from a German point of view in broader strategic perspective. At the end I will try to find an answer for the central question of this volume – whether Gallipoli was indeed 'a ridge too far' – and aim to provide an assessment of whether this allied offensive posed a strategic threat for the Central Powers in 1915.

The value of the Turkish alliance for German strategy

It was the Ottoman government's own decision to enter the struggle in November 1914. Of course, the Turks were pressured by the Germans, who were keen to have an additional ally.[3] When the Ottoman Empire joined the fighting, German political and military leaders nurtured contradictory expectations, which can be summarised as representing three great hopes and one big fear.

The first hope was that the Sultan, as the religious head of the Islamic world, would declare a 'holy war' (*jihad*) and provoke a Muslim revolution all over the Islamic world. In 1914 it was the British Empire, not the Ottoman Empire, that claimed the largest Muslim populations and included a substantial portion of the 'Islamic world'. The Chief of the German Imperial Military Cabinet, General Moriz von Lyncker, said on 2 November 1914: 'We hope from Turkey especially the uprising of Islam.'[4] The German government also hoped for Islamic insurrections in Egypt and in India.[5] This was not likely to happen. The First World War was not a religious war, and pressure for a world-wide 'holy war' was, as Liman von Sanders underlined in his memoirs, not convincing, because the Ottoman Empire was not fighting for reasons of religion, but side by side with Germany and Austria-Hungary – that is to say, with Christian powers against other Christian powers.[6]

The second hope related to the Balkan states. The German Foreign Office expected Turkish intervention on the side of the Central Powers to produce favourable repercussions among the Balkan neutrals – Bulgaria, Romania and Greece. They hoped that these countries might join the German side, or at least stay permanently out of the war.[7]

The third hope was that Turkish intervention would force upon the allies a diversion of their military forces. German military leaders hoped that the allied powers would be forced to deploy troops along the new Turkish fronts in Palestine, the Caucasus and Persia. They even hoped that the Ottomans might conquer Egypt, or at least the Suez Canal. But some people doubted whether this was possible, given the British military superiority in Egypt. All the sceptics were proved right: an Ottoman military force reached the Suez Canal in February 1915, but was easily repulsed and forced to retreat.

All these hopes were overshadowed by Germany's big fear, namely, that the Ottoman army would not be able to fight this war energetically. The military effectiveness of the Turkish army itself was considered to be very low, because the country had suffered defeat in the First Balkan War. In early 1914 the German Military Mission in Constantinople thought that the Ottoman Empire would need at least ten years of peace to recover. A complete military breakdown was expected, should Turkey become involved in yet another war. The fighting strength of the Turkish army (*Feldstärke*) was estimated to be only around 200,000 men.[8] On 13 March 1914 the German Chief of Staff, Helmuth von Moltke, wrote to his Austro-Hungarian colleague, Conrad von Hötzendorf: 'Turkey is a military nullity. The reports from our military mission are disastrous. The army is in an indescribable condition. Up to now we have referred to Turkey as a sick man; but now one has to consider it a dying man. It has lost every energy and vitality and is in a hopeless condition of agony.'[9]

This perception dominated most German attitudes. German officers serving in Turkey described the conditions of the Turkish troops as disastrous. According to German observers, the Turkish army was lacking everything: guns, rifles, uniforms, ammunition and all forms of transport. Ninety-five per cent of all Turkish soldiers could not read or write. There was a serious lack of trained non-commissioned officers. A typical German comment was also to complain about the laziness, the corruption, and the lack of energy and goodwill of Turkish officers. Incidentally, Ottoman observers of the Turkish army's defeat in the Balkan war of 1912–13 found similarly harsh words for the condition, morale and fighting abilities of their own army.[10] Such opinions, dating from the immediate pre-1914 period, remained unchanged until the date of Turkish intervention in the First World War. Typical is the comment from the war letters of General von Lyncker, who noted on 10 November 1914:

> A short time ago I spoke with the Turkish ambassador [Mahmud Mukhtar Pascha] on the Turkish military operations. It's looking very badly; they think that they can reach the Straits of Suez only in 4 months, and in Asia Minor snow and ice will soon inhibit every further operation. They don't help us at all. We are standing alone, as we did before. Maybe the Turkish intervention is a political help, but from the military point of view it's different. A German officer of our military mission in Turkey who is here in the Headquarter said that Turkey has only 1 per cent of our own strength. Well! This is quite nothing![11]

This was in fact a great error. Ottoman military effectiveness, especially at the Dardanelles, exceeded all expectations – German as well as allied. This was also the opinion of Sir Ian Hamilton, who said later before the Dardanelles Commission: 'I did not know, to tell you the truth, that they were nearly as good as they turned out to be.'[12] The underestimation of the Ottomans is one of the most remarkable aspects of the First World War and especially of the Gallipoli campaign. It is possible to draw a historical parallel with the Second World War: in 1940–41, everybody, German as well as British, French and American military experts, considered the Red Army to be weak and unable to resist a German attack, mainly on the basis of the poor performance of the Red Army in the war against Finland in 1939. In fact, the Red Army turned out to be much more proficient than most thought, and the same was true for the Ottoman army in the First World War. It proved much better than its reputation.

American historian Edward Erickson concluded from his analysis of the military effectiveness of the Ottoman army that it was, in the first half of the war, not only good but better than its British counterpart. There were a number of reasons for this: its ability to learn from its defeat in the Balkan war; its elastic structure; the drastic reforms introduced immediately before 1914; and German military aid, which was very important.[13] We must also consider an additional factor. The Ottomans had lost during the Balkan war not only because of poor organisation and low morale, but because they were seriously outnumbered. They had to face the allied armies of Serbia, Bulgaria, Greece and Montenegro: 290,000 Ottomans fought against a determined enemy, numbering in total 474,000.[14] It is perhaps little wonder they lost. During the Balkan war the Ottoman army showed on several occasions that it was a formidable force and defended some places with great tenacity, such as the Çatalca line before Constantinople, and Jannina – the Turkish commander there, Essad Pasha, would go on to play an important role in the Gallipoli campaign. It was not by chance that the Balkan states did not underestimate the Turks to the same extent as the great powers. Greek and Bulgarian experts, for example, considered military action against the Dardanelles Straits might succeed only without preparatory operations in order to take the Turks completely by surprise.[15]

In a word, the Turks were stronger than they seemed, they learned from their defeats, they had already made gains by the Second Balkan War of 1913, and they had renewed, with significant German assistance, their army and tried to make up for the losses already suffered.[16]

Despite serious deficiencies, the Turkish armed forces sent approximately 500,000 men to the front when the war began for them in November 1914. This number increased throughout the war. Several early Turkish offensives failed, like that against the Suez Canal or in Armenia. Some of them were great disasters, like the battle of Sarikamish.[17] Nevertheless, the Ottoman

Empire managed to engage, and tie down in campaigns, approximately 1.5 million British, French and Russian soldiers, who otherwise would have been free to fight on the major European fronts, notably on the Western Front in France and Belgium. From the summer of 1916 onwards Turkish troops were sent to other European fronts as well, to Macedonia and Galicia to support the Austrians.[18] Therefore, the Turkish intervention was of great military importance for Germany. The Turkish impact was not 1 per cent of the German strength, as General von Lyncker believed, but most likely around 10 per cent, and therefore significant.[19]

The Gallipoli campaign in German strategy

The Ottomans had a prominent place in German strategic planning, but they did not dominate it. It has to be emphasised that the Ottoman fronts remained for the Germans a secondary theatre of war – even during the Dardanelles campaign. It should be clear that even if this allied offensive had been successful, even if Turkey had surrendered and dropped out of the war in 1915, Germany and Austria-Hungary would have continued to fight.

Turkey was not considered to be a decisive element in German and Austro-Hungarian strategy, but it was a very important one, and therefore both powers did everything they could realistically do to keep the Ottomans in the war and to help Turkey to win the Dardanelles campaign. So far, I have considered the extent to which the Turkish contribution was important for Germany. Now I want to turn the question around and ask what Germany did to help Turkey withstand the allied attacks and win the Dardanelles campaign.

The allied offensive against the Straits worried the German headquarters. Politicians and generals feared, as a worst-case scenario, that Turkey would drop out of the war should the Dardanelles be lost. General Erich von Falkenhayn, Chief of the German General Staff, thought the Turkish government would keep on fighting in Asia Minor even if the capital was occupied by allied forces. General von Lyncker wrote on 9 March 1915: 'If things go badly [and the defence runs out of ammunition], the Dardanelles and Constantinople will be unable to defend themselves for long – but this will be in no way the end of Turkey's war!'[20] Of course, it was considered wise not to make this the test of Turkish determination to continue fighting.

The German Chancellor, Theobald von Bethmann Hollweg, and the Secretary of the Foreign Office, Gottlieb von Jagow, were very anxious to help the Ottomans. They feared the breakdown of the entire near-eastern policy of Germany (which included German investment in the strategic Berlin–Baghdad railway project). Furthermore, they were afraid that the fall of Constantinople might encourage the neutral countries of the Balkans – Greece, Romania and Bulgaria – to join the war on the side of the Entente and undermine the precarious European military balance in early 1915.

General Erich von Falkenhayn (former Chief of the German General Staff, September 1914– August 1916), inspecting the mosque of Omar in Bethlehem, Palestine, with Djemal Pasha, Commander in Chief of Turkish Forces, 1917. Although appointed to senior command in Palestine, Falkenhayn favoured the Western Front as Germany's principal strategic theatre.

AWM P00360.002

The Dardanelles were considered a strongly fortified region and the Germans were generally confident that the Turks would be able to defend the region as long as they did not run out of ammunition. And this seemed possible on several occasions: Winston Churchill and others claimed that if the allied powers had continued the naval attack in March 1915, the defending batteries along the Dardanelles would have been out of ammunition after the third day. This assertion has now been challenged. Recent research has shown that the Turkish defenders had shortages of some kinds of ammunition, especially the heavy calibre armour-piercing shells needed to attack armoured ships, but that they had more than enough ammunition to check the minesweepers whose success was crucial for the entire allied naval operation.[21] Notwithstanding concerns over shortages of ammunition at the Dardanelles, a 'can do' attitude dominated German planning. It was partly the result of the optimism of their Turkish brothers in arms. The Ottoman military attaché in Germany, Zeki Pasha, reassured the Germans in March 1915 that the situation at the Dardanelles was 'quite good'.[22] In April 1915 Field Marshal Colmar von der Goltz visited the German Headquarters 'in a very optimistic mood, saying that the ammunition question was not that bad even if there would be shortages for a long period to come'.[23] Lyncker summarised these opinions on 22 April 1915, saying that 'many people consider a breakthrough at the Dardanelles as impossible'. There were also no more talks about ammunition shortage: 'Calm confidence rules all of us.'[24]

This cautious optimism regarding the question of ammunition at the Dardanelles did not stop diplomats and generals reflecting daily in early 1915 on how to deliver weapons and ammunition to the Dardanelles. There were numerous difficulties: Serbia blocked the land route to Turkey since an Austrian offensive against Serbia had failed in autumn 1914; and neutral Romania obstructed the passage of German and Austrian military transports.[25] Bethmann Hollweg and Jagow urged Falkenhayn on numerous occasions to seize the crucial northeast of Serbia to open a route for supplies to Turkey.[26] In the spring of 1915 Falkenhayn denied these requests despite the fact that he was no less worried about the lack of ammunition at the Dardanelles than anybody else. But he was heavily engaged in dealing with the other fronts: he considered it more necessary to prosecute the war against Russia and France on Germany's Eastern and Western Fronts. His main worries in the first half of 1915 were the Russian front, the Austrian weakness, the loss of the fortress of Przemysl (which surrendered with 120,000 men in March 1915 to the Russians), and especially the question of Italian neutrality. The intervention of this last neutral European great power was considered to be a mortal threat for the Central Powers. Turkish War Minister Enver Pasha actually agreed with Falkenhayn. Both were convinced that the Dardanelles defence would finally succeed, despite all difficulties, and that other theatres of war in France and Russia were more crucial.

Germany refrained from launching a major offensive in early 1915 to clear the road to Turkey, but it did attempt to smuggle weapons, soldiers and ammunition through Romania, paying large bribes in the process. Twice Germany tried to send an ammunition convoy along the Danube through Serbia – both times it failed.

The Dardanelles defence was therefore closely connected with German strategic decision-making in 1915, even if Falkenhayn's final and successful decision was to fight in Russia in the spring of 1915 and not in Serbia, while calculating that the Turkish defence of the Dardanelles would hold. This decision paid off. The result was the German-Austrian victory at Gorlice Tarnow on 2 May 1915, which destabilised the entire Russian front, strengthened the Austrians and enabled the Central Powers to face Italy's intervention on 23 May 1915.

These successes also gave the Central Powers the opportunity to win over Bulgaria and, with Bulgarian help, to attack and conquer Serbia in the autumn of 1915. By late 1915 the road to Constantinople was open, even if the need for repairs to destroyed bridges hindered an immediate transport of troops and matériel to Gallipoli. The first train from Berlin arrived in Constantinople only on 17 January 1916.[27] Nevertheless the conquest of Serbia and the opening of the supply lines to Constantinople destroyed the very last allied hopes of a breakthrough on Gallipoli – assuming there was any hope left after August 1915. The imminent arrival of German and Austrian heavy artillery presented a dire threat to the vulnerable allied positions on the peninsula. The allied decision to build a new bridgehead in Salonika in order to reorganise the Serbian Army and to engage the Bulgarians made the decision easier to evacuate the Mediterranean Expeditionary Force (MEF) from Gallipoli: by early January 1916 the last allied troops had left their beachheads and were glad to withdraw without heavy losses. It was wise to leave before being driven out or overrun, but it remained a difficult decision to surrender ground for which tens of thousands of soldiers had given their lives. However, the final withdrawal from Gallipoli was a direct consequence of German strategic successes in 1915.

Direct German involvement at Gallipoli

Germany was also directly involved in the fighting on Gallipoli. Many important command positions in the Turkish army and navy were held by German officers. The German command structure in Turkey was quite complicated. In addition to General Liman von Sanders, there were at least six high-ranking German officers in Turkey with decision-making power (counting only those who had an *Immediatrecht* – that is, the right to write directly to the Kaiser). These commanders were, in ascending order of seniority: the influential German Military Attachés, Colonel von Leipzig and, following his early death, Colonel von Lossow; the Chief of the Turkish General Staff, General Bronsart von Schellendorf; the Chief of the Mediterranean Division, Admiral Wilhelm Souchon (Commander-in-Chief of the Ottoman navy); the Commander of the Coastal Defence of the Straits, Admiral von Usedom; Generalfeldmarschall (Field Marshal) Colmar von der Goltz; and, looking forward to 1917, the commander of the Turkish *Yildirim* (Lightning) armies (Heeresgruppe F) in Palestine, General Erich von Falkenhayn (after his dismissal in August 1916 as Chief of the German General Staff).[28]

On 24 March 1915 General Otto Liman von Sanders was offered the command of the 5th Ottoman Army, tasked with defending the Dardanelles and the Gallipoli Peninsula. His army initially had six divisions, although it would expand to more than three times that strength by the end of the campaign; his staff was

General Otto Liman von Sanders, pictured on 7 November 1914, aged 59, one week after the Ottoman Empire entered the war on the side of Germany. As head of the German military mission from December 1913, he worked to improve the Turkish army's fighting capabilities. From 25 March 1915 he commanded the Turkish 5th Army throughout the Gallipoli campaign, returning to his previous posting in Constantinople on 19 February 1916.

AWM J00200

Turkish, but several corps and divisional commanders were Germans, such as Generals Weber and Kannengiesser.[29] Before taking over his command at the Dardanelles, he was head of the German military mission in Turkey, work he had begun, in charge of approximately 50 German officers, in December 1913. The efficiency of his reform work before the war is subject to debate, even if a majority considers it a success.[30] But von Sanders was to become the most important German individual involved in the Gallipoli campaign.

Von Sanders and his work were judged critically by his contemporaries, as they have also been by historians. Before his appointment to the Ottoman Empire, he was a divisional commander in the German army and considered unsuitable to command a corps. He gained a reputation as a difficult and demanding officer, prone to sharp judgements and rarely shying away from extreme rudeness or endless quarrels to get things done his way, while stubbornly sticking to his own opinions. He was deeply disliked by many Germans themselves. The German ambassador in Constantinople, Baron von Wangenheim, said that for dealing with von Sanders, he would need 'a psychiatrist's training'.[31] German officers and diplomats intrigued against him in Turkey and Germany, and tried to get him replaced even during the Gallipoli campaign.

Leaving aside such controversies, the important question remains: What was von Sanders's impact on the Turkish victory at the Dardanelles? The answer is simple and predictable: as a supreme military commander, he most likely had a decisive impact on the outcome of a campaign. Von Sanders – and not Mustafa Kemal, as misguided popular Turkish opinion claims – was the father of the successful defence.[32] Several factors support that judgement.

The first was his preparation for the defence. Von Sanders planned and oversaw the disposition of Turkish troops on the Gallipoli Peninsula and on the Asia Minor littoral of the Dardanelles with a thoroughness that ensured success. The Turkish defenders' big problem was that they did not know the allies' precise intentions. Previous naval bombardments of the Straits defences and allied troop concentrations in Egypt and the Aegean had made it evident that either a further fleet action or an amphibious landing was imminent. But the defenders did not know exactly where and when. British naval superiority lent the allies the capability to concentrate their forces wherever and whenever they wanted. The Turks did not have sufficient troops to protect effectively the entire coast of Gallipoli and the Dardanelles – approximately 84,000 troops to defend almost 240 kilometres of coastline.[33]

The Dardanelles defence had achieved its first major victory by repelling the allied fleet on 18 March 1915. German advice and technology was essential in assisting the Turks in improving their coastal artillery as well as effectively mining the Dardanelles. But now it appeared that the allies would try to force the passage of the fleet by landing troops to subdue the Straits defences. When von Sanders assumed his command of the 5th Army, he found a quite impractical Turkish defence plan in place. This plan divided the Dardanelles defence into European and Asiatic theatres of war.[34] Von Sanders changed this immediately to make troop movements easier and to allow the 5th Army to defend both sides of the Dardanelles. Next, he abandoned the idea of Ottoman commanders, like Essad Pasha or Mustafa Kemal, to build a line of forward defence along the coast without holding considerable reserve forces.[35] He later wrote in his memoirs:

> The distribution of the available five divisions for both sides of the Marmora [*sic*] which had obtained until 26 March had to be completely altered. They had stood until this according to quite other principles, scattered along the whole coast like the frontier guards of the good old times. The enemy on landing would have found resistance everywhere, but no forces or reserves to make a strong and energetic counterattack.[36]

Therefore von Sanders formed three combat groups and stationed them adjacent to the most likely invasion areas, but further inland to protect them from naval gunfire. He placed two divisions – one-third of his troops – on the Asiatic shore, to cover the area around Kum Kale. He considered this the most dangerous landing point because a landing there could expose the main Turkish fortifications of the Straits on the Asiatic shore. Von Sanders stationed his second combat group of two divisions to defend the area around Cape Helles on the tip of the Gallipoli peninsula and along the Aegean coast. He concentrated his third combat group of two divisions at Bulair on the northern isthmus of Gallipoli, to cover supply lines between the battlefield and Constantinople.[37] Von Sanders choose this strategy to be able to react flexibly and with a certain minimal strength; this meant that in the case of a major invasion his troops would need to move quickly from one place to the other. He developed the roads on the Gallipoli peninsula to make the rapid deployment of troops and artillery possible. The price of this flexible scheme was that he could not defend the entire coastline, a deficiency which was criticised by some Ottoman officers such as Mustafa Kemal.

Yet it seems in hindsight that his strategy guaranteed the Turkish success. Von Sanders's mobile defence plan has been judged by Klaus Wolf, a German military officer, to be an 'appropriate' and 'very clever' defence scheme.[38] Wolf argues that criticism that von Sanders left unnecessarily strong troops in Asia Minor or at Bulair instead of deploying them at the southern part of the Gallipoli Peninsula and nearer the coast, ignores the fact that von Sanders could not know beforehand where the allied landings would be. The original static Turkish defence plan would have given greater opportunities for the allies to achieve and exploit a quick breakthrough.

Winston Churchill, one of the key instigators of the Dardanelles campaign, later wrote: 'There is no principle of war better established than that everything

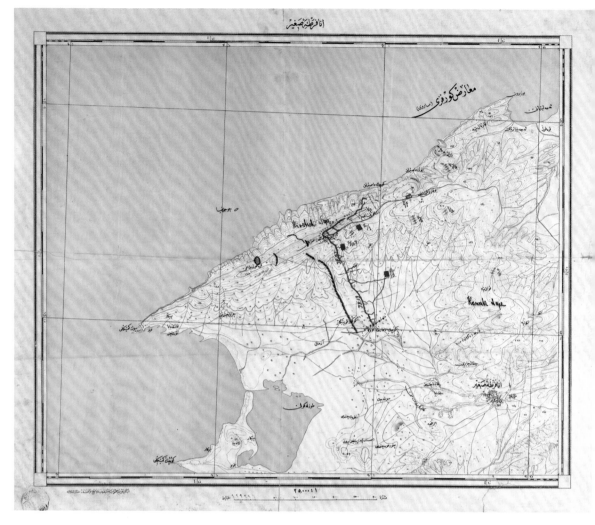

Map 8.1

General Otto Liman von Sanders's 1:25,000 map of the Suvla sector, showing allied and Turkish positions at the end of the main offensive operations in August 1915. Allied front-line trenches were indicated in blue and Turkish positions in red.

should be massed for the battle.'[39] Von Sanders planned accordingly. Once he was sure where the main landings were, he was not averse to taking risks and to leaving large areas uncovered. He has often been criticised for his decision to retain his two divisions at Bulair for too long during the 25 April landings, instead of sending them directly southwards as reinforcements. Canadian historian Tim Travers has claimed that misleading intelligence reports may account for von Sanders's so-called 'obsession' with Bulair.[40] An historical comparison should put this claim into perspective. During the landing in Normandy on 6 June 1944, due to the success of the allied deception plan the German defenders left an entire army of 19 divisions for an additional month at the Pas de Calais in expectation of a second landing, instead of throwing all their forces immediately into Normandy.[41] Compared with this, von Sanders must be considered to have responded quickly. Churchill acknowledged that during the Suvla Bay landings in August 1915, von Sanders rushed all of his available troops there, leaving the Asian coast and the Gulf of Saros practically undefended.[42]

Von Sanders was generally quick in making decisions, including his decisions to appoint and dismiss his senior commanders in the field. Indeed, his most famous decision was made at the height of the allied August offensive in appointing Mustafa Kemal as Northern Group commander of all Turkish formations fighting in the Anzac and Suvla sectors. The result was the Turkish victory of 10 August, celebrated annually in Turkey to the present day.

Despite his abilities, von Sanders was not immune to error, as he later admitted in his memoirs. One of his mistakes was to order on several occasions costly counter-attacks intended to throw the British back into the sea. Another was the unfair dismissal on 8 August 1915 of Colonel Fevzi Bey, commander of the Turkish Northern Group, who refused to execute a hasty counter-attack that probably would have ended in disaster. The benefactor of this decision was Mustafa Kemal. Von Sanders was also criticised for stubbornly holding the forward line instead of incorporating an elastic defence, able to surrender terrain under pressure. Some of his commanders – for example, General Weber Pasha, who commanded the Turkish Southern Group at Helles – believed that it would have been wiser to give up ground and to focus on the decisive heights only. Weber's dissent led to him relinquishing his command and being replaced by Mehmet Vehip Pasha.

Von Sanders made mistakes, but successful leadership does not depend upon making no mistakes – virtually impossible in the fog of war – but rather on making fewer mistakes than the enemy. Von Sanders did, however, avoid one mistake: inertia. He was absolutely determined to give his utmost and he also asked his men to give their utmost to defend key positions on the battlefield. Perhaps his defence plans were stubborn; General Hans von Seeckt later criticised them as such.[43] On the other hand, in confronting a determined attacker, a commander needs to be a very stubborn defender to resist.

Liman von Sanders should be considered the father of the Turkish success. The Austro-Hungarian Military Attaché in Constantinople, Feldmarschalleutnant Pomiankowski, wrote in his memoirs: 'There can be no doubt that Liman had the biggest share of the successful defence of the Straits.'[44] The German general was responsible for checking and repelling multiple allied attacks. But the price was high: the losses of the Turkish defenders exceeded those of the attackers. This may have been unavoidable, given allied superiority in artillery, especially naval artillery. Tim Travers argues that von Sanders himself, but also Kannengiesser, Willmer, Kiazim Bey, Esad Pascha, Halil Bey and Kemal Pascha, were ultimately better commanders than their allied counterparts and that this was the final factor which overcame the allies' advantages and resulted in the Turkish victory on Gallipoli.[45]

A number of less prominent German officers also contributed significantly to the Turkish defence of the Dardanelles: the German artillery specialist Lieutenant Colonel Wehrle trained the Turkish artillery at the Straits. His training helped to improve the Turkish gunnery and make it more effective. Kapitän Pieper organised the production of rifle ammunition in Constantinople. With the help of German soldiers and specialists, he also started to produce artillery ammunition for the Turkish army, a task that involved a number of German specialists, some of whom were smuggled in through neutral countries, as well as large numbers of munitions workers. Even if Pieper's ammunition had a big proportion of failures – many grenades failed to explode – it helped to overcome the most serious shortages. It should be mentioned that the Turkish shortage of ammunition was not a general phenomenon, but limited to certain types of heavy calibres. To the unpleasant surprise of allied troops who had hoped for the contrary, Turkish troops always had sufficient rifle ammunition.[46]

The Gallipoli campaign – a ridge too far?

Among the enduring battle narratives of Gallipoli is the perception that more energetic advances by allied troops – especially General Stopford's troops – would have secured the possession of the crucial heights. However, the German and Turkish commanders were absolutely determined to keep their positions. They reacted quickly and without regard for losses.[47] Perhaps

Comrades in the field. Flanked by a Turkish gun crew, a German liaison officer (second from right) on an inspection tour of a Turkish artillery battery on Gallipoli, accompanied by his Turkish liaison officer counterpart.

AWM P04411.031

this was not purely a military issue, but also one of psychology: Turkish and German commanders felt cornered and convinced that they were fighting for their existence. This was certainly true with Turkish commanders and soldiers, who were defending not only their own soil, but their capital and most likely the existence of their empire and culture. It was probably a mistake by the allies to attack the Ottomans at the very centre of their power; indeed, Lieutenant Colonel Maurice Hankey, Secretary to the British War Council, had proposed to attack instead Beirut or Haifa, where the resistance would surely have been less strong.[48] The allied planners should have considered that the Ottomans would fight to the last man, to the last grenade and to the last coin to defend the heart of their fatherland. Most likely even the loss of the Straits and Constantinople would not have deterred the Turks from continuing to fight. The history of Turkey after 1918 proved this: Turkey's new military leader Mustafa Kemal did not accept the Paris peace treaties and restarted the war to secure a settlement on Turkey's own terms.

The allied attempt to conquer the Straits culminated in three big efforts.

With the onset of winter, the end of the Gallipoli campaign seemed imminent. A group of Turkish and German senior officers in heavy greatcoats observe allied activities through a telescope from a vantage point on a ridge behind the front lines, late 1915.

AWM P04411.089

The naval assault failed on 18 March 1915. This attempt was never renewed, because of Admiral de Robeck's insight and also because of Admiral Fisher's stubborn protests. The second attempt was the landing of 25 April 1915, and the last was the August offensive breakout operations and landings at Suvla Bay. All three attempts failed to achieve their objectives. The staunchest proponent of the Gallipoli campaign, Winston Churchill, offered a compelling picture of lost opportunities in his book, *The World Crisis*.[49] He claims that success would have been possible if British planning had been bolder and seized opportunities to attack with significant numerical superiority. Churchill also made use of the memoirs of von Sanders, who claimed that the Turkish defenders were several times on the brink of defeat. The available evidence, however, does not support this.

In summary, the Gallipoli campaign looks in many aspects like a typical campaign of the First World War. Neither side had sufficient superiority to win, therefore every attack was doomed to lead to stalemate. So long as the attackers could not create significant local superiority, any attack would prove hopeless. Gallipoli became a race for tactical positions, for hills and ridges which promised to provide dominance over the valleys and the Straits.[50] It was, of course, of great military importance to control the heights and it doomed the allied efforts to failure that they were never able to capture them. But even the conquest of those most prized positions, heights such as Achi Baba, Chunuk Bair, Kiretch Tepe, and so forth, could not have led to full success, but only to a need then to conquer the rest. This approach recalls the battle of Verdun and its constant discussions about the importance of the forts and ridges of Douaumont and Vaux, Froide Terre, Tavanne, Souville, Hill 304 and Mort Homme. The history of the First World War shows that a battle either succeeded immediately – as, for example, Gorlice-Tarnow in 1915 – or else it became a hopeless stalemate. Gallipoli, no less than Verdun, falls into the second category. Once it had become a stalemate, it is very likely that the belated conquest of one or several of the heights or ridges would not have changed the outcome substantially. The fight would have continued, maybe a few kilometres eastwards.

Was, then, Gallipoli a ridge too far? The answer has to be that the mistake was much more fundamental; it lay in trying to conduct a campaign, and launch an offensive with insufficient forces. Only great luck, or major mistakes on the part of the defender, would have made success possible. The British Royal Commission into the campaign concluded that only much stronger forces, not only from Egypt but also from the Western front, would have helped materially.[51] But even then the prize of victory would have been small. In the best of all cases, the allied troops would have conquered the entire Gallipoli peninsula and might have shared the control of the Dardanelles with the Ottomans. Further gains would have been unlikely, even according to Churchill himself, who wrote:

> The temper of the Turkish Army in the Peninsula indicates that the forcing of the Dardanelles and subsequent appearance of the fleet off Constantinople will not, of itself, prove decisive.[52]

All other rationalisations, contemporary or later, were also illusions. The hope to open a supply line to Russia and to deliver war matériel to the Russians was unrealistic because the allies lacked a surplus to supply. The hope that Balkan neutrals would enter the war was similarly unrealistic. The Greeks expected Constantinople as a premium; but Russia wanted it for herself.[53] The Bulgarians were looking for revenge against Greece and Serbia, and allied success was unlikely to deter them, especially because Serbia rejected any attempt at compromise with Bulgaria.

In the case of the best possible outcome, the allied powers would have conquered Gallipoli and would have controlled a significant part of the Straits, but not achieved all of their aims. They would also have confronted the necessity to maintain an expensive bridgehead similar to Salonika, which was already an additional drain on British resources, transport and supply. The bridgehead of Salonika is generally considered by military historians to be an enormous waste of manpower – the biggest voluntary prisoner-of-war camp of the Great War – and the same would have been true in the case of any realistic 'victory' on Gallipoli.[54]

This makes it difficult to justify the losses: over 44,000 allied and almost 87,000 Turkish soldiers died in the Gallipoli campaign, and hundreds of thousands were wounded. The biggest mistake of the military planners involved in the campaign – as indeed on the other fronts of the First World War – was that they tried repeatedly to strike a decisive blow with insufficient forces. The greatest failure of military commanders in this war was not confined to the battlefield or some missed tactical opportunity, but rather the failure to concede that Europe was in a situation of strategic stalemate and that a reasonable chance of military success did not exist. The troops who fought on Gallipoli would likely have been sacrificed just as uselessly on the Western Front. The real alternative was not to fight on the Western Front rather than Gallipoli, but to admit that neither offensive would work and to press for a political solution instead of persisting in costly efforts to achieve the impossible. Similar misguided attempts were undertaken by the German command.[55] But British and allied leaders shared the universal opinion that a negotiated peace, the only thinkable outcome of the war until 1917, would have been tantamount to a German victory.[56] And so the stalemate and senseless slaughter continued for three more years until American intervention and radical developments on the battlefields of the Western Front finally determined the war's outcome.

Chapter 9

'No room for any lapses in concentration'

Ottoman commanders' responses
to the August offensive

Harvey Broadbent

A number of issues confronted the Ottoman (Turkish) High Command on the eve of the allied August offensive. Since incurring heavy casualties in the massed infantry attacks at Anzac on 19 May, the focus of the Turkish 5th Army Command had shifted from large-scale offensive operations to a reliance on defence and efforts to contain their enemy. From the first week of June 1915, the 5th Army Command had begun a reorganisation, intended to strengthen Turkish defences in the northern sector (the area from Kaba Tepe to the Anafarta Hills above Suvla Bay). This involved a number of changes in the deployment of Turkish units and positions, and the addition of reinforcements sent from the 2nd Army in Istanbul. Whatever the allies decided upon as their offensive tactics, the Ottoman High Command was determined to meet any possible attacks and contain them.[1]

Intelligence reports and observations had alerted all levels of Turkish command to signs of allied preparations for a major offensive operation. Both the 5th Army and the 3rd Corps needed to react to recent allied encroachments, such as that at No. 2 Outpost which had been occupied by the allies, by strengthening the defences in order to prevent any further advance.[2] They had begun to do this from the first week of June.

The 19th Division under Lieutenant Colonel Mustafa Kemal was strengthened by the addition of units from the 5th Division in the south and from Ece Harbour in the Anafarta Hills sector to the north. The result was an extension of the Turkish front.[3] Despite these efforts, some Turkish

field commanders felt that the defensive arrangements were not adequate. In various documents and memoirs they pointed to the difficulties they faced during the August offensive, claiming these could have been minimised by better defensive planning in this period. Mustafa Kemal was perhaps, not unexpectedly, the strongest critic of the High Command at this time.

But Kemal's authority was limited to that of a divisional commander, and as such he was forced to make the best of the situation as he found it. His first reaction to the possibility of a new allied offensive was to deal with the newly extended front. On 4 June he transferred the 19th Division headquarters to Duztepe (Battleship Hill). This brought his command post closer to the centre of the wider defensive front, although he recorded that this location also had significant disadvantages, in particular that it was not possible from there to view the whole front and monitor any enemy operation emerging from the Anzac Cove area.

Command of the Anafarta Hills sector, overlooking Suvla Bay, was assigned to the newly arrived German officer, Lieutenant Colonel Wilhelm Willmer, a move Mustafa Kemal deplored on account of the German's lack of local knowledge. This contrasted with Kemal's much more positive view of the capabilities of the 9th Division commander, Colonel Hans Kannengiesser. Moreover, Kemal was critical of the confusion surrounding the allocation of the boundaries of the two commands: he disapproved of the division of the Sazlidere area into two command zones because he believed it was strategically crucial, and hence should be kept under a single command. His misgivings were prescient: this was to be the route used by New Zealand troops in their successful, albeit brief, assault on the heights at Chunuk Bair.

Lieutenant Colonel Mustafa Kemal (fourth from left), commander of the Turkish 19th Division, with Ottoman officers and staff of the Anafarta Group which he commanded from August 1915. Far left is Major Izzettin Bey, Kemal's chief of staff who served with him in the operations during the allied August offensive.

AWM P01141.001

By the first week in August, General Otto Liman von Sanders, German commander of the 5th Army, had settled on a deployment of his force from north to south. The main feature of this deployment was that the force was fully stretched to cover as many eventualities as possible, as had occurred at the time of the original allied landings in April. Underlying this was his concern, which some commentators have described as an 'obsession', about the consequences of an attack in the north at Bulair (on the Gulf of Saros–Bolayir isthmus) – just as he had been concerned about this in April. This led to further disquiet at the supreme Ottoman Army Headquarters in Istanbul about von Sanders's tactical deployment of his divisions to cover a possible landing at Bulair. The Turkish commanders had not been happy with the effects of such a deployment in April. They felt the defences then could easily have failed, and the same situation seemed to be developing again. They wanted larger forces deployed near the coast to cover potential enemy landing beaches.[4]

Von Sanders resisted such pressure – at least, in the short term – but by doing so he again delayed deploying a fuller defence force in the Anzac sector. His deployment, which was to have an immediate impact on events as they unfolded in early August, was as in Table 9.1 below:

Table 9.1
Disposition of the Ottoman 5th Army at the beginning of August 1915

5th Army Commander: Liman von Sanders

		Approx. sector boundaries
Saros Group	Colonel Fevzi (Feyzi)	Bulair (Bolayir) Lines and Saros Gulf sector, including Gelibolu Garrison
Tayfur Area	Lieutenant Colonel Hamdi	Tayfur–Burgaz area to Ece Harbour
Anafarta Area	Lieutenant Colonel Willmer (German)	Ece Harbour to lower slopes of Hill 971, south of Buyuk Anafarta village
Northern Group	Brigadier General Esat Pasha; C.o.S (chief of staff): Lieutenant Colonel Fahrettin	Hill 971 (Koja Chimen Tepe) to southern edge of Kayal Tepe–Kilitbahir line
Southern Group	Brigadier General Vehip Pasha	South of Kilitbahir–Kayal Tepe line to Cape Helles
Asia Group	Major General Mehmet Ali Pasha	Kum Kale to Eski Istanbul Burnu, south of Ezine

At the outbreak of the offensive on the morning of 6 August, the Ottoman 5th Army Order of Battle was as in Table 9.2 below:

Table 9.2
Ottoman 5th Army Order of Battle as at the morning 6 August 1915

5th Army Northern Group
Brigadier General Esat Pasha
HQ: Kemalyeri [Scrubby Knoll]

		Sectors of deployment
19th Division 57th Regiment 72nd Regiment 27th Regiment	Colonel Mustafa Kemal; C.o.S (chief of staff): Major Izzettin	Northern and right flank: Between the line Sazlidere–Ağildere to Battleship Hill south to Steele's Post–Johnston's Jolly on Second Ridge.
18th Regiment		HQ: Topsirt [Cannon Ridge]. 500 metres south of Battleship Hill. Outposts on shore low ground only lightly defended.
16th Division 125th Regiment 77th Regiment 48th Regiment 47th Regiment	Colonel Rüştü; C.o.S (chief of staff): Captain Nazim	Left flank: Johnston's Jolly south to Azmak Dere (south of Kaba Tepe) HQ: Adana Bayir
9th Division 25th Regiment 26th Regiment 64th Regiment	Colonel Kannengiesser (German); C.o.S (chief of staff): Major Hulusi	South of Azmak Dere to Kum Tepe area, inland to Kayal Tepe HQ: Kayal Tepe
5th Division 13th Regiment 14th Regiment 15th Regiment	Lt.Col Hasan Basri; C.o.S (chief of staff): Captain Arif	As North Group Reserve north of Kojadere village HQ: North of Kojadere in valley behind Third Ridge

The Northern Group defence

From the outset, Brigadier General Esat Pasha's Northern Group had fewer numbers than it needed to defend the peninsula. This resulted in a level of desperation among all Turkish commanders once the allied offensive was under way. In particular, the deficiencies in strength impacted on those elements of the Northern Group, which would soon have to face the major thrusts of the allied assaults. By 6 August Esat Pasha was calling for reserves, resulting in a scramble to bring reserves in from all the surrounding groups—the Southern Group, the Asia Group and the Saros Group.

Initially, Esat Pasha had to deploy his inadequate force as best he could. He made his most effective defence lines by concentrating his existing main force strength, with Mustafa Kemal as divisional commander, in the old areas of greatest conflict: that is, along the Second Ridge from Pine Ridge in the south via Lone Pine and Johnston's Jolly, Steele's, Courtney's and Quinn's Posts, the Nek, the seaward slopes of Baby 700 and Battleship Hill (Kemal's Field HQ); then they were dispersed, more thinly, down the seaward spurs to the lower hills behind No. 1 and No. 2 Outposts and Sazlidere.

Significantly, Rhododendron Ridge (Şahinşirt) and Chunuk Bair (Conk-bayiri) were left unmanned. Northern Group Command (and ostensibly 5th Army Command) considered these positions to be less threatened at this time, and relied on forward defence on the lower slopes, spurs and in the *deres* (valleys). Even the field headquarters of the 16th Division, the Northern Group and the 19th Division were positioned to cover the southern

Brigadier General Esat Pasha (seated), commander of III Corps, Turkish 5th Army, holds a conference with his staff at their field headquarters on Third Ridge, overlooking the Anzac area. Esat Pasha commanded Turkish forces of Northern Group during the allied August offensive.

AWM A05295

approaches. This deployment suggests that the area from Chunuk Bair to Hill 971 was vulnerable to a determined allied attack if the Turkish front lines could be breached. Indeed, this was how events were later to develop, although the allies never effectively exploited their temporary success.

Kemal records how he unsuccessfully tried to persuade Esat to his view that the imminent allied assault would come from Anzac, via the lower ridges and valleys, with Hill 971, Hill Q and Chunuk Bair as their objectives. The result was the celebrated tactical discussion on Battleship Hill in which Kemal was asked to explain, overlooking the ground, the arguments he had put to Esat in writing:

> The Army Corps Commander stroked my shoulder, smiling and said: 'Don't worry, Beyefendi, they can't come!' When I realised that it wasn't possible to (convincingly) explain my view, I thought it pointless to prolong the discussion. I left off by saying 'Sir, I hope it will happen as you have foretold.'[5]

This was perhaps the first example of the disagreements arising at the Northern Group field command level that Esat had to deal with and which would continue to emerge throughout the first week of the allied offensive.

The main thrust of the offensive commenced at 5.30 pm on 6 August with the feint attacks at Lone Pine in the southern end of the Anzac sector. On this date the total Turkish force in the *Ariburnu* (Anzac) sector numbered 19,000, but there were only 2500 in the northern Suvla–Anafarta area.[6] Although the Turkish artillery had secured the optimum positions for their guns, at this stage the batteries were handicapped by a shortage of ammunition, which meant they had to conserve their shells, particularly those of the long-range guns firing from the south. The heavy guns on Palamut Sirt, on the edge of the Kilitbahir Plateau, were also largely ineffective because these batteries were sited at the limits of their effective firing range and the gunners were reluctant to waste ammunition. The commanders would therefore have to rely heavily on their infantry for counter-attacks in the tortuous Anzac terrain.

The allied offensive was also supported by two diversionary artillery bombardments: one in the Cape Helles sector and the other on Lone Pine. The latter led Esat to conclude that a serious attack was about to begin on the 16th Division's front. He assigned the 5th Division's 5/13th Regiment, which was located to the east of Kavaktepe (Anderson's Knoll), to the command of 16th Division. Additionally, he brought up his reserves from the rear.[7]

Esat reacted to the 1st Australian Brigade's attack at Lone Pine, which captured the first line of Turkish trenches (manned by the 16/47th Regiment), by deploying his reserves immediately and then by trying to supplement his force from other sectors. First, he sent in the 5/13th Regiment's 3rd Battalion as reinforcements. The other two battalions of the 5/13th Regiment were then also ordered to Lone Pine and they in turn were reinforced by the 1st Battalion of the 19th Division's 57th Regiment, which was then in the process of withdrawing for a rest. Esat also ordered 9th Division's commander, Colonel Hans Kannengiesser, who was further south at Kayaltepe on the Kilitbahir Plateau, to leave the 26th Regiment behind, guarding the Kaba Tepe and Kum Tepe coastline, and immediately deploy to Lone Pine with the 9/25th Regiment and the 3/64th Regiment, taking as much artillery with him as he could. Esat then ordered his brother, Vehip Pasha, commander of the Southern Group, to send any forces he could spare. Vehip nominated the 4/10th and 4/11th Regiments, and at 11 pm they set out for Kojadere under the command of Division Commander Lieutenant Colonel Cemil Bey.[8]

Despite repeated Turkish counter-attacks and continuous heavy fighting throughout the night, the Australians managed to hold onto their gains at Lone Pine. Only a section of the 16/47th Regiment's second-line trenches (trench number 77) was recaptured by a battalion of the 5/13th Regiment.[9] The memoirs of Fahrettin Bey, the Northern Group's Chief of Staff, and other documents reveal the desperation of the Turkish commanders' responses to the loss of their front-line positions at Lone Pine as they tried to plug the hole created by the Australian 1st Brigade attack, regain their lost trenches, and deal with the other allied attacks at Anzac. Colonel Rüştü, the 16th Division's commander, sent a message that the forces he had at hand were 'not even enough to sustain the present situation'.[10] Rüştü followed this message with a grim detailed report of the losses suffered by his men:

> I have been trying to re-establish the communication between the right and left flanks which has been down since last night and I am also trying to build a tunnel behind us, parallel to the enemy's front. Many times our soldiers who penetrated the enemy Division's trenches were wiped out. We need a disciplined force that will attack fearlessly and persistently towards the centre of the 47th Regiment's position and, as well, an operational space that will make this attack possible.
> 7 August 1915.[11]

So what can be gleaned about the Northern Group Command's reaction to the events at Lone Pine on 6 and 7 August? The records suggest that, based on his experience, instinct and training, Esat Pasha regarded any gap or weak point in the defence line as being potentially disastrous. This explains his initial preoccupation with regaining the lost Lone Pine positions. The documents also suggest that Esat showed signs of suffering from the pressure of events. In his own memoirs, the newly arrived 4th Division commander, Lieutenant Colonel Cemil, also recorded some aspects of the general atmosphere in the headquarters:

When I was going to the Northern Group Commander Esat Pasha's shelter [at 2 am on 7 August], I came across 9th Division Commander Kannengiesser Bey. The German was exhausted. He told me that he was going to curl up and sleep somewhere. I then went into Esat Pasha's shelter. There was a portable bed, a table and two or three chairs. In this hollow, the pasha was lying on his bed … So in such an important and perilous situation, an esteemed and serious commander like Esat Pasha was lying down silently in a tired, disgruntled and discouraged state. I (later) guessed that his condition might be due to the dissension with the 19th Division Commander Mustafa Kemal, who was under his command.[12]

After having clearly rallied somewhat, following a brief rest, Esat decided these fresh 9th Division reserves had to be sent to strengthen the defences further north, around Chunuk Bair, the allied assaults in that direction having by then made their objectives clear. The Turkish attempts to retake their Lone Pine positions would continue for another two days, but further losses, added to 16th Division's existing losses, forced Esat to finally agree to call off these efforts in favour of merely defending the new front line. Esat had clearly decided the limit for losses at no gains in that sector had been reached, and that events to the north were now more critical.[13]

Despite the strenuous feint at Lone Pine, some Turkish commanders had deduced late on 6 August that an assault on the Sari Bair ridge (Kocaçimentepe) was to be the main thrust of the allied attacks. However, it will be recalled that Esat had earlier dismissed Mustafa Kemal's concerns about an allied approach from the Ağildere (Aghyl Dere) and Sazlidere. As little activity had been observed in Ağildere and the Anafarta region so far, Esat still wanted to concentrate his defence along the centre of the Second Ridge with reserves being brought into the 19th Division's sector. It was not until news came that the enemy appeared to be reinforcing their outposts in Sazlidere that Esat reacted. He ordered the German commander of the Anafarta Group, Major Willmer, to bring his reserve battalion closer to the northern flank of the Ariburnu area (Anzac sector) and also other reserves to be deployed by 9 pm on 6 August.

So by the time the Anzac and Indian brigades advance in the Sazlidere and Ağildere area began, around 10 pm, the whole region was defended by only two battalions: the 5/14th Regiment's 1st Battalion and the 5/14th Regiment's 3rd Battalion. However, once the Turkish commanders were made aware of these developments, they reacted swiftly. Mustafa Kemal himself, who had moved back to Scrubby Knoll, relocated again to the Battleship Hill battery observation post during the night.

Events from 7 August onwards

It is possible to follow events closely as they rapidly developed from this point. As early as 1.10 am on 7 August, Mustafa Kemal gave orders to his local commanders and officers to be extra vigilant and determined, as the situation was extremely critical.[14] This was the first point at which the thin Northern Group defence line became a factor in the battle for Sari Bair: Rhododendron Ridge (Şahinsirt) and Chunuk Bair had been left almost unmanned because they were considered less vulnerable. Their security still relied upon the thin forces in the forward defence positions on the lower slopes, spurs and in the valleys.

The three peaks – Chunuk Bair, Hill Q and Hill 971 – did indeed appear vulnerable. Belatedly, Esat now had to try to plug that gap in the defences. But all he had at his disposal were Kannengiesser's 9th Division regiments, intended earlier for Lone Pine, and so he ordered these to head for Chunuk Bair. They left Scrubby Knoll at 5 am, just as the New Zealand troops of the right assaulting column was advancing on Rhododendron Ridge and the Australian 4th Brigade's left column was moving into the Ağildere from Catlakdere.

Following the ill-fated and costly attacks after 4.30 am by the Australians at the Nek and at several places along the Anzac front line on Second Ridge, Esat and Kemal continued to reinforce their front line on Second Ridge, as best they could.[15] After dawn, Chunuk Bair remained open to the allied assaults. Two companies from the 1st Battalion of the 19/72nd Regiment, which were on the southern slopes of Kabaksirt (the seaward slopes of Baby 700) and Sazlidere, were ordered to march in the direction of Rhododendron Ridge to occupy Chunuk Bair. By 6 am the 19/72nd's 1st Battalion had moved over Rhododendron Ridge to the lower slopes of Chunuk Bair and the 1st Battalion of the 5/14th Regiment, under its Commander Major Reşit Efendi, had moved onto Battleship Hill. Meanwhile, the Anzac and Indian columns advancing into the Ağildere had been delayed, allowing some time for the Turkish commanders to get their reserves in place to strengthen the defences at Chunuk Bair. Most of Rhododendron Ridge, however, was by now in the hands of the New Zealand Brigade. As Kemal recorded, just two companies of the reserve 1st Battalion of the Turkish 14th Regiment were deployed to Chunuk Bair:

> since the situation in the Ağildere sector wasn't regarded as important … the other two companies [were] being kept close to Battleship Hill. The incessant enemy fire at the division's front tied down the entire divisional forces that were only just adequate for maintaining this front. The division had no forces that could be sent to Chunuk Bair. Only two companies from the 1st Battalion of the 72nd Regiment could be dispatched to the south side of Sazlidere.[16]

Turkish and German commanders and staff officers who led Ottoman forces in operations in the Anzac and Suvla sectors during the August offensive. The group includes: front row, standing (from left), Colonel Rüştü Bey, commander 16th Division; Colonel Mustafa Kemal, commander 19th Division; Brigadier General Esat Pasha, commander III Corps. Standing behind Rüştü is Major Wilhelm Willmer, commander Anafarta Detachment; standing behind Esat is Colonel Hans Kannengiesser, commander, 9th Division.

AWM A05296

These Turkish soldiers became the first forces to block the allied advance to the ridgeline peaks from Chunuk Bair to Hill 971. But they were still awaiting the arrival of the 25th and 64th Regiments of Colonel Kannengiesser's 9th Division, which had not yet arrived at Chunuk Bair.

The 64th Regiment arrived at Hill Q sometime after 6 am, just before their 9th Division commander Kannengiesser. When he arrived he surveyed the situation and saw that the 64th occupied ground behind Wolf Pass (below Hill Q) but that the 25th was still approaching. He found that Hill Q was only lightly defended, and his arrival corresponded with the new threat posed by the appearance of the New Zealanders on Rhododendron Ridge. He engaged them as best he could.[17] By 8.30 am Kannengiesser's men had been pushed back onto the summit of Chunuk Bair, and allied 'skirmishing' troops were infiltrating Wolf Pass as the New Zealanders were beginning to advance again from the Apex feature. Kannengiesser himself received a wound serious enough for him to be evacuated, so he handed over command of the 9th Division troops to his second-in-command, Hulusi Bey. Kemal later wrote of Kannengiesser: 'He later served in my retinue as Army Corps commander. He was the most capable German officer in our army and he received wounds during the Chunuk Bair battles and was obliged to retire.'[18]

By 9 am on 7 August, a rapid-fire mountain battery under First-Lieutenant Besim had arrived at Hill Q. Taking up a position in the open, it began to lay down an accurate fire. Further reserves arrived, and the allied attack was completely halted.[19] By noon, however, the New Zealanders were close to the Pinnacle feature, below the summit of Chunuk Bair. Kemal strongly sensed that a critical point had been reached, and he and Esat brought up all their remaining reserves.[20]

There was a change in the Ottoman field command at 1 pm, when Lieutenant Colonel Cemil, 4th Division Commander, relieved Hulusi Bey to take command of the 9th Division. The Anafarta sector commander, Major Willmer, was also placed under his command.[21] In his memoirs, Cemil Bey recorded the resolute Ottoman defensive response:

> I couldn't see the battlefield. From Kordere [the dip between Chunuk Bair and Hill Q], it was impossible to either control or see this 10–12 kilometre-wide front on which English were landing in the middle of Suvla Bay. I therefore transferred my battle command position to Kurtgecidi (Wolf Pass), which also provided a view of the Anafartas … And in the event of our losing a position, we would re-occupy it with an immediate counter-attack or assault. In short, I was determined to persevere in this sector … I tried to continue the battle by placing more emphasis on my right flank, which was empty and exposed.[22]

Having called up his reserves from the south, Cemil awaited their arrival. This delay gave the New Zealanders their opportunity to move up to Chunuk Bair. It was not until 5 pm that the Turkish reserves, two battalions from the 11th Regiment, arrived. Meanwhile, Cemil held on. After his reserves arrived, Cemil ordered the 11th Battalion onto Chunuk Bair to defend the summit; he kept his 10th Regiment as the Northern Group reserve.[23] Fahrettin Bey records in his memoirs how Cemil Bey succeeded in halting the Australian 4th Brigade trying to approach Hill Q by combining ferocious rifle and machine-gun fire with artillery.[24]

The general situation at this stage was one of badly mauled Turkish units having been pulled back and replaced by fresh units from regiments brought in from the Anafarta and Southern Groups. There were crucial periods, however, when the defence of the heights remained thin.[25] The local field commanders were naturally focused on their own sectors, but army and corps commanders kept the overall view in their sights. By the end of 7 August, the main concern of 5th Army High Command was to keep up the overall strength of the defence against the offensive, across all fronts – at Suvla as well as in the Anzac sector and further south at Helles. Uppermost in commanders' minds was the need to bring up reserves of men and munitions from farther away and to ensure their security while in transit.

These concerns led Kazim Bey, the 5th Army's Chief of Staff, to call urgently for reserves from both the Saros Group and the Asia Group across the Dardanelles Straits:

> To the Director of War Operations
>
> The enemy's progress through the Ağildere was stopped at the west of Asmadere, Cakmak Pinari, Conbayiri and Duztepe (Battleship Hill). We have two divisions at the front. This night we are bringing only one regiment and one battery from Anatolia. In addition, the enemy is making fortifications to the east of Lalatepe (Lala Baba) and the Salt Lake. Our counter(attack) front against them is the Ismailoglu Tepe and Mestantepe (Chocolate Hill). We plan to make an attack on their left flank with forces from the north (Saros Group). I am not able to provide more information. Now we are well. But please send us munitions very quickly and for God's sake send us submarines. I wait your response for munitions and submarines.
>
> 7 August 1915,
>
> Kazim, Chief of Staff (Kazim is waiting for an answer at the telegraph machine)[26]

By now, the need to mount an effective defence against the British landings at Suvla Bay was beginning to constrain the Northern Group's activities and limit the Turkish commanders' options (also driving the desperate call for submarines to interfere with the Suvla landings). There was initially concern that the allies' intention of the landings was to make for Hill 971 in order to bolster the push from Anzac towards the peaks. The reaction around midnight on 7–8 August was to send the newly arrived reserves from the Saros Group (now positioned near the Anafarta villages) under Colonel Fevzi to bolster defences on the Koja Chimen (Sari Bair) heights. Meanwhile, von Sanders had ordered troops from the 7th and 12th Divisions of the 16th Army Corps to move from the Bulair–Saros area and deploy to the Anafarta sector – in what would become a 20-hour forced march.[27]

This led to a further instance of split command in the field. Despite Cemil Bey's defensive success so far, von Sanders ordered his 9th Division and Willmer's Anafarta detachment to be placed under the command of the newly arrived Fevzi, who, as the Anafarta Group commander, outranked Cemil. Fevzi's instructions were to attend to Suvla first and then move on to defend Chunuk Bair.[28] This led to the well-known crisis in field command in the Hill 971–Anafarta area, involving Fevzi, which would come to a head during the following day.

The allies renewed their assault up Rhododendron Ridge during the night of 7–8 August. Turkish losses continued to increase. The 19th Division positions were particularly affected, and Kemal had once again to call for reserves on his side of Chunuk Bair after the situation became critical early in the morning.[29] The surviving operational records and other documents point to 8 August as being a critical moment in a number of ways. Experienced field commanders continued to become casualties, so lines of command had constantly to be adjusted.[30] Moreover, the ferocity of the fighting on the approaches to Chunuk Bair caused major confusion, with the Ottoman chain of command in the field often breaking down. Kemal records:

> At the time it attracted my attention that some troop commanders under the command of 9th Division Commander were sending their reports to *me*. Moreover, the content of these reports did not depict the state of Chunuk Bair and the command and control there in any positive way. For example:
>
> 1. 'An attack on Chunuk Bair has been ordered. To whom shall I pass this order? I am looking for the battalion commanders, I can't find them. Things are in a mess and the situation is grave …'
>
> 2. 'The majority of the officers are dead or wounded. I don't even know the name of the place where I am located. I can't see anything by observing.'[31]

The documents indicate that Esat and other commanders were struggling to contain the allied advance owing to the width of the front, insufficient reserves, disruption of communications, and the losses being inflicted, which were now having an effect. From 7 August – and throughout the next three days – there were constant requests for reserves to be brought in from the Southern Group, the Saros Group and from the Asia Group on the Anatolian side of the Dardanelles. By the morning of 8 August there was a growing and pervasive sense of anxiety, although combined with a great determination to prevail.

It is clear from the records that the Turkish chain of command in the field had been affected seriously by the confused fighting. The field command had passed from one commander to another and the British landings at Suvla had also impacted on the chain of command. After Fevzi's 7th and

12th Divisions arrived from Saros, the Anafarta Group was put under his control and thereby was under direct command of the 5th Army and not the Northern Group. Great pressure was being placed on the shoulders of one or two main commanders in the field – Cemil, for example. After handing over control of the 9th Division, as ordered, to Fevzi, who seems to have been resting his reserve Saros force in the rear and so was essentially inactive, Cemil then spent the day moving from one part of his allocated front to the other, handing over temporary command in one sector while he dealt with another, then returning and assuming control again. Such effort took its toll, and by the end of the day Cemil was forced to withdraw, suffering from exhaustion.[32]

A further example of the stress exerted on the Ottoman field commanders was the dismissal of Colonel Fevzi after he arrived from Saros to assume command of the Anafarta Group. His reluctance to obey orders to attack the British at Suvla with the 7th and 12th Divisions from the Anafarta Hills on 8 August led to his dismissal: command of the Anafarta Group was transferred to Mustafa Kemal, who thereby became responsible for the entire area from Suvla Bay up to the heights of the Sari Bair ridgeline from Hill 971 to Chunuk Bair.[33] There are various accounts of the Fevzi dismissal.[34] Esat Pasha's recollection of the event suggests some sympathy for Fevzi while also making a passing criticism of Kemal. Esat's account serves as an example of the type of problems facing the Ottoman field commanders:

> A long and difficult walk had brought the [Saros] unit here in an exhausted state. The arrival of the regiments had not been completed either. Surely, it cannot be expected that an unprepared attack would produce the desired outcome. It was surprising that the German Army Commander could not think of this … Ahmet Fevzi Bey was in the right with respect to his view and behaviour. However, he was not strong enough to defend himself to the German Commander like Mustafa Kemal.[35]

Meanwhile, by dawn on 8 August, the New Zealand soldiers of the Wellington Battalion had reached the southern part of the summit of Chunuk Bair and occupied it. Esat regrouped and the fresh 8th Division, sent from Vehip Pasha's Southern Group, was assigned to the command of Northern Group under the command of Colonel Ali Riza. At around 10.30 pm Riza attacked the enemy on Chunuk Bair with the two battalions of 8/24th Regiment. However, he failed to push the enemy off, even though he twice repeated his attacks using reinforced units.[36]

The position by the end of 8 August was that Turkish forces, estimated to be 5000 strong on a 4500-metre-long front centered on Abdul Rahman Bair, had successfully halted the offensive in that sector, although the southern part of Chunuk Bair summit was in the hands of the Wellingtons. Mustafa

Kemal then received the order to take command of the Anafarta Group a couple of hours before midnight on 8 August and to attack the British forces now landed at Suvla Bay at dawn on the 9 August. He assigned the 27th Regiment's commander, Lieutenant Colonel Şefik Bey, to deputise as 19th Division commander, and informed him of his views on what needed to be done on the 19th Division's front. Kemal himself had endured three days and three nights without sleep, working incessantly. Ill with exhaustion, he took with him the division's chief physician, Huseyin Bey, when he left 19th Division headquarters for Suvla HQ at Çamlitekke half an hour before midnight on 8 August. Kemal relates that after he arrived from Chunuk Bair, initially on Abdul Rahman Bair, he pursued Fevsi's plan for a renewed attack on 9 August and had his forces prepare for the attack.[37]

Detailed accounts of Kemal's achievement in repulsing the British at Suvla on 9 August appear in both the Turkish official history and his memoirs. This account requires us to focus on the Chunuk Bair front, where 9 August can be described as a day when efforts to push the enemy back were frustrated by the allies' determination to hold onto their gains, and also by further disputes over field command – the last thing Esat needed as he strove to contain the allies. The latest dispute involved Esat's assigning of 9th Division troops to add weight to the 8th's next attempt at a counter-attack. However, the recently arrived new German commander of the 9th Division, Lieutenant Colonel Pötrih, disputed the deployment, thereby holding up both the 8th Division's preparations and the attack itself. Again, difficulties emerged with split and confused chains of command as well as with the relations between the Turkish and German commanders. Pötrih insisted that the 9th Division troops should be put under the command of the 8th Division, saying he could not possibly lead into battle troops he had no prior experience of commanding. The 8th Division command post also made some counter-suggestions. Esat's orders were therefore held up. When the situation was reported to 5th Army HQ, von Sanders and Kazim immediately overrode Esat, ordering that no counter-attack be attempted until Kemal could be brought back from his Suvla command.[38]

By nightfall on 9 August the Turkish forces were confronted by allied occupation of Rhododendron Ridge, a large section of the Sazlidere area and part of the southern, lower section of the Chunuk Bair summit. In the early hours of 10 August Kemal returned from Camliktepe in the Anafarta area to the 8th Division headquarters on Chunuk Bair. Having assessed the strength and condition of his force, he decided to launch a surprise attack at dawn with massed infantry, using most of the forces at his disposal. Some of his subordinate commanders pushed for a more cautious course, suggesting that he await the arrival of the reserves, then already on their way. Kemal is on record as agreeing with this logic, but he did not want to give the enemy more time to dig in. So he pushed for the swiftest possible counter-attack:

In fact, they were right. But I was seeing this success in not having more forces but in giving the existing forces faith and conviction … Any time wasted, would benefit the enemy more than us. Therefore, in spite of all the suggestions I was definitely going to attack.[39]

To support the attack, Kemal placed the 8/23rd Regiment's machine-gun company, then in position at Saddle Point, at the head of Kördere. The 8/23rd Regiment moved into position: two battalions at the front line, the other one at the rear with the 8/23rd Regiment's 1st Battalion, north of Chunuk Bair summit. The waves of troops assaulting with bayonets would be launched at 4.30 am on the signal of a raised shovel from the unit at Saddle Point from where the terrain features to the south could be observed. The plan called for the 28th Regiment, due to arrive later, also to attack Rhododendron Ridge (Şahinsirt) from between Baby 700 and Battleship Hill, and for the

Northern Group commander Colonel Mustafa Kemal (later Atatürk, fourth from left front, pointing with upraised right arm) explains the Anafarta battles to a visiting delegation of members of parliament from Constantinople, August 1915. Second from left is Kemal's chief of staff Major Izzettin Calislar. The Anafarta sector stretched from Chunuk Bair in the south to Kiretch Tepe, north of Suvla. The handwritten captions on the photograph are in traditional Ottoman 'Arabic' script (top left) and modern Latin script (bottom left) which was adopted in 1929.

AWM P01141.002

41st Regiment to form the reserve, because it was unable to arrive before the attack began. It was intended that the 8th Division forces, together with the recently arrived new forces, would push the enemy off the ridges from Chunuk Bair to Rhododendron Ridge and then pursue them as far as possible. The 7th and 12th Divisions would occupy and fortify the lines reached in the day's advance.[40]

The Turkish assault to re-take the summit of Chunuk Bair on 10 August 1915 has entered both Turkish and Anzac folklore. Kemal is reported to have led his troops in the attack, almost like a medieval warrior, using his whip to cue the signal for the advance and pressing on despite being hit by a shrapnel ball which was stopped by striking his watch. The outcome saw the Turkish forces once again in possession of Chunuk Bair and the surrounding heights of the Sari Bair ridge. The dreadful losses suffered by the allies are well documented. Less well known is that the battle raged for four hours before the 8/23rd and 8/24th Regiments completed their victory and the 28th Regiment occupied the summit of Rhododendron Ridge. They were unable to proceed any further owing to the effective New Zealand machine-gun fire coming from the saddle of the Apex on Rhododendron Ridge.[41]

Immediate efforts were made to consolidate Turkish gains by fortifying the new line and the captured emplacements. A fortifications company, and a couple of labour and construction companies were immediately ordered to gather 5000 sandbags and begin building trenches and liaison saps at the new forward lines.[42]

It appears that Liman von Sanders observed the events of 10 August from his 5th Army field headquarters at Suvla. Later in the day he sent news of the success to Enver Pasha, the Turkish war minister in Istanbul, not missing the opportunity to take full credit. However, he was doubtless aware that the allies would probably try again, certainly they were unlikely to evacuate. In any case, his depleted army needed urgent replenishment:

> As I reported, the allied attacks from the right flanks at the Anafartas and Koja Chimen (Hill 971) were completely repulsed. To achieve this I took all troops that I could from all groups. With God's favour, I hope to expel all enemies. I do not know exactly whether they are to receive reinforcements or not but we have to have reserve divisions. Please send new and fit divisions. This will be helpful.
> Submitted 10 August 1915, Liman von Sanders.[43]

As for Esat Pasha, he may have been sanguine in June and July about the likelihood of a determined allied attack on the heights, but the experience of the August offensive clearly tempered his optimism. In his message to 5th Army Command on 11 August, he reported that the threat was not yet over and that the enemy was:

determined to finalise this attack and finish the job before the end of August. Our duty is to thwart this attack ... Don't forget that retreating even one step before the enemy can lead to disaster ... I am sure of the courage and devotion of our soldiers and officers. May the Great Allah help our Army to a victory soon. I repeat that there is *no room for any lapses in concentration*.[44]

And so it was. No lapses followed and the dominant Sari Bair ridgeline of Conkbayiri (Chunuk Bair), Besimtepe (Hill Q), and Kocaçimentepe (Hill 971) remained 'the ridge too far' for Anzac, British and Indian troops.

In conclusion, Turkish military archival documents reveal a great deal about Ottoman command issues as well as about the commanders' personal capabilities and their actions that enabled the 5th Army to survive the August offensive – albeit barely – and to retain their hold on the high ground. First, the records show that, at the outset, the 5th Army Divisions were dispersed too widely to respond quickly to the major attack. This is because Esat Pasha was convinced the approach to the high ground via the eventual route of the Anzac right and left assaulting columns could not be attempted due to the difficult terrain. Second, Liman von Sanders himself had kept significant forces at the Saros–Bolayir isthmus away from the area of attack, and consequently Esat Pasha's Northern Group had fewer numbers than it needed to mount an effective defence. Third, these facts in turn caused difficulties when it came to deploying reserves quickly. Fourth, the commanders faced major artillery restrictions because of the terrain and distances involved as well as shortages of essential munitions. Fifth, the allied offensive inflicted swift losses and high casualty rates, which compounded the problem of supplying reserves and gave rise to chain of command difficulties, largely owing to the effects of the level of casualties and resultant tensions between Ottoman and German commanders. Sixth, the need for commanders to respond to successive crises produced a mounting sense of desperation in some headquarters – although Mustafa Kemal was reportedly the exception with his customary *sang-froid* and calm authority.[45] Most Turkish commanders responded with a determination to defend the ground at all costs, and ultimately the Turkish troops and their commanders prevailed.

Today, Sari Bair ridge possesses a legendary status among Turks as well as among New Zealanders for their ancestors' achievements there. The Anzac story is now part of the national foundation stories of Australia and New Zealand, but much still remains unknown about Turkish leaders and soldiers and their experiences in the Gallipoli campaign. Further research in the rich Ottoman archival sources should uncover records that reveal much more of the Ottoman side of the campaign, serving to complete the story for future generations.

The French on Gallipoli and observations on Australian and British forces during the August offensive

Elizabeth Greenhalgh and Colonel Frédéric Guelton

It comes as a surprise to many, to learn that French forces were involved in the Gallipoli campaign of 1915. Yet, over the course of the campaign, France sent to the Dardanelles a total of 79,000 men (approximately 42,000 at their peak strength) as well as 65 million rounds of rifle ammunition and 527,000 artillery shells; in addition, the French navy supplied four pre-dreadnought battleships, a cruiser, six torpedo boats and four submarines and the crews for all those vessels. These resources, although substantial, were smaller than the massive contribution by Britain (and its Empire), which had instigated the campaign, so overall command of both nations' expeditionary forces fell to General Sir Ian Hamilton, the British commander.

The context

The reason for this sizable French contribution may be explained very simply. The eastern Mediterranean represented a French sphere of influence, hence France would not permit the British to have a free hand there. A disgruntled member of France's small but influential colonial party complained in 1900: 'There is a tradition that France gets colonies so that England may take them over.'[1] Moreover, France was more interested in retaining that sphere of influence than in breaking up the Ottoman Empire, which might very well have been the result if the Dardanelles expedition had succeeded in driving the Ottomans from the war. The views of the colonial party's adherents were clear: for France to be true to her destiny she must 'spread wherever she is able her language, her culture, her arms, and her genius'. They were dismayed by the spread of the English language: 'Are we going to substitute for the pure, simple accents of our lucid language the mewings of the English?' Indeed, before the war, 'French was becoming the second language and the common language of all the Ottomans.'[2] On a more fundamental level, France's financial interest in the Ottoman Empire was large. By 1914 French investors held 60 per cent of the Ottoman public debt, a proportion that was three times greater than that held by Germany, the next largest investor.[3] It is not, therefore, surprising that once the French learned what the British were planning, the War Minister, Alexandre Millerand, should have written to his colleague, the Foreign Affairs Minister: 'You will, I think, judge that our traditional interests in Asia Minor demand that the English should not land there by themselves. We must therefore … be in a position to intervene rapidly without being invited to do so – if not at the same time as the English, then immediately in their wake.'[4]

Three factors in particular influenced France's decision to join the British in the expedition to the Dardanelles. The first was France's specific area of interest in the Ottoman Empire, namely Syria, Lebanon and the 'holy land' places in Palestine. France had long been recognised as the protector of the Ottoman Empire's Christian populations, a role that was formalised by a series of so-called 'Capitulations' granted to successive French monarchs from Francis I to Louis XIV. The Maronite Christians of Lebanon had fought with the Crusader armies and were supposed to have forged a special bond between the 'Franks of France' and the world of Islam. As late as 1860 a French expeditionary force had intervened to protect the Maronite Christians from massacre by the Muslim Druzes. Since the time of the Crusades, French missionaries had done considerable educational work in the area, and so it was fair to claim, as one historian of France's involvement in the Dardanelles expedition put it, that 'by 1914 French had become the language of culture and literature of all educated classes in the Levant'.[5] So the French connection was long-standing, but the official policy of the Comité de l'Asie Française was that the Ottoman Empire should remain intact: 'We prefer to make our contribution to the cultivation of a great Ottoman garden rather than to have a small plot in Syria to ourselves alone.'[6] Nevertheless, if the great Ottoman garden was to be broken up into allotments, France wanted her share. After the war, France received the mandates for Syria and the Lebanon from the League of Nations.

The second factor influencing France's decision to join the Dardanelles military expedition, was France's ally, Russia. If Russia were to gain access to the eastern Mediterranean through a defeat of the Ottomans, this would affect the balance of power there. The fear became more acute following the Straits Agreement: on 12 March the British Secretary of State for Foreign Affairs,

Sir Edward Grey, formally acceded to Russia's claim to Constantinople; consequently, two days later his French counterpart, Théophile Delcassé, asked for Russian recognition of a French sphere of influence in Syria as a *quid pro quo*. Russia was opposed to French control over the holy places, and on 10 April Delcassé accepted defeat and conceded Russia's claim to Constantinople.

The third factor influencing France's decision to join the expedition was naval. At the outbreak of war in 1914, a Franco–British agreement had divided the Entente responsibility for coastal protection by giving the Royal Navy that task in the North Sea and along the Atlantic coast of France, while the French Navy took command in the Mediterranean. This eliminated duplication and enabled a more efficient use of naval resources, especially in safeguarding the crossings between North Africa (a source of colonial manpower) and mainland France. Despite France's nominal naval command in the Mediterranean, however, the British were proceeding with their planning completely independently. Moreover, the French navy minister, Victor Augagneur, judged from a naval intelligence report he had received that using a purely naval force to attack the Dardanelles was unlikely to succeed and would serve no useful purpose.[7]

For all these reasons the French politicians were determined not to allow the British a free hand. Nevertheless, there was considerable opposition from the military to a diversion of resources from France. The French commander-in-chief, General Joseph Joffre, was utterly opposed to the plan to join the British in a military adventure in a peripheral theatre. With ten of France's northern *départements* and their rich mineral resources occupied, and their inhabitants deported, Joffre believed that his task was to expel the invader from France's territory, and he directed several offensives in northern and eastern France during the course of 1915 precisely to accomplish this aim.

Despite this opposition, a Corps Expéditionnaire d'Orient was constituted under the command of General Albert d'Amade. It consisted of two brigades: a *brigade métropolitaine* (two regiments, one from French *dépôts* [175 Régiment d'Infanterie] and the second a mixed regiment of *zouaves* [Algerian light infantry] and Foreign Legion); and a *brigade coloniale* (two regiments, each containing one European and two Senegalese battalions). In this way, Joffre lost no troops from his forces in France by the creation of the new corps. In addition, there was a regiment of cavalry; three groups of artillery (six batteries of the standard French artillery piece, the 75-millimetre gun, and two batteries of 65-millimetre mountain guns); and all the necessary administrative and medical services. Thus the expeditionary corps became the equivalent of slightly more than one standard division. The corps arrived at Mudros Harbour on the Greek island of Lemnos on 18 March, but then returned to Alexandria to await developments.

At the same time, the French battleship, the *Bouvet*, took part in the

French troops on board the French transport ship SS *Havraise*, some hoisting their kepis on rifles, on their way to the Gallipoli Peninsula.

AWM G00392

combined British and French abortive attempt to force the Dardanelles on 18 March, but was sunk with the loss of more than 600 men when it ran into an undetected minefield. The failure of the naval operations meant that amphibious landings would go ahead.

Later a second division was sent to join the corps when there was a change of commander. In early May, General Henri Gouraud replaced d'Amade as corps commander, and he arrived with reinforcements. These constituted the second division, composed in a similar way to the first, but without any Foreign Legion troops and minus mountain artillery, under the command of General Maurice Bailloud. After Gouraud was wounded on 30 June and evacuated to France, Bailloud took over command of the whole corps. The British did not have a very high opinion of Bailloud. He was, in the view of Sir Maurice Hankey (Secretary to the War Council of the British Cabinet), the 'most confirmed pessimist' he had met thus far in the war and was 'a stupid old man' who 'ought to be superseded'.[8] On the other hand, Gouraud was highly thought of, and Hamilton looked upon him 'more as a coadjutor than a subordinate'.[9]

Following the decision to land men on the peninsula, the corps re-embarked from Egyptian ports on 15 April and by the 21st had concentrated once again at Mudros. The task assigned to the French by Hamilton for 25 April was a diversionary landing on the Asiatic side of the Straits in order

French Army Generals Bailloud (sitting, left) and Gouraud (right), astride one of the large Turkish guns damaged in the early months of the campaign at the Seddülbahir Fort, photographed on the day before General Gouraud was severely wounded, 29 June 1915.

AWM H10295

to subdue the Turkish heavy guns at Kum Kale from firing across the Straits into the rear of the British landings at Cape Helles, and to prevent Turkish reinforcements from crossing the Straits to assist in defending the peninsula against the British troops landing there. This French operation was the only one to gain its objectives on that day, although the troops suffered heavy casualties. Two days later, on 27 April, they evacuated the Asiatic shore as planned, and rejoined the British on the peninsula.

During the remainder of the campaign, the French forces took part in the three successive and ultimately futile 'battles of Krithia', aimed at capturing that village and the dominating hill of Achi Baba. Because they were deployed on the right of the British line at Helles, they were exposed to the fire of the Turkish guns from the Asiatic side, and suffered heavy casualties. British complaints that the Senegalese especially were ill-disciplined and tended to run away when their European officers were killed or wounded were ungenerous, as the exposed positions the French were holding were regularly shelled by Turkish gunners firing across the Dardanelles.

For the August operations, the French remained in the Helles sector, where their role was to support the northern breakout operations and the Suvla landing with a diversionary attack in the south. Both Gouraud (before he was wounded and evacuated back to France) and Bailloud had argued for

another landing on the Asiatic shore in preference to what became the Suvla landings, but Hamilton disagreed. Yet the Turkish batteries were inflicting great damage on the allied troops, as Bailloud knew only too well; silencing those batteries by landing troops on the Asiatic shore would have been of enormous benefit. Furthermore, the French commanders contended that the risks of an epidemic on the peninsula, stemming from the endemic dysentery and enteric fever, might have been alleviated if the area of operations were to be extended across the Straits.[10]

These arguments did not prevail, and so the French troops attacked the Kereves Dere ravine on 7 August after the British VIII Corps had launched their assault the previous day. Against well-entrenched Turkish troops, neither British nor French made much headway. Yet, despite insignificant gains of territory, they had achieved their principal aim, namely tying down large numbers of the enemy while the operations to the north of Anzac and the simultaneous Suvla landing operations were under way. The reason for the failure to make any significant advance lay in the poor artillery preparation that preceded the infantry attack, despite the French having realised early on that adequate artillery support was the key to enabling the infantry to progress. Fierce fighting continued until 10 August, but little ground changed hands.[11]

After the failure of the August fighting, Joffre's arguments against the French commitment to the Gallipoli campaign became unanswerable. He was planning a large double offensive in France in September to attack the German positions from two sides: from the east in Champagne and from the north in Picardy, where the French line was extended by the British in what

Preparations for a long campaign. Part of the French army's wine store of hundreds of barrels stored at Mudros Harbour on Lemnos island, December 1915. During the Gallipoli campaign French soldiers were allocated a daily ration of wine. In the background is the French military hospital.

AWM G00649

became the Battle of Loos. In addition, the entry of Bulgaria into the war on the side of the Central Powers on 11 October 1915 enabled direct transfers of equipment from Germany and Austria-Hungary to Turkey, and put Serbia in even greater danger. French forces were diverted to Salonika in a failed attempt to save the Serbian ally. On 28 September one of the two French divisions on Gallipoli had left for Salonika, although the second remained until the allied evacuation from the Helles sector began in early January 1916.

The soldiers and sailors of French forces who died in the Gallipoli campaign are commemorated in a unique French military cemetery above the former S beach in Morto Bay: the cemetery contains the graves of 3000 officers and men, gathered from eight separate cemeteries established during the campaign, as well as the remains of an estimated 12,000 unknown soldiers buried in four ossuaries.[12] Official sources record over 27,000 French army casualties, including almost 10,000 dead and missing.[13] Additional naval casualties include over 600 men who drowned with the sinking of the battleship *Bouvet* on 18 March 1915 and sailors on smaller vessels and submarine crews.

Australian and British forces – from the perspective of a French liaison officer

On 26 March 1915 a French army officer, Major de Bertier, was assigned to the British Army operating in the Dardanelles as liaison officer with General Sir Ian Hamilton, Commander-in-Chief of the Mediterranean Expeditionary Force. Between that date and the end of December, he sent to Colonel Hamelin, chief of the African section of the French army's General Staff in

A French soldier looks out warily through a barbed-wire entanglement above his trench towards the Turkish lines, Helles sector, 1915.

AWM G00472

Paris, 29 private letters which are preserved in the French military archives. The reason why de Bertier sent his letters to the African section lies in the pre-war organisation of the French army's General Staff. This comprised four bureaux, the second of which (the *Deuxième Bureau*) dealt with intelligence matters, plus an African section, because most of France's military action overseas concerned North Africa (Algeria, Tunisia and Morocco). During the war, the African section also dealt with the occupation of Egypt, Arabia, the East in general and the Balkans. Between April 1915 and March 1917, an Eastern office was attached to the African section.[14]

It is these letters, written to Paris by de Bertier, that provide the basic source for this chapter.[15] The letters afford both an advantage and a disadvantage. The disadvantage is intrinsic to the historian's profession. Obviously, when Major de Bertier wrote his letters, he could not have known that, nearly a century later, they would be analysed and examined for evidence of interest to historians. Thus, for example all the particular pieces of information concerning the activities and operations at Anzac and regarding Australian troops are generally submerged in other, more numerous pieces of information about French, Turkish and broadly speaking 'English' forces and actions.[16] Therefore this comparative analysis extracts data about the Australian forces, which, it must be remembered, represent but a small proportion of the whole.

Despite this disadvantage, these letters are of great interest for two reasons: first, the writing has an immediate force, and second, as they are private letters, they escaped both French and British censorship and tell us exactly what de Bertier sees and what he reports to Paris. Their frankness is revealed clearly when they are compared with the official reports that Colonel Hamelin wrote, based on de Bertier's letters. As a consequence this chapter is organised around two main themes: first, the Australians are presented exactly as de Bertier depicted and compared them with other British troops throughout the whole campaign; second, the Australians are described as one part of British strategy. The Australians are not the main focus of de Bertier's letters, rather they are the unfortunate actors in a British strategy which fails, although it was not predestined to fail, in de Bertier's view – quite the opposite.

Major de Bertier (his full name, Marie René Jean de Bertier de Sauvigny) was aged 38 in 1915. Related to the old French nobility from Lorraine in eastern France,

Major Marie René Jean de Bertier de Sauvigny, cavalry officer and French Military Attaché to Washington in 1914.

Photograph provided by Colonel Frédéric Guelton, courtesy of *Service historique de l'armée de terre* (SHAT), Vincennes.

he graduated from the French Ecole spéciale militaire de Saint-Cyr in 1898 (where he ranked 22nd out of 522 cadets), and became an officer in the heavy cavalry. He took part in the Moroccan campaign of 1908–12, and then was assigned to the Second Bureau (Intelligence) of the General Staff. In 1913, as a captain, he was sent to Washington as Military Attaché. On the outbreak of war, he returned to France and became a liaison officer with the British Expeditionary Force up to the time when he left France for the Dardanelles. In summary, de Bertier, fluent in English, was both a cavalry soldier and an intelligence officer.

De Bertier's letters to Paris escaped detection by both the local French military hierarchy and British censorship. As he explained in his letter of 20 April: 'Although the method I use to send this letter is unusual, not to say strange, it is safer and full of advantages. So I do not hesitate to use it. [Otherwise], it would be seen either by the British censors or submitted to General d'Amade, who would not appreciate the way I keep in touch with you without his knowledge!' But exactly how de Bertier managed to send his letters remains unclear, even if there are some indications that he was using covert intelligence mail.

The Australians as depicted by de Bertier

De Bertier arrived in Alexandria on about 15 April 1915 from the Flanders battlefield, via Paris, Marseille, Algiers and Bizerta. In Alexandria he discovered – as did General d'Amade, who was under Hamilton's operational command – that Hamilton had disappeared. He reported that Hamilton had 'left two days ago. But which way did he go? Well, as strange as it seems, nobody knows!'[17]

During his short stay in Alexandria, de Bertier learned about the Australians from accounts of the way they had misbehaved in Cairo a couple of weeks earlier. And what he heard reminded him of his own experience with the French Foreign Legion in Morocco. The Australians, he wrote:

> are criminals! They behaved horribly. In Cairo, because some of them had caught venereal disease they burnt down the 'red-light district'. And when regular forces arrived in order to get the situation under control, they fought a regular battle and some soldiers were killed … on both sides![18]

Moving on to the battle zones, de Bertier reports that, according to Turkish prisoners of war, Australian and French soldiers had the same bad reputation of 'not taking prisoners'. 'French and Australian soldiers', he wrote, 'are said not to take prisoners, whereas the others inflict on them poor treatment and hard labour.'[19] Nevertheless de Bertier admired the Australians' composure in the face of adversity. He visited them in their defensive positions by the only available means of transportation (a boat) and wrote: 'The wharf is under fire all day long. And, even if many boats have been sent to the bottom, nevertheless 25,000 isolated Anzacs live under fire and have enough supplies for at least a month.' And de Bertier concluded with some admiration: 'It's a good example for nervous people to meditate upon!'[20]

All de Bertier's references to Australians are positive and admiring, including even their general behaviour in Cairo. He was particularly interested in the way troops stood up to many local illnesses. After the August fighting and the start of autumn, de Bertier pointed out the robustness of the Anzacs when compared with the other British troops. He stressed that, according to the British medical services' own figures, the Anzacs' rate of evacuation for illness was 4.5 per cent per week, whereas it reached 6.5 per cent in other British units, although the wounded evacuation rate was the same (0.75 per cent per week) for both. These figures remained true to the end of October, despite the appearance of 'many cases of jaundice, among them some very serious, but neither typhus nor cholera'.[21]

With regard to Anzac military capabilities, de Bertier considered that corps officers 'who have all been promoted since the beginning of the war, lack authority with their men'.[22] But he noted the same situation in the English units, whose young officers had 'suffered huge casualties since the beginnings of the war [and, as a consequence were] neither professionally efficient nor morally committed'.[23] He added that he knew some 18-year-old sub-lieutenants 'fresh out of school and appointed after a short five-month period of training'.

On the other hand, de Bertier, whose judgements are often harsh, praises the Anzac soldiers for their bravery and their endurance. 'Full of energy and initiative,' he wrote, 'Australians and New Zealanders are excellent soldiers who fight well in the steep and hilly terrain.'[24] Finally, de Bertier considered General Birdwood to be one of the best British officers (if not the best) in the Dardanelles: 'Anzac troops', de Bertier wrote, 'are under General Birdwood's command. He is a remarkably energetic commander who has succeeded in keeping his troops hanging onto a cliff that drops sheer to the sea, and linked only precariously to the other forces, because the wharf is regularly shelled.'[25]

Anzac forces and British command and strategy

Although de Bertier regarded the Anzacs highly, at the same time he looked critically at the British command system and at the way the Anzacs were used. These criticisms began as early as the April landings, when he joined the units to be sent 'to the beach S.W. of Kapa Tepe where the Anzac landing has been planned'. In the planning phase, he was highly impressed by the 'mechanics of the landings, which were carefully studied and well rehearsed'. But he became deeply concerned about other arrangements: the lack of supplies, mainly of artillery munitions, and the poor preparation of the later attacks. He writes: 'Everything seems to depend on chance and luck. Here, just as in Flanders, the British high command is only able to get the right measure of the enemy's defences after crashing into them, when it is too late!'[26] Reporting on the landing to Colonel Hamelin on 29 April he added in a laconic and military style: 'Australians. Thrown onto the coast in front of a cliff 150 metres high, they met a lot of difficulties in forcing their way through. Today, they are holding a position between Fisherman's Hut and Kapa Tepe, having advanced about 1500 metres from the coast.'[27]

In subsequent letters, de Bertier denounced the futile casualties and the meagre gains won by the sacrifice of lives in the face of Hamilton's demands. There could be no improvement until reinforcements arrived. He reported allied casualties between 25 April and 9 May of '683 officers and about 16,000 men',[28] and once again spoke very highly of the actions of the Anzacs, especially during the Turkish attacks on 19 and 20 May.[29]

Soon after his arrival to replace d'Amade, and after a complete battlefield tour aboard a torpedo boat, General Gouraud, the new French commander, thought that it would be 'opportune' to use the beach south (sic) of Kapa Tepe, the very one where the Anzacs were first scheduled to land, in order to regain the initiative. He thought that the new Anzac positions could be used as a strong point in support of 'an attack towards Maidos in order to cross and conquer the isthmus, which is there only 8000 metres wide, [that is] to return Hamilton to his first idea, but with more forces and on the proper axis'.[30]

Gouraud and de Bertier explained this proposal to Hamilton. The Anzac forces plus the reinforcements coming from Great Britain, a total of about eight infantry divisions, attacking from Kabatepe towards Maidos, 'could upset the balance in favour of the allied forces'.[31] However, shortly afterwards, wondering how to regain his 'freedom of action', Gouraud changed his mind. Originally opposed to an 'Asiatic solution', he became an ardent defender of it: on condition, however, that 100,000 men should be committed. His successor, General Bailloud – after Gouraud was wounded and evacuated to France – continued to support the 'Asiatic solution', but Hamilton refused. He 'hopes', wrote de Bertier, 'to be successful with a landing at Kapa Tepe near the Australians' positions.'[32]

Gouraud was so worried by Hamilton's attitude, and his views on how to proceed on the peninsula, that from his hospital bed in Paris he dictated a letter, preserved in de Bertier's papers, to Hamelin: 'I have been informed that Hamilton refuses to listen to anybody who is in favour of a landing in Asia. I no longer understand him!'[33]

In the face of this lack of understanding between the two staffs, relations deteriorated. From mid-July the British staff withheld from the French all information concerning the forthcoming August operations. Confidence was badly affected. De Bertier wrote that the British staff remained 'completely silent. General Bailloud is more and more irate. But they allege that a shared secret is no longer a secret!' Nevertheless, de Bertier was a good intelligence officer. In the very same letter in which he speaks of the British 'silence', he reports all the details of the forthcoming landing, which he managed to obtain despite what he calls the new British attitude 'based on suspicion'.[34]

Now, in this new period based on 'suspicion', de Bertier's' criticisms became unrestrained. On 10 August he wrote: 'in short, even without any vigorous Turkish opposition, the night landing was extremely confused.' In IX Corps, there were a 'lack of orders, lack of artillery on the battlefield, nobody to run the battle, staff at ease on a cruiser up to the evening of the 8th', and so on. The only corps which is not criticised is ANZAC: 'The Australians, side by side with the Indians and with the 13th Division under General Birdwood's command, launched a frontal attack against well defended strong points built on a steep ridge whose capture would permit cutting the isthmus into two … Fighting well, sometimes hand to hand, they lost, in 4 days, 3000 killed and 5000 wounded … Unfortunately this morning they had to abandon the Abd-el-Rhaman Bair and Chunuk Bair positions because they could only be held if the units alongside [British 10 and 11 Divisions] made progress.'[35]

General Sir Ian Hamilton, Commander-in-Chief, Mediterranean Expeditionary Force (right), and Major-General Walter Braithwaite, his chief of staff, being rowed ashore at Cape Helles in a warship's boat.

AWM G00328

Moreover, according to de Bertier, victory was at that time within reach. But the British staff failed to command, and the poor performance of the 10th (Irish) Division and 11th (Northern) Division meant that the Australians were not supported. Hamilton's staff did not give precise orders:

> In brief, we find in the British command wishes, vague impulses but no precise indication as to the aim … Yesterday evening I was with Hamilton. Although he still had at his disposal 5 completely fresh brigades, he asked the front units to walk to Kavak Tepe 'if they were not too tired' … They realise what ought to be done but do not know how to put it into orders. It is appalling! For this is an opportunity that will not recur … Tomorrow Turkish reinforcements will arrive and once again the front will be blocked.[36]

De Bertier emphasised these points when he gave his personal opinion of both Ian Hamilton and his chief of staff, General Walter P. Braithwaite. Hamilton was 'not at all prepared to command such a big expeditionary force', and Braithwaite 'only sees war through what he learned on the Indian frontier'. De Bertier added that:

> both lack military knowledge, method, strength of will and capacity for work … At the beginning of August the Anzacs launched the main attack against well defended positions, whereas the IX Corps on its left faced a weak defence. But instead of pushing the IX Corps forwards in order to overrun the enemy's right flank, nothing happened … Nowhere did the commander impose his will; nowhere was the aim declared and objectives determined; there appeared nowhere the simultaneous or successive means to coordinate efforts – in a word, no command.[37]

Despite these underlying tensions, on the surface the relationship between the British and French staff officers was cordial. Hamilton recorded in his diary a 'gay little ceremony' on 29 September 1915 in which he decorated de Bertier with a DSO and the other two French staff liaison officers, Lieutenants de la Borde and Pelliot, with MCs. The three 'were led in smiling like brides going up to the altar', Hamilton wrote. 'All three officers are most popular, and there were loud cheers' from the guard of honour made up of Surrey Yeomanry, Royal Naval Division and Australian soldiers.[38]

To conclude, de Bertier's letters tell us little we don't know already, especially about Australian troops and their behaviour. However, these letters, extracted and summarised here, suggest to us a different approach, an approach both distant and close to our concerns. Obviously 'distant', because very often de Bertier focuses more on the French and on the Turks than on British and Australian units. But also 'very close' because all the letters are written so close to the event. And nothing obstructs the clarity and forthright character of their writing. For de Bertier, the privileged observer, defeat on Gallipoli was not inevitable; and the only ones who escape his critical and severe judgements and are regularly congratulated by him are the Anzacs, that is to say, mainly the Australian soldiers.

The wider context

Some wider conclusions may be drawn from the analysis of the French liaison officer's reports to Paris. The first concerns the value of such testimony from liaison officers. If it is always better to 'see ourselves as others see us', then de Bertier's observations help us to reach more balanced conclusions. In this case, most of the comments are complimentary to the Anzacs, hence they are easily accepted. This does not exclude, however, the possibility that de Bertier's criticisms could be valid and provide useful lessons.[39] Liaison officers are privileged observers, especially when, as in de Bertier's case, they are trained and experienced intelligence officers. Their reports provide for later historians a useful 'back channel', free from censorship or the desire to paint an overly optimistic picture.

A second point concerns the conduct of a coalition war. The fact that the French contribution to the Gallipoli campaign has been so thoroughly forgotten by anglophone historians tends to hide the tensions that fighting a coalition war can provoke, especially over questions of command. (Lower down the chain of command, relations could be easier, with the choice of 'Entente cordiale' as the password used by British VIII Corps and French troops to avoid 'friendly fire' accidents in the confined areas of the Helles front.[40]) Since the British had conceived and instigated the expedition and supplied the greater number of resources, it was natural that overall command should be in General Sir Ian Hamilton's hands. General Gouraud was, however, an experienced soldier who had fought in France's colonial wars, even if d'Amade and Bailloud were less impressive. The French accepted British control at the Dardanelles and expected, in return, French control on the Western Front, where Field Marshal Sir John French was proving a prickly commander of the British Expeditionary Force. The French war minister, Alexandre Millerand, wrote to his British counterpart, Lord Kitchener, on 21 March (over one month before the Gallipoli landings) to ask whether it would not be in their 'common interest that Field Marshal French, who is happy to address General Joffre as a general-in-chief of the allied armies, should deal with him as such and consequently take instructions from him'.[41] So the fact that unified command existed on Gallipoli affected the Franco–British relationship elsewhere.

Moreover, it is possible to draw a further conclusion by considering whether it might have been better if the French had played a larger role on

French soldiers take up position at Cape Helles while men pitch tents in the background. A long earthwork has been thrown up (centre), while behind it (right) a man is digging a trench or foxhole. A mattock lies on the ground in front of him. A machine-gun wrapped in a protective cloth stands on a tripod (left). In the foreground are some dixies, with some other utensils resting in a wooden crate.

AWM P02282.027

Gallipoli, especially as regards the August operations. When Gouraud arrived on Gallipoli to take over from General d'Amade, he concluded immediately that a different method of proceeding was required. He wrote to Hamilton on 18 May, suggesting either a landing on the Asiatic shore or on the flatter ground south (*sic*) of Kabatepe, where the Anzacs were to have landed originally. The best use of the reinforcements from England, Gouraud continued, would be in extending the base that the Anzacs had already created.[42] Hamilton's unenthusiastic response cited the lack of reinforcements to undertake any new operations. Certainly Kitchener in London was surprised that Hamilton had not asked for further units; furthermore, as regards munitions, Sir John French in France was crying 'shell shortage' as a way of explaining his failures.

Despite this rejection of his suggestion, Gouraud re-stated these ideas in a letter to Hamilton on 13 June, well before any final decision was taken on future operations. He now proposed three alternatives to the Suvla landings. The first involved a landing on the neck of the peninsula at Bulair, but Gouraud did not develop this idea because it depended upon British naval forces being able to cover the landings and he had no control over these resources. The second involved a landing on the Asiatic shore which would free the allies from the Turkish gunfire that affected the French in particular, since the French occupied the allied lines next to the Straits. Gouraud accepted that a landing on the Asiatic shore would be a purely defensive measure, since it would not constitute a step further towards Constantinople.

Gouraud's third proposal, as we have seen, was reported by de Bertier to Paris. This third proposal would probably involve Anzac troops, since Gouraud suggested a landing on the flatter ground south (*sic*) of Kabatepe, which was only eight kilometres distant from the eastern side of the Gallipoli peninsula at Maidos (present-day Eceabat). Gouraud identified correctly that the French and British troops advancing on Krithia would still have the Kilid Bahr (Kilitbahir) plateau to scale even after (or if) they captured the heights of Achi Baba. A successful crossing of the peninsula to Maidos would skirt the north side of the Kilid Bahr plateau, give the allies a base on the Dardanelles north of the Narrows, and cut off the Turkish troops further south. As Ashley Ekins has made clear (in chapter 3 of this volume), the Kilid Bahr plateau was crucial high ground to capture, and cutting it off from Turkish reinforcements further north would make the difficult task much easier. Hamilton's lame response was to express his thanks and his pleasure that he and Gouraud were in agreement.[43]

It was, however, the Asiatic shore option that Gouraud developed, despite the British lack of enthusiasm. A memorandum in Millerand's papers sums up his thinking. First, the Turkish batteries on the Asiatic shore threatened the existence of the French troops on the peninsula; next, only a bridgehead could be contemplated because there were not enough troops to do more. Three or four divisions were a minimum requirement even for a bridgehead with a landing at Besika Bay, well south of Kum Kale, where the French had landed on 25 April, but opposite the allied base on the island of Lemnos. To hold the bridgehead, heavy artillery was required, and the Senegalese, who had proved unreliable on the peninsula, should only be employed once that bridgehead had been established. Clearly Gouraud had thought through the operational implications of the proposal.[44]

Gouraud was thinking not only on the operational level. At the tactical level too he made decisions that proved useful and, moreover, showed the value of fighting with an ally. He had realised the need, if any success was to be won, to concentrate artillery resources on a sector of the front, limited to what the guns could attack. In a series of small operations at the end of June and the beginning of July, Gouraud and his neighbouring commander, Major-General A.G. Hunter-Weston (commanding the British 29th Division) combined their artillery resources and used them to attack a limited sector of the front in order to obtain local superiority. Thereby, small gains of territory at acceptable cost were achieved.[45]

It was during one of these 'bite-and-hold' operations that Gouraud was gravely wounded by a Turkish shell and was evacuated back to France. The 1 Division commander, General Bailloud, took over command of the French Expeditionary Corps. He maintained pressure to get authorisation for an Asiatic shore landing, while Gouraud supported him from his hospital bed in Paris, as noted above. He had begged Millerand to intervene personally, so pressure was exerted at the highest level, with Millerand writing to Kitchener about the 'preservation of the very existence of the French Expeditionary Corps'.[46] Kitchener's response, however, indicated his unwillingness to 'impose' on a commander-in-chief an operation that differed from the latter's own carefully worked out plan. Kitchener counted on the 'good relations' between Hamilton and Bailloud to permit a 'frank' exchange of views on the matter.[47]

Yet frankness was not a characteristic of their relationship. We have already seen that de Bertier reported to Paris a degree of British secrecy about the forthcoming operations that was angering Bailloud. Indeed, Bailloud had already sent a secret letter to the war minister, over a week earlier than de Bertier's report, in which he warned of an influx of Turkish troops following the forthcoming end of Ramadan, and of the slow British response to making good their losses with reinforcements. Bailloud stated that Hamilton's plans were secret, and that he did not know what the plans were for the Australians, whom he had just visited. They held good defensive positions, he reported, but would be unable to break out successfully without more artillery resources. The conclusion that Bailloud drew from these considerations was that the British should be persuaded to use their reinforcements for the Asiatic shore proposal in order to prevent the Turks from becoming yet stronger and threatening the allied position on the peninsula even more.[48]

French suggestions were discounted. No landing was made on the Asiatic shore; the Suvla landings were made instead. Certainly Hamilton had the command authority to choose between the two options, but the secrecy involved did not indicate a good working coalition relationship. The British commander appears to have spent little time considering his coalition partner's reasoned proposals. Bailloud remained bitter. On leaving Gallipoli, he wrote again to Millerand on 1 October, complaining of British selfishness and failure to keep promises. He had excellent personal relations, Bailloud wrote, with British commanders – and he included glowing letters from Hamilton and from Lieutenant-General F.J. 'Joey' Davies, commanding VIII Corps, to prove his point – but such considerations counted for nothing when 'the interests or simply the prestige [of Britain] entered the equation'.[49] So ended the French participation in the Gallipoli campaign.

There are many 'what ifs' associated with the Dardanelles and Gallipoli. What might have happened if the Suvla operation had been rejected in favour of the French proposal for an attack from Kabatepe eastwards towards Maidos and the Straits, or else by a landing on the Asiatic shore, is yet another to add to the list.

Chapter 11

Their mercenary calling

The Indian army on Gallipoli, 1915

Rana Chhina

The Indian expeditionary force that served in the Dardanelles was not very large in numbers: barely 5000 men in a campaign that swelled from 75,000 to nearly half a million allied troops engaged by the end of the campaign.[1] Yet the Indian force had a significant impact upon the course of the operations, and no account of the campaign can ignore the contribution of the 14th Sikhs in the third battle of Krithia, or the 1/6th Gurkha Rifles in the climactic battle of Sari Bair.

However, despite the fact that she served with honour on Gallipoli – not just with, but as a part of, the Australian and New Zealand Army Corps (ANZAC) from August onwards – this contribution has been relegated largely to a passing mention in most accounts of the campaign.[2] Part of the reason for this lies in the political history of British India. On the eve of the First World War, India was still a colony, agitating for self-governing Dominion status within the Empire, a status that the colonial authorities were loath to confer.

In India, therefore, the war was seen as an opportunity to press for home rule by proving her loyalty to the Empire. As a measure of her support to the Imperial cause, India provided Britain with not just men and material, but money as well. Apart from the 1,440,437 men recruited, and the 1,381,050 men sent for service overseas,[3] India also bore the cost of these troops which were being used largely for Imperial rather than Indian purposes, and in 1917 she made an outright gift of £100 million towards the cost of the war. The British Indian army, often derided by educated nationalists as a mercenary force in a veiled attack on British policy in India, and on the British presence itself, was to serve with distinction in nearly every theatre of war.[4] However, in spite of India's sterling contribution to the war effort, it would be nearly three decades before her demands for political representation, by then hardened from home rule to complete independence, would come to fruition.

By then, world events had been overtaken by another world war, and with Indian independence, the regiments and batteries that had served on Gallipoli were split between three armies – those of India, Pakistan and Britain – and the memory of those soldiers who had served a now-discredited empire was all but lost in the post-colonial world. The lack of a political identity in 1915 thus served to rob Indian soldiers not just of an acknowledgement of their role, or of a commemoration of their sacrifice, but also of their place in history.

India and the Dardanelles

In this chapter I do not intend to touch upon the grand strategy of the Dardanelles campaign. The follies that preceded it and the missed opportunities that accompanied it are likewise treated with a Nelson's eye unless these impacted directly upon the fortunes of the Indian detachments on Gallipoli.

As far as India was concerned, events in the Dardanelles were more directly linked to domestic security issues than to grander Imperial strategic concerns. The somewhat vague emotional attachment of Indian Muslims to the Sultan of Turkey as *Khalifah* was being exploited by political agitators in India, who were publicising the ideal of a pan-Islamic movement that laid stress upon the kind of international solidarity and unity of all Muslims, or *Ummah*, that had been fostered by the Sultan for decades. The Viceroy of India, Lord Hardinge, noted with concern early in 1915 that if the allies suffered any more reverses in the Dardanelles he feared 'serious results' in India.[5] The *Khilafat* movement also had its impact upon the Indian army, and there were numbers of desertions from among Muslim soldiers that were thought to be the work of extremist elements in India, working to undermine the loyalty of Indian troops and endeavouring to advance pan-Islamic propaganda to the detriment of British Imperial interests. This was held to be especially the case with Pathans and other Pushtu-speaking classes, who were supposedly more susceptible to such influences than other Indian Muslims.[6]

The Indian army on Gallipoli in 1915

As the German general Hans Kannengiesser, who commanded a Turkish Division at Gallipoli, wryly remarked, 'seldom have so many countries of the world, races and nations sent their representatives to so small a place with the praiseworthy intention of killing one another.'[7] Hence along with the Australians, New Zealanders (both Pakeha and Maori), British, Zionists, French, Senegalese, Turks and Germans among others, India added some of the finest classes of its fighting men to the mix at Gallipoli.

In the second half of the nineteenth century, the British in India formulated the 'martial races' theory according to which only certain ethnic or religious groups (or classes) were considered eligible to bear arms, on the basis of their perceived hardiness or value as soldiers. The Indian army was accordingly organised into units consisting of 'class' companies or squadrons, each unit with its own distinct composition. An important aspect of this classification was loyalty to the Empire, since the British were taking no chances after the Sepoy Mutiny of 1857 when a large portion of the Indian army revolted against colonial rule. In a classic application of *Divide et Impera* (divide and rule), the composition of the various ethnic classes in a unit was maintained in such a way as to ensure that the troops were unlikely to combine in a general uprising against the colonial authorities, and so that they could be used as a counter to one another, if required. A few favoured communities were enlisted into single or 'pure' class regiments. These were often the *crème de la crème* since they exuded enormous clan spirit, and the homogeneity generated by the close-knit Indian regimental system, in which sons followed fathers into the same regiment, ensured that very high standards could be set and obtained under dedicated officers. Indian units that served on Gallipoli therefore were composed of soldiers from various ethnic groups or classes, comprising Sikhs, Punjabi Muslims and Gurkhas.[8]

However, the class system of organisation had its drawbacks as well. With the entry of Turkey into the war, it was not considered prudent to send units

Four Indian army soldiers at Walden Point near Aghyl Dere, a position captured by New Zealanders during the night advance on Sari Bair on 6–7 August 1915. The soldier on the right is a Gurkha. The third soldier from the left is wearing an Australian jacket and forage cap.

AWM C00730

with a significant proportion of Muslim troops into action against the Turks on the peninsula. As a result, two of the original battalions of the Indian brigade, the 69th[9] and 89th[10] Punjabis, which had landed at Helles on 1 May, were withdrawn from this theatre within a fortnight and sent to fight in France. These two battalions were among the oldest units of the Indian army. They had a high proportion of Muslim troops, the 69th having four companies of Punjabi Muslims (PMs) while the 89th had three. Both units subsequently served with distinction, and without compunction, against the Turks in Mesopotamia; a Punjabi Muslim Rajput soldier of the 89th, Naik Shahmad Khan, won the Victoria Cross near Sannaiyat in April 1916.

Apart from political considerations relating to operational deployment, the class-company system with its narrow recruiting base also encountered severe problems of replenishment of manpower as a result of casualties on a scale that was both unprecedented and unanticipated. The totally inadequate system of reserves completely broke down, as did the localised regimental recruiting. The manpower demands of the Great War led to an expansion of the recruiting base for the duration of the war at least. At the same time it raised the awareness, and the expectations, of large sections of the Indian public about the very significant role of the Indian army in Imperial defence – and the political concessions that they hoped would follow as a result.

During the war India functioned as an Imperial strategic reserve. The global nature of its commitments is exemplified by none other than the

Below the dugouts of Indian troops, an Indian soldier tends sheep at Anzac. Live sheep and goats were supplied as part of the meat rations for the Indian troops on the Gallipoli Peninsula and slaughtered in accordance with Muslim religious traditions.

AWM C01614

89th Punjabis, who had been turned away from Gallipoli to fight the (non-Islamic) Germans in France. The battalion had the distinction of serving in more theatres of the war than perhaps any other single battalion in the Commonwealth. Having sailed from India in November 1914, by the time it returned home in September 1920 it had served in southwest Arabia, in Egypt, on Gallipoli, in France, in Mesopotamia, on the northwest Frontier, in Salonika, in the Caucasus, and finally at Constantinople with the Army of the Black Sea.

The Indian army was represented on Gallipoli by the 7th Indian Mountain Artillery Brigade, the Indian Mule Corps, a medical establishment and the 29th Indian Infantry Brigade.[11] The infantry served in the Helles area from 1 May until 10 July, and were transferred to Anzac after a brief period of rest and reorganisation at Imbros, just in time to take part in the August offensive. The artillery landed at Ari Burnu with the Australian and New Zealand troops and shared all the travails and vicissitudes of the ANZAC corps, from the day of the first landings on 25 April until the final evacuation in December.

The 7th Indian Mountain Artillery Brigade

After the great uprising of 1857, the British had disbanded all Indian artillery except for the mountain batteries. The 7th Indian Mountain Artillery Brigade[12] that proceeded to Gallipoli from Egypt was composed of the 21st Kohat[13] and 26th Jacob's Mountain Battery,[14] manned by Sikh and Punjabi Muslim gunners. The latter were the only allied Muslim troops in action against the Turks on the peninsula. The brigade was a complete formation with ammunition column, field ambulance section, ordnance field park, supply section and post office.

The batteries were armed with 10-pounder breech-loading (BL) screw guns which were brought into action disassembled on a seven-mule gun line. Each battery had six guns organised into three sections. The Indian mountain batteries served throughout the campaign on the peninsula, without even a day's relief, as an integral part of the ANZAC formation; 26th Jacob's Battery prided itself on being the first in and last out among the artillery units on Gallipoli. The services of this battery during the landing at Anzac on 25 May were described as being of inestimable value. Its fire gave encouragement to the Australian troops at a critical time when they were hard pressed to hold the line on their own, and the battery relieved the infantry of a good deal of pressure by drawing enemy fire upon itself.[15] The Australian official war correspondent and later official historian, C.E.W. Bean, witnessed such actions and made many admiring observations in his diary and his history about the fighting qualities and fortitude of Indian troops on Gallipoli.[16]

Before embarking for Gallipoli a defect was noticed in the BL 10-pounder shrapnel shell: the shrapnel broke up badly as the resin was too hard. As a

result, 7.5 per cent of the shells fired burst defectively. No action was taken by the ordnance 'as the defect complained of is inherent in the design of the BL 10 pr Shrapnel'.[17] Ultimately the armourer's ingenuity prevailed and the problem was resolved by *boiling* the shells before use, which had the desired effect! The 10-pounder gun was ill-adapted for the work required on Gallipoli, as the hilly topography and the very short ranges demanded the use of a howitzer. The problem was resolved by cutting the cartridges in two to make half-charges and by using improvised range tables.

By the third week of May the guns were showing signs of wear and replacements were urgently sought from India, as none were said to be available in England. Six of those that arrived were replaced a month later. During the August offensive on the Sari Bair ridge, the two Indian mountain batteries, less one section each, formed part of the two assaulting columns and rendered full support to the infantry. In the third week of September, the MEF commander-in-chief requested that in view of the 7th Mountain Artillery Brigade's invaluable work, it be re-armed with the new 12½-pounder gun. But the guns were not available. By all accounts, however, the Indian mountain batteries made a mark for themselves and were long remembered with affection and regard by their former Anzac comrades.[18]

Indian mule transport

It may come as no surprise that when the Gallipoli expedition was planned in January 1915, transport was not included, since Lord Kitchener expected that the landing force would be required only to march over the narrow peninsula. The history of the Royal Army Service Corps notes that Kitchener was persuaded to include a quota of transport to accompany the troops, by 'the reminder that on active service a properly organised supply of ammunition was essential'. The history goes on to candidly observe, 'Now among Lord Kitchener's qualities, and they were both numerous and eminent, knowledge of transport was not included.'[19]

However, even with his authorisation, the lack of roads on the peninsula rendered motorised transport useless. The transport difficulty was largely resolved by the allotment of an Indian mule transport train from France, consisting of 4316 mules and 2000 carts.[20] The transport was organised into four Mule Cart Corps, each consisting of ten troops; and each of these had 108 mules and 50 carts with 60 drivers. The total strength of a corps was 650 men and 1086 mules. Ten thousand tons of hay, barley and maize from India accompanied the force for animal fodder.

Service in the Mule Corps was not one of the most soldierly activities; but in no other theatre of war did the lowly mules or their gallant drivers share more equally in the hardships and dangers of their front-line comrades than on the beaches and in the gullies of Gallipoli. Just before the landings it became obvious that the mules would also have to be used in a pack role, for which the Mule Cart Corps were neither equipped nor organised. Luckily the design of the Indian saddlery permitted conversion of the saddle from draught to pack role by certain modifications that were carried out by the drivers. The mules were landed on Gallipoli on the very first day. One Mule Cart Corps was to land at Cape Helles with the 29th Division and the rest were to go ashore with the ANZAC troops at Gaba Tepe.

It took three days to complete the landing of the entire Mule Cart

Corps. The carts, which were the last to be brought ashore, had to be assembled in the cramped, dingy and ill-ventilated holds of the ship. However, the Indian Mule Corps soon established themselves in what came to be known as 'Mule Gully', beneath the prominent feature the Anzacs named the Sphinx. For the rest of the campaign, the mules and their drivers were a familiar and welcome sight to the soldiers holding onto their precarious perches in the heights above, as the Mule Corps cheerfully went about their task of delivering ammunition and supplies to the trenches. However, there was no let-up from enemy fire, and even Mule Gully was under constant sniper fire during the day, which led to most of the movements being carried out under cover of darkness.

In spite of all precautions, the transport suffered daily shelling in its camps and during the trips to the front lines. The entire stretch of the track from Mule Gully up to the first-line mule camp was under direct enemy fire and every convoy was machine-gunned. On the upward trips the drivers would stack their loads on the exposed side and hunch behind this flimsy cover, but on the return journey even this protection was unavailable. It was not uncommon to see mule and driver dashing at full gallop across particularly bad stretches. At Anzac alone, the transport suffered 177 men and 858 mules killed or wounded.

A unique feature was the construction of a light railway using wagons pulled by mules, all with carefully worked-out timings and halts. After the allied landings at Suvla Bay, the headquarters of the Indian Mule Train was established there. When the force was finally withdrawn from the peninsula under cover of darkness in December, 50 of the squeakiest carts were used in the last convoy before evacuation, to give the impression that the convoys were operating as usual. Before embarking, a large number of mules and horses were shot in their stalls to prevent them from falling into the hands of the enemy.

Following their evacuation from Gallipoli, the mule transport was returned to India for further deployment with British forces in Mesopotamia.[21] However, there is another segment of the story of Indian supply and transport on Gallipoli that remains to be told.

Indian Mule Corps teams in Mule Gully, loading mules with supplies for the troops, May 1915. Lines of mules are tethered further up the valley.

AWM A03809

Indian Labour Corps

On 1 September 1915, Austen Chamberlain, the Secretary of State for India, cabled Delhi with an urgent request on behalf of the War Office to provide an organised corps of Indian coolies from the Punjab, as they would be 'invaluable' for service on Gallipoli. He estimated that for work on roads and railways 2000 Hazaras would be required, and for unloading on beaches, 1000 workers. A semi-military organisation was suggested, and liability to work under fire was to be included in the indentures of the men selected. He noted that 'Greek and Egyptian labour on the peninsula have proved impossible. All soldiers are required to fight and imbroglio [confusion] goes on on many beaches.'[22]

In reply the Secretary of State was informed that it would not be possible to raise a coolie corps of Hazaras, as men of this class[23] were required for the Indian army. The Viceroy also opposed the policy of having such a homogeneous corps of Muslims to face the Turks. He pointed out that there had been cases of Hazara soldiers deserting to the Turks in Egypt; besides, the Hazara would demand a very high rate of pay, and to grant it would have a bad effect on the Indian army. Instead he offered to raise 3000 coolies, both Muslim and Hindu, from the Punjab, provided that the men were not of the same class as those enlisting for the Indian army.

Australian soldiers of the 10th Battalion watch Indian mule drivers as they lead their mule train carrying boxes of stores around the base of a hill, past a covered trench, to a storage area. Shrapnel Valley, Anzac, May 1915.

AWM P00326.011

Moreover, it was emphasised that he could not 'guarantee, in view of the above, that men of the classes we are prepared to endeavour to obtain for the cooly corps will, unarmed, stand fire or be suitable for such imbroglios as you describe', and asked London for definite instructions on these points.[24] The Viceroy was informed that the commander of the Mediterranean Expeditionary Force was quite willing to accept 3000 Punjabi coolies of any description, and that the proportion of Muslims to Hindus did not matter: the essential point was to get men to take the risk of coming under fire, and to obtain the men as soon as possible. The General Officer Commanding (GOC) ended with the plea, 'Labour is an urgent necessity with us.'[25]

To meet this urgent demand for military labour for the Mediterranean Expeditionary Force, the Director General of Military Works in India organised two Labour Corps for railway and road construction, of about 1000 men each, under an experienced Royal Engineer officer. Each corps was organised in four companies, each company being under a selected Indian army reserve officer. The organisation of the corps was semi-military, and included regular Indian officers (VCOs).[26] Some British military upper subordinates from the Military Works Service were attached for supervision. Non-commissioned officers, or 'gangers', were mainly from the labour class. Labourers were enrolled and attested and liable for duty, under fire, and would be eligible for wound, injury, and family pension at three-quarters of sepoy rates.[27] Arm badges '1st (or 2nd) LC' were to be worn by all non-commissioned officers, artificers and labourers, instead of the more military shoulder title.[28]

A 1000-strong Porter Corps was also raised along the same lines in the Punjab under the command of a captain of the Supply and Transport Corps (STC). To allow the corps to be split up into smaller complete units, subdivisions of 500 each were to be commanded by senior warrant officers of the STC temporarily employed as officers, on special rates of pay, with a proportion of Indian officers and supervising personnel.[29] The cost of clothing and equipment was estimated at £3000; initial pay of all ranks about £1200 monthly.[30]

On 18 November, 596 porters of the Porter Corps with necessary supervising personnel sailed from Karachi for Force 'G', via Suez; the remainder were to follow by the middle of December.[31] The 1st Labour Corps were ready for embarkation at Rawalpindi by 30 November;[32] they sailed from Karachi on 14 December.[33] However, these men, who may have been invaluable if available during the August offensive at Anzac, were never destined to reach Gallipoli. The evacuation of all allied troops from Anzac and Suvla was completed by 20 December and the remaining troops at Helles were to be withdrawn in early January. On Christmas Day 1915, the Inspector General of Communications, Mudros, informed India that the balance of the Porter Corps and part of 2nd Labour Corps, due to sail from Karachi on the 26th, were no longer required for the Mediterranean Expeditionary Force.[34]

The 29th Indian Infantry Brigade

Although apparently overawed by the personality of his former commander, Lord Kitchener, Secretary of State for War, the commander-in-chief of the Mediterranean Expeditionary Force, General Sir Ian Hamilton, was conscious of the inadequate size of the force at his disposal for the task at hand. Though extremely reluctant to ask for the additional troops that were required, he did provide himself with a safety margin by requesting one Gurkha brigade from Egypt, in exchange for which he offered to leave four mounted brigades in Egypt.[35]

Ian Hamilton had done most of his service in India, during which time he had developed an admiration for the Gurkhas and was not slow to realise that they would be ideally suited to warfare in the hilly Gallipoli terrain. In a letter to Lord Kitchener dated 25 March 1915, he said:

> I am very anxious, if possible, to get a brigade of Gurkhas, so as to complete the New Zealand divisional organisation with a type of man who will, I am certain, be most valuable on the Gallipoli peninsula.
>
> The scrubby hillsides on the south-west faces of the plateau are just the sort of terrain where these little fellows are at their brilliant best. … Egypt, in fact, so far as I can make out, seems stiff with troops and each little 'Gurkh' might be worth his full weight in gold at Gallipoli.[36]

Prompted by Sir Ian Hamilton's request, Lord Kitchener instructed the GOC in Cairo to be prepared to assist Hamilton with additional troops if required. The result was the despatch of the Indian Brigade to Gallipoli:

> When in Cairo at the end of March he [Hamilton] had told General Maxwell how much he wanted it. On the evening of the 6th April he sent him a parting telephone message, begging him 'to jog K's elbow "about the Gurkhas"', and two days later, just as he was sailing from Alexandria, an answer was received that General Maxwell 'would do his best to meet his wishes'.[37]

There was no purely Gurkha brigade serving in Egypt at the time and hence the 29th Indian Infantry Brigade of the 10th Indian Division was ordered to Gallipoli. As originally constituted in October 1914, the brigade consisted of the 14th King George's Own Ferozepore Sikhs, 69th Punjabis, 89th Punjabis and the 1/6th Gurkha Rifles. It sailed from Karachi for Egypt on 2 November 1914 under the command of Brigadier General H.V. Cox.[38] For the next six months it was engaged in the defence of the Suez Canal before it sailed for Gallipoli, arriving off Cape Helles at midday on 30 April. Disembarking at V Beach on the 1 May, it was attached as an extra brigade of the much depleted

29th Division. It moved into the front line on the 9th, relieving the British 87th Brigade on the extreme left of the line. It was to occupy this sector throughout its stay at Helles.

The first significant action of the brigade was the capture of 'Gurkha Bluff', on 12 May, thereby extending the line of the allied defences down to the sea. On 14 May the 69th Punjabis and 89th Punjabis were withdrawn from the line, and on the 15th embarked for Egypt, en route to France[39], as they contained a significant proportion of Muslim troops. In the short period that these units had been on the peninsula, the 89th Punjabis had suffered over 100 casualties, while the 69th Punjabis, which had not been engaged in the front line, lost 10 killed and 23 wounded. These units were replaced by the 1/5th[40] and the 2/10th[41] Gurkha Rifles, but not until 2 June; in the meantime the brigade was brought up to strength by the temporary addition of two British battalions.[42]

During its stay at Helles the brigade was involved the Third Battle of Krithia and the action of Gully Ravine. In the battle of Krithia on 4 June, the 14th Sikhs, one of the few non-Gurkha pure-class battalions of the Indian army, composed entirely of seasoned Jat Sikh soldiers from the Punjab, launched repeated attacks, in the face of murderous machine-gun fire, against the Turkish positions astride Gully Ravine. Held up by the barbed wire that was unaffected by the allied artillery bombardment, a section of men leapt the wire as if it were a hurdle on a sports field and charged the Turks with the bayonet. However, human valour was unavailing against modern weapons of war, and on that day the battalion's casualties amounted to 82 per cent of the men actually engaged in the battle. Only three battalion officers were left unwounded. Writing to the commander-in-chief in India a few weeks after the event, General Hamilton paid noble tribute to the heroism of all ranks:

> In the highest sense of the word extreme gallantry has been shown by this fine Battalion. … In spite of these tremendous losses there was not a sign of wavering all day. Not an inch of ground gained was given up and not a single straggler came back. The ends of the enemy's trenches leading into the ravine were found [after the successful British advance on 28 June] to be blocked with the bodies of Sikhs and of the enemy who died fighting at close quarters, and the glacis slope is thickly dotted with the bodies of these fine soldiers all lying on their faces as they fell in their steady advance on the enemy.
>
> The history of the Sikhs affords many instances of their value as soldiers, but it may be safely asserted that nothing finer than the grim valour and steady discipline displayed by them on the 4th June has ever been done by soldiers of the *Khalsa*. Their devotion to duty and their splendid loyalty to their orders and to their leaders make a record their nation should look back upon with pride for many generations.[43]

The heavy casualties suffered in the previous fighting were somewhat offset by the equally heavy punishment inflicted upon the Turks during their gallant counter-attacks on 3 and 5 July.

The repulse of the Turkish attacks on 5 July marked the end of serious fighting for the Indian Brigade in the Helles area, and after a few days spent in bivouac on the coast it was moved to the island of Imbros for rest and reorganisation on 9–10 July. By then the brigade had dwindled to a skeleton. The 1/5th and 1/6th Gurkha Rifles had been temporarily amalgamated, and the 14th Sikhs were by now so depleted in numbers (1 battalion officer (BO), 1 VCO and 117 ORs) that they were attached to the 2/10th Gurkhas for rations and maintenance. Like the 14th, the 1/5th also had only one battalion officer left. Indeed the 5th Gurkhas' history records that only eight battalion officers remained in the brigade as a whole, including the staff, and every unit was greatly reduced in numbers.[44] The shortage of British officers was the primary reason for withdrawing the brigade from the firing line.[45]

During its stay at Imbros, the brigade was once again brought up to strength by the arrival of drafts from linked battalions and from depots in India. Reinforcements for class regiments like those employed on Gallipoli were proving to be a problem. Sir Ian Hamilton rejected a suggestion that reinforcements of other classes should be sent for the 14th Sikhs, saying that he deprecated the 'introduction of foreign element into famous class regiment'. He said that for this kind of trench warfare, young recruits with two or three months' training would do well if put into seasoned cadres, and that Jat Sikh recruits of this type 'would be invaluable here'.[46]

However, in the event, a double company (DC) of Patiala Imperial Service Infantry[47] arrived as reinforcements on 7 July and a second followed on 25 September 1915.[48] Like the 14th Sikhs this was also a class regiment consisting of only Jat Sikhs. However, unlike the 14th it was not a regular unit of the British Indian army, but belonged to the army of the princely state of Patiala in the Punjab. The Maharaja of Patiala, H.H. Lieutenant Colonel (later Lieutenant General) Bhupindar Singh, was concerned that the famous Ferozepore Sikhs would overshadow any glory coming the way of the Patiala troops. He specifically requested that the attached double companies should be maintained as a separate unit or, if this was not possible, that their identity should be preserved and that all casualties should be reported as occurring in the Patiala Infantry and not in the 14th Sikhs. Although attempts were made to mollify the Maharaja by stating 'that he had the honour of being the only [Indian] ruler who had troops in the Dardanelles',[49] history bears witness that the Maharaja's apprehension was indeed well founded. The Patiala Infantry find no mention in accounts of the Dardanelles campaign.[50]

In addition to other ranks, the shortage of British officers continued to be acutely felt. In response to an urgent telegram from Sir Ian Hamilton to say that Cox's Brigade had scarcely any officers left and requesting replacements, the GOC Egypt informed India that he had already despatched every available Gurkhali-speaking officer and others in addition, and was in consequence himself 'reduced to the minimum required for safety'. He urged that 'the maintaining of this Brigade in a state of efficiency calls for serious consideration.'[51]

There is no doubt that officer casualties in British army formations were very high, but they were nowhere more keenly felt than in Indian units. It became exceedingly difficult to find replacements for officers who could not only speak the men's language but were also deeply respected and implicitly trusted by the troops. In keeping with their regimental traditions, officers made it a point to set an example, often leading to unnecessary loss of life. On one occasion, an officer of the 1/5th Gurkhas drew his sword – he was perhaps the only officer on the peninsula who wore one in battle – and led his men in a gallant, though doomed, charge against the enemy.

On 21 July the Indian troops with the Mediterranean Expeditionary Force (MEF) were designated Indian Expeditionary Force (IEF) 'G'.[52] However, as late as the first week of August, the GOC in Egypt was unaware of this designation, asking the commander-in-chief in India by telegram on 6 August 'What is Force "G" please?'[53] Brought up to strength by reinforcements in July, Force 'G' it was that took the field as a part of the August offensive on the Anzac front, and fought side by side with the Anzacs till the final evacuation from the peninsula in late December. Table 11.1 outlines what the force was ultimately to consist of.

Table 11.1 Composition of the Indian Expeditionary Force (IEG) 'G'

Fighting units

7th Indian Mountain Artillery Brigade

Headquarters

21st (Kohat) Mountain Battery (Frontier Force)

26th (Jacob's) Mountain Battery

Mountain Artillery Section, Divisional Ammunition Column

29th Indian Infantry Brigade

Headquarters

14th King George's Own Ferozepore Sikhs

2 Double Companies, Patiala Imperial Service Infantry (attached 14th Sikhs)

1/5th Gurkha Rifles (Frontier Force)

1/6th Gurkha Rifles

2/10th Gurkha Rifles

1/4th Gurkha Rifles and details[54]

Administrative units

Transport

Indian Mule Cart Train, comprising the following:

Mule Corps (each a complete corps): 1st, 2nd, 9th, 11th, 15th, 28th, 31st and 32nd

Mule Corps (detachments from): 3rd, 6th, 7th, 8th, 10th, 12th, 14th, 18th, 19th, 20th, 21st, 22nd, 23rd, 24th, 26th, 27th, 29th, 33rd, 34th, 35th, 36th and 37th

Detachments from:

Gwalior Imperial Service Transport Corps

Bharatpur Imperial Service Transport Corps

Indore (Holkar's) Imperial Service Transport Corps

Hospitals

108th Indian Field Ambulance (with 29th Indian Infantry Brigade)

110th Indian Field Ambulance (Clearing Hospital) (with Convalescent Depot)

'C' Section (Indian) 137th Combined Field Ambulance (with Indian Mountain Artillery Brigade)

'C' Section (British) 137th Combined Field Ambulance (on a transport)

Postal

IAPS Field Post Office (FPO) No. 34

This was the composition of the approximately 4800-strong Indian detachment that was to serve at the northern flank of Anzac, after the 29th Indian Brigade landed at Anzac cove on 5–6 August in order to take part in what would become the last major attempt to break the stalemate with a bold and, in retrospect, overambitious plan. This called for a vigorous offensive from Anzac (ANZAC, 13th Division and 29 Independent Brigade) combined with a surprise landing at Suvla Bay (IX Corps), under cover of a diversionary attack in the Helles area to pin down the Turkish forces and prevent reinforcements being sent to the north. 'Zulu' day for the breakout from Anzac, as well as the Suvla landings, was fixed for the night of 6–7 August.

The first step and the key to the plan was an assault at dawn on 7 August after a night advance by two columns to capture the summit of the Sari Bair ridge and gain command of the Narrows. To effect this, the Anzac forces under Major General Sir Alexander Godley, commanding the New Zealand & Australian Division, were organised into two covering and two assaulting columns. The left assaulting column, under Brigadier General H.V. Cox, commanding the 29th Indian Infantry Brigade, consisted of the 4th Australian

Brigade, the 29th Indian Brigade, the 21st (Kohat) Mountain Battery (less one section) and a field company of New Zealand Engineers. This column was to advance up the Aghyl Dere along a route previously chalked out by an ANZAC officer, Major J.P. Overton, and then divide at a pre-arranged point. This allowed the 4th Australian Brigade to make a detour via the Damakjelik Ridge, across the Azma Dere to a forming-up place on Abdul Rahman Bair, in order to assault Koja Chemen Tepe (Hill 971), while the Indian Brigade went straight on to the central height of the Sari Bair ridge, Hill 'Q'. Indian regimental accounts, based on contemporary views, are clear that the success of the venture was dependent upon the co-operation of the Suvla Bay divisions, although later historians contend that this was not necessarily so.

The Indian Brigade was assigned to the left assaulting column, whose allocated task was the most arduous, as it had the greatest distance to traverse to reach its objective. The route to the objective lay over 'a tangled network of twisting spurs and ravines, rugged and steep and covered thickly with prickly scrub'. Not only was the route largely unreconnoitred – it had only been surveyed by the brigade staff and 12 Gurkha scouts from the decks of a destroyer on the 5th – but the local guides picked to lead the columns had little real knowledge of the ground.[55] The objective was to be reached on a dark night over unfamiliar terrain, using maps that were known to be incomplete and inaccurate, and many of the officers lacked the training to conduct a successful night march. The plan did not inspire much confidence among those who had to execute it. The commander of 1/6th Gurkha Rifles, Major Cecil Allanson, remarked in his diary, 'when I was told that we were to break through the opposing outpost lines at 10 pm ... march along the sea coast for three miles, then turn at right angles and attempt to get under this big ridge about two miles inland, by dawn ... I felt, what would one have done to a subaltern at a promotion exam who made any such proposition?'[56]

The Indian Brigade embarked from Imbros on 5 August, and units continued landing at Anzac all night until daylight on the 6th. The beach was then shelled, and half the 14th Sikhs and the 108th Field Ambulance were not able to land until the night of 6 August. They were still at sea when the brigade column marched out from its starting point at No. 5 Supply Depot by 11.15 pm. The troops had had little rest in the past 24 hours. They would now be continuously in action, with little rest or sleep, until 10 August.

The order of march of the left assaulting column was as follows: 4th Australian Brigade, headquarters of the column; 29th Indian Brigade, less 14th Sikhs; No. 2 Company, New Zealand Engineers; 14th Sikhs, less escort to guns; 21st (Kohat) Mountain Battery; one double company of the 14th Sikhs. No animals other than gun mules accompanied the column. The total distance to be covered by the column was about three miles and it was hoped that the summit would be reached by 3 am. However, this quickly proved to have been an over-optimistic estimate and the timing went awry from the start. The head of the column, which should have started at 9.45 pm was delayed by one and a half hours, and progress was so slow that the 14th Sikhs at the rear of the column did not move forward until nearly 4.00 am on the 7th. The column was to march along the beach at the foot of the hills towards the bluff known as Walden Point, from where it was to turn right into the Aghyl Dere. However, unfortunately, in spite of the strong remonstrations of Major Pepys of the Indian Brigade, the New Zealand officer who was leading the column, Major Overton, was persuaded by the local guide to leave the coastal track earlier than intended and take a supposed shortcut through a narrow gorge, subsequently known as Taylor's Gap. Although only 600 yards long, the gap was so narrow and overgrown with scrub that the engineers had to be sent forward to clear a way, and even then the troops were able to proceed only in single file at a snail's pace. The head of the column took nearly three hours to get through the gorge, where they came under scattered fire.

By daybreak the leading Australian troops were on the Damakjelik Spur, barely a mile east of the mouth of the Aghyl Dere. Here they halted, under the impression that they had reached the Abdul Rahman ridge, and that they were within assaulting distance of Hill 971. They were in fact on the right of the left covering force on Damakjelik Ridge, and spent the day reorganising and calling up reserves. Though the Indian Brigade pressed on, battalions lost direction and cohesion in the semi-darkness. By dawn two companies of 2/10th Gurkha Rifles and one double company of 1/5th Gurkha Rifles, which had lost its battalion, found themselves in the vicinity of Rhododendron Spur, where they established contact with the New Zealanders of the right assaulting column. Three double companies of 1/5th Gurkha Rifles struggled up the slopes towards the summit of Hill Q before falling back to a line half a mile from the bifurcation of the Aghyl Dere, while the 1/6th Gurkha Rifles, one of the battalions originally detailed to assault 971, reached a point about 500 yards below the crest of Hill Q. The 14th Sikhs were on the left between the Australian brigade and 1/5th Gurkha Rifles. Throughout the rest of the day, the force clung on to the ground gained on the western slopes of Sari Bair, suffering heavy casualties from artillery- and rifle-fire. The day ended with communication barely established and the troops exhausted from the hard work and the thirst endured under a blazing sun.

The attack was resumed the next day, 8 August. The Australians on the left lost very heavily and the attempt on Hill 971 was abandoned. The Indian Brigade was also unable to make any headway in their advance on Hill Q, other than gaining some ground in the neighbourhood of the Farm. The troops, suffering heavily from thirst and exhaustion, then dug in on the line which they then held. Orders were received late in the evening for a renewal of the attack at 5.15 am the next morning by fresh troops after a heavy bombardment.

The climax of the battle of Sari Bair was to take place on the morning of

9 August, when the ridge was crested for the last time by any allied troops in the campaign. This occurred when the 1/6th Gurkha Rifles, with small detachments from the 6th South Lancashire and 9th Warwickshire Regiments, led by Major Allanson, CO of the Gurkha Rifles, charged up the steep slope. As dawn broke over Asia Minor across the Dardanelles, for a short while they had the object of the offensive in their sight. Twenty years later, one of the earliest historians of the campaign, Major John North wrote that 'the lonely advance of these British and Gurkha skirmishers to the crest of the ridge when the battle was already lost must always remain one of the most gallant episodes in the whole campaign.'[57]

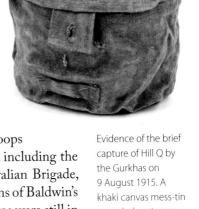

The plan for the attack that morning was for five fresh New Army battalions under Brigadier General A.H. Baldwin, commanding the 38th Brigade, to advance from Rhododendron Spur under cover of 45 minutes of intense bombardment. The troops which had occupied the foremost line during the previous day, including the 1/6th and 2/10th Gurkha Rifles, together with the 4th Australian Brigade, were to demonstrate only. But at the appointed hour the battalions of Baldwin's column were nowhere in sight. At 6.15 am, three of the battalions were still in the Aghyl Dere, and one was halfway up the slope to the small plateau named 'the Farm'; all were completely out of their proper alignment and positions, and over an hour late. In the meantime the 1/6th Gurkha Rifles, as ordered, with three companies of British troops, had worked up to close under the ridge. When the artillery bombardment stopped, they got to the top of the ridge and after a fierce struggle drove the Turks from the crest. They then advanced on the enemy, who were retreating down the opposite slope.

Evidence of the brief capture of Hill Q by the Gurkhas on 9 August 1915. A khaki canvas mess-tin cover belonging to an unknown soldier of 1/6th Gurkha Rifles, found on the crest of Hill Q by members of the Australian Historical Mission on 3 March 1919 while they were investigating the actions of August 1915 around Chunuk Bair.

RELAWM00397.001

Further evidence of the brief capture of Hill Q by the Gurkhas on 9 August 1915. A section of khaki cotton webbing ammunition pouches belonging to an unknown soldier of 1/6th Gurkha Rifles, found on the crest of Hill Q by members of the Australian Historical Mission on 3 March 1919 while they were investigating the actions of August 1915 around Chunuk Bair. The 1908 Pattern Mark II ammunition pouches each held three clips holding five rounds of .303 ammunition (15 rounds per pouch) and the complete webbing had five pouches on each side, holding a total of 150 rounds.

RELAWM00397.002

But just as they had moved some 300 yards down the reverse slope, they were suddenly hit by a salvo of artillery shells, combined with heavy fire from the direction of Abdul Rahman Bair and a Turkish counter-attack, which drove them from the summit. They were eventually rallied on the line held the previous night, but all the British officers of 1/6th Gurkha Rifles except the medical officer were casualties. The main attack, which should also have taken place at 5.15 am, did not develop until about 9 am. By this time it was fairly evident it would not succeed, and permission was obtained to hold and consolidate the line on which the troops stood. However, the battle for Sari Bair was by now lost, and strong Turkish counter-attacks on 10 August managed to push the allies to a line along the lower slopes of the great ridge, which the Turks entrenched and held until the end of the campaign.

Soldiers of the Indian Brigade were further actively involved in the subsidiary action of Hill 60 on 21 August, their last battle of any magnitude on the peninsula. After the fighting stalled on the slopes below the summit of Hill 60 one week later, the entire line settled down to the routine of trench war. The Indian Brigade held a front on the extreme left flank of the Anzac defences, extending northward from Hill 60 and joining up with the right of

A group of Gurkha soldiers with bandaged frostbitten feet, waiting to be evacuated from Anzac after the blizzard and snowfalls in late November 1915 badly affected troops exposed to the severe conditions.

AWM C02448

IX Corps at Suvla. It remained in these positions until the final evacuation on 20 December. Paradoxically, this was the most successful of allied operations during the campaign. Executed with meticulous planning, and accomplished with a measure of success beyond expectation, the evacuation of Gallipoli was to become one of the Punjabi soldiers' defining memories of the *laam ki larai*, the long war. The stories of rifles fitted with delayed-action contrivances that enabled them to fire long after the *morchas*, or trenches, were empty, ranked with those of the ill-fated Indian garrison of Kut-al Amara, where the troops were reduced to eating horse flesh in order to survive.[58]

Conclusion

On Gallipoli, the Indian contingent, in common with the rest of the British force, was short of most of the equipment required for the type of warfare to which it had been committed. There were shortages of machine-guns and of artillery shells, and the guns and their ammunition were not suited to the short ranges over which they had to be employed. An acute shortage of grenades (or 'bombs' in the language of the soldiers) handicapped the troops and caused numerous avoidable casualties in the close-proximity combat at Helles. During the main battle of Sari Bair, which has been described as one of the great soldiers' battles of all time, the Indian Brigade more than held its own. Ultimately, a shortage of officers, poor communications, inadequate command and control of the tactical battle, and a plan far too ambitious in its ambit lost the battle for the allies. While one argument suggests that it would have been necessary to capture all three high points of Sari Bair for the whole operation to succeed,[59] the official history offers the judgement that the chief mistake of the British plan was the 'choice of so wide an objective' by including the capture of Hill 971 in the first night's plan. That view is supported by the brigade major of the Indian Brigade, who wrote that the plan was much too complicated for successful execution even during peace: 'in war it was impossible'.

The source of the half-dozen fateful shells that drove Allanson and his small band from the crest of Sari Bair is one of the great 'whodunits' of the Gallipoli campaign. Where did these shells come from? Lieutenant Colonel Allanson 'was at the time convinced that they were from British naval guns'.[60] However, a more recent, excellent account of Gallipoli, argues this was:

> unlikely, given Allanson's position over the crest, allowing a view of the Straits. However, the ship's log of *Bacchante*, supporting the operation, shows that she opened fire at 5.20 am on 9 August on Hill Q with 6-inch shells and the 12-inch shells of a monitor might also have been responsible. But what historians have overlooked is that the *pre-arranged artillery time table* called for Anzac howitzers to search

the forward crest *at 5.15 am* on 9 August, obviously to defend Hill Q against Turkish counterattacks, and for the Navy to switch to flank fire at this time. Since Allanson and his Gurkhas were hit on the forward crest *at about 5.35 am*, the responsibility for this unfortunate 'friendly fire' incident obviously lies with poor staff work, while the 'very excitable' but brave and energetic Allanson unintentionally put his Gurkhas at risk after 5.15 am. Clearly, Allanson did not know what the Allied fire plan was.[61]

In his footnote to this paragraph the author, Tim Travers, further notes that 'Godley, Birdwood and Cox all saw Allanson as an unreliable witness and excitable' and that Temperley (the New Zealand brigade major) 'thought it was Anzac howitzers that did the damage'.[62] Travers goes on to observe:

> Strangely, Allanson's story of naval shelling was later undercut by his own letters to Aspinall in 1930. In these Allanson says that he did not stay on the summit (or saddle) of Hill Q on 9 August, not because of naval shelling or other friendly fire, but because of the extreme exposure of the summit, where a few shells would dislodge them. He does not actually refer to any naval shelling.[63]

However, this observation is inaccurate, as in his letter Allanson refers to the statement in the draft history that said the Turks had occupied the ridge without a struggle. He clarifies this as follows:

> The actual ridge was not occupied by any one until about 4 to 5 pm of that afternoon, the 9th, and then only temporarily, when the succession of counter-attacks was made over it, and all completely repulsed. Had the summit been occupied we, immediately below, just [*sic*] have known it, and I do not believe that we should have remained; my reason for not attempting to go back on to it was the extreme exposure of the position, from which a few shells would dislodge us.[64]

The entire thrust of Allanson's explanation in this paragraph pertains to the reasons why the ridge was not physically occupied, either by him or the Turks on 9 August, until his battalion withdrew, under orders, on the following day. He does not refer to the shelling that earlier drove him off the ridge because that is not the issue he is addressing. Whatever the origin of the artillery shells, there is no doubt that at the time Allanson was under the impression that the bombardment came from naval guns. Apart from his oft-quoted diary, in a note sent to the headquarters of the 29th Indian Brigade at 9.30 am Allanson says, 'Unfortunately at 5.25 artillery reopened fire (I think it must have been ours) and a good many casualties occurred among the men.' This is borne out by the war diary of the 29th Indian Brigade which states, 'Unfortunately the artillery, no doubt seeing that the main attack was hopelessly late, reopened fire on the ridge, and caused many casualties.'

In the larger scheme of things, the Indian contingent that served on the peninsula was but a small fraction of the total troops employed. It was sorely tried but emerged from the fray with credit, having suffered a total of 4130 casualties during the campaign. The high point of its deployment at Gallipoli was undoubtedly its conduct during the battle for Sari Bair, when one of its battalions gained the crest of the mighty ridge and for a short time, it is still widely believed, may have held the key to victory in its grasp. The forlorn hope of this small band, as it waited in vain for reinforcements which never came, and before it was hurled off the crest by a storm of Turkish fire and an unfortunate salvo of friendly artillery fire, must remain one of the most poignant images of the entire campaign.

Yet there are other images as well – though, unlike the Australian and New Zealand armies, which turned the historian's gaze upon the involvement of their individual soldiers, the story of the Indian army at Gallipoli, and indeed in the Great War as a whole, received no such separate scrutiny. The Indian story, and it was a substantial one, must therefore be unravelled from among the larger official accounts of the war. There are almost no records that preserve the subaltern voice of the Indian rank and file, apart from the fortuitous but fragmentary collection of letters passed down by the Indian censors in France. The Gallipoli narrative gets a human touch from the accounts of a few British officers of the Indian army, who recount the doings of their men in passing. From such we have the enduring snapshot of the Gurkha subedar major, literally weeping in frustration as his wounds forced him to leave his battalion and be carried off the battlefield during the assault on Hill 60; of the Indian gunner, Karam Singh, continuing to relay fire orders from the observation officer to the guns of his battery, long after he had been rendered blind by shrapnel; of Gunner Jan Mohamed pumping 17 out of 22 shells into the gun ports of a Turkish battery opposite Quinn's Post, even though his gun emplacement had been knocked down by high explosive; of the grieving mule drivers bringing wreaths of wild flowers to lay on the grave of the noble-hearted John Simpson Kirkpatrick or his donkey 'Murphy'; and numerous others that serve to remind us that behind the dry statistics and official reports there lies another story that can perhaps now never be told.

Chapter 12

Supplying the offensive

The role of allied logistics

Rhys Crawley

In 1979 the renowned British military historian Sir Michael Howard noted, 'no campaign can be understood, and no valid conclusions drawn from it, unless its logistic problems are studied as thoroughly as the course of operations'.[1] When we look at the literature of the August offensive, or the entire Gallipoli campaign for that matter, it is evident that Howard's assertion has fallen on deaf ears. To date there remains no logistic analysis of these military operations. On the one hand, this absence is understandable, given the technical nature of logistics studies in comparison with the popular appeal and human drama of battle narratives; on the other, it is difficult to fathom, given that one of the principal strategic objectives of the Gallipoli campaign was – however unrealistic it may have been – to open a logistic supply line to Russia through the Black Sea.[2]

Logistics, referring to 'the practical art of moving armies and keeping them supplied', are an important component of war.[3] Without the basic necessities of food, water and ammunition, an offensive – particularly a major one like the August offensive at Gallipoli – stands a very slender chance of succeeding. Put simply, without these essential items, troops cannot fight, at least at their full capacity, for prolonged periods.[4] There are examples throughout history that point to the direct impact that logistics have had on both the success and the failure of military operations. Take, for example, the highly efficient logistic system of the British Expeditionary Force (BEF) on the Western Front in 1918, which gave Douglas Haig the strategic flexibility that he desired and required for victory; and compare that with Germany's failure to provide sufficient transport (or indeed, fuel and spare parts) to move its troops during Operation Barbarossa in 1941.[5] Although on a much smaller scale, the logistic systems in place for the August offensive are no less significant, and deserve their place in history.

The principal aim of this chapter is to examine whether the Mediterranean Expeditionary Force (MEF) could be maintained and sustained during a prolonged period of offensive operations on Gallipoli in August 1915. In doing so, it will analyse whether the August offensive was a logistically viable operation of war. As it was an *allied* offensive, this paper will focus on the structure, processes, and complexities of the allies' logistic system, but not on those of the Ottoman army. That said, it should be noted that the MEF's supplies – both in quantity and quality – were far greater than those available to their enemy, who were constantly plagued by shortages throughout the campaign. This is not to say that the allied logistic system was easier to implement. Indeed, it can be argued that with its home base nearly 3500 sea miles (6500 km) from the theatre of operations, and with the difficulties of sea-borne supply in amphibious operations, the MEF's logistic system was inherently more complex and difficult than their enemy's.[6]

This chapter will focus on three major components of logistics during the August offensive: first, the processes of getting supplies from the United Kingdom to the Gallipoli Peninsula; second, the processes of disembarking these items onto the beaches and then distributing them forward to the units; and finally, the logistic elements of medical evacuation. I shall not attempt to quantify what was landed during the August offensive. The historical record, which is imperfect and incomplete, simply does not allow such calculations.

Lines of communication

The MEF's logistic system was, according to the quartermaster-general (QMG) at the War Office, 'abnormal and peculiar'.[7] It differed greatly from that employed on the Western Front, where the BEF was backed by a sympathetic civilian population, pre-existing and established lines of communication (L-of-C) in the form of road and rail networks, and a short sea passage between the United Kingdom and the Continent.[8] With such a foundation, the maintenance of the BEF, even with all its difficulties, was essentially assured.[9] On Gallipoli, however, the allies had none of these elements.[10] A further contrast between the two fronts was the process by which stores and supplies were requested and then delivered. On Gallipoli, the MEF employed what can be described as a 'pull' logistic system, whereby units submitted daily requests to General Headquarters (GHQ), outlining what items they believed would be required in the immediate future; GHQ then forwarded these requests to the War Office in London. Although this worked, it was an inefficient system. Indeed, the amount of administrative paperwork required to keep a 'pull' system functioning was the very reason why the BEF abandoned this process in July 1915, and introduced a 'push' system in its place, under which the BEF was automatically forwarded (or pushed) a regular 'divisional pack', which contained their average daily requirements. This measure greatly reduced the amount of red tape and administrative time-lapse experienced by the BEF.[11]

The administrative system of requesting, acquiring and despatching items to the Dardanelles was complex (see Diagram 12.1). The deputy quartermaster-general (DQMG) at GHQ directed all requests for supplies (such as food, provisions, etc.) to one officer at the War Office in London, and all requests for stores (equipment, munitions, clothing, etc.) to another.[12] It is important to note, however, that these official channels were often bypassed, and requests were instead made through private correspondence.[13] The existence of these parallel official and unofficial channels caused both confusion and delay. Indeed, in the lead-up to the August offensive the QMG at the War Office complained to the MEF's inspector general of communications (IGC) that there was still confusion as to who was responsible for requesting items, and informed him that 'it is impossible to deal with demands unless they all come through one recognized channel'.[14] Both channels were still being used when the August offensive commenced.

Once informed of the MEF's requirements, it was the duty of the War Office to acquire these items. The absence of a 'push' system, however, meant that the War Office was unable to give adequate forethought to what would be

Diagram 12.1
Request, acquisition, and disembarkation cycle

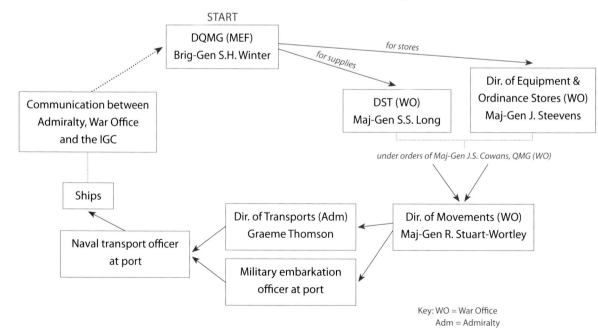

required. Arrangements, therefore, were not made until a request was received – the result being further delay.[15] With the acquisition complete, the War Office then organised for the transportation, mainly by train, of these items to their ports of embarkation.[16] This necessitated a considerable amount of co-operation with the Admiralty, which was responsible for providing, loading, and then despatching the ships overseas.[17] The items were loaded in bulk, and the *aim* was to place one type of item on one or as few ships as possible. It did not always work like this, however.[18]

The Mercantile Marine, under the direction of the Naval Transport Department, undertook the majority of the transportation to the Dardanelles. The vessels were protected, and often manned throughout the voyage, by the Royal Navy (RN).[19] After leaving the UK, ships travelled to Alexandria via Gibraltar and Malta.[20] On rare occasions, and only in times of great urgency, a dual L-of-C was opened, whereby items were sent to the MEF from France, thus shortening the voyage by up to 2,100 miles (3,360 km).[21] General Sir Ian Hamilton (GOC, MEF) described the former, main route as the 'biggest and most difficult Line of Communication … the world has probably seen since the day of Xerxes'.[22] At such distances, and subject to further complexities caused by unfavourable weather, hostile submarines and delays at the various ports of call, the difficulties of supplying the MEF 'were beyond description or possibility of exaggeration'.[23]

Gibraltar and Malta were merely ports of call. Alexandria, however, was the MEF's main base, and almost all shipping from the UK was sent there rather than straight to the advanced base.[24] With its infrastructure of wharves, piers, jetties, railway lines and cranes for unloading large ships, Alexandria was described by Hamilton's most senior staff officer as having 'everything one wants in reason'.[25] Because of a lack of similar facilities closer to the front, most ships bound for Gallipoli had to be disembarked, re-sorted, re-packed (into ration sizes rather than bulk) and reloaded at Alexandria before being forwarded to the intermediate base at Mudros Harbour (Lemnos Island).[26] This was a time-consuming process, and caused considerable delay to the logistic system.

Owing to the German submarine menace, allied ships over 1500 tons were prevented from travelling direct from Alexandria to the Gallipoli Peninsula. Instead, they had to proceed first to Mudros Harbour – a journey which was itself particularly vulnerable to German U-boats.[27] After reaching the safety of the harbour, the ships would transfer their cargoes into smaller craft (as these were less vulnerable to the enemy's submarines), which would then make the voyage to the peninsula.[28] It was at Mudros, however, that the greatest delay and confusion in the L-of-C was experienced.[29]

The first issue that caused delay at Mudros was a lack of port facilities. When he arrived on 22 July to take over as IGC, Lieutenant General Edward Altham informed the War Office that the harbour was in a state of 'appalling confusion'.[30] He later expanded on this, noting that while it was 'a magnificent harbour' it was 'totally undeveloped in the matter of piers, landing places, storehouses [and] buildings'.[31] In addition, water supply on the island was poor, there were minimal engineer stores, roads were non-existent and local transport was insufficient.[32] Mudros was thus in great need of improvement. Altham and his team got straight to work to address this, but, while many positive changes were made, Mudros had barely improved as a port by the time of the August offensive.[33] Indeed, according to the Superintendent Transport Officer (STO) at Mudros, it would take at least six months to get Mudros into a satisfactory state.[34]

The second problem faced at Mudros was congestion. In mid-July, when preparations were under way for the August offensive, there could be as many as 200 deep-water ships (but no deep-water piers for them to dock alongside) and countless small craft crowded into the harbour.[35] By 1 August the numbers had increased to such an extent that the King's Harbour Master doubted whether he could accommodate them all.[36] When he arrived at Mudros on 4 August, the Commanding Officer (CO) 59th Brigade, Royal Field Artillery, described the harbour as 'a most interesting sight at this time, crammed as it was with all sorts of vessels ... amongst which was a wooden bogus battleship'.[37] In such overcrowded conditions, collisions were not uncommon and communication was difficult.[38]

Given the absence of deep-water piers, and a lack of facilities on the island

Logistics preparations for the initial amphibious operations on Gallipoli. Huge piles of French army stores organised for shipping from Mudros Harbour, Lemnos Island, March 1915.

AWM H10398

in which to store items as they arrived, the MEF had to rely on 'floating depots' (converted store ships) to store its goods.[39] In theory, the idea was that a supply ship would go alongside a floating depot, unload its cargo, and then return to Alexandria or the UK for further work. Items would be stockpiled on board the floating depots, and when required, transferred to smaller craft for the voyage to the peninsula.[40] In practice, this did not work. There were only five floating depots (three British, two French) to service all supply ships and the multitude of smaller craft during August.[41] Further hindering the process was a lack of knowledge of what items each supply ship carried. Most, for example, arrived at Mudros without a manifest of goods on board. This made it difficult to locate specific items, or to prioritise which ships should be unloaded first.[42] It was not uncommon for supply ships to remain unemptied for weeks on end, or to be sent away before being cleared.[43] This both delayed the arrival of essential items and kept ships from duties elsewhere.

Port facilities were not the only problem at Mudros. Delays were further compounded by the lack of available labour to load and unload cargoes during the trans-shipment process. Even with the addition of Greek and Egyptian labourers, Turkish prisoners of war and an order that all butchers and bakers not presently working in their trade were to assist, the MEF's L-of-C always suffered from a lack of manpower.[44] The labour problem was acute during the August offensive. Numbers were so short that IX Corps was stripped of its fortress companies for work on the L-of-C.[45] By 5 August – the day before the offensive began – the labour situation was so dire that the IGC requested that an entire infantry battalion of the 53rd Division be allotted to him for fatigue work.[46] This was initially approved, but later retracted after opposition from IX Corps, which desperately needed all the troops it could get for operations at Suvla Bay.[47]

Mudros also suffered from a lack of small craft. There were not enough motor launches for maintaining communications between ships, while a shortage of lighters adversely affected trans-shipping.[48] The Admiralty realised the gravity of the situation, and sent out a representative 'to ascertain in detail the requirements of the Army in small vessels for [the] forthcoming operations'.[49] This representative, however, did not arrive until 22 July: too late to influence or have an impact on the August offensive. The Admiralty subsequently informed Vice-Admiral John de Robeck (Commander-in-Chief, Eastern Mediterranean Squadron) that they were 'squeezed dry, as regards small vessels' and it was difficult to acquire more in the theatre, for they were scarce and expensive.[50] Yet de Robeck was not anxious, and informed the Admiralty that 'the Navy has always been able to meet any demands that have been made on it by the Army up to the present, and I see no reason that we will not continue to do so.'[51] He was only able to meet these demands, however, by employing vessels that should have been used in other roles. In doing so, de Robeck reduced the fighting efficiency of the naval forces.[52]

The pressures faced at Mudros were partially relieved by the smaller advanced base at Kephalos Harbour (Imbros Island). This location, however, faced even more problems than Mudros, owing to its poorer facilities and greater exposure to the weather.[53] Kephalos was much closer to the peninsula than Mudros, though.[54] It was therefore used as a thoroughfare for small vessels travelling from Mudros, which could wait in its smaller harbour before proceeding to the beaches with their cargoes at night.[55] In reality, though, Kephalos was little more than an overflow for Mudros, and its prime function was as the site of GHQ, and as accommodation for reinforcements.

The journey to the peninsula, whether from Mudros or Kephalos, was generally undertaken under the cover of darkness, which offered protection from both submarines and enemy shelling as the vessels approached and lay off the beaches.[56] Due to the distances involved, and the fact that unloading could only be done at night, it was not usually possible to make more than one round trip daily.[57] Through this process the navy was able to deliver 300–400 tons to the peninsula daily. This 'best case' tonnage, which depended upon good weather and the arrival of all lighters, was insufficient for the August offensive, which would require an increase to 700–800 tons per day; and a further increase to 2000 tons daily should the MEF have advanced across the peninsula to Maidos, in accord with its operational objectives of the August offensive.[58]

Before considering the process of disembarking these items onto the peninsula, it is necessary to examine the administrative structure of the L-of-C already discussed. From the moment items left Britain, until they reached the advanced bases on the Gallipoli Peninsula, no fewer than six separate individuals (and their respective staffs) were in charge of the naval transport for the MEF.[59] This was too many to allow the system to work effectively. The army believed that the system would have worked better if control had been vested in a single individual, as was the case with their service.[60] While the military's logistic system was theoretically less complex than the naval model – since administration of the L-of-C fell under one individual, the IGC – it was no more efficient in practice. In effect, the IGC co-ordinated the L-of-C, which, because of its reliance on ships, meant close co-operation with the navy.[61] The IGC, more than anyone else, was therefore fundamental to the efficiency of the L-of-C, and as such needed to be an excellent administrator and organiser. Unfortunately for the MEF, the original IGC, Major General Wallace, who was described by the CGS, Major General Braithwaite, as 'an apology for an IGC', was no such man.[62] Wallace was replaced before the August offensive by the more experienced and capable Edward Altham, who was described at the time as 'one of the most able administrators we have in the Army'.[63] Altham immediately made changes to the L-of-C (both in terms of administration and facilities), but he arrived too late to have any distinct impact on the August operations.[64]

Left

British, Indian and Australian soldiers unloading supplies from a 'K' lighter at Anzac and loading transport mules during the August offensive. The armoured lighters (nicknamed 'beetles') were capable of carrying up to 500 men and were equipped with landing ramps for rapidly disembarking troops; not available for the April landings, they were used at Suvla from August.

AWM A00882

Below

Barges landing supplies amid soldiers piling stores at X Beach, Cape Helles, in May 2015.

AWM P02647.029

Supply and transport on the Gallipoli Peninsula

Just as on the Western Front, the real difficulties were faced when transporting supplies from the advanced base (or the railheads on the Western Front) to the troops.[65] On Gallipoli, the first part of this process was disembarking the necessary goods at the advanced base. None of the beaches, which made up the advanced bases, was logistically suitable. Those at Helles and Anzac were narrow, with little room for storage, and were overcrowded.[66] The naval chief of staff complained about this after the August offensive had failed, and noted, 'The lack of space for safe storage in the vicinity of the beaches was frequently given as a reason for refusing to accept stores … and for requests to re-embark stores and beasts already landed.'[67] He particularly singled out the narrowness of Anzac Cove, believing that 'this is still a bar to the accumulation of a large reserve' in that sector.[68] The beaches at Suvla were large enough, but were too vulnerable to the enemy's artillery fire to be deemed satisfactory. The unsuitability of these beaches, combined with a lack of men for fatigues, meant that items could not be landed and stockpiled quickly enough. This in turn led to bottlenecks and serious delays in landing supplies.

Further adding to the delay was the confusion surrounding who was responsible for disembarking the items. Neither Britain's *Field Service Regulations* (1914), nor the *Manual of Combined Naval and Military Operations* (1913) clearly defined the boundaries of responsibility between the army and navy.[69] Moreover, in the case of the August offensive, the division of these duties differed between sectors. In the Helles and Anzac sectors, for example, where the advanced bases were already established and their staff experienced, the beach commandant – who acted as the IGC's representative – was responsible for disembarkation and any work on the beaches.[70] At Suvla, however, where there was a need to establish a new advanced base with minimal delay, GHQ adopted a different and considerably more complicated system. Rather than placing direct control under a beach commandant, and therefore within the realm of the IGC, GHQ instead decided to split it between two officers: one naval (the principal beach master) and the other military (principal military landing officer).[71] This decision, however, injected a level of confusion into the process of disembarkation at Suvla that was not present in the other sectors, and one that could have been avoided.[72]

Given the lack of suitable piers extending from the advanced bases, it was necessary again to trans-ship items into lighters upon their arrival at the peninsula. Being smaller than the supply ships, lighters could approach the piers and unload the goods. For this task, it was necessary to have an adequate number of lighters, as well as the requisite labour. Opinion as to whether there were sufficient lighters for the task was divided. The army believed there were not, while the navy was adamant that numbers were sufficient and that the problem lay with the military's capacity to clear and free them up for additional

Soldiers moving among the stores and equipment lining the full length of the narrow beach of Anzac Cove, looking south towards Hell Spit and Kabatepe, 1 August 1915. At left is the corner of No. 3 Depot, beyond which is the Ordnance Depot and stacks of ammunition. The piers have been stacked with boxes for protection from shrapnel as the numerous lighters and barges unload cargo.

Pack mules being loaded with cans of water on the beach at Anzac Cove for transport to the front line. In the left foreground crates of stores are stacked; on the right is a pile of fodder for the animals, along with timber discarded after unpacking stores and used later in constructing dugouts.

AWM C02147

work.[73] While they disagreed on this matter, both services agreed that there were not enough personnel available to undertake the difficult and exhausting work of manhandling the items from the lighters onto the piers, and thence onto the shore, where they were stockpiled and organised for distribution.[74]

Unlike the Western Front, or the MEF's rear bases in Egypt and on the Greek islands, there was very little civilian labour available for work on the Gallipoli Peninsula. In addition, the available labour could not be put to any practical use because workers refused to work while the beaches were being shelled.[75] This meant that troops desperately needed for the operations, and exhausted from a lack of rest, had to be employed instead. GHQ realised the problems associated with this – not least of which was the fact that it depleted the MEF's strength in the trenches – but the August offensive had been fought and had failed before any real solution could be found.[76]

Further hindering the disembarkation process were two elements outside the control of the MEF. Each allied beach (with its exposed stores and personnel) was vulnerable to Ottoman artillery fire. The war diary of the 40th Depot Unit of Supply clearly highlights the dangers faced on the beaches. This unit, which was responsible for transferring supplies from HMT *Edenmore* to lighters off Suvla Bay, noted that it was under shellfire almost every day in August.[77] This problem was unique to Gallipoli. Unlike their equivalent positions on the Western Front, the advanced bases at Gallipoli were constantly exposed to artillery fire.[78] To combat this, supplies were mostly disembarked at night, using darkness as a screen against Ottoman observation. Though this

A Turkish shell bursting near the beached SS *River Clyde* at V Beach, Cape Helles, during preparations for the British evacuation from the Helles sector, December 1915.

AWM H10393

Anzac Cove under shellfire from the Turkish artillery battery at 'the Olive Grove', summer 1915. The Turks at Kabatepe could observe daylight activity around the piers unloading stores in Anzac Cove. A shell is bursting near the ANZAC headquarters at the end of Watson's Pier.

AWM PS1494

was partially successful, it was only Turkish shortages of ammunition that prevented a complete breakdown of allied supplies on the beaches.[79]

The second and equally important element was the weather. With its exposed beaches, and its complete reliance on sea-borne supplies, the MEF's entire logistic chain was dependent on favourable weather. Fortunately for the MEF, the weather was generally good throughout the August offensive. But, as was proven in early October, had the August offensive progressed beyond the Sari Bair ridge and into its subsequent 'phases', the MEF would have only a nine-week window before the weather turned and wrought havoc on their advanced bases.[80]

Once disembarked at the beach, the various supplies were stockpiled at locations chosen by each corp's senior administrative officer, the deputy adjutant and quartermaster-general (DA&QMG).[81] Despite being responsible for all administrative arrangements in his sector, the DA&QMG's role was primarily managerial, and consisted largely of reporting to GHQ and co-ordinating the supply and transport arrangements of his respective divisions. The substantive arrangements for distributing items from the beaches to the front line were undertaken at the divisional level by the assistant adjutant and quartermaster-general (AA&QMG).[82] This officer, who controlled both the 'A' (personnel) and 'Q' (maintenance) functions of his formation, was not chosen on the basis of individual knowledge or expertise, but more by way of a rotational quota. Being the representative of both branches of the administrative staff, one AA&QMG was selected by the Deputy Quartermaster-General, and then next by the Deputy Adjutant-General. As such, this officer – the person responsible for ensuring that divisions received their supplies – did not necessarily have specific experience in 'Q' work (nor in 'A' work, for that matter).[83]

Despite all of the difficulties discussed above, the MEF was able to build up significant reserves prior to the August offensive. By mid-July a reserve of 24 days' rations for 45,000 men existed at Helles, and 23 days' rations for 25,000 men at Anzac.[84] By 23 July Helles had reached its target of 30 days' rations.[85] Reserves in the Anzac sector, however, were already dwindling by the end of the month. As the reserves grew at Helles, those at Anzac were depleted.[86] While the number of troops stationed at Anzac increased in preparation for the offensive, there was no proportional increase in supplies, so the reserves had to be used to meet daily usage. The depletion of reserves was not helped by an order on 3 August which put a ten-day freeze on sending supplies to Anzac and stipulated that the corps would instead live on the reserve already accumulated.[87] By 13 August the reserve at Anzac had reduced to nine days, compared with one month at Helles.[88] The troops in the Anzac sector were increasingly living a hand-to-mouth existence. The early accumulation of a reserve was also a priority at Suvla. It was planned to land seven days' supplies and forage for IX Corps as soon as possible.[89] Things did not go to plan, though, and one week passed before there was any accumulation ashore.[90] Their target still eluded them on 21 August.[91]

As stated earlier, logistics on Gallipoli were unique. Owing to the unsuitability of the terrain, the lack of roads, and a lack of fuel, there was no mechanised transport at Gallipoli, except for a small number of vehicles used by the British at Cape Helles.[92] Therefore, instead of employing supply columns (a fundamental element of supply and transport on the Western Front) to transport its requirements, the MEF had to rely almost solely on mules and men.[93] These, in effect, were obliged to take the place of the 3-ton motorised transport vehicles that were standard in British supply columns

Opposite

Anzac Cove, looking south, showing the damage caused by a heavy storm on 17 November 1915. Barges were washed up on the shore, and piers were extensively damaged; a long section of trestle construction at Watson's Pier, in the centre, was torn away when a lighter broke through it. The stockpiled stores and supplies were subsequently moved to North Beach or higher up onto the constructed terraces.

AWM P05227.007

on the Western Front.[94] This was ineffective, as there were not enough mules, and units could scarcely afford to release men from the trenches for fatigue work.

The number of mules allotted to a formation was based on the number of men who had to be supplied.[95] For the operations at Anzac and Suvla in August, GHQ determined that supply arrangements should be calculated to ensure that mules made a maximum of two trips per day.[96] There were 950 mules at Anzac prior to the offensive, but by the time the attack commenced these mules, and particularly their drivers, were exhausted.[97] They had worked continually for weeks, with practically no rest, preparing the Anzac sector for the offensive. The drivers were, according to one officer of the Indian Mule Cart Train, 'done to a turn'.[98] It was intended to land an additional 3500 mules at Anzac and Suvla on 7–8 August to supplement this transport.[99] This intention, though, did not become a reality. None were landed on 7 August owing to Ottoman shellfire, and only 541 were disembarked the following

In preparation for the increasing number of troops at Anzac for the August offensive, soldiers haul a steel water-storage tank to a terrace near the summit of Plugge's Plateau, 25 July 1915. By the end of July, most wells at Anzac had begun to dry up and troops were dependent upon water barges towed from Alexandria and Malta for their meagre supply of one-third of a gallon (1.5 litres) per day.

AWM G01117

day.[100] Thus, in the early stages of the offensive, the MEF was only able to land 15 per cent of its target transport. The deficiency had to be met by the troops, who were required to carry supplies while at the same time fighting desperately to establish and consolidate their positions.[101] This task was beyond their capabilities. The result was a complete breakdown in the logistic process, and, by extension, of offensive operations at Suvla. In effect, without sufficient numbers of mules, there was 'no means of transporting food, water, or ammunition'.[102]

Aside from their deficiency in number, the task allotted to the mules was made increasingly difficult by Turkish fire and a lack of water and forage for the animals. A mule convoy was a particularly valuable and vulnerable target to a Turkish gunner, and losses sustained from gunfire throughout the August offensive were significant.[103] The pressure on the mules greatly increased once the hot weather arrived and the local wells dried up.[104] Watering the mules became particularly difficult. At Anzac, the drivers initially scraped small holes in the ground to provide for their beasts, but the amount of water produced by this method was insufficient, and it quickly became brackish.[105] The drivers were eventually given permission to draw water at night from a well south of Brighton Beach, but this was not suitable, as the work of transporting supplies also took place at night.[106] It was a similar situation at Suvla, where, at the end of the month, the deputy director of veterinary services (DDVS) reported that the water arrangements for the mules were still inadequate.[107]

While there were some positive reports at a local level, these were generally limited to those within close proximity to the beach. When viewed from a broader perspective, there can be little doubt that the difficulties faced during disembarkation, stockpiling and distribution resulted in a near-complete breakdown of the logistic system during the 'first phase' of the August offensive. This, at least, was the opinion of the IGC, who, after analysing the array of reports (both positive and negative) received throughout the offensive, informed the War Office that the transport system was a shambles, and concluded that as a whole the supply situation during the August offensive was 'unsatisfactory'.[108] Evidence for this view is ample. Water supply, particularly at Suvla, failed.[109] Similarly, while a lack of water at Chunuk Bair did not directly lead to its loss on 10 August, the war diaries of those units concerned clearly show that it hampered operations and the fighting ability of the troops.[110] It is doubtful, therefore, whether the MEF would have been able to supply itself as it advanced across the peninsula to Maidos (present day Eceabat) in accord with the operational objectives of the August offensive. There were simply too few men and animals to transport supplies across such extended distances and difficult terrain. Lord Kitchener realised this, and informed Prime Minister Asquith that obtaining proper lines of communication 'is the main difficulty in carrying out successful operations on the Peninsula'.[111]

Logistics of medical evacuation

It should be realised that logistics is a two-way process. While supplies are being pushed forward, there is also a need to collect the wounded and evacuate them for medical treatment. It is noteworthy, however, that while troops might legitimately expect to receive prompt evacuation if wounded, a failure in this regard has little direct bearing on the ability of a force to achieve its objectives.[112] Put simply, not enough of those who are evacuated return to have any significant impact on immediate operations.

In planning the medical evacuation for the August offensive, many improvements were made on the original model that had failed during the landings in April 1915. Arrangements for hospitals were based on an estimate of 30,000 casualties, and while these numbers were not met, the system was much more efficient than that employed in April.[113] The second improvement was an increase in the number of ships to accommodate and transport the wounded. A total of 15 hospital ships, nine transports converted into temporary ambulance carriers (known as 'black ships') and a range of small craft were employed in evacuating 30,890 cases from the peninsula between 6 and 21 August, inclusive.[114]

The process of evacuating the wounded was similar to that employed in April. After being collected by a regimental stretcher-bearer, casualties

The crowded evacuation of wounded soldiers from Anzac Cove, summer 1915. Those able to stand or sit were transported to hospital ships on the steam launch *Keraunos*.

AWM C02679

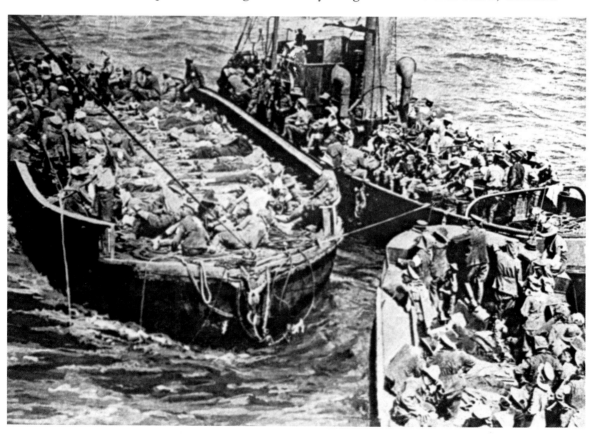

would make their way, via a regimental aid post (RAP), advanced dressing station, and main dressing station, to a casualty clearing station (CCS) on the beach.[115] This entire process was hindered by a lack of medical personnel. The routes used when removing the wounded to the beach were the same as those used for supply and transport purposes. The routes were therefore perpetually congested and movement was slow.[116] Once they reached the CCSs, the navy and GHQ took responsibility for evacuating the wounded from the peninsula.[117] This was generally done during the day so as not to interfere with the disembarkation of men, guns, and stores, which generally occurred at night. But it was not always possible to get the wounded men to the ships.[118] No casualties, for example, were evacuated before midnight on 6 August. This caused severe congestion on the beaches, and further delayed the landing of supplies. The reason for this was a lack of small vessels to transport the wounded from the beach to the waiting ships.[119] Aside from the first few days, however, when the system struggled to come to grips with the situation and the scale of casualties, the evacuation of the wounded during the August offensive was a logistic success. Apart from slowing down anchorages, and at times congesting the beaches and supply routes, the evacuation of the wounded during the August offensive was largely carried out during daylight hours, and therefore had only a minimal influence on the logistic and battlefield operations.

Conclusion

Was the August offensive a logistically viable operation of war? The simple answer is no. The entire Line of Communication from the UK to the Gallipoli Peninsula was an administrative nightmare, and was hindered by a lack of facilities. It was a lengthy process, and was organised by too many people. The combination of all these elements resulted in considerable delays, which meant that many items requested were often no longer required by the time they arrived at the Dardanelles.[120] The real problem, however, was experienced once supplies reached the peninsula. The supply and transport system was incapable of disembarking, stockpiling and then distributing the necessary daily requirements, and in effect broke down during the fight for the Sari Bair ridge and the consolidation of Suvla Bay. With insufficient numbers of personnel for fatigues, and a deficiency in mules for transport, it would have required a miracle for the supply and transport arrangements to cope with any advance across the peninsula. And while the medical evacuation process worked throughout August, this was at a stage when the operations stretched little more than a kilometre from the beaches. One is left to ponder whether this system, like the supply and transport system, could have coped – especially given its shortage of medical personnel – with 'successful' offensive operations requiring logistic support for major advances across the peninsula.

Part 4

Legacies

Chapter 13

Walking the ground

Gallipoli revisited, 1919

Janda Gooding

In early 1919, the Australian Historical Mission, a small team led by Australia's official war correspondent Charles Bean, visited Gallipoli. The Mission's main aims were to resolve some of the enduring questions relating to the events of 1915 for Bean's proposed official war history, to collect historical artefacts for a national Australian war museum, and to document for all Australians, through photography and painting, the battlefield landscape and history of the Gallipoli campaign.[1] This chapter focuses on the latter aim of the Mission, the visual collection – and specifically, on a series of photographs by the official photographer Hubert Wilkins and paintings by the official artist George Lambert, all related to the costly Australian attack at the Nek during the August offensive. The work of the Australian Historical Mission illuminates Charles Bean's direction of the official photographers and artists, and how insights into Bean's pursuit of his ideal of 'truth' can be found in the Memorial's collection of images.

By October 1917, Australia's official war correspondent Charles Bean had already formulated his principles for the gathering of material that would become the core collection of a future Australian national war museum.[2] He identified three kinds of records that would help people understand Australia's part in the war: the written record in diaries, letters and official documents; the visual record, comprising photographs, paintings, sketches and moving film footage; and relics collected from the field, still bearing the marks of battle. Bean's idea was that people would need to view all these records to gain the best understanding of what had happened during the war, especially those aspects of soldiers' experiences that were so remote from ordinary civilian life. He held a conviction that 'truth' was not just about providing the most

Previous pages

A British soldier visits a comrade's grave at sunset on the cliffs above Cape Helles, Gallipoli, 1915. A photograph taken by the official British Admiralty photographer Ernest Brooks.

AWM G00363

accurate written report possible: each item in its unique way would reveal something of the essence of an event, and, when combined together in a great museum, they would present Australians with a comprehensive and powerful account of the war.

Official artists were encouraged to paint reliable representations of the landscapes across which Australians fought and to show accurate details of events. But at the same time Bean wanted them to present their own interpretation of the drama and emotional intensity of war; if they wanted to change a small historical detail to deliver a more powerful message, he supported them. A key point to note about paintings produced for the official war art scheme was that Bean believed that 'emotional truth' carried weight as evidence, because it was just as important for Australians who would visit the museum to get an insight into what people might have felt as it was to understand the details of specific actions.

However, photography was something different. Bean felt that Australians should be able to rely implicitly on the veracity of official photographs as evidence of places and the events in which Australian troops were involved. Inevitably, when the Australian official photographer Frank Hurley created composite photographs to represent the awesome nature of modern warfare, Bean's ideal for scrupulous honesty in all aspects of the official photographic record was severely challenged. His preference was that the photographs convey 'the plain simple truth', pure and unadulterated.[3]

In 1915, when Charles Bean was Australia's official correspondent on Gallipoli, there had been limited opportunities to systematically photograph allied soldiers' activities and few chances to learn what the Turks could have seen from their positions. Events of the August offensive were no exception: although the British Admiralty official photographer, Ernest Brooks, was on hand, the taking of photographs at the Nek was so dangerous that it meant all he could do was hold a camera above the trench, click, and hope that something of interest would be captured. When Anzac forces abandoned Gallipoli, many details of the campaign remained unclear. Indeed, some things would prove to be unknowable. Record-keeping had been inadequate, and apart from the many photographs taken by Bean, and others he collected from soldiers in the field, the visual record was initially very limited.[4]

Examining and recounting Australia's part in the war was to become Charles Bean's life's work, and he laboured tirelessly to gather as much information as possible. He built up a web of details, cross-checking stories and events against records of dates, times and geographic features, as well as using operation orders and reports to gain insights into commanders' actions and their outcomes. But Bean recognised that images would play an important role in making the war visible to Australians, and the establishment in 1917 of the Official War Art and War Photography schemes was part of his overall project to assemble research material for later interpretation.

From early 1917 onwards, war artists were appointed to document the activities of Australians fighting in Europe and the Middle East. George Lambert served as an official war artist with the Australian Light Horse in Egypt, Palestine, and the Sinai Peninsula in early 1918. Despite his earlier reputation as a society portrait artist with a flamboyant public persona, Lambert was an inspired choice. He immediately felt at home travelling with Australian mounted units, in whose company he felt both humility and admiration. He wrote that he was surrounded by 'magnificent men & real top hole Australian horses' and all around him the light and landscape of the Middle East presented him with opportunities for 'pictures by the yard'.[5]

To assist him to explore the specific landscapes of significance to Australia's military history, he was guided everywhere by veterans from battles such as Romani, Beersheba, Gaza or El Arish. For Lambert, the clear and bright little paintings he made were a tribute to 'the brave men of all ranks out there …[and] the wonderful military feats they have achieved'.[6] Lambert did not have an opportunity to witness Australian troops in battle, but he did learn an important lesson. He realised that veterans would only value and respect his paintings if he got the details right. Whether it was the topographical accuracy of the old battlefield, the uniforms worn, or the light at the time of day when an incident happened, Lambert knew that these were crucial components that he needed to represent correctly. However, he also went a step further and concentrated on trying to grasp the emotion of an event. At Beersheba for instance, the site of the celebrated mounted charge by the Australian Light Horse on 31 October 1917, he borrowed an officer's horse and charged at full gallop across the plain to experience something of the excitement of the charge and, as he said, 'to get the spirit of the thing'.[7]

The Australian-born Hubert Wilkins had a dramatically different experience as an official photographer on the Western Front from mid-1917. As part of a small team of photographers, he criss-crossed the areas where Australians were fighting, taking photos of anything he felt could be of interest – men going into and coming out of battle, corpse-littered battlefields, equipment, billets, camps, key events and important people. This was to be a comprehensive collection that Bean intended would record the 'sacrifices, and the sacred memory of the great men'; the photographs would ultimately be a monument to their memory.[8]

Wilkins was already an experienced cameraman and reporter before his appointment as a war photographer in 1917. He had been employed by the London newsreel company Gaumont in 1912 to report on the Balkan War from the Turkish side; immediately after that, in 1913, he joined an expedition to the Arctic as photographer. After hearing about the war, Wilkins enlisted in the AIF in May 1917. He was commissioned as a second lieutenant, initially as a pilot in the Australian Flying Corps, but by August he was serving at I Anzac Corps headquarters on the Western Front. Roaming around the allied front lines in the Ypres area, Wilkins was frequently exposed to danger. In September and October 1917 he was in the front line with fighting troops at Polygon Wood, Broodseinde Ridge and Zonnebeke, taking every opportunity to record Australian troops in action. It was during this time that he was recommended for a Military Cross for his exemplary courage and, as the recommendation noted, 'procuring invaluable pictures of the front line during the period of fighting in Polygon Wood ... [and] pressing daily through barrages, without relief, during a period when almost all other officers engaged in work of equal danger were relieved.'[9]

In April 1918 he was appointed as Australian official photographer, charged with making 'an accurate and complete record of the fighting and other activities of the AIF'. Thereafter he worked closely with Bean. The only Australian official photographer to be decorated, in the following year Wilkins was awarded a Bar to his Military Cross. On at least six occasions during a two-month period in 1918, Wilkins went 'over the top' with attacking troops. On 29 September during a German counter-attack at the Hindenburg Line, he even rallied and led a group of inexperienced American troops whose officers had been killed.[10] Wilkins was in the thick of it most days, and he came to the conclusion that 'human beings seemed insignificant in the midst of all this [and] it didn't seem possible that men could go through it and live.'[11]

The work of the Australian official artists and photographers from 1917 to the end of 1918 represented invaluable information about Australians at war, but the events at Gallipoli were always at the back of Charles Bean's mind. On 12 November 1918, the day after Germany signed the armistice and the war ended, Bean was in London to seek formal approval to return to Australia via Gallipoli. He asked permission to take an artist and a photographer to help him complete a thorough survey of the battlefields. He selected men he knew and trusted: Hubert Wilkins and George Lambert were his first choices. They understood Bean's working methods and shared his commitment to accuracy in their work. Through his fine documentary work, Wilkins had demonstrated his determination to make reliable and truthful photographs, 'so accurate', Bean later wrote, 'that they could be, and often were, relied on as historical evidence'.[12] Bean offered him the trip to Gallipoli partly as a reward for his hard work.[13] And although there was a long list of Australian artists to choose from, Bean was insistent that George Lambert be appointed. He considered Lambert one of Australia's finest landscape and figure painters, and Bean knew that he would make an outstanding contribution to the pictorial collection.

Bean was keen to gather as many eyewitness accounts as possible, and getting a Turkish perspective was particularly important. Passing through Constantinople on the way to Gallipoli, he requested from the Turkish General Staff the assistance of an experienced Turkish officer to walk the ground with him and help in the investigations. He was assigned Major Zeki Bey, who had commanded the 1st Battalion of the 57th Turkish Regiment (19th Division) on Gallipoli, and subsequently commanded the 21st Regiment, seeing almost continuous action against Australian and New Zealand forces from the time of the ANZAC landing in April until the evacuation in December 1915. Major Zeki stayed with Bean's party for over a week. As he and Bean wandered together across the old Anzac area, conversing in broken French, Bean was able to get a fuller understanding of specific incidents, Turkish troop dispositions and activities, and their command structure in 1915.

The Australian Historical Mission spent just over three weeks on Gallipoli. The peninsula had been abandoned by allied forces three years earlier. During the war, there had been few opportunities to bury bodies properly, and in the intervening years the remote Anzac and Suvla areas had been scavenged thoroughly by wild dogs. In many places, human remains lay everywhere. An Australian graves registration unit had arrived only a month before the Historical Mission and was doing its best to locate Australian bodies, identify them and reinter them in marked graves. The work was grisly and depressing. The sad atmosphere of the place affected everyone, with someone even renaming Plugge's Plateau, 'Spooks Plateau'.[14]

The men of the Historical Mission spent most of their days surveying the battlefields, making sketches, taking notes, drafting maps and taking a large number of photographs. Wilkins worked alongside Bean, and photographed places that Bean considered important to Australia's military history. The

Members of the Australian Historical Mission at lunch on Hill 60, 22 February 1919. From left: Lieutenant Herbert Buchanan; Turkish officer Major Zeki Bey; official war photographer Captain Hubert Wilkins; official war correspondent (later official historian) Captain Charles Bean; and official war artist Captain George Lambert.

AWM A05258

camera Wilkins used took delicate glass-plate negatives; although by today's standards it appears cumbersome and unsophisticated, it produced beautifully sharp and nuanced images.

Bean directed Wilkins in his choice of subjects. On 17 February, their first full day in the old Anzac area, the party walked from the beach at Anzac Cove up to the Baby 700 feature, noting significant sites on the way. Bean pointed out the Turks' shallow trenches that Australians had came across on their first rush up from Ari Burnu to Plugge's Plateau on 25 April. Wilkins photographed the shore from this point to show the view the Turks would have had of Australians landing and approaching the position.

The photographic record being compiled was intended to document the marks and evidence that remained on the landscape. These would be the clues to help others interpret events; and by locating an event or an object in an actual landscape, Wilkins's photographs provided supporting evidence for Bean's historical interpretations. The theory was that once people could see where something happened, they might more easily understand how it had happened. This was important at the Nek, where so many Australian Light Horse soldiers had died in the first light of dawn on 7 August 1915. When he walked across that saddle of ground for the first time, Bean was surprised at the small size of the battlefield which was much narrower than he had imagined.

Looking from Turkish trenches near German Officers' Trench towards the Australian trenches, 24 February 1919.

Photographer: George Hubert Wilkins, AWM G01940

Wilkins photographed the Nek area from all angles, taking particular care to show what the Turks could have seen. From Baby 700 he was able to show the strength of the Turkish machine-gun positions that had been a crucial factor in stopping the Australian charge at the Nek. An attack on German Officers' Trench during the night of 6 August had failed, and Australian light horsemen met the full force of enfilading machine-gun fire from that position too. Bean remembered the Turkish fire as sounding like 'one continuous roaring tempest'.[15] One observer described how the Turkish machine-guns 'just poured out lead and our fellows went down like corn before a scythe'.[16] Providing photographs of the gun positions would allow Australians to imagine what it might have been like.

Human bones still lay on the surface of the landscape as more tangible reminders of the cost of the campaign, and they became an important motif in many of Wilkins's photographs. The brief ceasefire on 24 May 1915 had allowed the bodies of many men from both sides to be buried. But those who died in no man's land later in the campaign lay where they fell until the graves registration unit started its gruesome work. At the Nek, the unit 'found and buried more than three hundred Australians in that strip the size of three tennis courts', Bean later wrote.[17]

Conveying to Australians the physical landscape at the Nek would be important to assist their understanding of the events. To capture more accurately the wide sweep of the landscape, and to illustrate the dominance of Baby 700 and Battleship Hill, Wilkins created a double-plate panoramic photograph. He positioned his camera just behind the Australian lines, looking across to the recently erected Turkish memorial that now marked the opposing trenches, from 15 metres to 50 metres distant. Even though the panorama takes an expansive view, the narrowness of the piece of no man's land between the trenches is very evident.

But as in so many of Wilkins's photographs, it is detail in the foreground that reveals the tragedy of the place. His photograph makes it possible to see inside the Australian trenches, where the men had waited before leaping out

Looking across the Nek from the Australian trenches towards Baby 700, 17 February 1919. A Turkish monument is in the background and a whitened skull and bones are in the foreground. Combined image from a two-part panorama of double glass half-plate negatives.

Photographer: G.H. Wilkins, AWM G02013P (composed from AWM G02013A and G02013B)

in their mad dash. Fragments of clothing are still caught in the parapets, and just beyond them, bleached bones and a skull are physical reminders of the great loss of both Turkish and Australian life at this place.

Wilkins was also asked to photograph the opposing Australian and Turkish trenches that had been the scene of bloody, close-quarters fighting during the four-day-long battle at Lone Pine in August 1915. He took numerous photographs, but two most effectively represented the nature of the subterranean struggle there. The first shows the trenches from the Australian side. Here men had fought a ferocious, pitched battle for days, dodging Turkish bombs, occasionally even catching and hurling them back at the enemy.

In the second photograph, taken on the same day, Wilkins emphasises the proximity of the opposing trenches by using human figures to give a sense of scale: five members of the Historical Mission stand astride the tiny strip of no man's land dividing the Turkish and Australian improvised bombing posts.

The photographs that Wilkins made on Gallipoli in 1919 provided visual evidence of the military events and lent support to the official history later written by Charles Bean. Wilkins also repeatedly tried to show what a soldier might have seen. By taking a soldier's perspective, his photographs mirrored Bean's own approach to military history through an emphasis on the front-line soldiers' experiences, and bound the photographic and the historical accounts into a cohesive and consistent narrative. Even though by

The remains of trenches and overhead cover at Lone Pine where Australian and Turkish soldiers fought intense bombing duels. A Turkish memorial, which marks the spot where the Turks halted the Anzac advance, is on the left, and Turkish officer Major Zeki Bey is standing on the skyline to the right of the monument, February 1919.

Photographer: G.H. Wilkins, AWM G01939

1919 nature had started to reclaim the scarred earth and the eroded trenches were subsiding, the signs of battle were still everywhere. As Bean intended, Wilkins's Gallipoli photographs stand as an eyewitness record of the traces of battle that remained on the landscape. His enduring images would help ensure that Australians never forgot these events.

Apart from developing and printing up his glass-plate negatives, Wilkins's work was largely done when he left Gallipoli. For George Lambert the work was only just beginning, and with the prospect of commissions for large paintings, it would continue for many years. Bean had already promised Lambert at least two major commissions: one to depict the Anzac landing on 25 April, and the other to show the charge of the Third Light Horse Brigade at the Nek on 7 August 1915. It was important that these large studio paintings presented factual information, but Bean was equally concerned that they conveyed the emotional intensity, bravery and tragedy of the events.

While on Gallipoli, as part of his preparation for the later paintings, Lambert needed to capture the light, atmosphere and feel of the place. The small oil sketches he produced on the spot were finished paintings in their own right and not necessarily studies for the later battle paintings. They served as 'memory notes' to remind him of the colour, light and character of the landscape. He sketched and painted directly onto small wood panels, often allowing the wood grain to remain as part of his composition. The weather

was bleak and cold; there was even a substantial snowfall just as the Historical Mission arrived. Lambert's hands and fingers were freezing, yet he produced extraordinarily fine work, such as the little panel painting *The Sphinx from Plugge's Plateau*. He painted the panel in three morning sessions, sitting, as he described himself, 'perched up on the edge of what you would call a precipice and wait[ing] for the sun to shine & occasionally getting in a dash now and again.'[18]

On their first full day in the field, Lambert and Wilkins both chose to record a view of the Nek from the same vantage point behind the old Australian lines. As Wilkins took his photographs and moved on towards Baby 700, Lambert set himself up to make a quick oil sketch of the scene – *The Nek, Walker's Ridge, site of the charge of the Light Horse*. A fierce wind forced him to work very quickly and he lay in areas of sky, ground, and churned earth where the trenches remained. Lambert described the landscape as a 'wonderful setting to the tragedy' but the bleached bones lying scattered across the ground reminded him of the terrible sacrifice.[19] He accentuated the melancholy mood by painting a lone soldier looking across the narrow field, and at his feet, a skull and human thigh bone poke out of the earth.

Lambert's desire for authenticity was paramount. On 6 March he rose before dawn so he could be painting at Lone Pine at the same time of day as the charge at the Nek.[20] Although the wintry season in February 1919

George Lambert, *The Sphinx from Plugge's Plateau*, 18 February and 4–5 March 1919, oil and pencil on wood panel, 24.8 x 35.6 cm.

AWM ART02846

was very different to that in August 1915, he felt he had the right light for painting the scene; but in 1919 the ground was still littered with human bones that stood out white in the early morning light. The jackals, as he described them, were 'chorusing their hate' and he commented that 'the worst feature of this after battle work is that the silent hills & valleys sit stern, unmoved callous of the human and busy only in growing bush, and sliding earth to hide the scars left by the war disease.'[21]

Lambert's mood was sombre and made more so by the presence of both the human remains and the constant labour of the graves registration unit proceeding alongside the Historical Mission. He wrote to his wife, 'The dead or rather their bones spoil it of course and the melancholy is ready for him who lets his thoughts wander.'[22] Finding the place sad yet very beautiful, he commented 'I cannot tell you how pleased I am at getting clear of this graveyard, beautiful as it is, nor can I explain how satisfied I am to have done what work I have done.'[23]

George Lambert, *The Nek, Walker's Ridge, site of the charge of the Light Horse*, 17 February 1919, oil on wood panel, 24.1 x 35.6 cm.

AWM ART02856

Lambert's field work produced just over 30 small paintings, watercolours, and drawings; by comparison, the photographic material created during the Historical Mission was comprehensive. Hubert Wilkins made about 200 glass-plate negatives and Bean's own photographs numbered about 65. In addition, Bean filled notebooks with topographical sketch maps and made

detailed diary entries. Maps made on the spot, and those gathered from other sources and checked against the landscape, added another layer of intricate knowledge of the land across which Australian soldiers fought. This collection of images formed a core collection in the war museum that Charles Bean proposed and helped to found. Paintings, photographs and the relics collected in 1919 were extensively used in the years immediately after the war to demonstrate to audiences the powerful stories associated with Australians at Gallipoli.

Hubert Wilkins's photographs became essential aids to Bean when he commenced writing the first volumes of the official history. When he arrived back in Australia in late 1919, Bean had Wilkins's photographs pasted into large albums and began annotating them. Anyone who has worked with the research materials compiled by Bean and his assistants understands how particular he was in arranging, indexing and cross-referencing the working material. He worked on Wilkins's photographs with the same scientific precision, plotting key geographic features, angles and distances, and the location of specific units and military objectives across the surfaces of the photographs. As he wrote his epic multi-volume account of Australians at war, he used these photographs as primary references.[24] Some became the basis for sketch maps and diagrams, while others were reproduced as part of the account of specific actions published in the official history.

Like all thorough historians, Bean knew that his written version of any event must be congruent with the geography of the landscape. Words and images had to match and he never relied solely on one source. As he wrote up the relevant part of his history, he often checked eyewitness statements against photographs. The images provided him with visual evidence of the landscape and helped to confirm people's accounts of an event. In this way, Wilkins's photographs served as frameworks on which to reconstruct a story.

Bean had always considered art to be a central component of the prospective museum, as art had the capacity to unite strong storytelling with powerfully emotive symbolism. In 1922, when the fledgling Australian War Memorial put up temporary displays in Melbourne, an important feature was the massive painting by George Lambert of the Anzac landing on Gallipoli.[25] And in 1925, when the museum transferred to Sydney, Lambert's second large painting, *The charge of the 3rd Light Horse Brigade at the Nek, 7 August 1915*, was a celebrated new addition.

During his visit to Gallipoli in 1919, Lambert painted only one small study at the Nek; but he had clearly been thinking about the composition for this large painting as the Historical Mission left Gallipoli. During the next few weeks of travelling towards Cairo, he made a rough sketch of the main theme of the painting on the back of a panel. Another study in pencil, completed in London, gives an indication of what the final painting would look like.[26] He started to sketch some figures that he would use in the final composition and

George Lambert, *The charge of the 3rd Light Horse Brigade at the Nek, 7 August 1915,* painted in 1924, oil on canvas, 152.5 x 305.7 cm.

AWM ART07965

asked Charles Bean what men looked like when bullets struck them. Bean described how their 'knees seemed to go like string' or they crumpled and sank forward before sliding onto the ground.[27] Lambert made other enquiries about the uniforms and kit worn on the day and was given details, such as that many of the men had worn hats or sun helmets and were in summer-weight breeches or shorts. Shirtsleeves were rolled up or cut off above the elbow, and many wore white cloth armbands and white patches sewn on their backs so they could be recognised by their comrades in the early morning half-light.[28] All these details would be essential in producing the final painting.

For his composition, Lambert adopted the viewpoint of a soldier – one reviewer said it was a soldier of the second line – just on the edge of the Australian trenches. In front, men are falling, spun around by the force of the bullets, as someone noted, 'like marionettes jerked into eternity'.[29] Others lie wounded or dead on the field, while only a metre or so in front of the Turkish front line, men are being shot down. A man on his knees in the centre right of the picture looks stunned and disbelieving as he raises a wounded hand to his head. In the middle of the painting, smoke and dust kicked up by the Turkish rifle and machine-gun fire adds to the sense of confusion. It is a scene of terrible carnage, made more powerful by the dominant blood-red colours of the earth and the churned-up ground. Lambert deliberately painted the bodies and the earth in the same tone, to make them nearly indistinguishable in the dawn light. From his own experience of walking the ground on Gallipoli, he was only too aware that the earth had literally swallowed up many of these men and obliterated their identity.

The picture brought together elements of the Gallipoli story in ways that other visual material and objects could not, and it was tremendously popular: it captured the entire sweep of the story, and the enormous canvas created a dramatic and emotional experience for veterans and general visitors alike. It clearly satisfied many viewers as an authentic representation of the charge at the Nek, despite the fact that the artist had not been an eyewitness. Lambert believed it was 'the biggest job of [his] life' and he wrote to Bean that it epitomised 'the Gallipoli spirit' of the Australian forces.[30] The painting went on show to the public when the Australian War Memorial Museum opened in Sydney in April 1925, and Bean, Wilkins and Lambert were all in attendance to see thousands of people start to move through the displays. Over 8000 people visited the displays on one day in the week after the museum opened.[31]

Many items collected by the Historical Mission, or created as a result of it, were on show by 1925, and they still remain central and iconic features of the Australian War Memorial's First World War displays. Lambert's paintings are featured in the Gallipoli gallery, and alongside them are examples of Wilkins's photographs taken on the peninsula in 1919. Objects picked up by the Historical Mission as they walked the ground are also on view, including logs retrieved from the overhead cover of the Turkish trenches at Lone Pine. One of the salvaged lifeboats from the Anzac landing was shipped back to Australia and is currently displayed as a highlight of the Memorial's Orientation Gallery.[32] Gathered from the beaches, trenches, ridges, and valleys around the Anzac area, these are all part of the evidence that was collected to help answer some of the lingering riddles concerning Australia's role in the Gallipoli campaign.

Bean was well aware that no single narrative could tell the whole story of the war. The museum would engage and attract people if it told not one story, but multiple stories, each contributing a particular aspect of the overall narrative. Whether it was a photograph of the battle site or a painting bringing together many stories into one cohesive whole, each had its own truth that would help Australians remember, understand, and reconcile themselves to the tragic events of Gallipoli.

Like all primary source material, the Australian War Memorial's collection remains open to new interpretations, and its continuing use in publications and exhibitions is clear evidence that the collection has remained relevant for successive generations. Surely its continued presence in the permanent displays of the Memorial indicates that, as Charles Bean intended, it has become a lasting memorial to the tragedy of war, as well as to the achievements and sacrifices of Australian servicemen and women.

Chapter 14

Gallipoli
Foreshadowing future conflicts

Robert O'Neill

In this chapter I intend to examine some of the significant lessons and consequences of the Gallipoli campaign. Shifting the focus from the actions of Australian, New Zealand, British, French, Indian, Newfoundland, Turkish and German soldiers and sailors and their commanders in those hard-fought operations, this chapter will look at five of the broader policy issues raised by the campaign. They are all perennial problems in military interventions and thus have continuing resonance and application to recent conflicts and wars in which we are currently involved. How we handle these challenges today and in the future will exercise a powerful influence on our future fortunes, both as nations and as individuals.

I have been studying military history for most of my working life, and two conclusions stand out very clearly: first, if you lose a war, you suffer, often acutely and for a long time; second, if you start a war which you then lose, your fate will be made all the more excruciating by the revenge-taking and exultation in moral superiority that the victors will be free to indulge in. Let me now proceed to look at each of these five issues, how they were dealt with in 1914–15, and how they relate to strategic choices of the 21st century.

1. Military assistance to states with strategic leverage: how Britain and Germany built the seaward defences of the Dardanelles in 1909–15, and what profit it brought them

All the major European powers could see the strategic importance of Turkey in the late nineteenth and early twentieth centuries. To the Russians, Turkey was the guardian and controller of their sea route from the Black Sea ports to the wealth that could be earned by their exports on world markets. For the Germans, Turkey was a means of throttling Russia should the need arise. Turkey was also a land bridge to the Persian Gulf, a conduit for wealth, strategic power and political influence to flow to Germany, aided by strategic investments such as the Berlin to Baghdad railway. For France, Turkey was a potential ally in supporting the Russians, both by limiting German influence in the Near and Middle East in peace and by applying direct pressure in war.

For Britain, Turkey's importance was declining but it was still worth some investment of money and effort to fend off worse scenarios before 'the sick man of Europe' was swept away and replaced by some other power which might prove hostile to British interests, including access to oil supplies from the Persian Gulf. Also the thought of a controlling British hand on the Dardanelles in times of tension was attractive to some politicians in Westminster, despite its illusory nature. Winston Churchill, even while President of the Board of Trade in 1908–09, took a particularly keen interest in the Turkey that emerged from the revolt of the Young Turks, led by Enver Pasha.

Perceptively, as early as 1909, Churchill had sought out and made the acquaintance of Enver. It is perhaps significant that their meeting took place in Germany, at the German army's Imperial manoeuvres near Würzburg. Thereafter Churchill took the trouble to maintain personal contact with Enver, and visited him in Constantinople in the summer of 1911. But the record of Churchill's writings indicates that he did not discover until too late that Enver was a convinced Germanophile, who intended to take Turkey into partnership with the Germany in the event of a major war, regardless of British blandishments. Another relevant event of that summer was the signing of a contract for the construction of two battleships for the Turkish navy by Armstrongs in Britain over the following two years. This project had been approved not long before Churchill succeeded McKenna at the Admiralty.

Churchill, when he became First Lord of the Admiralty in September 1911, could see the dangers that the Turks would pose to the balance of power in a war-divided Europe if they sided with Germany and Austria-Hungary. He took special pains in the pre-war years to try to dissuade the Ottoman Empire from joining with the central powers. He chose to offer the carrot rather than the stick.

The new First Lord, having taken the initiative to switch the key fuel of the Royal Navy from coal to oil, understood very clearly the importance of secure access to supplies from the Persian Gulf and the ability of the Turks to impede it. This was a huge change, transforming the strategic importance of the Middle East not just for Britain but for the whole world. Churchill sought to protect these assets by strengthening political relations with Turkey, particularly by continuing the policy of his predecessor, McKenna, of providing an admiral and supporting staff to command the Turkish navy and drive it towards modernisation. This naval mission, whose strength built up to some 30 members, was in operation for nearly six years, the last three of which were on Churchill's watch at the Admiralty. It had been led by Rear Admirals Gamble (1909–10), Williams (1910–12) and Limpus (1912–14).

Between 1909 and 1915 the British naval mission transformed an antiquated and poorly administered Ottoman navy into a recognisably modern, well administered and supported force, with several new warships and hundreds of newly trained technical personnel to its credit. The most vulnerable element in this supportive relationship was the construction of the two Turkish battleships in British shipyards, to be delivered in July 1914. While the ship builders were able to meet their deadlines, Churchill could not let them go to a potential enemy power just as a major war was about to erupt. Widespread public hostility towards Britain erupted across Turkey because these ships had been paid for by public subscription.[1]

The most important contribution that the British naval mission made to Turkey's maritime defences from the perspective of the Dardanelles campaign was in the fields of mine warfare and coastal defence. The Turks had mined the Narrows during the Balkan Wars of 1912–13. The mines were not very

The supreme symbol of British naval power, the Royal Navy battleship HMS *Queen Elizabeth* in Mudros Harbour, Lemnos, March 1915. With a fully loaded displacement of 36,500 tons, a speed of 24 knots and equipped with eight 15-inch guns, this super-dreadnought was the most modern warship in the world and the first British vessel of its class to be powered by oil instead of coal. As flagship, the *Queen Elizabeth* participated in the naval bombardment of Turkish defences on Gallipoli from February to May 1915.

AWM H12931

good. Many of them broke from their moorings under the force of the 4–6 knot current which ran through the Narrows. In 1913 Admiral Limpus, the then head of the British naval mission, commissioned the replacement of the old mines with new and more powerful munitions and moorings. Stores and workshops for the mines were built and technical personnel were trained. New lines of mines were designed to bar the Straits, and Limpus also planned the installation of torpedo tubes to destroy any enemy ships which survived the minefields. At least three tubes were in place by early 1915.

The Turks were not content to leave the strengthening of the defences of the Dardanelles solely to Limpus. While he was away on home leave in May and June 1914, a German admiral, Wilhelm von Schack, arrived with the express mission of strengthening the seaward defences of the Dardanelles. The British government had to accept this *fait accompli*. Schack's term was limited to six months and he was not supposed to wear uniform in his new posting – but everyone soon knew who he was. And after six months he was replaced by a further two German admirals, Johannes Merten and Guido von Usedom. The latter was a particularly powerful addition to the German team in Constantinople. Winner of the *Pour le Mérite*, equivalent to a German VC, for his bravery during the Boxer Rebellion in China in 1902, when he earned the title 'Hero of Kiaochow', von Usedom energetically set about strengthening the mine warfare resources at the Dardanelles. Nineteen wagon-loads of mines were brought in by rail from Germany. He took the calculated risk of transferring most of the heavy artillery shells from the Bosphorus forts to those on the Dardanelles. Technical support for mine warfare was increased, German technical personnel were introduced, and when Enver ordered

Turkish gunners loading a 276-kilogram shell into a Krupps L/35, 35.5-centimetre (14-inch) calibre heavy gun, part of their interlocking defensive network of coastal artillery and mobile howitzer batteries on both sides of the Dardanelles, combined with extensive minefields within the straits.

AWM P04411.033

the closure of the Dardanelles in September 1914, it was done quickly and thoroughly.

The Turkish navy operated the mines and torpedo tubes. The army, under Merten's guidance, modernised and manned the coastal forts, deployed more medium gun batteries on the peninsula, built dummy guns and emplacements for deception, and provided mobile batteries of howitzers to attack smaller vessels attempting to sweep the mines.

All of these systems were backed up by the aerial reconnaissance capabilities of a flight of German aircraft. Six were sent from Germany in the guise of medical equipment in February and March of 1915, via the neutral countries, Romania and Bulgaria. Air and ground crews followed, and a flight of three aircraft was deployed to cover the Gallipoli Peninsula while a second was sent to the Palestine front. The air build-up continued apace, and by 1918 the Germans had sent 460 combat aircraft to Turkey. During 1915, bombs for the aircraft were also smuggled through the two neutrals, not in the guise of medical equipment but out of sight in beer barrels. This ploy worked until in summer a thirsty Romanian railway official decided to tap the beer. Throughout the Gallipoli campaign Turkish commanders had the benefit of aerial photographs of the allied front lines and rear areas.

This fourfold combination of mines, forts equipped with heavy, long-range guns, stationary medium artillery and mobile howitzer batteries ashore made a formidably tough, mutually supporting combination of elements that individually were not overwhelmingly powerful. Inexpert, improvised British minesweepers were driven back from the mines by the howitzers. The guns of the forts made it dangerous for the battleships to halt in order to take a really accurate shot at the embrasures of the forts, so the big ships could not readily close with the forts. The ten individual lines of mines were covered and protected by medium coastal artillery. The minefields themselves had been freshly re-laid in 1914 on the basis of Limpus's preparations, and there were also numbers of floating mines dropped in by the Turks as an unknown menace to the big warships. And because of the depth at which the mines had been positioned, aerial reconnaissance by the British fleet yielded erroneous intelligence.

As the events of February and March 1915 were to show, the seaward defences of the Dardanelles were very effective. Churchill should have been aware of the firmness of the foundations laid by Limpus, and not attempted to send the fleet through until these defences had been overcome by other means. Yet Churchill's operational planning and subsequent failure to exploit Limpus's unique knowledge show that the First Lord of the Admiralty really had not thought hard enough about what the British naval mission had accomplished under his authority at the Dardanelles in 1913–14. And for reasons not fully clear, Churchill's subordinates at the Admiralty neither brought Limpus back to London to advise in October 1914 nor tried to convince the First Lord that

the defences of the Dardanelles could prove too much for the Royal Navy to penetrate. Churchill had left Limpus in place for six weeks after the onset of hostilities between Britain and Germany, but on 15 August the Turks stood him down and the command of the Turkish fleet passed to the Germans. Limpus left Constantinople on 15 September, but then was parked out of the way in Malta rather than being brought straight back to the Admiralty. He carried in his head the clearest picture of the Dardanelles naval defences and their capabilities, and that is where it remained. Churchill gives Limpus only two brief mentions in his volume, *The World Crisis*, and totally fails to give his readers any information on what Limpus's mission had achieved.

The other key contributor to the Dardanelles defences, Germany, had by mid-1914 frustrated the foreign policy objectives of British assistance. Casting one's mind forward to the era of Saddam Hussein and the role of Western countries and agencies in helping him to make war against Iran with access and assistance, and in helping other states with arms, even assistance in developing nuclear weapons, it is readily apparent that these problems are still with us. Like Churchill in 1915, our governments need to think harder about the possible consequences when they give military assistance to foreign countries.

2. Strategic planning: the relevance of expertise for those intending intervention

Churchill began to make plans for penetrating the Dardanelles and seizing Constantinople as early as August 1914. While this idea had been considered by the Committee of Imperial Defence in 1906, the plan which shaped the 1915 operations originated with the First Lord. He became fascinated by his grand design and drove it relentlessly through the higher levels of both the Admiralty and the War Office, and then the government, over the following months until it became national policy. His initial concept was for a powerful naval attack on the Dardanelles, neutralising the minefields and silencing the forts, combined with the landing of troops, hopefully to be provided by the Greeks. As he wrote to Foreign Secretary Edward Grey in early September 1914: 'A good army of 50,000 men and sea-power – that is the end of the Turkish menace.'

The Greeks declined to oblige, as did the Russians and the Bulgarians, so where was this 'good army' to come from? Churchill tells us in *The World Crisis* that at the end of November he knew of the arrival of the two Anzac divisions in Egypt. With a gleam in his eye he wrote to Kitchener on 30 November 'Had we not better keep enough transports concentrated [in Egypt] for 40,000 men, or shall we disperse them ready to assemble at short notice?' Kitchener was not ready to jump and adopt Churchill's suggestion, so the Anzacs were spared the commitment until they had found their land legs again in Egypt. Churchill was forced to fall back on planning for a purely naval operation against the Turks.

But Churchill brushed aside the challenges of the Dardanelles defences by reading a brief telegram from his admiral in the eastern Mediterranean, Sackville Carden, to his ministerial colleagues. Was this deliberate deception? Probably not: more likely it was passionate counsel based on his ignorance of the true situation and his lack of expertise in knowing what to focus on in taking these key decisions.

Churchill, in *The World Crisis,* quotes Bean's verdict on his strategic planning: 'So through Churchill's excess of imagination, a layman's ignorance of artillery, and the fatal power of a young enthusiasm to convince older and slower brains, the tragedy of Gallipoli was born.' Churchill then comments: 'It is my hope that the Australian people, towards whom I have always felt a solemn responsibility, will not rest content with so crude, so inaccurate, so incomplete and so prejudiced a judgement, but will study the facts for themselves.' Having spent many years studying the facts, I think Dr Bean had it about right!

The result of Churchill's drive was the series of naval bombardments of the Turkish coastal fortifications along the Dardanelles, up to the minefields, which began on 19 February and ended with the loss of three battleships and serious damage to three other ships on 18 March. Why did Churchill not know the situation better? There was adequate information in the Admiralty for him to have done so, and some of his staff must have known of its existence. It surely would have been wise to have brought Limpus back to London to report directly on what he knew. Could it have been that Churchill knew of the information which suggested that the course he was putting forward was risky and decided simply to bury it? He was to pay a high price for his errors of judgement in following years, but probably he learned from these events and made a better leader than otherwise would have been the case in the Second World War. But the tens of thousands of British, French and colonial troops who were to die as a result of his faulty strategic planning had no second chance.

There were significant strategic planning capabilities in the Admiralty and the War Office in 1914–15, but they were not properly engaged in the vital time leading up to the taking of the main decisions by the government. Above all the decision-making process was driven by a man who was ignorant of what he was ordering others into and did not fully avail himself of the expertise of those who had a much better understanding. He was then joined by Kitchener who, in seeking to save the naval effort from disaster and humiliation, escalated the operation by making the army available for a landing on the peninsula.

And sadly, as the events of 2002–3 have shown, this tendency on the parts of forceful and determined political leaders, such as Richard Cheney and

Donald Rumsfeld, is still with us. The weakness of Prime Minister Asquith in controlling debates in the War Council may also have been paralleled by the incapacity of President George W. Bush to judge between sound advice and illusion. State leadership requires high competence in strategic judgement.

3. What happens when the assisted power asserts itself: preparation of the land defences of the Dardanelles

There can be no doubt that the Turkish army was in poor shape in 1908, and that this weakness was recognised by the Young Turks in undertaking their coup. Hence they asked their long-standing provider of military expertise, Germany, for increased assistance in training and modernisation. The Kaiser was keen to sustain Turkey's vision of Germany as its principal European ally. The mission to the Ottoman Empire, which had begun with the Prussians in 1835, was re-focused and expanded in 1909. The immediate result was disappointing. The Turkish army performed poorly in the wars of 1911–13 against the Italians and the Balkan states. In late 1913 the Turkish government, impelled by Defence Minister Enver Pasha, requested a new German military mission. The era of General Otto Liman von Sanders in the Ottoman Empire had begun.

Von Sanders, as he looked at the strategic situation in Turkey, was seized by the urgent need to improve the defences of the Gallipoli Peninsula.[2] He could see the strength of the seaward defences of the Dardanelles and recognised that an enemy wanting to open the sea passage to Russia would need to invade the peninsula in order to neutralise the coastal fortresses and their batteries, and to sweep the mines that would have been by then laid in the Narrows. Initially von Sanders had been given command of the 1st Turkish Army, entrusted with the key defences of Constantinople. He had pressed hard for the deployment of more forces in the Gallipoli Peninsula itself, and on 24 March 1915 Enver gave him command of the 5th Army, then being deployed on both sides of the Narrows.

The 5th Army was supported by the 2nd Army in Thrace, just around the head of the Gulf of Saros, and while Constantinople itself was not under attack, the 5th could also draw on reinforcements and support from elements of the 1st Army. Thus there were in effect three Turkish armies of over twelve divisions in total, or 200,000 men, available within a few days to contain an invader on the north side of the Straits and the peninsula. To attack a force of these dimensions with some 80,000 men was to show contempt for the enemy when on his home ground, or perhaps just gross ignorance of the Turks' real capabilities.

At the centre of von Sanders' strategic appreciation of the situation was the fortress and communications centre of Chanak. Without controlling

Chanak, the seaward defences of the Dardanelles would be difficult for an invader to overcome. He could see four principal landing points for an invading army: Bulair at the neck of the Gallipoli Peninsula, Kum Kale on the southern side of the entrance to the Dardanelles, Cape Helles at the tip of the peninsula, and Gaba Tepe on the northern side. He, his staff and his Turkish subordinates were concerned to minimise the problems of uncertainty that they faced because the attackers had such a wide choice of landing points. So in late March and early April they re-shaped the original Turkish defences from a thin line all around the peninsula to a series of concentrations from which troops could be quickly deployed forwards to the landing areas and then counter-attack.

The Turkish army was not liberally supplied with modern artillery but it had some, and it could also rely on the mobile batteries supporting the naval defences when they were not engaged in that role. The obvious landing points were defended with wire obstacles and trenches, but in the main the defences relied on tough, brave, aggressive infantrymen who would be sent forward in time of need. The attackers might have several hours of relative freedom to advance once they had come ashore, provided that they achieved surprise, but once their thrusts had been detected, they could expect, after a few hours, to receive solid counter-attacks.

As we know, the Anzacs had the particular misfortune of encountering Kemal's 19th Division and were held in check by the afternoon of 25 April. By desperate efforts they clung onto the steep upper slopes of gullies and in some places had a foothold on relatively level high ground. But gone were any prospects of being able to achieve the strategic aims of the landings. The challenge now was to retain their tiny footholds – which at ANZAC fell within a perimeter that takes just two hours to walk around. Hence Bridges and Birdwood made their query to Hamilton to see if the Anzacs could not be evacuated from the Peninsula that night, to which came Hamilton's stout response that the Anzacs had to dig in and hold on. A night evacuation, under Turkish pressure, would have risked chaos, even panic. They had to stay and hang on in the hope that the Turks would weaken or that greater force might be brought to bear. The Anzacs had missed their one slender opportunity and, from now on, the superior strength of the Turks, the weather, lack of water, and dysentery would grind them down.

Once again, clever people in national capitals had failed utterly to learn how other armies might be able to defend their own territory, and compensate for their lack of firepower and communications by the bravery and determination of individual troops, their NCOs and officers. More recently we have learned through painful experience in Vietnam and Iraq, and now in Afghanistan, that such blindness and miscomprehension is still to be encountered regularly in our own governments and their agencies.

4. The use of amphibious warfare: a defining prerogative of really great powers

The technique chosen by Churchill for the assault on the Gallipoli Peninsula was amphibious warfare – probably the most difficult and demanding type of operation to put into practice successfully. It requires special landing craft to put soldiers and their equipment ashore together and speedily. The ships in which they and their equipment and supplies travel need to be reverse-loaded, i.e. the people and items needed first must be the last to be loaded. The landing beaches need to be spacious and have adjacent cover in which the landing troops can sort themselves out and assemble in their platoons, companies and battalions, ready to advance as fast as possible and fully secure their beachhead. The beaches themselves need to be controlled by officers who can reassemble units out of their component boatloads of men and equipment. Once the beachhead is secured, these operations have to be followed by reinforcement of the landing force to the point at which they can successfully attack the enemy's main defences and gain control of the hinterland. Medical arrangements, especially for the safe location of wounded, their treatment onshore and rapid evacuation onto waiting hospital ships, must be planned ahead of the landing.

I shall not go into further detail on the requirements of effective amphibious operations. Clearly the Royal Navy and the British army had not developed the basic essentials – which, given Churchill's belief that one of the key functions of the navy was to transport and launch the army into the suppression of local rebellions or the acquisition of new imperial territories, is more than a little surprising. British experience of amphibious operations in the nineteenth century included the Walcheren expedition, a disaster of 1809 in which the Royal Navy landed 40,000 British soldiers on the coast near Antwerp; the final operations of the war of 1812, aimed at seizing Washington and New Orleans in late 1814; and the Crimean War. All of these landings, unopposed by strong defences, ended in withdrawal. Yet Churchill, writing in *The World Crisis* of his thinking in early 1915, described Britain as 'the Great Amphibian'. What self-delusion he was indulging in! Britain perhaps had a fish, in the form of the Royal Navy, and a hardy land animal in the form of the army, but it entirely lacked anything which could truly fit the category of the frog, at home in both environments! If he thought Britain was the Great Amphibian, he was well detached from reality.

In the case of Gallipoli not only did the forces involved know little about amphibious warfare, but also the Anzacs were put ashore too far to the north. While Ari Burnu may have been compatible with the imprecise orders that the first landing elements were given, it was out of accord with the lie of the land. When I gave the address at the dawn commemorative service on Ari Burnu in 1997, I invited the participants to raise their eyes and discern the heights of the Sphinx, Russell's Top and the ridges behind, and then turn their gaze to the right where the lower headland of Gaba Tepe could just be made out in the growing light. From that landing point they could have got off to a much faster start, advanced to the centre of the peninsula and given the Turks a more severe problem in containing the invasion. Yet, as luck would have it, the Anzacs were put ashore facing heights of 300–400 feet, on beaches a few yards wide. For a while they certainly had the advantage of surprise because the Turks had not imagined that a main thrust would come ashore at Ari Burnu. But by mid-afternoon on the first day, the Anzacs had been halted and the strategic purpose of the landings had been vitiated. The same was also true of the landings at Cape Helles. The Turks showed that they could rally under pressure and fight hard to defend their own territory.

The US Marine Corps studied the lessons of Gallipoli seriously in the 1920s and 1930s. Their doctrines and techniques, applied to such decisive effect in the Second World War and later in Korea, owe a debt to the inadequacies shown up in the Gallipoli landings. This knowledge was also exploited by the British in 1941–42 as they developed the techniques they were to apply in Europe in 1944. But for the men who had to cope with the inadequacies of their equipment, supplies, planning and system of control in 1915, these later developments were of no consolation.

5. Islamic aspects of the conflict: a complication for the non-Islamic powers involved

European nations have been at war with Turkish, Arab, Iranian and Central Asian nations and peoples for millennia. The outcomes of these struggles from the days of the Roman Empire to the Crusades and beyond to Afghanistan in the nineteenth century should have made it abundantly clear to European leaders that going to war against such enemies, especially on their home territories, was likely to be costly, protracted and ultimately to end in defeat. How strange it is, therefore, that Winston Churchill, a voracious student of military history, thought that a force of some 60,000 men, landed on the shores of the Gallipoli Peninsula and backed by the Royal Navy, would rapidly induce a Turkish collapse leading to the seizure and occupation of Constantinople. What did he imagine the Turks were made of? He saw the Ottoman Empire as moribund. Again in *The World Crisis* he declared: 'From every quarter the nations and races who for five or six hundred years had waged war against the Turkish Empire, or had suffered the fate of Turkish captives, turned their gaze in measureless hatred and hunger upon the dying Empire from which they had endured so much so long.' Unfortunately, the Ottoman Empire in 1915 had plenty of fight left in it, and was not about to collapse just because a British fleet penetrated the Dardanelles. It is even more strange that Churchill should have had such erroneous thoughts after British naval experts had just spent nearly six years in improving Turkey's naval defences, especially those of the Dardanelles.

And as more recent events in Iraq and Afghanistan have shown, this tendency to under-rate Islamic opponents and see them as houses of playing cards ready to collapse at the least external stress is still very much alive. It is perhaps not as thriving in 2010 as in 2003, but nonetheless, Islamic incapacity seems to be one of the assumptions on which current military interventions are based. Why was this the case in 1914–15 as the British government was making up its mind to knock the Ottoman Empire out of the war by means of a naval and military attack?

In early twentieth century Europe there was a kind of conceit that the great Christian empires were superior and therefore had overridden the Islamic states, either making them subject to imperial authority or side-lining them so effectively that they did not really register as major international forces. Writing to Grey on 4 November 1911, Churchill said, 'we are the greatest Mahometan power in the world'. He took this conceit further in a letter to the leading Young Turk Djavid Bey, two weeks later: 'In the future the enormous interests which unite the two great Musselman Powers should keep us in touch.' He meant Britain and the Ottoman Empire, writing as if the 60 million Muslims in India were simply a loyal resource ready to do Britain's bidding around the world, and the Turks would naturally accept Britain's leadership as the greatest Muslim power of the world. But once hostilities had been opened in Europe in 1914, the voices of those more experienced in affairs touching Islam, such as those of Kitchener and Lord Crewe, Secretary of State for India, were raised in concern about the consequences for Muslims in British India and Egypt of putting pressure on Turkey. In their minds, and probably in Asquith's also, there was an unarticulated anxiety that Islam was already an influential factor in international politics, and that Britain could be vulnerable to its power.

Islam formally became a factor in the conflict once the Entente powers had declared war on Turkey on 5 November 1914. The Turkish government reciprocated formally on 11 November, and two days later the Sultan, Mehmet V, presided over a ceremony in the hall of Topkapi Palace, where the remains of the Prophet Mohammed were kept. A fatwa was read, proclaiming *Jihad*. This was followed on 23 November by a decree from Mehmet V, in his authority as the Caliph, that jihad should be proclaimed and the call published throughout the Muslim world.

While this call did not lead immediately to mass uprisings through the Middle East and in India, it raised tensions in Egypt. The Khedive, Abbas Hilmi, was strongly opposed to British rule in Egypt and he also called for jihad. The British government ousted Abbas and imposed martial law. The British Commander in Egypt, General Sir John Maxwell, who had to maintain law and order, was concerned that too much of his force was being drawn off to meet wider commitments, jeopardising his ability to maintain authority over the 70,000 Turks in Egypt by frequent demonstrations of military power.

The call for jihad by the Caliph in late 1914 even had a response in Australia on New Year's Eve when the well-known incident of the two 'Turks', who were actually Afghans, occurred near Broken Hill. These two individuals, one of whom had been an Ottoman soldier for several years, in the tradition of the jihadi willing to sacrifice his life for his faith, opened fire on a trainload of picnickers, killing three and wounding several others. They in turn were shot and killed by police. After rioting and the destruction of the local German Club, the situation was calmed, but authorities were worried by the incident as they recognised a way in which jihad could reach into Australia itself.

The Islamic faith provided a unifying bond across an Ottoman Empire which stood in danger of disintegration under the forces of nationalism. Relations between Arabs and Turks varied from passive acceptance of each other to coolness and even hostility. This led to battlefield desertions such as that by the 77th Regiment (largely made up of conscript Arabs) of Kemal's division on the night of 25 April. Brave Anatolian soldiers replaced them, enabling him to form a stronger line against the invaders. Despite that episode, the 19th Division fought solidly and well. Kemal noted the importance of the motivation provided by Islam to his soldiers. Writing to his lady friend Corinne Lütfü on 20 July 1915 he said, somewhat facetiously:

> Life here is truly hellish. Fortunately, my soldiers are very brave and tougher than the enemy. What is more, their private beliefs make it easier to carry out orders which send them to their deaths. They see only two supernatural outcomes: victory for the faith, or martyrdom. Do you know what the second means? It is to go straight to heaven. There, the houris, God's most beautiful women, will meet them and will satisfy their desires for all eternity. What great happiness!

Such humour aside, Kemal's men were indeed brave – as were the majority of Turkish soldiers – and their religion played a strengthening role. While British, Australian, New Zealand and French soldiers were also brave, the degree of risk that an allied commander could regularly subject his troops to was probably not as high as that to which Kemal and his colleagues could subject their Ottoman troops. British and Anzac officers did not order their men expressly to die. Kemal famously said he did. And while there were instances in the Gallipoli campaign where Turkish units collapsed or withdrew suddenly, there were many others, especially under the weight of the main allied offensives in August 1915, where Turkish doggedness deprived the allies of a decisive success. And the margins of Turkish success were often very thin – and they knew it was.

This quiet strength conferred by Islam on its soldiers is a far cry from the panic-prone tendencies which were high in European public, and probably political, perceptions of the Turks. Yet panic and collapse were what the authors of the Dardanelles campaign believed would occur if the Royal Navy entered the Sea of Marmara. The experience of the Gallipoli campaign suggests that even if British warships had been able to shell Constantinople, the war on land would have been hard-fought, bitter, protracted and very costly in allied lives. In any event Enver had his own plans should he have to surrender Constantinople: there would have been a re-grouping of Turkish forces across the Bosphorus from where a harassing campaign would have been conducted for as long as the allies wanted to fight. And let us also not forget the stubbornness of the Turkish defence in the Mesopotamian and Palestine campaigns. It took three battles for Gaza, over seven months, before the British could march on Jerusalem in 1917. Not much evidence for the 'panicking fanatics' school of thought is offered by these Turkish battles.

And yet in 2003 the Bush administration still appeared to share this view of Muslims. 'Shock and awe' was the name of their campaign against Saddam Hussein. As we have seen in the years since then, 'Shock and awe' was sufficient to get a technologically powerful set of armed forces into Iraq, and there they still are, with only limited successes to show for a huge effort and heavy loss of life on both sides. The concept of 'jihad' and the 'jihadi' has acquired a new relevance for us. The Bush Administration had to acknowledge that the principal security threat to the United States was not another nation state but a small group of jihadis with weapons of mass destruction. And there are thousands of potential 21st century jihadis out there, waiting to be given the call, the weapons to be used and the right opportunity to engage their foes.

In conclusion

The Gallipoli campaign has certainly cast a long shadow – already 98 years if one takes the landings as a starting point – and a round century if one looks at the foundation of the Fleet Club in Turkey to conduct that popularly supported fundraising drive which successfully raised the money to pay for the two battleships that Churchill confiscated in July 1914. In taking on Turkey, the allies were also taking on the Turkish people, and those people were not about to dissolve into tiny groups of panicking fanatics who would bow down to the mighty will and complex weapons systems of the Entente powers. A long shadow indeed, and it still stretches before us. The lessons from history's page are obvious, but do we have politicians who are prepared to take the time necessary, and do the hard studying, to develop real expertise in the management of international security policy? The experience of the past decade suggests that we are as far away from that goal as were the national leaders of 1914–15.

Notes

Preface

1 Robert Rhodes James, *Gallipoli*, Pimlico, London, 1999, author's preface to the first edition of 1965, p. xv; Robert Rhodes James, *Churchill: A Study in Failure 1900–1939*, Penguin, Harmondsworth, 1973, p. 81.

2 John Robertson, *Anzac and Empire: The Tragedy & Glory of Gallipoli*, Hamlyn, Port Melbourne, 1990, ch. 34, esp. p. 244; Jenny Macleod, *Reconsidering Gallipoli*, Manchester University Press, Manchester, 2004, ch. 1.

3 Cmd 371 Final report of the Dardanelles Commission, 4 December 1917, 'General review', reprinted as *Defeat at Gallipoli: The Dardanelles Commission Part II, 1915–16*, The Stationery Office, London, 2000, p. 287.

4 Alan Moorehead, *Gallipoli*, Macmillan, Melbourne, 1989 (first published 1956), pp. 32, 300–3. This positive view of the campaign's strategic importance followed that of the British and Australian official historians, C.F. Aspinall-Oglander and C.E.W. Bean, and continues to have its adherents. See for example, Peter Chasseaud and Peter Doyle, *Grasping Gallipoli: Terrain, maps and failure at the Dardanelles, 1915*, Spellmount, Staplehurst, Kent, 2005, pp. xx–xxi, 267–9.

5 Robin Prior, 'Gallipoli', in Peter Dennis, Jeffrey Grey, Ewan Morris, Robin Prior with Jean Bou (eds), *The Oxford Companion to Australian Military History*, Oxford, South Melbourne, Second edition, 2008, pp. 223–32, 230, 232; Robin Prior, *Gallipoli: the end of the myth*, UNSW Press, Sydney, 2009, pp. 237–52.

Introduction

1 C.F. Aspinall-Oglander, *Military Operations: Gallipoli*, Vol. 2, *May 1915 to the Evacuation*, William Heinemann, London, 1932, p. 308. According to Turkish official sources, Turkish casualties were 9200 at Chunuk Bair and Hill 971, 2000 at Baby 700 and the head of Monash Gully; and 6930 at Lone Pine. C.E.W. Bean, *The Story of Anzac, from 4 May 1915 to the Evacuation of the Gallipoli Peninsula*, Vol. 2, The Official History of Australia in the War of 1914–1918, Angus & Robertson, Sydney, 1924 (edition of 1944), p. 713 n. 56.

2 General Sir Ian Hamilton, *Gallipoli Diary*, 2 vols, Edward Arnold, London, 1920, Vol. 2, 23 August 1915, p 136.

3 Ellis Ashmead-Bartlett, letter written to British Prime Minister H.H. Asquith, 8 September 1915, carbon copy in Ashmead-Bartlett papers, Mitchell Library, State Library of New South Wales. Ashmead-Bartlett intended his original letter to be delivered by Australian journalist Keith Murdoch but it was confiscated by British military authorities who intercepted Murdoch in Marseilles *en route* to London.

4 *Ibid.*

5 Bean, *The Story of Anzac*, Vol. 2, p. 908.

6 Total allied casualties are estimated at approximately 265,000, including over 44,000 killed or died of wounds and disease. Some 500,000 Turkish soldiers served on Gallipoli and their casualties are estimated at over 250,000, including almost 87,000 dead.

7 This passage derives from P.H. Liddle, 'The Distinctive Nature of the Gallipoli Experience', *Journal of the Royal United Service Institute*, no. 122, 2, June 1977, pp. 51–6. Liddle identified other aspects of this distinctiveness: the absence of adequate rest areas away from the fighting or provisions for leave, in contrast with the Western Front; the inadequate medical arrangements to deal with the wounded and the high incidence of sickness from disease and malnutrition amongst soldiers on the peninsula (features more commonly associated with the British Imperial wars of the nineteenth century); the multinational character of the Mediterranean Expeditionary Force and the relative informality of the military experience on Gallipoli; the comparatively small numbers of men and units involved, the tactics and weapons used and the limited duration of the campaign, giving it a scale which made it more intelligible to ordinary soldiers than the experience of the Western Front.

8 Hamilton, *Gallipoli Diary*, Vol. 1, 15 June 1915, pp. 304–5. Emphasis in original.

9 C.E.W. Bean, *Gallipoli Mission*, ABC Enterprises in association with the Australian War Memorial, Crows Nest NSW, 1990 (first published 1948), p. 278.

10 Hamilton, *Gallipoli Diary*, Vol. 1, pp. 104, 192, 212; Vol. 2, pp. 226, 253.

11 Richard S. Fogarty, *Race and War in France: Colonial Subjects in the French Army, 1914–1918*, Johns Hopkins University Press, Baltimore, 2008, esp. ch. 2, pp. 82–95.

Chapter 1

1 John Maynard Keynes, *The General Theory of Employment, Interest and Money*, Macmillan, London, 1936, pp. 383–84.

2 C.E.W. Bean, *The Story of Anzac: From 4 May, 1915, to the evacuation of the Gallipoli peninsula*, Vol. 2, The Official History of Australia in the War of 1914–18, Angus & Robertson, Sydney, 1924, p. 717.

3 Bean, *The Story of Anzac*, Vol. 2, p. 910.

4 Winston S. Churchill, *The World Crisis*, Vol. 2, Thornton Butterworth, London, 1923, p. 452.

5 Churchill, *The World Crisis*, Vol. 2, p. 17.

6 David Lloyd George, *War Memoirs*, Vol. 1, Ivor Nicholson & Watson, London. 1933, pp. 438–89.

7 C.F. Aspinall-Oglander, *Military Operations: Gallipoli*, Vol. 2, *May 1915 to the Evacuation*, William Heinemann, London, 1932, p. 481.

8 Aspinall-Oglander, *Military Operations: Gallipoli*, Vol. 2, p. 309. The obelisk described by Aspinall-Oglander was the New Zealand memorial erected on the summit of Chunuk Bair (Turkish: Conkbayiri) in May 1925.

9 Quoted in Aspinall-Oglander, *Military Operations: Gallipoli*, Vol. 2, p.328.

10 B.H. Liddell Hart, *Through the Fog of War*, Faber and Faber, London, 1938, p. 291–92.

11 Liddell Hart, *Through the Fog of War*, pp. 293, 295.

12 John North, *Gallipoli: The fading vision*, Faber and Faber, London, 1936.

13 North, *Gallipoli*, pp. 54, 57.

14 North, *Gallipoli*, p. 101.

15 North, *Gallipoli*, ch. III, pp. 101–24.

16 Hansard 7/5/40.

17 Hansard 7/5/40.

18 From Churchill's famous 'blood, toil, tears and sweat', speech in the House of Commons, 13 May 1940.

Chapter 2

1 M. Aksakal, 'War as the Savior? Hopes for War and Peace in Ottoman Politics before 1914', in H. Afflerbach and D. Stevenson (eds), *An Improbable War? The outbreak of World War I and European political culture before 1914*, Berghahn Books, Oxford, 2007, pp. 287–302.

2 The National Archives of Great Britain, Kew [hereafter TNA], CAB 21/69 Statutory Commission on the Dardanelles and Gallipoli Operations, 1915, Lord Kitchener's orders to GOC MEF, March 13, 1915.

3 I. Hamilton, *Gallipoli Diary*, 2 vols, Edward Arnold & Co, London, 1930, Vol. 1, p. 197.

4 TNA, CAB 19/1 Dardanelles Commission Final Report Cd 371 Part II Conduct of Operations Etc., 1919, p. 25; C.F. Aspinall-Oglander, *Military Operations: Gallipoli*, Vol. 2, *May 1915 to the Evacuation*, William Heinemann, London, 1932, pp. 56–57.

5 TNA, CAB 21/69 Statutory Commission on the Dardanelles and Gallipoli Operations, 1915, Letter from Hankey to the Secretary of the Dardanelles Committee, 26 September 1916; TNA, CAB 22/2 Dardanelles Committee, Meeting 7 June 1915.

6 T. Travers, *Gallipoli 1915*, Tempus, Stroud, Gloucestershire, 2001, p. 262 n. 18.

7 Hamilton, *Gallipoli Diary*, Vol. 1, p. 267.

8 C. Lee, *Jean, Lady Hamilton 1861–1941: A Soldier's Wife*, published by author, 2001, p. 129.

9 Hamilton, *Gallipoli Diary*, Vol. 2, pp. 12–14.

10 Hamilton, *Gallipoli Diary*, Vol. 1, p. 374; and Vol. 2, pp. 14–24, quotation from p. 15.

11 M. Gilbert, 'Churchill and Gallipoli', in J. Macleod (ed.), *Gallipoli: Making history*, Frank Cass, London, 2004, p. 15.

12 N. Fergusson, *Empire: How Britain made the modern world*, Penguin, London, 2004, p. 247; I.F.W. Beckett, *The Victorians at War*, Hambledon and London, New York, 2003, p. 216; N. Fergusson, *The Cash Nexus: Money and power in the Modern World 1700–2000*, Basic Books, New York, 2001, pp. 44–45; A.J.P. Taylor, *The Struggle for Mastery in Europe 1848–1918*, Oxford University Press, Oxford, 1954, p. xxvii.

13 O. Esher (ed.), *Journals and Letters of Reginald Viscount Esher: Volume 3 1910–1915*, Ivor and Nicholson, London, 1938, p. 221; R. Holmes, *The Little Field Marshal: Sir John French*, Cape, London, 1982, pp. 302–5; N. Lloyd, *Loos 1915*, Tempus, Stroud, Gloucestershire, 2006, pp. 54, 64.

14 TNA, CAB 24/1 'The Dardanelles: Memorandum on the Situation, August 30, 1915', p. 16.

15 Hamilton, *Gallipoli Diary*, Vol. 2, p. 29; J. Lee, *A Soldier's Life: General Sir Ian Hamilton 1853–1947*, Macmillan, Basingstoke, 2000, p. 181.

16 E. Köroğlu, *Ottoman Propaganda and Turkish Identity: Literature in Turkey During World War I*, I.B. Tauris, New York, 2007, pp. 82–85.

17 Hamilton, *Gallipoli Diary*, Vol. 1, p. 304.

18 Hamilton, *Gallipoli Diary*, Vol. 2, pp. 83–5; K. Fewster (ed.), *Bean's Gallipoli: The diaries of Australia's official war correspondent*, Allen & Unwin, Sydney, 2007, pp. 196–7.

19 TNA, CAB 24/1 'The Dardanelles: Memorandum on the situation, August 30, 1915', p. 15.

20 K. Fewster, V. Başarin and H. Hürmüz Başarin, *Gallipoli: The Turkish story*, Allen & Unwin, Sydney, 2003, p. 117; E.J. Erickson, *Ordered to Die: A history of the Ottoman Army in the First World War*, Greenwood, Westport CT, 2001, pp. 90–91.

21 S. Grimes, 'The Baltic and Admiralty War Planning 1906–7', *The Journal of Military History*, Vol. 74, No. 2, April 2010, pp. 407–38.

22 P.A. Towle, 'The influence of the Russo-Japanese War on British military and naval thought 1904–14,' PhD thesis, University of London, 1973, pp. 340–59.

23 TNA, WO 33/644 *Manual of Combined Military and Naval Operations* 1913; J. Bou, *Light Horse: A history of Australia's mounted arm*, Cambridge University Press, 2010, p. 107; *A Soldier's Life*, pp. 111–22.

24 G.H. Cassar, *Kitchener's War: British strategy from 1914 to 1916*, Brassey's, 2004, p. 140; M. Gilbert, 'Churchill and Gallipoli', in Macleod (ed.), *Gallipoli: Making history*, p. 21.

25 Lee, *A Soldier's Life*, pp. 113–48.

26 Cassar, *Kitchener's War*, pp. 19–22.

27 French, quoted in G. French, *The Life of Field Marshal Sir John French First Earl of Ypres*, Cassell, 1931, p. 221.

28 Holmes, *The Little Field Marshal*, pp. 262–64.

29 TNA, ADM 1/8884 'Extract from the minutes of the 92nd meeting of the Committee of Imperial Defence regarding war with Turkey, 26th July 2906'.

30 G.H. Cassar, *Kitchener's War*, pp. 50–57.
31 TNA, CAB 22/1 Committee of Imperial Defence, 'Secretary's Notes of a War Council, Meeting January 8, 1915'; Cassar, *Kitchener's War*, pp. 146-52; G.H. Cassar, *The Tragedy of Sir John French*, University of Delaware Press, 1985, pp. 196–97; J. Grigg, *Lloyd George: From Peace to War 1912–1916*, Methuen, 1985, pp. 194–97.
32 TNA, CAB 24/1 'The Dardanelles: Memorandum on the Situation, August 30, 1915', p. 74.
33 G. Sheffield and J. Bourne, (eds), *Douglas Haig: War Diaries and Letters 1914–1918*, Weidenfeld, 2005, p. 170.
34 Letter from Charles Repington to Andrew Bonar Law, 24 November 1915, reproduced in A.J.A. Morris (ed.), *The Letters of Lieutenant Colonel Charles à Court Repington CMG: Military Correspondent of The Times 1903–1918*, Sutton, 1999, p. 244. General Sir John Nixon was commander-in-chief of the Indian Expeditionary Force in Mesopotamia.
35 K. Jeffrey, *Field Marshal Sir Henry Wilson: A Political Soldier*, Oxford University Press, 2006, pp. 92–93.
36 Quoted in Holmes, *The Little Field Marshal*, p. 285.
37 A. Bristow, *A Serious Disappointment: The battle of Aubers Ridge 1915 and the munitions scandal*, Leo Cooper, 1995, pp. 143–78.
38 Lloyd, *Loos 1915*, pp. 21–8.
39 TNA, CAB 22/2 Dardanelles Committee, 'Meeting June 17, 1915'; Esher (ed.), *Journals and Letters of Reginald Viscount Esher: Volume 3 1910–1915*, pp. 252–53; Lloyd, *Loos 1915*, pp. 22–23.
40 S. Roskill, *Hankey – Man of Secrets, Volume I: 1877–1918*, Collins, 1970, p. 153.
41 TNA, CAB 22/1 Committee of Imperial Defence, 'Secretary's Notes of a War Council, January 1, 1915'.
42 N. Stone, *The Eastern Front 1914–1917*, Hodder and Stoughton, 1975, pp. 144–64; French, *British Strategy and War Aims 1914–1916*, pp. 105–06; Cassar, *Kitchener's War*, pp. 187–201.
43 TNA, CAB 21/69 Statutory Commission on the Dardanelles and Gallipoli Operations, 1915, Letter from Hankey to Asquith, July 24, 1916.
44 Gilbert, 'Churchill and Gallipoli', in Macleod (ed.), *Gallipoli: Making History*, pp. 15–16.
45 D. French, *British Strategy and War Aims 1914–1916*, Allen & Unwin, 1986, p. 81.
46 French, *British Strategy and War Aims 1914–1916*, pp. 78–79.
47 Hamilton, *Gallipoli Diary*, Vol. 1, p. 230.
48 Lee, *Jean, Lady Hamilton 1861–1941*, p. 124.
49 Hamilton, *Gallipoli Diary*, Vol. 1, pp. 235–6.
50 Hamilton, *Gallipoli Diary*, Vol. 2, pp. 39–40.
51 Hamilton, *Gallipoli Diary*, Vol. 1, pp. 262–5, 311–13; Lee, *A Soldier's Life*, p. 181; Lee, *Jean, Lady Hamilton*, p. 122.
52 French, *British Strategy and War Aims 1914–1916*, p. 109.
53 TNA, CAB 24/1 'The Dardanelles: Note by the Secretary of the Committee of Imperial Defence', 16 June 1915.
54 R.T. Foley, *German Strategy and the Path to Verdun: Erich von Falkenhayn and the Development of Attrition 1870–1916*, Cambridge University Press, 2005, pp. 127–55; Stone, *The Eastern Front 1914–1917*, pp. 128–42; E.J. Erickson, *Gallipoli and the Middle East 1914–1918*, Amber, 2008, pp. 37–39 and p. 118; French, *British Strategy and War Aims 1914–1916*, pp. 109–10.
55 Holmes, *The Little Field Marshal*, pp. 288–92.
56 Lee, *Jean, Lady Hamilton*, pp. 123–25; Aspinall-Oglander, *Military Operations Gallipoli*, Vol. 2, pp. 59–61.
57 Hamilton , *Gallipoli Diary*, Vol. 1, pp. 302–6; Lee, *A Soldier's Life*, pp. 189–91.
58 Cassar, *Kitchener's War*, p. 208.
59 Aspinall-Oglander, *Military Operations Gallipoli*, Vol. 2, p. 57.
60 French, *British Strategy and War Aims 1914–1916*, pp. 102–03.
61 Cassar, *Kitchener's War*, pp. 206–08.
62 Corbett, *History of the Great War Based on Official Documents: Naval Operations, Volume III*, pp. 24–36 and pp. 56–8; P.G. Halpern, *A Naval History of World War I*, Naval Institute Press, 1994, pp. 298–9.
63 Aspinall-Oglander, *Military Operations Gallipoli: Volume II May 1915 to the Evacuation*, pp. 60–62; J.S. Corbett, *History of the Great War Based on Official Documents: Naval operations*, Vol. 3, HMSO, 1928, pp. 42–45, 56–59.
64 F. Maurice, *The Life of General Lord Rawlinson of Trent*, Cassell, 1928, pp. 135–36.
65 Holmes, *The Little Field Marshal*, p. 294.
66 French, *British Strategy and War Aims 1914–1916*, p. 107.
67 Roskill, *Hankey – Man of Secrets: Volume I: 1877–1918*, p. 188.
68 Lee, *Jean, Lady Hamilton*, p. 129; Cassar, *Kitchener's War*, pp. 209–11.
69 Esher (ed.), *Journals and Letters of Reginald Viscount Esher: Volume 3 1910–1915*, pp. 252–53.
70 Lloyd, *Loos 1915*, pp. 29–40; Holmes, *The Little Field Marshal: Sir John French*, pp. 296–98; French, *British Strategy and War Aims 1914–1916*, pp. 107–8.
71 Hamilton, *Gallipoli Diary*, Volume II, pp. 13–14 (emphasis in the original). Hamilton's comment about high-explosive and shrapnel is military shorthand for high explosive shell being largely used to destroy enemy defences to assist an attack, while shrapnel shell was largely used against enemy troops in the open as they attacked, and that he believed that he should get greater priority in receiving high explosive shell than the BEF.
72 Roskill, *Hankey – Man of Secrets: Volume I: 1877–1918*, pp. 188–97.
73 Quoted in Lee, *A Soldier's Life*, p. 199; see also M. Soames, *Clementine Churchill: The Biography of a Marriage*, Cassell, 1979, pp. 147–48; Lee, *Jean, Lady Hamilton*, pp. 129–30.
74 Lee, *Jean, Lady Hamilton*, p. 130.
75 Roskill, *Hankey – Man of Secrets: Volume I 1877–1918*,

pp. 198–99; TNA, CAB 24/1 'The Dardanelles: Memorandum on the Situation, August 30, 1915', p. 4.

76 TNA, CAB 22/2 'Dardanelles Committee, Meeting August 20, 1915'; Grigg, *Lloyd George: From peace to war 1912–1916*, pp. 311–12; French, *British Strategy and War Aims 1914–1916*, p. 111; Cassar, *Kitchener's War: British strategy from 1914 to 1916*, pp 218–19.

77 Lloyd, *Loos 1915*, pp. 29–40; Holmes, *The Little Field Marshal*, pp. 296–98.

Chapter 3

1 Cecil Malthus, *Anzac: A Retrospect*, Whitcombe & Tombs, Christchurch, 1965, pp. 118–19. The Canterbury Battalion suffered heavy casualties on Rhododendron Ridge during the preliminary advance on Chunuk Bair. Malthus based his incisive account on his own and comrade's personal letters, diaries and reminiscences as well as published official histories.

2 General Sir Ian Hamilton, *Gallipoli Diary*, Edward Arnold, London, 1920, Vol. 2, 9 August 1915, pp. 105–6. Hamilton's 'diary' was actually a memoir in diary form, based on notes he made during the campaign and later compiled as a narrative to defend his actions in command during the Gallipoli campaign. Robert Rhodes James, *Gallipoli*, Pimlico, London, 1999, pp. 52–53 n.; Jenny Macleod, *Reconsidering Gallipoli*, Manchester University Press, Manchester, 2004, pp. 180–83.

3 Christopher Pugsley, *Gallipoli: The New Zealand Story*, Hodder & Stoughton, Auckland, 1984, p. 271.

4 James, *Gallipoli*, p. 250.

5 Theodore Ropp, *War in the Modern World*, Collier-Macmillan, New York, 1965, Preface to revised edition, p. 5; John Keegan, *The American Civil War: A military history*, Hutchinson, London, 2009; see also, Keegan. *Fields of Battle: the Wars for North America*, Viking, London, 1996. Ropp was Professor of History at Duke University, formerly Professor of Maritime History at the US Naval War College and a member of the Secretary of the Army's Advisory Committee on Military History; Sir John Keegan was one of Britain's most eminent military historians. Obituary, *Telegraph* (London), 2 August 2012.

6 '[N]o battleground so easily lends itself to retrospective sentimentality', wrote John North, *Gallipoli: The fading vision*, Faber & Faber, London, 1966 (first published 1936), p. 20.

7 This chapter summarises the findings of extensive historical research and study *in situ* of the former battlefields and terrain of the Gallipoli Peninsula, stemming from the author's earlier article: Ashley Ekins, 'A ridge too far: military objectives and the dominance of terrain in the Gallipoli campaign', in Kenan Çelik and Cehan Koç (eds), *The Gallipoli Campaign: International Perspectives 85 Years On*, Atatürk and Gallipoli Campaign Research Center, Çanakkale Onsekiz Mart University, Çanakkale, Turkey, 2002, pp. 5–34.

8 The British names were misnomers resulting from errors in the first British maps issued to troops. The correct name of Achi Baba was Alçitepe (Turkish for 'plaster hill') but the hill retained the name Achi Baba throughout the campaign. Sari Bair was the Turkish name for the seaward-facing cliffs and slopes above the beaches north of Ari Burnu, whereas the correct name for the entire 'Sari Bair' range of hills and its highest peak was Kocaçimentepe. Brigadier General C.F. Aspinall-Oglander, *Military Operations: Gallipoli*, Vol. 1, *Inception of the campaign to May 1915*, William Heinemann, London, 1929, p. 37 n. 3, n. 4.

9 C.E.W. Bean, *The Story of Anzac: From 4 May, 1915, to the Evacuation of the Gallipoli Peninsula*, Vol. 2, The Official History of Australia in the War of 1914–1918, Angus & Robertson, Sydney, 1944 (first published 1924), pp. 432, 437.

10 Churchill, writing in his multi-volume history, *The World Crisis 1911–1918* (1923), quoted by Robert Rhodes James, *Churchill: A Study in Failure 1900–1939*, Penguin, Harmondsworth, 1973, p. 99 n. 54.

11 Robert Rhodes James, 'A visit to Gallipoli, 1962', *Stand-To* [Journal of the ACT Branch of the (Australian) Returned Services League], Vol. 9, No. 2 (March–October 1964), pp. 4–6.

12 GHQ, MEF, Force Order No. 1, 13 April 1915, Vol. I, *Maps and Appendices*, Aspinall-Oglander, *Military Operations: Gallipoli*, p. 7.

13 'Lord Kitchener's Instructions to Sir Ian Hamilton', 13 March 1915, p. 1, para. 5, Vol. 1, *Maps and Appendices*, Aspinall-Oglander, *Military Operations: Gallipoli*, Vol. 1, p. 37.

14 The original objective was stated as 'a line across the Peninsula through "Achi Baba peak" and this was not altered in the later instructions'. C.E.W. Bean, *The Story of Anzac: From the outbreak of war to the end of the first phase of the Gallipoli campaign, May 4, 1915*, Vol. 1, The Official History of Australia in the War of 1914–1918, Angus & Robertson, Sydney, 1921, Preface to Third Edition (1934), p. xl, n. 2.

15 Bean, *The Story of Anzac*, Vol. 1, Preface to Third Edition (1934), p. xl; descriptive notes, Map 2, 'Helles and the Narrows', Ordnance Survey Office, 1928, Vol. 1, *Maps and Appendices*, Aspinall-Oglander, *Military Operations: Gallipoli*, Vol. 1.

16 Aspinall-Oglander, *Military Operations: Gallipoli*, Vol. 1, p. 37.

17 Typical of some influential accounts was that by Lieutenant General Horace Robertson who had served on Gallipoli as a captain with the 10th Australian Light Horse Regiment. He argued in his military lectures that possession of Achi Baba for an advance on the Kilid Bahr plateau would have provided a valuable observation point and artillery positions to dominate enemy batteries on both sides of the Dardanelles. Lieutenant General H.C.H. Robertson, *Notes on the Gallipoli Campaign* (Army Headquarters, Canberra, 1948), lectures prepared in 1937–1938 for

Royal Military College, Duntroon, Lecture 4, p. 5, Item 33.68/29410, CRS A1194, National Archives of Australia (NAA).

18 Five such sources are cited by Robin Prior, *Churchill's 'World Crisis' as History*, Croom Helm, London, 1983, pp. 126, 299.

19 C.E.W. Bean, *Gallipoli Mission*, ABC Enterprises in association with the Australian War Memorial, Crows Nest, NSW, 1990 (first published 1948), pp. 283–4, 303–6, sketch p. 307.

20 Bean, *The Story of Anzac*, vol. I, Preface to Third Edition (1934), p. xl.

21 Major W.R.E. Harrison, 'Gallipoli revisited', *The Journal of the Royal Artillery*, Vol. LIX, No. 3, October 1932, pp. 286–99, 293.

22 Sir Roger Keyes, *The Naval Memoirs of Admiral of the Fleet Sir Roger Keyes: The Narrow Seas to the Dardanelles 1910-1915*, Thornton Butterworth, London, 1934, p. 325. Emphasis added.

23 Sir Julian S. Corbett, *Naval Operations*, vol. III, *History of the Great War based on official documents by direction of the Historical Section of the Committee of Imperial Defence*, Longmans, Green and Co., London, 1923, pp. 222, 242; James, *Gallipoli*, pp. 336–8.

24 C.E.W. Bean, *The Story of Anzac*, Vol. 2, pp. 432, 437. In seeking to gain ground at moderate cost, Hunter-Weston's tactics anticipated the effective 'bite and hold' operations developed later on the Western Front. Robin Prior, *Gallipoli: the end of the myth*, UNSW Press, Sydney, 2009, pp. 152–9, 245–6.

25 Bean, *The Story of Anzac*, vol. II, p. 907.

26 Bean, *The Story of Anzac*, vol. II, p. 432.

27 Order issued to VIII Corps, 6 August 1915, quoted in C.F. Aspinall-Oglander, *Military Operations: Gallipoli*, Vol. 2, *May 1915 to the evacuation*, Heinemann, London, 1932, p. 169.

28 Colonel Izzettin Calislar (chief of staff to Lieutenant Colonel Mustafa Kemal, Commander of the Turkish 19th Division), diary, 31 May 1915, translated and compiled by Ahmet Arda, 'Extracts from the Diary of a Turkish Officer', *[Australian] Defence Force Journal*, No. 81, March/April, 1990, pp. 83–98, 91.

29 Major Sherman Miles, 'Notes on the Dardanelles Campaign of 1915', part 3, *The Coast Artillery Journal*, Vol. 62, No. 2 (February 1925), pp. 119–43, 134. In the course of his detailed study Miles visited the Gallipoli battlefields four times and received assistance from the British historical section of the Committee of Imperial Defence (CID) and the Turkish General Staff, as well as from General Sir Ian Hamilton.

30 Brigadier General C. Cunliffe Owen (chief artillery officer on Birdwood's HQ staff), 'Artillery at Anzac in the Gallipoli Campaign, April to December 1915' (lecture delivered at the Royal Artillery Institution, 22 January 1920), *The Journal of the Royal Artillery*, vol. XLVI, no. 12, 1920, pp. 535–55, 543.

31 'Statement on artillery' by Brigadier General Sir Hugh Simpson Baikie, in Hamilton, *Gallipoli Diary*, vol. II,

Appendix I, pp. 279–91, 285. Baikie commanded the British artillery at Helles from 29 May to September 1915.

32 Hamilton, *Gallipoli Diary*, vol. I, p. 330. Hamilton used the name Hill 305 for Hill 971.

33 Corbett, *Naval Operations*, vol. III, p. 68.

34 Major W.R.E. Harrison, 'Gallipoli revisited', *The Journal of the Royal Artillery*, vol. LIX, no. 3 (October 1932), pp. 286–99, 293–4.

35 The distance from Hill 971 to Fort Çimenlik at Çanakkale is 16,500 yards (15,088 metres); from Hill 971 to Kilid Bahr is 15,160 yards (13,862 metres).

36 The issues of reinforcement, resupply and fire support to troops holding the heights, as well as the question of subsequent operations, are covered in Prior, *Gallipoli: the end of the myth*, pp. 185–9.

37 Hamilton, *Gallipoli Diary*, Vol. 2, 8 August 1915, p. 57.

38 For a comprehensive analysis of the development of British artillery capabilities in the First World War see Robin Prior and Trevor Wilson, *Command on the Western Front: The Military Career of Sir Henry Rawlinson 1914–18*, Blackwell, Oxford, 1992, pp. 36–43, 163–6, 292–5.

39 Bean, *The Story of Anzac*, Vol. 2, pp. 83–4.

40 Major-General Sir C.E. Callwell (former Director of Military Operations), *The Dardanelles*, Constable and Company, London, 1924, p. 189. Statistics on numbers of guns on Gallipoli vary, but these figures are generally corroborated in 'Dates of Arrival and Emplacement of Artillery, Australian and New Zealand Army Corps, Anzac, Gallipoli', Cunliffe Owen, 'Artillery at Anzac in the Gallipoli Campaign', p. 555.

41 Prior and Wilson, *Command on the Western Front*, pp. 163, 41.

42 Bean, *The Story of Anzac*, Vol. 2, ch. III.

43 Cunliffe Owen, 'Artillery at Anzac in the Gallipoli Campaign', p. 543.

44 The following information is from the statement on artillery by Baikie, in Hamilton, *Gallipoli Diary*, Vol. 2, Appendix I, pp. 279–91. There is considerable variation in numbers of guns and ammunition recorded in different sources.

45 Aspinall-Oglander, *Military Operations: Gallipoli*, Vol. 2, pp. 392–3.

46 Statement on artillery by Baikie, in Hamilton, *Gallipoli Diary*, Vol. 2 pp. 282–3.

47 Statement on artillery by Baikie, in Hamilton, *Gallipoli Diary*, Vol. 2, Appendix I, pp. 284–5; see also John Lee, *A Soldier's Life: General Sir Ian Hamilton 1853–1947*, Macmillan, London, 2000, caption to plate 16. The British official historian states that the four 60-pounder guns of 91st Heavy Battery, RGA, arrived but all were out of action by August owing to trouble with faulty recoil springs. Aspinall-Oglander, *Military Operations: Gallipoli*, Vol. 2, p. 168 n. 1.

48 Michael Crawshaw, 'The Impact of Technology on the BEF and its Commander', in Brian Bond and

Nigel Cave (ed.), *Haig: A Reappraisal 70 Years On*, Leo Cooper, Barnsley, 1999, pp. 155–75, 162, 173–4.

49 I.V. Hogg, and L.F. Thurston, *British Artillery Weapons and Ammunition 1914–1918*, Ian Allen, London, 1972, p. 160; S.N. Gower, *Guns of the Regiment*, Australian War Memorial, Canberra, ACT, 1981, pp. 176–77. By comparison, the 8-inch howitzer, introduced in 1916, weighed over 13 tons (14,000 kg) and a later 8-inch howitzer introduced in 1917 weighed over 8 tons (9000 kg).

50 Cunliffe Owen, 'Artillery at Anzac in the Gallipoli Campaign', p. 547. The weight in action of a 4.7-inch field gun was just under four tons (3870 kilograms), Gower, *Guns of the Regiment*, pp. 164–5.

51 Hamilton, *Gallipoli Diary*, Vol. 2, pp. 10–11.

52 The 'effective' ranges of the artillery discussed here and listed in the tables were considerably less than the maximum ranges given.

53 Bean, *The Story of Anzac*, vol. II, pp. 171–72; Callwell, *The Dardanelles*, pp. 339–42.

54 The allied fleet mounted a total of 274 medium and heavy guns. Aspinall-Oglander, *Military Operations: Gallipoli*, Vol. 1, p. 78.

55 CB 1550 'Report of the Committee [Mitchell Committee] appointed to investigate the attacks delivered on and the enemy defences of the Dardanelles Straits', 1919, Admiralty Naval Staff, Gunnery Division, April 1921, AWM 51 [39], esp. pp. 72–9, Appendix A to chapter 4, 'Factors governing ships' fire on the Dardanelles forts'.

56 Hans Kannengiesser, *The Campaign in Gallipoli*, Hutchinson, London, 1938, p. 81

57 CB 1550 'Report of the Committee [Mitchell Committee] . . .', 1919, pp. 76, 509, 524–7.

58 'The Turkish General Staff History of the Campaign in Gallipoli', Part I, *The Army Quarterly*, Vol. XI, No. 2 (January 1926), pp. 343–53, 351.

59 Aspinall-Oglander, *Military Operations: Gallipoli*, Vol. 1, pp. 86–7 n. 2.

60 Bean, *The Story of Anzac*, Vol. 1, pp. 314–15, 392–5, 480.

61 Major General Kiazim Pasha, Chief of the Turkish General Staff (Chief of Staff to Liman von Sanders, commander of the Turkish 5th Army on Gallipoli in 1915), responses to questions by Australian official historian Charles Bean, 1919. Bean, *Gallipoli Mission*, p. 352.

62 Major Zeki Bey (former commander of the 1st Battalion of the 57th Turkish Regiment and the 21st Regiment during the Gallipoli campaign). Bean, *Gallipoli Mission*, pp. 251–2.

63 Cunliffe Owen, 'Artillery at Anzac in the Gallipoli Campaign', p. 539. On the provenance of the issued map, its topographical inaccuracies and faulty compass bearing, see the defence of British mapping by Peter Chasseaud and Peter Doyle, *Grasping Gallipoli: Terrain, maps and failure at the Dardanelles, 1915*, Spellmount, Staplehurst, Kent, 2005, pp. 157–68; also pp. 213–14,

221–2, 234, 297 on the deficiencies of the map which was 'useless for the direction and control of fire'.

64 Bean, *The Story of Anzac*, Vol. 2, p. 164, n. 46.

65 Turkish 1:25,000 maps were based on a topographical survey of the peninsula in c. 1912/13. Chasseaud and Doyle, *Grasping Gallipoli*, pp. 59, 72, 149–50, 262.

66 Chasseaud and Doyle, *Grasping Gallipoli*, pp. 40, 71–2, 157–62, 227.

67 Bean, *The Story of Anzac*, Vol. 1, p. 242.

68 Aspinall-Oglander, *Military Operations: Gallipoli*, Vol. 1, pp. 166 n. 3, 167.

69 R.A. Jones, *The War in the Air: Being the Story of the part played in the Great War by the Royal Air Force*, Vol. II, Oxford University Press, Oxford, 1928, p. 2.

70 For examples of the effects of map inaccuracies on operations, see Aspinall-Oglander, *Military Operations: Gallipoli*, Vol. 1, pp. 137 n. 1, n. 2, 282 n. 1, 204 n. 2, 226, 229 n. 2, 282 n. 1.

71 See the extensive maps and strength and establishment information in the Turkish General Staff official history: *Çanakkale Cephesi Harekati* ('Gallipoli front operations'), 3 Vols, *Birinci Dunya Harbi'nde Turk Harbi* (Turkish War during the First World War), *Genelkurmay Basimevi* (General Staff Printing House), Ankara, 1978, 1980, 1993; Turkish General Staff, *A Brief History of the Çanakkale Campaign in the First World War (June 1914–January 1916)*, Turkish General Staff Printing House, Ankara, 2004.

72 Bean, *The Story of Anzac*, Vol. 2, pp. 497–8, 508–9 n. 23.

73 The claim that 'some of the perceived inadequacies of the printed maps were overcome' before the landing by such measures as layer-colouring of reliefs is fanciful. Chasseaud and Doyle, *Grasping Gallipoli*, p. 161.

74 Map of Gallipoli, Sheet 2, AWM G7432/G1, S65v.2a. Ross sent the map to Bean in June 1928. A similar map, minus annotations of Turkish defences, was apparently issued before the landing to the commander of the 1st Australian Brigade, Colonel H.N. MacLaurin. AWM G7432/G1, S65v.2c

75 Aspinall-Oglander, *Military Operations: Gallipoli*, Vol. 2, p. 242 n. 1, 248, 140–1.

76 Rhodes James, *Gallipoli*, p. 246.

77 'Final instructions from GHQ to IX Corps for Suvla operations', 29 July 1915, para. 4, Appendix 3 in Vol. 2, *Maps and Appendices*, p. 19, Aspinall-Oglander, *Military Operations: Gallipoli*. GHQ instructions and operation orders are reproduced as Appendices 2, 3, 4, 5.

78 Aspinall-Oglander, *Military Operations: Gallipoli*, Vol. 2, chs X, XVII.

79 'First instructions from GHQ to IX Corps for Suvla operations', 22 July 1915, para. 2, Appendix 2 in Vol. 2, *Maps and Appendices*, pp. 15–18, Aspinall-Oglander, *Military Operations: Gallipoli*. Hamilton noted that success in this aim would depend upon the capture of Hill 971 and the capture of Suvla Bay as a base of operations. *Ibid.*, para. 4.

80 James, *Gallipoli*, pp. 33, 79, 239.

81 Prior, *Gallipoli: the end of the myth*, pp. 197–200.

82 Robert Rhodes James described his experience of walking the difficult terrain in 'A visit to Gallipoli, 1962', *Stand-To* [Journal of the ACT Branch of the Returned Servicemen's League], Vol. 9, No. 2 (March–October 1964), pp. 4–6, 5.

83 Suvla 1:10,000 scale map, stamped 26, sheet nos 118/119, compiled by Intelligence Branch, General Staff, GHQ, MEF, September 1915, trenches based on information available up to 14 October 1915, AWM map collection.

84 'Very Urgent' message by Mustafa Kemal, 11 August 1915, quoted in Tim Travers, 'The other side of the hill', *MHQ: The Quarterly Journal of Military History*, Vol. 12, No. 3, March 2000, pp. 6–19.

85 Bean, *The Story of Anzac*, vol. II, pp. 183–4, 466 n. 59; Aspinall-Oglander, *Military Operations: Gallipoli*, Vol. 2, p. 130.

86 Aspinall-Oglander, *Military Operations: Gallipoli*, Vol. 2, p. 308.

87 Lieutenant Colonel The Hon Aubrey Herbert, *Mons, Anzac and Kut by an MP*, Pen & Sword, Barnsley, 2009 (first published 1919), p. 139.

88 Hamilton, *Gallipoli Diary*, Vol. 2, pp. 105–6.

89 Hamilton, *Gallipoli Diary*, Vol. 2, p. 157.

90 Hamilton, quoted in James, *Gallipoli*, p. 311.

91 Sir Ronald East (ed.), *The Gallipoli Diary of Sergeant Lawrence of the Australian Engineers*, Melbourne University Press, Melbourne, 1983, p. 82.

92 A.J. Hill, Introduction to UQP edition, Bean, *The Story of Anzac*, Vol. 2, University of Queensland Press in association with the Australian War Memorial, St Lucia, Queensland, 1981, p. xxix.

Chapter 4

1 The encircled beach and land area of Australian and New Zealand operations also took the name 'Anzac Cove' and the 'old Anzac' area.

2 The Vickers gun, an improved version of the Maxim, had limited distribution on Gallipoli.

3 Sir Ian Hamilton, 'Lack of guns in Gallipoli campaign', *Reveille*, 1 September 1932, p. 2.

4 Sir Ian Hamilton, *Gallipoli Diary*, 2 vols, Edward Arnold & Co, London, 1930, vol. II, p. 57.

5 (Sir) Nevill Smyth, 'The storming of Lone Pine', *Reveille*, 1 August 1932, p. 7.

6 Peter Burness, 'Hooky Walker, the English general', *Wartime*, 50, 2010, p. 29.

7 I.G. Mackay, 'Lonesome Pine: called after song', in *Reveille*, 1 August 1932, p. 14.

8 Smyth, 'The storming of Lone Pine', p. 7.

9 Mackay, 'Lonesome Pine: called after song', p. 14. (Other accounts also state that this was done.)

10 No. 3 Operational Order, 1st Infantry Brigade, 5 August 1915: 'The signal will be ... three (3) short whistle blasts by the Bde Major in the entrance of B5 tunnel at 1730', 1st Australian Brigade War Diary, AWM 4; Eric Wren, *Randwick to Hargicourt: History of the 3rd battalion, AIF*, Ronald G. McDonald, Sydney, 1935, p. 100.

11 (C.E.W. Bean), Reports received from the official press representative with the Australian forces. Published in, Commonwealth of Australia, *Military Order 530 of 1915*, p. 73.

12 F.W. Taylor and T.A. Cusack, *Nulli Secundus: A history of the Second Battalion, AIF, 1914–1919*, John Burridge, Swanbourne, WA, 1992 (original edition 1942), p. 141.

13 Peter Chasseaud and Peter Doyle, *Grasping Gallipoli: Terrain, maps and failure at the Dardanelles, 1915*, Spellmount, Staplehurst, Kent, 2005, p. 246.

14 2nd Australian Battalion War Diary, 6 August 1915, AWM4 23/2/6.

15 C.E.W. Bean, *Two Men I Knew: William Bridges and Brudenell White, founders of the AIF*, Angus and Robertson, Sydney, 1957, p. 104.

16 Hamilton, *Gallipoli diary*, vol. II, p. 57.

17 2nd Brigade War Diary, August 1915, AWM4, 23/2/6.

18 The Anzac war diary says the attack went at 3.15 am (the official history does not give the time). AWM4 (1/25).

19 Forsyth continued on from Gallipoli, and led the battalion next year at Pozières in France; after that, he had a nervous breakdown.

20 Glasford was a British officer serving in the AIF; he was later killed in France.

21 2nd Brigade War Diary, August 1915, AWM4 23/2/6.

22 Bean, *Two Men I Knew*, p. 105.

23 There is evidence that watches were synchronised, but perhaps only within the brigade.

24 C.E.W. Bean, *The Australian Imperial Force in France during the allied offensive, 1918*, vol. 6, Official History of Australia in the War of 1914–18, Angus and Robertson, Sydney, 1942, p. 1083.

25 Australian Red Cross Society Wounded and Missing Enquiry Bureau. AWM 1DRL/0428.

26 G.H. Bourne, *The history of the 2nd Light Horse Regiment*, John Burridge, Swanbourne, WA, 1994, p. 25.

27 1st ALH Brigade War Diary. AWM4 10/1/13 PART 1.

28 C.E.W. Bean, *The story of Anzac: from 4 May 1915 to the evacuation of the Gallipoli peninsula*, vol. 2, Official History of Australia in the War of 1914–1918, Angus and Robertson, Sydney, 1941, p. 633.

29 Ross McMullin, *Pompey Elliott*, Scribe, Carlton North, Vic., 2002, p. 165.

Chapter 5

1 The exchange, quoting from Allanson's 'confidential, unpublished account', is recounted in R. Rhodes James, *Gallipoli*, Random House, London, 1999, p. 272.

2 C.F. Aspinall-Oglander, *Military Operations: Gallipoli*, Vol. 2, *May 1915 to the evacuation*, Heinemann, London, 1932, p. 185. For a fuller discussion of the plan for the Sari Bair assault, see also C.E.W. Bean, *The Story of Anzac, from 4 May 1915 to the Evacuation of the Gallipoli Peninsula*, Vol. 2, The Official History of Australia in the War of 1914–1918, Angus & Robertson, Sydney, 1924 (edition of 1939), pp. 457–63.

3 Monash to Bertha Monash (daughter), 8 May 1916,

Monash papers (hereafter MP), National Library of Australia (NLA), MS1884.

4   Monash to Bean, 4 May 1931, Item 27/3, 3DRL/7953, AWM38. This file contains Bean's correspondence regarding the British Official History of the Gallipoli campaign.

5   New Zealand & Australian Division Order 11 (and instructions), 5 August 1915, NZ & A Div War Diary (hereafter WD), August 1915, 1/53/5 Part 1, AWM4. This is Godley's operation order, which sets out the tasks and routes for all the columns.

6   Cox's evidence to Dardanelles Commission. See *Final report*, London, 1919, p. 33.

7   The author retraced the 4th Brigade's route in April 1981 and in April 1990.

8   Bean, *The Story of Anzac*, Vol. 2, p. 461. See also pp. 462–3.

9   Bean to J.E. Edmonds, 17 June 1931, Bean Collection, Item 27/3, 3DRL/7953, AWM38.

10 Cox's instructions, dated 6 August 1915, are in Folder 20, Series 3, 3DRL/2316, Australian War Memorial (hereafter AWM). (3DRL/2316 is the collection of Monash's papers held by the AWM.) See also Bean, *The Story of Anzac*, Vol. 2, p. 567 and Aspinall-Oglander, *Gallipoli*, Vol. 2, p. 191.

11 Dated 5 August 1915, the timetable is in Folder 20, Series 3, 3DRL/2316.

12 NZ & A Div G834 dated 3 August 1915, NZ & A Div WD, 1/53/5 Part 1, AWM4; General Staff, *Field Service Regulations, Part I: Operations*, HMSO, London, 1909 (reprint 1914), p. 187 (hereafter *FSR*).

13 Monash, 'Notes on operations', 2 August 1915, Folder 19, Series 3, 3DRL/2316, AWM.

14 Monash's notes, orders etc on the Sari Bair operations are in Folders 19–20, Series 3, 3DRL/2316, AWM.

15 Cox's instructions, dated 6 August 1915, Folder 20, Series 3, 3DRL/2316.

16 Monash to Bean, 4 May 1931, Item 27/3, 3DRL/7953, AWM38. In his planning, Cox assumed that there would be no opposition until the Aghyl Dere was reached. The advance to that location was to be a 'march in one column'. See Cox's planning notes of 3 August 1915, headed 'General Plan', in Folder 19, Series 3, 3DRL/2316, AWM.

17 *FSR*, p. 134.

18 See P.A. Pedersen, *Monash as military commander*, Melbourne University Press, Melbourne, 1985, p. 94.

19 NZ & A Div G834 dated 3 August 1915, NZ & A Div WD, 1/53/5 Part 1, AWM4.

20 Cox's instructions, dated 6 August 1915, Folder 20, Series 3, 3DRL/2316.

21 C.E.W. Bean, *The Australian Imperial Force in France 1917*, Vol. 4, The Official History of Australia in the War of 1914–1918, Angus & Robertson, Sydney, 1933 (edition of 1938), p. 488n.

22 Monash to Godley, 6 June 1915, Folder 17, Series 3, 3DRL/2316, AWM.

23 Bean, entry for 19 July 1915, Diary 10, 3DRL/606/10/1, AWM38.

24 Monash to NZ & A Div, 21 July 1915, Folder 19, Series 3, 3DRL/2316, AWM.

25 Capt. J. Gellibrand to Walter (brother), 4 November 1915, Item 2, 749/37/1, 3DRL/6541, AWM.

26 A.G. Butler, *The Gallipoli Campaign*, Vol. 1, Part 1, The Official History of the Australian Army Medical Services in the War of 1914–1918, Australian War Memorial, Melbourne, 1938, pp. 252–3.

27 Geoffrey Serle, *John Monash: A Biography*, Melbourne University Press, Melbourne, 1982, p. 278; photographs of Monash on embarkation from Melbourne on 22 December 1914, facing p. 248.

28 Bean, *The Story of Anzac*, Vol. 2, p. 584.

29 Dated 4 August 1914, the 'Longitudinal Section' is in Folder 20, Series 3, 3DRL/2316.

30 4th Brigade Operation Order No. 5, 6 August 1915, 4th Bde WD, 23/4/1 Part 2, AWM4.

31 Monash's notes for these meetings and the text for his briefing address in Reserve Gully are in Folder 20, Series 3, 3DRL/2316, AWM.

32 Aspinall-Oglander, *Gallipoli*, Vol. 2, p. 192.

33 These officers were visiting Gallipoli in 1990 as part of the Australian government-sponsored Anzac veterans' pilgrimage to commemorate the 75th anniversary of the campaign.

34 Bean, *The Story of Anzac*, Vol. 2, p. 664. Writing to the British Official Historian in 1931, Bean remarked that 'In France, when we had twice the experience, we should have considered about half this task practicable, and would never have dreamed of setting more with any hope of success.' Bean to Edmonds, 17 June 1931, Item 27/3, 3DRL/7953, AWM38. In 1915, though, Bean thought that the risks involved in the attempt on Hill 971 were worth taking. Entry for 6 August 1915, Diary 11, 3DRL/606/11/1, AWM38.

35 Bean, *The Story of Anzac*, Vol. 2, p. 585. Bean states that the head of Monash's 4th Brigade was forced to halt at No. 2 Outpost 'while the 40th Brigade moved from seaward across its path at the crossing of the Chailak Dere.'

36 *FSR*, p. 51.

37 This paragraph is based on the account in Pedersen, *Monash as military commander*, pp. 100–101.

38 Monash to Bean, 4 May 1931, Item 27/3, 3DRL/7953, AWM38. Lt Col C.M. Dare (14th Battalion) remarked to Bean, that 'General Monash was personally responsible for getting the column moving again'. See Bean to Edmonds, 17 June 1931, Item 27/3, 3DRL/7953, AWM38.

39 Pedersen, *Monash as military commander*, p. 101.

40 Monash's account to Bean, 20 August 1915, Bean Diary 14, 3DRL/606/14/1, AWM38.

41 Monash's account to Bean, 20 August 1915, Bean Diary 14, 3DRL/606/14/1, AWM38.

42 See Birdwood to Bean, 21 April 1922, Item 24, Series 5, 3DRL/8042, AWM38 (Bean's Historical Notes – Gallipoli: Suvla Bay); Cox in Brudenell White to Bean, 27 February 1931, Item 27/2, 3DRL/ 7953, AWM38; Godley in J. North to Allanson, 12 December 1935,

North papers, Item I/3/26, Liddell Hart Centre for Military Archives, King's College, University of London (hereafter LHC).

43 Entry for 8–9 August 1915, Bean Diary 11, 3DRL/606/11/1, AWM38.

44 Serle, *John Monash*, p. 236. Rhodes James's *Gallipoli* was first published in 1965. His account of the Monash/Allanson episode in the 1999 edition, for which he wrote a new preface, remained unchanged.

45 Entry for 7 August 1915, Bain diary, Item 23, Series 5, 3DRL/8042, AWM38 (Bean's Historical Notes – Gallipoli: Battle of Sari Bair).

46 For Monash's outbursts at Anzac on 3 May 1915 and during the Hindenburg Line attack in September 1918, see Pedersen, *Monash as military commander*, pp. 76, 288–90.

47 Allanson to North, 18 December 1935 and North to Bean, 9 June 1936, North papers, Items I/3/28 and 76, LHC. Monash's letter, dated 16 August 1916, is in F.M. Cutlack (ed.), *War letters of General Monash*, Angus & Robertson, Sydney, 1934, pp. 62–3.

48 Allanson to North, 18 December 1935, North papers, Item I/3/28, LHC.

49 Rhodes James to North, 28 February 1964, North papers, Item I/3/402, LHC.

50 Serle, *John Monash*, pp. 236–7. Serle's assessment of the incident and the sources relating to it are in his Appendix II, pp. 534–5, 582n.

51 Besides C.S.M. Bain, they included Chaplain F.W. Wray (13th Bn), Capt. H. Loughran (14th Bn) and the members of the 4th Brigade staff. Pedersen, *Monash as military commander*, pp. 105–6. See also H.V. Howe to Rhodes James, 7 November 1964, Bazley Collection, Folder 118, 3DRL/3520, AWM. Howe had landed with the 11th Battalion at Anzac on 25 April 1915 and revisited Gallipoli with Charles Bean in 1919. He reviewed Rhodes James's drafts and was highly critical of his version of the Allanson/Monash encounter. Rhodes James's description was, as Howe said in this letter, 'I am sure quite untrue'.

52 Dated 19 January 1917, Allanson's evidence is in File 16/1/1, Hamilton papers, LHC.

53 Bean wrote up his discussions with Allanson in entries for 29 and 30 August 1915 in Diary 10, 3DRL/606/11/1, AWM38. Nor is there any mention of Monash in the relevant entries, 6–8 August 1915, in Allanson's diary, which is in Item 23, Series 5, 3DRL/8042, AWM38. An abridged printed version, fifty copies of which were produced for private circulation by Allanson, is held by the National Army Museum in London.

54 Bean, *The Story of Anzac*, Vol. 2, p. 589.

55 Monash's account, 20 August 1915, in Bean Diary 14, 3DRL/606/14/1, AWM38.

56 NZ & A Div to 4th Brigade, 6.35 pm 7 August 1915, Folder 20, Series 3, 3DRL/2316, AWM.

57 Entry for 7 August 1915, Monash diary, File 9/D16, MP, NLA.

58 See E. Margolin (16th Bn) to Bean, 9 August 1922, and D.R. McDermid (14th Bn), 'The August 1915 fighting at Gallipoli', p. 9, both in Item 23, Series 5, 3DRL/8042, AWM38.

59 Pedersen, *Monash as military commander*, p. 108.

60 Bean, *The Story of Anzac*, Vol. 2, p. 656.

61 Dare to Bean, 3 March 1931, Item 27/3, 3DRL/7953, AWM38.

62 A transcript of Pope's messages during the attack is in Item 23, Series 5, 3DRL/8042, AWM38.

63 C. Smith, 'The fighting at Suvla', n.d., in Item 23, Series 5, 3DRL/8042, AWM38.

64 See Monash to F. Swinburne, 20 July 1925, MP, NLA.

65 4th Brigade strength state for 29 August 1915, Folder 22, Series 3, 3DRL/2316.

66 See the second of Monash's three lectures to the officers of the 3rd Australian Division, dated 25 October 1916, in Folder 44, Series 3, 3DRL/ 2316, AWM.

67 Pedersen, *Monash as military commander*, p. 204.

Chapter 6

1 This title of this chapter, 'From the uttermost ends of the earth', is taken from the poignant epitaph on the New Zealand National Memorial on the summit of Chunuk Bair (Conkbayiri), unveiled in May 1925. Ian McGibbon, *Gallipoli: A Guided to New Zealand Battlefields and Memorials*, Reed Publishing, Auckland, 2004, pp. 94–100.

2 Lieutenant Colonel W.G. Malone's diary 3 August 1915, MSX 2547, in John Crawford (ed.), *No Better Death: The Great War Diaries and Letters of William G. Malone*, Reed Publishing, Auckland, 2005, p. 294.

3 Christopher Pugsley, *Gallipoli: the New Zealand Story*, Hodder & Stoughton, Auckland, 1984 p. 283.

4 Crawford (ed.), *No Better Death*, pp. 306–7.

5 Malone to OC NZ Infantry Brigade, 7 August 1915, Malone Family Collection, in Crawford (ed.), *No Better Death*, p. 307; Pugsley, *Gallipoli*, p. 277.

6 Pugsley, *Gallipoli*, pp. 284–85.

7 Pugsley, *Gallipoli*, p. 285.

8 Pugsley, *Gallipoli*, p. 285.

9 Pugsley, *Gallipoli*, p. 285; Crawford (ed.), *No Better Death*, pp. 306–07.

10 Malone diary entry 4 August 1915 MSX2547, Alexander Turnbull Library, in Crawford (ed.), *No Better Death*, pp. 294–95.

11 Crawford (ed.), *No Better Death*, p. 307.

12 C.E.W. Bean, *The Story of Anzac, from 4 May 1915 to the Evacuation of the Gallipoli Peninsula*, Vol. 2, The Official History of Australia in the War of 1914–1918, Angus & Robertson, Sydney, 1924 (edition of 1944), p. 637.

13 Bean, *The Story of Anzac*, Vol. 2, pp. 637–8; Crawford (ed.), *No Better Death*, p. 307; Pugsley, *Gallipoli*, p. 285; David W. Cameron, *Sorry, Lads, But the Order is to Go*, UNSW Press, Sydney, 2009, pp. 206–7.

14 Pugsley, *Gallipoli*, p. 285; Crawford (ed.), *No Better Death*, p. 308.

15 Pugsley, *Gallipoli*, pp. 285–86; Crawford (ed.), *No Better Death*, p. 308.

16 Pugsley, *Gallipoli*, p. 286; Crawford (ed.), *No Better Death*, p. 308.

17 C.S. Algie, diary, 7 August 1915, MS1374, Alexander Turnbull Library.

18 Pugsley, *Gallipoli*, p. 286.

19 Interview, Christopher Pugsley with Charlie Clark, TVNZ 1982, in Pugsley, *Gallipoli*, pp. 286–87.

20 Pugsley, *Gallipoli*, p. 287.

21 Pugsley, *Gallipoli*, p. 287.

22 Pugsley, *Gallipoli*, p. 287; Cameron, *Sorry, Lads*, pp. 223–24.

23 Pugsley, *Gallipoli*, p. 288.

24 Crawford (ed.), *No Better Death*, pp. 310–11.

25 Ben Smart, diary, 8 August 1915, in Crawford (ed.), *No Better Death*, p. 311; Pugsley, *Gallipoli*, p. 288.

26 Pugsley, *Gallipoli*, p. 288.

27 Pugsley, *Gallipoli*, pp. 288–89; Crawford (ed.), *No Better Death*, p. 311.

28 Pugsley, *Gallipoli*, pp. 289–90; Crawford (ed.), *No Better Death*, p. 311; Archives New Zealand, WA/73/1, Report of Fighting on Chunuk Bair; letter, Bill Cunningham to Robert Hughes, 23 February 1916, in Robert Hughes Collection MS Papers 4192, Alexander Turnbull Library.

29 Pugsley, *Gallipoli*, p. 290; Crawford (ed.), *No Better Death*, pp. 313–14.

30 Crawford (ed.), *No Better Death*, p. 315; Pugsley, *Gallipoli*, pp. 291–93.

31 Letter, Cunningham to Hughes, 23 February 1916, MS Papers 4192, Alexander Turnbull Library.

32 Letter, Cunningham to Hughes, 23 February 1916.

33 Crawford (ed.), *No Better Death*, p. 317; Pugsley, p. 302.

34 Hastings's account in Crawford (ed.), *No Better Death*, p. 317; Pugsley, *Gallipoli*, p. 302.

35 Pugsley, *Gallipoli*, p. 298.

36 Pugsley, *Gallipoli*, p. 314.

37 Pugsley, *Gallipoli*, p. 303.

38 Pugsley, *Gallipoli*, p. 303.

39 Pugsley, *Gallipoli*, p. 303.

40 Pugsley, *Gallipoli*, pp. 303–4.

41 Lieutenant Colonel W. Meldrum, quoted in Ted Andrews, 'Kiwi Trooper: The Story of Queen Alexandra's Own', *Wanganui Chronicle*, 1967; Pugsley, *Gallipoli*, p. 306; Terry Kinloch, *Echoes of Gallipoli*, Exisle Publishing, Auckland, 2005, p. 221.

42 Kinloch, *Echoes of Gallipoli*, p. 221.

43 Meldrum in Andrews, 'Kiwi Trooper'.

44 Kinloch, *Echoes of Gallipoli*, p. 223.

45 Bean, *The Story of Anzac*, Vol. 2, p. 705; Cameron, *Sorry, Lads*, p. 301.

46 Meldrum in Andrews, 'Kiwi Trooper'.

47 Harry Ernest Browne Collection, MS3519, Alexander Turnbull Library.

48 Kinloch, *Echoes of Gallipoli*, p. 226; Pugsley, *Gallipoli*, p. 311.

49 Pugsley, *Gallipoli*, p. 311.

50 Cameron, *Sorry, Lads*, p. 303; Pugsley, *Gallipoli*, p. 312.

51 Cameron, *Sorry, Lads*, p. 303–04; R. Stowers, *Bloody Gallipoli: The New Zealanders' Story*, David Bateman, Auckland, 2005, p. 191.

52 Pugsley, *Gallipoli*, p. 312. The Australian official history reports the Turkish assault consisted of 'three or four regiments'. Bean, *The Story of Anzac*, Vol. 2, p. 709. The British official history estimates the Turkish strength as 'six battalions'. C.F. Aspinall-Oglander, *Military Operations: Gallipoli*, Vol. 2, *May 1915 to the Evacuation*, William Heinemann, London, 1932, p. 306.

53 Pugsley, *Gallipoli*, p. 312.

54 Aspinall-Oglander, *Military Operations: Gallipoli*, Vol. 2, pp. 306–8.

55 General Sir Alexander Godley, *Life of an Irish Soldier*, John Murray, London, 1939, pp. 187–88.

56 Bean, *The Story of Anzac*, Vol. 2, aerial photograph of New Zealand positions held on 8–9 August and later Turkish redoubts on the main ridge at Chunuk Bair, September 1915; also map with key, p. 719 and facing page.

Chapter 7

1 In a speech Churchill delivered to his parliamentary constituency in Dundee, Scotland on 5 June 1915, he urged a continuing military effort on Gallipoli, stating that the campaign offered 'some of the shortest paths to a triumphant peace'.

2 The narrative of events and commentary in this chapter draws primarily on Turkish publications, including the following: Turkish General Staff official history, *Çanakkale Cephesi Harekati* (Gallipoli front operations), *Haziram 1915–Ocak 1916* (June 1915 –January 1916), *V Nci Cilt 3 Ncii Kitap* (Vol. 5 Book 3), *Birinci Dunya Harbi'nde Turk Harbi* (Turkish War during the First World War), *Genelkurmay Basimevi* (General Staff Printing House), Ankara, 1980; Mustafa Kemal, *Arıburnu ve Anafartalar Raporları* (Ari Burnu and Anafartalar Reports), Tarih Kurumu Yayınları, Ankara, n.d.; Ismet Inönü, *Memoirs*, Bilgi Yayınevi, Ankara, 2006.

3 For details see Edward J. Erickson, *Gallipoli: The Ottoman Campaign*, Pen & Sword, Barnsley, 2010, pp. 128–31.

4 Vehip was Esat Pasha's younger brother and had previously commanded the Ottoman 2nd Army before he was appointed in July 1915 to command the Southern Group. Erickson, *Gallipoli*, p. 129.

5 Erickson, *Gallipoli*, pp. 134–5.

6 The various accounts of this famous exchange all derive from Mustafa Kemal Atatürk's memoirs. See, for example, Robert Rhodes James, *Gallipoli*, Pimlico, London, 1999, pp. 254–5; Tim Travers, *Gallipoli 1915*, Tempus, Stroud, 2001, p. 115; and the chapter by Harvey Broadbent in this volume.

7 Quoted in James, *Gallipoli*, p. 255.

8 C.E.W. Bean, *The Story of Anzac, from 4 May 1915 to the Evacuation of the Gallipoli Peninsula*, Vol. 2, The Official History of Australia in the War of 1914–1918, Angus & Robertson, Sydney, 1924 (edition of 1944), pp. 450–53.

9   Contrary to claims in earlier histories, more recent studies have argued that the area from Chunuk Bair to Hill 971 was not undefended, but in fact occupied by relatively strong Turkish forces who were simply in need of a coherent command structure and battle plan. Erickson, *Gallipoli*, pp. 150–51.

10 Fahri Belen, *20nci Yüzyılda Osmanlı Devleti Tarihi* (Ottoman History in the 20th Century), Remzi Kitapevi, Istanbul, 1973; Fahri Belen, *Çanakkale Savaşı'ndan Alınan Dersler* (Lessons learned from the Gallipoli Campaign), Yeditepe Yayınevi, Istanbul, 2009.

11 When Fahri Belen taught at the military academy, he organised a war game which demonstated that three divisions were not enough for this task. At least two more divisions were needed, plus a naval attack to stop the transportation of Turkish troops across the Dardanelles: only then might that plan have succeeded. He also argued that a landing and attack from Bolayır would have faced similar problems.

12 All the following extracts are from Lieutenant Colonel G.S. Patton Jr, *The Defence of Gallipoli: A General Staff Study*, Headquarters Hawaiian Department, Fort Shafter TH, 31 August 1936. In the First World War Patton had commanded a tank brigade of the US Army in France and was wounded in action in September 1918.

Chapter 8

A note on archival sources:

The Prussian Military Archive (Heeresarchiv) in Potsdam was destroyed in 1945, so most of the relevant files are no longer available (for example, the papers of Liman von Sanders). Some papers survived in the Bavarian and Württembergian military archives in Munich and Stuttgart. A wealth of relevant material is to be found in the Archive of the Foreign Office (PA/AA Berlin), some of which has been drawn on by Jehuda Wallach (see below). Some files from the Kriegsgeschichtliche Forschungsanstalt des Heeres (formerly the Reichsarchiv) were captured in 1945 by the Red Army. The major portion of this material is now in the Military Archive in Freiburg (BA/MA Freiburg, the so-called 'W 10' files). A smaller portion is still in Moscow, in the so-called Special Archive (Centre for Historical Documentary Collections).

1   Otto Liman von Sanders: *Fünf Jahre Türkei*, Berlin, 1919, p. 125, speaks of 500 German soldiers at Gallipoli in 1915; Carl Mühlmann, *Der Kampf um die Dardanellen: Schlachten des Weltkrieges in Einzeldarstellungen*, vol. 16, Berlin, 1927, p. 164, mentions 700; Klaus Wolf, *Gallipoli 1915: Das deutsche-türkische Militärbündnis im Ersten Weltkrieg*, Sulzbach/Ts. and Bonn, 2008, p. 195, follows Mühlmann, (Mühlmann was von Sanders's *aide de camp* or Rittmeister during the Gallipoli campaign and later worked in the interwar period for the Reichsarchiv).

2   Wolf, *Gallipoli 1915*, p. 139.

3   For the Ottoman perspective, see: Mustafa Aksakal, 'War as the Savior? Hopes for War and Peace in Ottoman Politics before 1914', in Holger Afflerbach and David Stevenson (eds), *An Improbable War? The Outbreak of World War I and European Political Culture before 1914*, Berghahn Books, New York and Oxford, 2007, pp. 287–302.

4   'Von der Türkei hofft man besonders den Aufstand des Islam, und vielleicht eine direkte Einwirkung auf Rußland durch Landung im Schwarzen Meer', in Holger Afflerbach (ed.): *Kaiser Wilhelm II als Oberster Kriegsherr während des Ersten Weltkrieges – Quellen aus der militärischen Umgebung des Kaisers 1914–1918*, München, Oldenbourg, 2005 (*Deutsche Geschichtsquellen des 19. und 20. Jahrhunderts*, vol. 64), p. 190.

5   Egmont Zechlin, 'Friedensbestrebungen und Revolutionierungsversuche im Ersten Weltkrieg', in *Aus Politik und Zeitgeschichte*, B 20/1961; B 24/1961; B 25/1961; B 20/1963; B 22/1963; Hew Strachan, *The First World War*, vol. 1: *To arms*, Oxford University Press, Oxford, 2001, pp. 694–814 ('Germany's Global Strategy').

6   Von Sanders, *Fünf Jahre Türkei*, pp. 48ff.

7   See especially Mühlmann, *Oberste Heeresleitung*, and Karl-Heinz Janßen: *Der Kanzler und der General. Die Führungskrise um Bethmann Hollweg und Falkenhayn, 1914–1918*, Göttingen, 1967.

8   Mühlmann, *Oberste Heeresleitung*, pp. 22–23.

9   Mühlmann, *Oberste Heeresleitung*, p. 22: 'Die Türkei ist militärisch eine Null. Die Berichte unserer Militärmission lauten geradezu trostlos. Die Armee ist in einer Verfassung, die jeder Beschreibung spottet. Wenn man früher von der Türkei als dem kranken Mann sprach, so muß man jetzt schon von dem sterbenden sprechen. Sie hat keine Lebenskraft mehr und befindet sich unrettbar im Zustand der Agonie.'

10 Eyal Ginio, 'Mobilizing the Ottoman Nation during the Balkan Wars (1912–1913): Awakening from the Ottoman Dream', in *War in History*, 2005, 12:2, pp. 156–77.

11 'Eben war der Türkische Botschafter bei mir; ich sprach mit ihm über die Operationen der Türken. Nun das sieht allerdings sehr schlecht aus; vor 4 Monaten glauben sie nicht über den Suez-Kanal zu kommen; und in Klein Asien macht sehr bald Eis und Schnee allen Operationen ein Ende. Die helfen uns also gar nicht. Wir stehen nach wie vor allein da. Es ist lediglich vielleicht eine politische Hilfe, militärisch bedeutet es nach Ansicht eines auch hier anwesenden deutschen Offiziers, der zur Militärmission gehört, 1% unserer eigenen Kraft. Na! Das ist so gut wie Nichts.' Afflerbach, *Kaiser Wilhelm II als Oberster Kriegsherr während des Ersten Weltkrieges II*, pp. 196ff.

12 Edward J. Erickson, *The Strength of an Army: Ottoman Military Effectiveness in the First World War*, Dissertation, University of Leeds, 2005, p. 1.

13 Erickson, *The Strength of an Army*; see also, Edward J. Erickson, *Ordered to Die: A history of the Ottoman Army in the First World War*, Greenwood Press, Westport CT,

2001. Jehuda L. Wallach, *Anatomie einer Militärhilfe. Die preußisch-deutschen Militärmissionen in der Türkei 1835–1919*, Düsseldorf 1976. Wolf considers German assistance was indispensable for the Turkish victory at the Dardanelles in 1915. Wolf, *Gallipoli 1915*, pp. 201ff.

14   Katrin Boeckh, *Von den Balkankriegen zum Weltkrieg. Kleinstaatenpolitik und ethnische Selbstbestimmung auf dem Balkan*, München 1996 (Südosteuropäische Arbeiten, 96), p. 35.

15   Edward Albert Hall, *The Abortive Partnership: Britain and Greece in World War I, 1914–1915*, PhD Thesis, Lancaster, 1996, pp. 349ff.

16   Erickson, *The Strength of an Army*, pp. 10–23.

17   Strachan, *To Arms*, pp. 722–29.

18   Holger Afflerbach, *Falkenhayn. Politisches Denken und Handeln im Kaiserreich*, Munich (2), 1996 (Beiträge zur Militärgeschichte, vol. 42), pp. 421ff.

19   It would be possible to compare the figures of allied soldiers fighting at the Turkish front and at the German front, but this would be a complex task because of constant changes and also because the fighting power of the troops which both sides employed on the Turkish front were not equal. To give an estimate: the German armies had in the summer of 1916 a strength of roughly 8.2 million men (*Feldheer* and occupying troops alone were 5.3 million men); number taken from: *Deutschland im Ersten Weltkrieg. Hrsg. von einem Autorenkollektiv des Zentralinstituts für Geschichte der DDR*, 3 vols., Berlin, (2) 1970, vol. 2, p. 531 f. The Turkish army had in 1916 a nominal strength of approximately 1 million men; but this figure is most likely exaggerated according to the German official history, *Der Weltkrieg 1914–1918. Die militärischen Operationen zu Lande*. Bearbeitet im Reichsarchiv, 14 vols., Berlin 1925–1944, vol. 10, p. 604. The German official history (*Der Weltkrieg*, vol. 10, p. 603–16) adds additional information on the Turkish fighting strength in 1916. The nominal difference in numbers (8.2 million versus 1 million men) would be 12 per cent; but the German official history (*Der Weltkrieg*, vol. 10, p. 604) explains that because of the Turkish lack of equipment the fighting power of German and Turkish troops could not be taken as 1:1. Therefore, a purely numerical comparison does not help. It seems that 10 per cent is a very approximate but realistic guess of the relation between Turkish and German military strength in the First World War.

20   Lyncker on 9 March 1915: 'Im ungünstigen Falle können sich Dardanellen und Constantinopel nicht lange halten; keineswegs aber wäre der Krieg der Türken dann zu Ende.' Afflerbach, *Wilhelm II*, p. 222.

21   Tim Travers, *Gallipoli 1915*, Tempus, Stroud, 2004, pp. 36ff.

22   Lyncker, 17 March 1915, Afflerbach, *Wilhelm II*, p. 226.

23   Lyncker, 2 April 1915, Afflerbach, *Wilhelm II*, p. 235.

24   Lyncker, 22 April 1915, Afflerbach, *Wilhelm II*, p. 246.

25   Lyncker, 9 March 1915, 'Sehr schlimm für die Dardanellen ist es, daß Rumänien die

Munitionstransporte zwar zu sich hereingelassen hat, aber nicht wieder herauslassen will. Das ist auch so eine Räuberbande. Sie sollen nun, da es mit Güte nicht geht, etwas bedroht werden.' Afflerbach, *Wilhelm II*, p. 222.

26   Volker Ullrich, 'Entscheidung im Osten oder Sicherung der Dardanellen. Das Ringen um den Serbienfeldzug 1915', *Militärgeschichtliche Mitteilungen* 32 (1982), pp. 45–63.

27   Strachan, *To Arms*, p. 693.

28   Wallach, *Anatomie*, pp. 206–7.

29   Hans Kannengiesser, *The Campaign in Gallipoli*, London, 1927.

30   Erickson, *The Strength of an Army*; Wolf, *Gallipoli 1915*.

31   Wallach, *Anatomie*, p. 174.

32   Wolf, *Gallipoli 1915*, p. 104.

33   Robert Rhodes James, *Gallipoli*, Pimlico, London, 1965, p. 71.

34   Von Sanders, *Fünf Jahre Türkei*, p. 72f.

35   Wolf, *Gallipoli 1915*, p. 102.

36   Winston Churchill: *The World Crisis*, London, 1968, vol. 1, p. 459, gives von Sanders's text in English translation. The German original is in Liman, *Fünf Jahre Türkei*, p. 81f.

37   Von Sanders, *Fünf Jahre Türkei*, p. 80.

38   Wolf, *Gallipoli 1915*, p. 105.

39   Churchill, *The World Crisis*, vol. 2, p. 548.

40   Travers, *Gallipoli*, pp. 39–42.

41   Omar N. Bradley, *A Soldier's Story*, New York, 1999, p. 344f.

42   Von Sanders, *Fünf Jahre Türkei*, p. 89: 'Die Entblößung des oberen Sarosgolfes von sämtlichen Truppen war ein ernster und weitgehender Entschluß für mich als verantwortlicher Führer.' See also Churchill, *The World Crisis*, vol. 2, p. 556.

43   Wallach, *Anatomie*, p. 191.

44   Joseph Pomiankowski, *Der Zusammenbruch des Ottomanischen Reiches*, Graz, 1969.

45   Travers, *Gallipoli*, p. 237.

46   Travers, *Gallipoli*, p. 174.

47   Travers, *Gallipoli*, p. 300.

48   Travers, *Gallipoli*, p. 42.

49   On the importance of Winston Churchill's *The World Crisis* for the entire Gallipoli debate, see: Edward Spiers, 'Gallipoli', in Brian Bond (ed.), *The First World War and British Military History*, Oxford University Press, Oxford, 1991, pp. 165–88, pp. 168–70, especially: 'The *World Crisis* proved a watershed in the historiography of Gallipoli.' (p. 169).

50   Concerning the battlefield, see Peter Doyle and Matthew R. Bennett, 'Military Geography: the influence of terrain in the outcome of the Gallipoli Campaign, 1915', *The Geographical Journal*, vol. 165, no. 1, March 1999, pp. 12–36.

51   The Dardanelles Commission concluded: 'We are of the opinion that, with the resources then available, success in the Dardanelles, if possible, was only possible upon condition that the Government concentrated their efforts upon the enterprise and limited their

expenditure of men and material in the Western theatre of war. This condition was never fulfilled.' Travers, *Gallipoli*, p. 297.

52 Churchill, *The World Crisis*, vol. 2, p. 504.

53 Hall, *Abortive Partnership*, p. 347–431.

54 Institute for Balkan Studies (ed.), *The Salonica Theatre of Operations and the Outcome of the Great War*, Thessaloniki 2005.

55 Holger Afflerbach, *Falkenhayn. Politisches Denken und Handeln im Kaiserreich* (Beiträge zur Militärgeschichte. Bd. 42), München, 1994, pp. 198–210.

56 Churchill, *The World Crisis*, vol. 2, p. 769: 'and the war would have ended in a Peace by negotiation or, in other words, a German victory'.

Chapter 9

1 This chapter draws on research in Turkish sources by the Gallipoli Centenary Research Project, managed by the author as principal researcher and administered by Macquarie University's Department of Modern History, Politics and International Relations in partnership with the Australian War Memorial and with funding assistance from the Australian Research Council. The project has identified and translated records held in the Turkish General Staff (hereafter TGS) Archives, the Ottoman Archives, the Presidential Archives, the Red Crescent Archives, and private collections, as well as Turkish publications. Material examined for this chapter, which provided insights into the situation faced by Ottoman commanders on Gallipoli and their responses to the August offensive of 1915, included: Turkish General Staff Archival material released to the project by courtesy of the administration and staff at the Military Archives in Ankara (ATASE); the Turkish General Staff official history of the First World War, particularly Volume 3, which covers the period of the August offensive; Volume 1 of the collected works of Colonel Mustafa Kemal Atatürk; and the memoirs of Brigadier General Esat Pasha, Lieutenant Colonel Cemil Conk and Lieutenant Colonel Fahrettin Altay, among others.

2 On 28/29 May 1915 New Zealand troops seized a newly established Turkish post 450 metres inland from No. 2 Post; on 30 May Turkish troops recaptured the position which the allies subsequently renamed 'Old No. 3 Post'. C.E.W. Bean, *The Story of Anzac, from 4 May 1915 to the Evacuation of the Gallipoli Peninsula*, Vol. 2, The Official History of Australia in the War of 1914–1918, Angus & Robertson, Sydney, 1924 (edition of 1944), pp. 191–6, 568–9.

3 Mustafa Kemal Atatürk, *Complete works*, Vol. 1, Kaynak Yayinlari, Istanbul, 1999, pp. 386–94.

4 Turkish General Staff (TGS) Archives, Military History Archives and Strategic Institute (hereafter ATASE), Ankara, File 182, Dossier 105/782, Index 20.

5 Atatürk, *Complete works*, Vol. 1, p. 420.

6 Yusuf Hikmet Bayur, *History of the Turkish Revolution*,

Vol. 3, Section 2, Turkish Historical Society Printing House, Ankara, 1991, p. 337.

7 Turkish General Staff official history (hereafter TGSH): *Çanakkale Cephesi Harekati* (Gallipoli front operations), *Haziram 1915–Ocak 1916* (June 1915–January 1916), *V Nci Cilt 3 ncii Kitap* (Vol. 5 Book 3), *Birinci Dunya Harbi'nde Turk Harbi* (Turkish War during the First World War), *Genelkurmay Basimevi* (General Staff Printing House), Ankara, 1980, p. 332.

8 TGSH, Vol. 5 Book 3, p. 336, quoting Hayri.

9 During this attack, 16/47th Regiment commander Major Tevfik and 5/15th Regiment commander Lieutenant Colonel Ibrahim Sukru were both killed by a bomb. TGSH, Vol. 5 Book 3, p. 337.

10 TGSH, Vol. 5 Book 3, p. 338.

11 ATASE, File 3402, Dossier 72, Index 10–25.

12 Lieutenant Colonel Cemil Bey, quoted in *The memoirs of Esat Pasha*, Örgün Yayinevi, Istanbul, 2003, pp. 269–75; also Cemil Conk, in *Çanakkale Hatirlari*, Arma Yayinlari, Istanbul, 2002, p. 198.

13 *Memoirs of Esat Pasha*, pp. 286–89; TGSH, Vol. 5 Book 3, p. 332.

14 Atatürk, *Complete works*, Vol. 1, p 422.

15 Turkish sources estimate that allied losses were approximately 3000 and Turkish loss around 1000 in the assaults at Anzac (in addition to the much heavier losses to both sides at Lone Pine). Atatürk, *Complete works*, Vol. 1, pp. 175–76.

16 Atatürk, *Complete works*, Vol. 1, pp. 175–76.

17 Kannengiesser later noted in his memoirs his linguistic and cultural difficulties with commanding Ottoman officers and troops. Similar problems are recounted in Edward J. Erickson, *Gallipoli: The Ottoman Campaign*, Pen & Sword, Barnsley, 2010, p. 163.

18 Atatürk, *Complete works*, Vol. 1, p. 424.

19 TGSH, Vol. 5 Book 3, p. 350.

20 Atatürk, *Complete works*, Vol. 1, p. 424.

21 On 8 August Lieutenant Colonel Pötrih was assigned to the command of 9th Division. TGSH, Vol. 3, p. 351.

22 Cemil Conk, *Çanakkale Savaşlari*, Arma Yayinlari, Istanbul, 2002, p. 208.

23 Conk, *Çanakkale Savaşlari*, p. 209. See also TGSH, Vol. 5 Book 3, p. 353; ATASE, File 4798, Dossier H4, Index 1–137.

24 Fahrettin Altay, *10 Yil ve Sonrasi*, Eylem Yayinlari, Ankara, 2008, p. 111

25 Atatürk, *Complete works*, Vol. 1, p. 424–25.

26 ATASE, File 182, Dossier 782, Index 63.

27 An order sent to North Group Command instructed that 2nd Army Corps Commander Brigadier General Faik Pasha should immediately go to Gelibolu to undertake the duty of Saros Group Command. Hence the position which became vacant after Colonel Fevzi went to the Anafarta Group Command had been filled. TGSH, Vol. 5 Book 3, p. 398.

28 TGSH, Vol. 5 Book 3, p. 356.

29 Atatürk, *Complete works*, Vol. 1, pp. 424–25.

30 TGSH, Vol. 5 Book 3, p. 357.

31 Atatürk, *Complete works*, Vol. 1, p. 403.
32 TGSH, Vol. 5 Book 3, p. 360.
33 The units that remained in Asmalidere region were assigned to the command of 5/14th Regiment Commander Lieutenant-Colonel Ali so that the 4th Division front (Kocacimen region) was separated under the responsibility of two commanders. Conk, *Çanakkale Savaşlari*, p. 162; TGSH, Vol. 5 Book 3, pp. 357–58.
34 Atatürk, *Complete works*, Vol. 1, p. 428.
35 *Memoirs of Esat Pasha*, p. 285.
36 *Memoirs of Esat Pasha*, pp. 287–88; TGSH, Vol. 5 Book 3, p. 361.
37 Atatürk, *Complete works*, Vol. 1, pp. 433–34.
38 TGSH, Vol. 5 Book 3, p. 369.
39 Mustafa Kemal, interview with Kadri Perk, in *Çanakkale Savaşının Tarihi*, Parts 2 and 3. Askeri Basimevi, Istanbul, 1940, p. 120. See also TGSH, Vol. 5 Book 3, p. 373.
40 TGSH, Vol. 5 Book 3, p. 374.
41 TGSH, Vol. 5 Book 3, p. 374.
42 TGSH, Vol. 5 Book 3, p. 375.
43 ATASE, File 182, Dossier 782, Index 77, 'Ottoman Imperial Consul, Number 6231, Cipher arrived from 5th Army to Ministry of Supreme Military Command'.
44 ATASE, File 3402, Dossier 72, Index 14–4.
45 As reported by Major Zeki Bey to Australian official historian Charles Bean. C.E.W. Bean, *Gallipoli Mission*, Australian War Memorial, Canberra, 1948, p. 224.

Chapter 10

1   Christopher M. Andrew and A.S. Kanya-Forstner, *France Overseas: The Great War and the Climax of French Imperial Expansion*, Thames and Hudson, London, 1981, p. 9.
2   Andrew and Kanya-Forstner, *France Overseas*, p. 26.
3   Andrew and Kanya-Forstner, *France Overseas*, p. 40.
4   Millerand to Delcassé, 5 January 1915, cited in Andrew and Kanya-Forstner, *France Overseas*, p. 70.
5   George H. Cassar, *The French and the Dardanelles*, George Allen & Unwin, London, 1971, pp. 34–35; also Andrew and Kanya-Forstner, *France Overseas*, pp. 40–41.
6   Andrew and Kanya-Forstner, *France Overseas*, p. 65.
7   Cassar, *The French and the Dardanelles*, p. 57.
8   Hankey's comments quoted in Robert Rhodes James, *Gallipoli*, Angus and Robertson, Sydney, 1965, p. 232.
9   Sir Ian Hamilton, *Gallipoli Diary*, 2 Vols, Edward Arnold, London, 1920, Vol. 1: pp. 295–6.
10 Robert A. Doughty, *Pyrrhic Victory: French Strategy and Operations in the Great War*, The Belknap Press of Harvard University Press, Cambridge, MA, 2005, p. 210.
11 *Les Armées Françaises dans la Grande Guerre*, 103 vols, Paris, Imprimerie nationale, 1922–38, tome 8, vol. 1, p. 104.
12 Phil Taylor and Pam Cupper, *Gallipoli: A Battlefield Guide*, Kangaroo Press, East Roseville NSW, 2nd revised edition, 2000, pp. 114–16.

13 Total casualties are listed as: 573 officers (183 killed, 348 wounded, 42 missing) and 26,431 other ranks (3555 killed, 16,827 wounded, 6049 missing). 'Effort de la France aux Dardanelles', 15 September 1916, in *Les Armées Françaises dans la Grande Guerre*, tome 8, vol. 1, note p. 126, with correction of p. 573.
14 Jean-Claude Devos, Jean Nicot, Philippe Schillinger, Pierre Waksman, *Inventaire sommaire des archives de la guerre, Série N 1872–1919*, Imprimerie La Renaissance, Troyes, 1974, vol. 2, pp. 166–67.
15 Lettres et rapports du commandant de Bertier, agent de liaison auprès du commandant anglais du corps expéditionnaire des Dardanelles, 7N 2170, Service historique de la Défense, Département de l'Armée de Terre, Château de Vincennes, France. Unless stated otherwise, all the French documents cited below are taken from this source.
16 Colonel Guelton uses 'English', because the French archival record reveals that the French in 1915 used 'British' and, more frequently, 'English' to subsume all British and Empire and Dominion forces.
17 Letter 1, 15 April 1915.
18 Letter 18, 18 September 1915.
19 Letter 16, 3 August 1915.
20 Letter 17, 10 August 1915.
21 Letter 22, 6 November 1915.
22 Letter 18, 18 September 1915.
23 Letter 18, 18 September 1915.
24 Letter 18, 18 September 1915.
25 Letter 18, 18 September 1915.
26 Letter 2, 20 April 1915.
27 Letter 3, 29 April 1915.
28 Letter 5, 13 May 1915.
29 Letter 6, 21 May 1915.
30 Letter 6, 21 May 1915.
31 Letter 9, 12 June 1915.
32 Letter 12, 8 July 1915.
33 Handwritten letter, Gouraud to de Bertier, 19 July 1915.
34 Letter 15, 29 July 1915.
35 Letter 17, 10 August 1915.
36 Letter 17, 10 August 1915.
37 Letter 20, 20 October 1915.
38 Hamilton, *Gallipoli Diary*, Vol. 2, p. 220; John Lee, *A Soldier's Life: General Sir Ian Hamilton 1853–1947*, Macmillan, Basingstoke, 2000, photographs 10, 11, show the award ceremony.
39 For further examples of the value of the testimony of liaison officers, see Elizabeth Greenhalgh, 'Liaisons not so Dangerous: First World War Liaison Officers and Marshal Ferdinand Foch', in Jennifer D. Keene and Michael S. Neiberg (eds), *Finding Common Ground: New Directions in First World War Studies*, Brill, Leiden/Boston, 2011, pp. 187–207.
40 Cited in Tim Travers, *Gallipoli 1915*, Tempus, Stroud, 2001, p. 180.
41 For a discussion of the negotiation over command on the Western Front, see Elizabeth Greenhalgh, *Victory*

Through Coalition: Britain and France during the First World War, Cambridge University Press, Cambridge, 2005, p. 26.

42 Gouraud to Hamilton, 18 May 1915, in *Les Armées Françaises dans la Grande Guerre*, tome 8, vol. 1, annex 201. There is a brief summary of Gouraud's letter in a footnote in the British official history, where it is described as 'a document of unusual interest': C.F. Aspinall-Oglander, *Military Operations: Gallipoli*, Vol. 2, Heinemann, London, 1932, p. 34 note 2.

43 Copies of Gouraud's letter and Hamilton's response are in the Millerand papers, 470AP/15, Archives nationales, Paris.

44 Avis du Général Gouraud, 24 July 1915, ibid., 470AP/16.

45 For these limited 'bite-and-hold' operations, see Robin Prior, *Gallipoli: The End of the Myth*, UNSW Press, Sydney, 2009, pp. 152–59.

46 Note, Hamelin to War Ministry, 19 July 1915, and Millerand to Kitchener, 20 July 1915, in *Les Armées Françaises dans la Grande Guerre* , tome 8, vol. 1, annexes 284, 285.

47 Kitchener to Millerand, 28 July 1915, *Les Armées Françaises dans la Grande Guerre*, tome 8, vol. 1, annex 294.

48 Letter, General Bailloud to War Minister, 1 October 1915, in Millerand papers, 470AP/16, Archives nationales, Paris.

49 Bailloud to Millerand, 1 October 1915, with 2 enclosures.

Chapter 11

1 The exact figure is 4950. Government of India, *India's Contribution to the Great War*, Calcutta, 1923, p. 98. Another table in the same publication gives the figure as 4428.

2 The 29th Indian Brigade was attached to the New Zealand & Australian Division in August 1915.

3 Up to 31 December 1919. *India's Contribution to the Great War*, pp. 79–80.

4 For an examination of the motives behind the service of Indian soldiers during the Raj, see David Omissi, *The Sepoy and the Raj: The Indian Army, 1860–1914*, Macmillan, London, 1994, and Philip Mason, *A Matter of Honour*, Penguin, Harmondsworth, Middlesex, 1974.

5 DeWitt C. Ellinwood and S.D. Pradhan, *India and World War 1*, Manohar, New Delhi, 1978, p. 30.

6 National Archives of India (hereafter NAI). WWI/145/H. General War Diary (WD), Vol. 15 Part II. Appdx 321 (Diary No. 6507). From the GOC, Canal Defences, Ismailia, to GOC the Force in Egypt. Also, Appdx 161 (Diary No. 5637), Telegram P, 15 March 1915 from the Viceroy (Foreign and Political Department) to the Secretary of State for India (henceforth SOSI). Return of desertions till 15 March 1915 was: Desertions 2121. Reservists failed to join 1344. Percentages desertions: Cis-frontier Pathans 1.6, Trans-frontier Pathans 6.7, other Mahomedans 9.0, Gurkhas 1.6, Hindus 9.0. Percentages reservists

absent: Cis-frontier 4.5. Trans-frontier 22.2, other Mahomedans 2.2, Gurkhas 12.8, Hindus 2.2.

7 John North, *Gallipoli: The Fading Vision*, Faber and Faber, London, 1966 (first published 1936), p. 21.

8 These classes served in the artillery and infantry units on the Gallipoli Peninsula. Punjabi Hindu, Brahmin and Rajput infantrymen also served briefly in early May 1915. Gurkha soldiers were indigenous people from central and western Nepal.

9 Raised 1765 as 10th Bn Coast Sepoys; 1824: 9th Madras Native Infantry; 1903: 69th Punjabis; 1922: 2/2nd Punjab Regiment; to India August 1947. Currently 1st Bn, Brigade of The Guards, Indian Army.

10 Raised 1798 as 3rd Extra Madras Bn; 1901: 29th Burma Infy; 1903: 89th Punjabis; 1922: 1/8th Punjab Regt, captured on Singapore Island in February 1942. Reformed in 1946 by redesignation of 9/8th Punjab; to Pakistan August 1947. Currently 1st Bn, The Baluch Regiment, Pakistan Army.

11 NAI, Army Dept, WW1/146/H. General WD, Vol. 16 Part I (1–15 April 1915). Appdx 232 (Diary No. 7271). Telegram No. 871-Z dated 9 April 1915 from GOC Egypt to C-in-C in India.

12 There were 12 mountain batteries in the Indian Army at the outbreak of the Great War, apart from nine British batteries, also on the establishment of the Army in India. Some batteries were grouped into brigades of two batteries each but most of them were independent.

13 Raised at Bannu in 1851 as No. 2 Punjab Light Field Battery, Punjab Irregular Force, from Horse Artillery troops of the Lahore Durbar.

14 Raised as 10th Company Bombay Golandaz Battalion of the HEICs Bombay Presidency Army in 1843.

15 Anon., *A Short Account of the Indian Mountain Artillery, for Use in Battery Schools*, by Ordnance Mule, c.1924. The battery suffered 17 casualties in 11 hours.

16 For examples, see C.E.W. Bean, *The Story of Anzac, from 4 May 1915 to the Evacuation of the Gallipoli Peninsula*, Vol. 2, The Official History of Australia in the War of 1914–1918, Angus & Robertson, Sydney, 1924 (edition of 1944), p. 158 n.37, and numerous references in index at pp. 944-45.

17 NAI. AD WWI/292/H. WD, IEF 'E', Vol. 7, (1–30 April 1915.), Appdx 55 (Diary No. 8349). Memo No 146-OB, dated 10 March 1915, from the Assistant Director of Ordnance Stores, 11th (Indian) Infantry Division Zagazig, to the Director of Ordnance Stores in India; NAI. AD. WWI/292/H. WD, IEF 'E', Vol. 7, (1–30 April 1915.) Appdx 56 (Diary No. 8350), Letter No. 5502-1 (O-9), dated 20 April 1915, from the DG of Ordnance in India to the GOC, Force 'E'.

18 The Indian troops appear to have got along very well with the Anzacs. In interviews with Indian veterans of the Great War about their interaction with soldiers of other nationalities, DeWitt Ellinwood noted that 'the most enthusiastic comments were about the Australians, who apparently treated them heartily and with a spirit of equal comradeship.' Ellinwood

and Pradhan, *India and World War 1,* p. 197. See also MacFetridge and Warren (eds.), *Tales of the Mountain Gunners,* Edinburgh, Blackwood, 1973, pp. 93–5.

19   Lt Col R.H. Beadon, *A History of the Royal Army Service Corps: A History of Transport and Supply in the British Army,* p. 157, quoted in Brig V.J. Moharir, *History of the Army Service Corps (1914–1938),* Sterling, New Delhi, 1982, p. 107.

20   Brigadier-General C.F. Aspinall-Oglander, *History of the Great War: Military Operations: Gallipoli,* Vol. 1, Heinemann, London, 1929, p. 122. The Zion Mule Corps (750 mules) was also raised in Egypt for service on Gallipoli. The British Army provided the ASC transport to supply the Indian Corps in France consequent to the despatch of the Indian transport train to the Mediterranean Force. NAI. WW1/146/H. Army Dept, General WD Vol. 16 Part I (1–15 April 1915). Appdx 30 (Diary No. 6780).

21   NAI. WWI/154/H. General WD, Vol. 24, (1–31 December 1915). Appdx 249 Diary 32371 Tgm no H-10107 dated 26 December from Viceroy (AD) to SOSI.

22   NAI. WWI/151/H. General WD, Vol. 21 (1–30 September 1915). Appdx 9 (Diary No. 20077); Telegram P No 3038, dated 1 September 1915 from the SOSI to the Viceroy (AD). For a scholarly account of the use of Indian military labour in the First World War, see Radhika Singha, 'Finding Labor from India for the War in Iraq: The Jail Porter and Labor Corps, 1916–1920', *Comparative Studies in Society and History,* 49 , 2007, pp. 412–45.

23   The Hazaras are Shia Muslims of Tartar origin, settled in the highlands of Afghanistan by Mongol invasions in the 13th century. A battalion of Hazara pioneers existed in the Indian Army from 1914 to 1933.

24   NAI. WWI/344/H. WD Diary IEF 'G', Vol. 3 (1–30 September 1915), Appdx 11 (Diary No. 20537). Telegram P No. H 7535, dated 6 September 1915 from Viceroy (AD) to SOSI.

25   NAI. WWI/151/H. General WD, Vol. 21 (1–30 September 1915). Appdx 80 (Diary No. 21824). Telegram P No. 3055, dated 18 September 1915, from SOSI to Viceroy (AD).

26   The officer establishment of each consisted of 1 Commandant (Major or Captain), 4 Company Commanders (Lieutenants or 2nd Lieutenants) with 1 Subedar Major and 1 Jemadar (Quartermaster). The four companies each had: 4 Subedars, 4 Jemadars, 8 Military Works Services and Public Works Department Military Upper Subordinates. Indian ranks comprised 3 Clerks at Headquarters while each of the 4 Companies had 1 Pay Clerk, 1 Writer, 1 Storekeeper, 4 Havildars (Sergeants), 8 Naiks (Corporals), 2 Carpenters, 4 Smiths, 4 Hammermen, 4 Bellows-boys, 12 Masons, 208 Labourers, 4 Bhistis (water carriers), 4 Sweepers and 4 Langris (cooks).

27   NAI. WWI/333/H. WD, IEF 'E' and 'G', Vol. 13, 1–31 October 1915, Appdx 33 (Diary No. 23793).

Telegram P No. H-8365-H, dated 9 October 1915, from Viceroy (AD) to SOSI.

28   NAI. WWI/333/H. WD, IEF 'E' and 'G', Vol. 13. Appdx 36 (Diary No 23825), Letter No. H-8363, dated 9 October 1915, from the Secretary to the Government of India, Army Department to the Director General of Military Works.

29   Under paragraphs 1062 and 1074, Army Regulations, India, Vol. I.

30   NAI. WWI/333/H WD, IEF 'E' and 'G', Vol. 13, Appdx 70 (Diary No 24618). Telegram P No. H-8587, dated 18 October 1915, from Viceroy (AD) to SOSI.

31   NAI. WWI/334/H. WD, IEF 'E' and 'G', Vol. 14, 1–30 November 1915, Appdx 102 (Diary No. 28761). Telegram P No. H-9412, dated 27 November 1915, from Viceroy (AD) to SOSI.

32   NAI. WWI/334/H. WD, IEF 'E' and 'G', Vol. 14, Appdx 119.

33   NAI. WWI/335/H. WD, IEF 'E' and 'G', Vol. 15, 1–31 December 1915, p. 80. QMG's embarkation statement, December 1915, Appdx 140. They had a strength of 5 British officers, 1 British warrant officer, 7 British other ranks, 13 Indian officers, 12 clerks, 49 Indian other ranks and 995 followers.

34   NAI. WWI/335/H. WD, IEF 'E' and 'G', Vol. 15. Appdx 113 (Diary No 32030), dated 25 December 1915.

35   This proposal was first put forward by Gen Birdwood on his return to Cairo from the Dardanelles in early March. Realising that the terrain on Gallipoli was not suited to mounted warfare, he suggested exchanging them for an Indian infantry brigade of the Egypt garrison. Aspinall-Oglander, *Military Operations: Gallipoli,* Vol. 1, pp. 122–23.

36   Col B.R. Mullaly, *Bugle and Kukri: The Story of the 10th Princess Mary's Own Gurkha Rifles,* Vol. 1, Naval & Military Press, London, 1993, p. 65.

37   Aspinall-Oglander, *Military Operations: Gallipoli,* Vol. 1, p. 124.

38   Later General Sir H.V. Cox, GCB KCMG CSI. Commissioned 14 January 1880; Commandant 69th Punjabis 1903–7; Commander 29th Indian Infantry Brigade 1914–15; Military Secretary, India Office; Colonel 69th Punjabis 1919. Brigade staff were: Bde Maj: Captain G.L. Pepys 57th Wilde's Rifles; Staff Capt: Capt H.G. Wilmer 14th Sikhs; Bde S&T Officer: Capt W.K. Rebsch, S&TC.

39   NAI. Army Dept WW1/293/H. WD IEF E Vol. 8. 1–31 May 1915. Diary No. 10562, Appdx 81. 69 and 89 Pujabis ordered to Force A, 20 May 1915.

40   Raised 1855 as a unit of the élite Punjab Irregular Force, the unit continues to serve as 1/5 GR (F.F.) in the Indian Army.

41   Raised 1908. Transferred to the British army as part of the Brigade of Gurkhas, August 1947. Disbanded 1968.

42   The 1st Battalion The Inniskilling Fusiliers and the 1st Battalion The Lancashire Fusiliers.

43 Col P.E.G. Talbot, *The 14th King George's Own Sikhs 1846–1933*, Royal United Service Institution, London, 1937, pp. 81–82.

44 Anon., *History of the 5th Royal Gurkha Rifles (Frontier Force) 1858 to 1928*, Aldershot, Gale and Polden, p. 244. However, in a telegram dated 2 July, Sir Ian Hamilton gave the strength of remaining BOs in the brigade as: 6th Gurkhas 5; 10th Gurkhas 7; 14th Sikhs 2; 5th Gurkhas 2. NAI. WWI/149/H. General WD, Vol. 19, Part I, 1–15 July 1915. Appdx 9 (Diary No. 13821). Telegram P., No. 1381-E, dated 2 July 1915.

45 TNA. WO95/4272. WD 29 Ind Inf Bde 1–31 July 1915. Memo 1688/M from Brig Gen H.V. Cox to HQ 29 Div dated 9 July 1915.

46 NAI. WW1/148/H. General WD AHQ, India. Vol. 18 Part II (16–30 June 1915). Diary No. 12588. Appdx 172. Telegram No. C-1328 dated 17 June 1915 from GOC Egypt to C-in-C in India, informed the latter of proposals for the reinforcement of the 14th Sikhs in the Dardanelles.

47 1st Patiala IS Infantry (Rajindra Sikhs). Raised 1783. The unit today survives in the Indian army as the 15th (Patiala) Battalion, The Punjab Regiment.

48 NAI. Foreign and Political (For & Pol) Dept – Internal – Deposit. Proceedings (Progs) August 1915, No. 7, 'Despatch of a double company of Patiala Imperial Service Infantry as reinforcements to the 14th Sikhs at Dardanelles'; also NAI, For & Pol Dept – Internal – B Progs Oct 1915, Nos 371–73 'Despatch of a double company of Patiala Infantry as reinforcements for the 14th Sikhs with Force "G"'. Telegram No. 315-H dated 2 October 1915 from GOC Egypt to C-in-C in India: BOs: 2 (Maj Campbell, Guides, and Lt Clark, IARO); Maj Ishar Singh and 4 IOs; Rank and file 181. Also NAI, WW1/333/H. Army Dept, WD IEF 'E' and 'G' Vol. 13 (1–31 October 1915). Appdx 8 (Diary No. 23172).

49 NAI. For & Pol Dept – Internal – Deposit. Progs August 1915, No. 7. This was not strictly true, as detachments of the Gwalior, Bharatpur and Indore Transport Corps formed a part of the Indian transport train serving on Gallipoli.

50 The men returned to duty with the 1st Patiala Infantry in January 1916. Telegram No. 2447 dated 16 January 1916 from the GOC Egypt, Suez Docks, to C-in-C in India.; NAI For & Pol Dept – Internal – B Progs, February 1916, No. 133. 'Return to duty with their own regt of the men of 1st Patiala Infantry temporarily attached to 14th Sikhs'.

51 NAI. WWI/149/H. General WD, Vol. 19, Part I, 1–15 July 1915. Appdx 9 (Diary No 13821). Telegram P, No. 1381-E, dated 2 July 1915. From GOC, Army of Occupation, Egypt to C-in-C in India.

52 NAI. WW1/342/H Army Dept, WD, IEF 'G' Vol. 1, 21–31 July 1915. Appdx 1, (Diary No. 15736). Also NAI. WW1/343/H Army Dept, WD IEF 'G' Vol. 2 (1–31 August 1915). Appdx 48, (Diary No. 19167).

53 NAI. WW1/343/H. Army Dept, WD IEF 'G'

Vol. 2, 1–31 August 1915. Appdx 20, (Diary No.17310). Telegram No. H-258, dated 6 August 1915.

54 Sent to the Dardanelles from France, 25 August 1915. 1/4 GR: 16 BOs, 21 IOs, 975 ORs, 32 followers; 2 GR: 11 ORs, 8 followers; 1/9 GR: 4 ORs. NAI. WW1/343/H. Army Dept, WD IEF 'G' Vol. 2 (1–31 August 1915). Appdx 52, (Diary No. 19370).

55 The guides were drawn from local Greek villagers who had been displaced by the Turkish military and wandered as refugees into the northern Anzac lines. Bean, *The Story of Anzac*, Vol. 2, pp. 182, 586.

56 Lt Col C.J.L. Allanson, *Diary* (privately printed, n.d.), p. 18.

57 North, *Gallipoli: The Fading Vision*, p. 119.

58 Interviews with the author by Dfdr Lakha Singh, 21 PAVO Cavy (FF), Village Ekalgadda, and Dfdr Hardit Singh, 9 Hodson's Horse, Village Raja Sansi; both veterans of the campaign in Mesopotamia, from District Amritsar, Punjab, 1976.

59 Tim Travers, *Gallipoli 1915*, Stroud, Gloucestershire, Tempus, 2002, p. 136.

60 The National Archives (TNA). WO95/4272. War Diary 29 Ind Infy Bde, Notes on Battle of Sari Bair by Col G.L. Pepys, DSO, dated 9 January 1931, folio 3. Pepys was the brigade major of 29 Ind Bde on Gallipoli. Also, 1–31August 1915, folio 24. Appdx IV, 'Copy of msg from OC 1-6 GR dated 9.8.15 (6.30 a.m.)'

61 Travers, *Gallipoli 1915*, p. 132. Emphasis in original.

62 Travers, *Gallipoli 1915*, p. 247 n. 35. Major (later Maj Gen) A.C. Temperley, Brigade Major of the NZ Bde.

63 Travers, *Gallipoli 1915*, p. 132.

64 TNA WO95/4272. WD 29 Ind Inf Bde: 1/6 GR September 1915 – January 1916. Para G, Letter of Col C.J.L. Allanson dated 8 December 1930 to Director, Historical Section (Mily Br).

Chapter 12

1 M. Howard, 'The forgotten dimensions of strategy', *Foreign Affairs*, Vol. 57, No. 5, Summer 1979, p. 976.

2 For more on the lack of logistic studies in military history, and the reasons for this see, A.P. Wavell, *Generals and Generalship: The Lees Knowles lectures delivered at Trinity College, Cambridge in 1939*, Penguin Books, Harmondsworth, 1941, p. 26; M. van Creveld, *Supplying War: Logistics from Wallenstein to Patton*, Cambridge University Press, New York, 2004, pp. 1–2; R. Prior, *Churchill's 'World Crisis' as History*, Croom Helm, Canberra, 1983, p. 140; J. Thompson, 'Principles: The disciplines of war', in M. Coles (ed.), *Military Logistics: A primer on operational, strategic and support level logistics*, Australian Defence Studies Centre, Canberra, 1996, p. 195; M. Kress, *Operational Logistics: The art and science of sustaining military operations*, Kluwer Academic Publishers, Boston, 2002, p. ix.

3 This definition of logistics by Martin van Creveld is based on that given by Jomini. See van Creveld, *Supplying War*, p. 1.

4 D. Chapman-Huston and O. Rutter, *General Sir John*

Cowans C.G.B., G.C.M.G.: The Quartermaster-General of the Great War, Hutchinson & Co., London, 1924, p. 107.

5   For more on the improvements made to the BEF's logistic system in 1916–17, and which of them – with other factors – helped lead to victory in 1918 see, I.M. Brown, British Logistics on the Western Front 1914–1919, Praeger, Westport, 1998, pp. 142–48; for more on the logistics of 'Operation Barbarossa' see van Creveld, Supplying War, pp. 142–80.

6   A. John, 'Lost Opportunity: An operational level analysis of the August offensive of the Gallipoli campaign 1915', Australian Army Journal, 2002, p. 3; Evidence of Sir John Cowans [Quartermaster-General, War Office] to the Dardanelles Commission, 30 March 1917, The National Archives (hereafter TNA), United Kingdom, Series CAB 19/33, p. 1330.

7   Evidence of Sir J. Cowans to the Dardanelles Commission, p. 1330.

8   E.A. Altham [Inspector General of Communications, MEF] in D. Chapman-Huston and O. Rutter, General Sir John Cowans, p. 108.

9   E.A. Altham in D. Chapman-Huston and O. Rutter, General Sir John Cowans, p. 108.

10 E.A. Altham in D. Chapman-Huston and O. Rutter, General Sir John Cowans, p. 108.

11 I.M. Brown, 'Growing Pains: Supplying the British Expeditionary Force, 1914–1915', in P. Dennis and J. Grey (eds.), Battles Near and Far: A century of overseas deployment, Army History Unit, Canberra, 2005, p. 44.

12 Evidence of Major-General S.S. Long [Director of Supplies and Transport, War Office] to the Dardanelles Commission, 22 March 1917, TNA, CAB 19/33, pp. 1246–47; Evidence of Major-General Sir J. Steevens [Director of Equipment and Ordnance Stores, War Office] to the Dardanelles Commission, 4 January 1917, TNA, CAB 19/33, pp. 385–86.

13 General Sir I.S.M. Hamilton (General Officer Commanding, MEF) often bypassed these official channels by making personal requests for men and munitions to Lord Kitchener (Secretary of State for War). Hamilton, however, was not the only individual to do so. His Chief of the General Staff (CGS), Major-General W.P. Braithwaite, for example, discussed supply and transport arrangements in his private letters to Sir J. Cowans (QMG, War Office). See, Letter, Braithwaite to Cowans, 27 July 1915, TNA, WO 107/43.

14 Telegram, Cowans to Altham [IGC], 24 July 1915, Papers of General Sir Ian Standish Monteith Hamilton (hereafter Hamilton Papers), Liddell Hart Centre for Military Archives (hereafter LHCMA), King's College, London, Series HAMILTON 7/4/8.

15 G. MacMunn, 'The Lines of Communication in the Dardanelles', The Army Quarterly, Vol. 20, No. 1, April 1930, p. 52.

16 Evidence of Major-General The Hon. R. Stuart-Wortley [Director of Movements, War Office] to the Dardanelles Commission, 19 January 1917, TNA, CAB 19/33, p. 599.

17 Evidence of Graeme Thomson [Director of Transports, Admiralty] to the Dardanelles Commission, 20 March 1917, TNA, CAB 19/33, p. 1207.

18 Letter, Hankey to Asquith, 4 August 1915, TNA, CAB 17/123, p. 10.

19 A. Hurd, History of the Great War: The Merchant Navy, Vol. 2, John Murray, London, 1924, p. 99; 'Admiralty Transport Service', [n.d.], TNA, MT 23/427, T50185/1915.

20 Notes of Dardanelles Committee meeting, 17 June 1915, TNA, CAB 22/2; Unpublished manuscript, 'The lines of communication: August 1915 – January 1916', Rayfield Papers, Imperial War Museum [IWM], 69/61/4; P.G. Halpern, The Naval War in the Mediterranean 1914–1918, Allen & Unwin, London, 1987, p. 49.

21 Unpublished manuscript, 'The lines of communication: August 1915 – January 1916', Rayfield Papers, IWM, 69/61/4.

22 Letter, Hamilton to Maxwell [GOC, Egypt], 27 June 1915, Hamilton Papers, LHCMA, HAMILTON 7/1/15.

23 G. Ellison, The Perils of Amateur Strategy as Exemplified by the Attack on the Dardanelles Fortress in 1915, Longmans, Green and Co., London, 1926, p. xxii.

24 'The Mitchell Report', Australian War Memorial (hereafter AWM), Series 124, Item 3/48, p. 212.

25 Letter, Braithwaite [CGS, MEF] to Cowans [QMG, War Office], 22 June 1915, TNA, WO 107/43.

26 Telegram, Altham [IGC, MEF] to War Office, 22 July 1915, Hamilton Papers, LHCMA, HAMILTON 7/4/8; Letter, Hankey to Asquith, 4 August 1915, TNA, CAB 17/123, p. 10.

27 'The Mitchell Report', AWM 124, 3/48, p. 212.

28 Telegram, Hamilton to War Office, 12 June 1915, Hamilton Papers, LHCMA, HAMILTON 7/4/8; Unpublished manuscript, 'The lines of communication: August 1915 – January 1916', Rayfield Papers, IWM, 69/61/4.

29 Memorandum, 'The Dardanelles: Memorandum on the situation, August 30, 1915', prepared for the Committee of Imperial Defence by Maurice Hankey, Hamilton Papers, LHCMA, HAMILTON 7/4/33.

30 Telegram, Altham to War Office, 22 July 1915, Hamilton Papers, LHCMA, HAMILTON 7/4/8.

31 E.A. Altham [IGC, MEF] in D. Chapman-Huston and O. Rutter, General Sir John Cowans, p. 108.

32 G. MacMunn, 'The Lines of Communication in the Dardanelles', The Army Quarterly, Vol. 20, No. 1, April 1930, p. 57; Evidence of Lieutenant-General Sir E.A. Altham to the Dardanelles Commission, 10 January 1917, TNA, CAB 19/33, p. 822; Diary entry, 27 July 1915, Director of Supplies and Transport (DST) War Diary, GHQ MEF, TNA, WO 95/4269.

33 G. MacMunn, 'The Lines of Communication in the Dardanelles', p. 57.

34 Letter, Simpson [STO, Mudros] to Thomson [Director of Transports, Admiralty], 1 August 1915, TNA, MT 23/431, T51236/1915; Evidence of Captain H.V. Simpson to the Dardanelles Commission, 2 February 1917, TNA, CAB 19/33, p. 822.

35 Letter, Simpson to Thomson, 18 July 1915, TNA, MT 23/427, T50185/1915; Diary entry, 22 July 1915, Papers of Lieutenant-General Sir Gerald Ellison, National Army Museum (hereafter NAM), Item 8704/35/214.

36 Letter, Simpson to Thomson, 1 August 1915, TNA, MT 23/431, T51236/1915.

37 Unpublished memoir of W.J.K. Rettie [CO 59th Bde, RFA], Rettie Papers, IWM, 81/9/1, p. 21. The 'bogus battleship' was one of two British merchant ships disguised as battle-cruisers intended to deceive the Germans about the strength and disposition of Royal Navy warships.

38 The MEF's only refrigerator ship, the SS *Pfalz*, was put out of action after a collision on 18 July. A replacement was not found until 27 August, thus depriving the MEF of frozen meat throughout the August offensive. See, Diary entries, 18 July, and 4, 7, 8, 18, 27 August 1915, DST War Diary, GHQ MEF, TNA, WO 95/4269.

39 Memorandum, 'Navy Transport Service', [n.d.], TNA, MT 23/427, T50185/1915.

40 Unpublished manuscript, 'The lines of communication: intervention of German submarines to July', Rayfield Papers, IWM, 69/61/3, p. 32.

41 Unpublished manuscript, 'The lines of communication: intervention of German submarines to July', pp. 32–33.

42 Letter, Hankey to Asquith, 4 August 1915, TNA, CAB 17/23, p. 10; Telegram, Altham to War Office, 22 July 1915, Hamilton Papers, LHCMA, HAMILTON 7/4/8; V. Rudenno, *Gallipoli: Attack from the sea*, UNSW Press, Sydney, 2008, p. 151.

43 Evidence of Brigadier-General A. Joly de Lotbinière [Director of Works, GHQ] to the Dardanelles Commission, 23 January 1917, TNA, CAB 19/33, pp. 632–33; J.S. Corbett, *Naval Operations*, Vol. 3, Longmans, Green & Co., London, 1923, p. 81.

44 Diary entry, 6 July 1915, DDST War Diary, TNA, WO 95/4270; Diary entries, 11 and 15 July 1915, DST War Diary, GHQ MEF, TNA, WO 95/4269; Letter, Maxwell to Hamilton, 16 July 1915, Hamilton Papers, LHCMA, HAMILTON 7/1/14; Diary entry, 25 July 1915, 'A' and 'Q' Branch War Diary, HQ L-of-C, TNA, WO 95/4355; Diary entry, 26 July 1915, DADS War Diary, TNA, WO 95/4270; Letter, Hankey to Asquith, 4 August 1915, TNA, CAB 19/123, pp. 10–11.

45 Telegram, GHQ to IX Corps, 20 July 1915, Appendix, General Staff War Diary, IX Corps, TNA, WO 95/4276.

46 Diary entry, 5 August 1915, General Staff War Diary, GHQ MEF, AWM 4, 1/4/5 Part 1.

47 Diary entries, 11 and 14 August 1915, General Staff War Diary, GHQ MEF, AWM 4, 1/4/5 Part 1.

48 Evidence of Lieutenant-General Sir E.A. Altham to the Dardanelles Commission, 10 January 1917, TNA, CAB 19/33, p. 464.

49 Memorandum, 'Steamers and small craft for the Dardanelles', 7 July 1915, TNA, MT 23/427, T50247/1915; Telegram, Admiralty to de Robeck, 12 July 1915, TNA, ADM 137/155.

50 Letter, Jackson to de Robeck, 27 July 1915, de Robeck Papers, Churchill Archives Centre (hereafter CAC), Series DRBK, Item 4/30; Letter, Wemyss to de Robeck, 14 July 1915, de Robeck Papers, CAC, DRBK 4/32; Letter, Thursby to Limpus, 15 July 1915, Limpus Papers, National Maritime Museum (hereafter NMM), Series LIM, Item 65.

51 Letter, de Robeck to Balfour, 28 July 1915, de Robeck Papers, CAC, DRBK 4/69.

52 Letter, Hankey to Asquith, 4 August 1915, TNA, CAB 17/123, p. 12.

53 Corbett, *Naval Operations*, Vol. 3, p. 82.

54 Unpublished manuscript, 'The lines of communication: August 1915 – January 1916'.

55 Diary entry, 19 August 1915, DST Supply diary, GHQ MEF, TNA, WO 95/4269.

56 Unpublished manuscript, 'The lines of communication: intervention of German submarines to July', pp. 31–32.

57 Unpublished manuscript, 'The lines of communication: intervention of German submarines to July', pp. 31–32.

58 For more on the operational objectives of the August offensive see R. Crawley, 'The myths of August at Gallipoli', in C. Stockings (ed.), *Zombie Myths of Australian Military History*, New South, Sydney, 2010, pp. 50–69.

59 Evidence of Lieutenant-General Sir E.A. Altham to the Dardanelles Commission, 10 January 1917, TNA, CAB 19/33, p. 468; Memorandum, 'Admiralty Transport Service', [n.d.], TNA, MT 23/427, T50185/1915.

60 Evidence of Lieutenant-General Sir E.A. Altham to the Dardanelles Commission, 10 January 1917, TNA, CAB 19/33, p. 468.

61 General Staff (War Office), *Field Service Regulations, Part II: Organization and Administration*, His Majesty's Stationery Office, London, 1909 (reprinted, with amendments, 1914), p. 32; Brown, 'Growing Pains', pp. 34–35.

62 Letter, Braithwaite to Cowans, 27 July 1915, TNA, WO 107/43.

63 Letter, Smith-Dorrien to Hamilton, 28 July 1915, Hamilton Papers, LHCMA, HAMILTON 7/1/37.

64 Letter, de Robeck to Jackson [First Sea Lord, Admiralty], 16 September 1915, de Robeck Papers, CAC, DRBK 4/70.

65 I.M. Brown, *British Logistics on the Western Front 1914–1919*, Praeger, Westport, 1998, p. 117.

66 P. Doyle and M.R. Bennett, 'Military Geography: The influence of terrain in the outcome of the Gallipoli campaign, 1915', *The Geographical Journal*, Vol. 165, No. 1, March 1999, p. 30.

67 Memorandum, 'Notes on piers and naval transport', [n.d.], de Robeck Papers, CAC, DRBK 4/70.

68 Memorandum, 'Notes on piers and naval transport', [n.d.], de Robeck Papers, CAC, DRBK 4/70.

69 General Staff (War Office), *Field Service Regulations, Part I: Operations*, His Majesty's Stationery Office, London, 1909 (reprinted, with amendments, 1914), p. 69; 'Manual of Combined Naval and Military Operations', 2 September 1913, Hamilton Papers, LHCMA, HAMILTON 7/4/2, pp. 8–9.

70 Diary entry, 4 August 1915, 'A' and 'A' Branch War Diary, HQ L-of-C, TNA, WO 95/4355; Diary entry, 5 August 1915, General Staff War Diary, GHQ MEF, AWM 4, 1/4/5 Part 1.

71 Memorandum, [no title] Braithwaite to Western, 4 August, Appendix, General Staff War Diary, GHQ MEF, AWM 4, 1/4/5 Part 2.

72 'Narrative of operations by Major-General J.H. Poett', [n.d.], TNA, CAB 45/244. The arrangements were again changed in late August, this time putting the landing places and their administrative services solely under the orders of the corps commanders. Letter, Altham to Cowans, 22 August 1915, TNA, WO 107/43.

73 There are numerous examples of arguments presenting both cases. For a detailed account of these see Chapter 7 in R. Crawley, '"Our second great [mis]adventure": A critical re-evaluation of the August Offensive, Gallipoli, 1915', PhD thesis, University of New South Wales, 2010.

74 Some examples that acknowledge the shortage of personnel allotted to fatigue work include: Memorandum, 'Notes on piers and naval transport', by Roger Keyes, [n.d.], de Robeck Papers, CAC, DRBK 4/70; Ellison, 'War Diary Summary for the month of August, 1915', 20 September 1915, Appendix, DQMG War Diary, GHQ MEF, TNA, WO 95/4266.

75 Letter, Ellison [DQMG] to Cowans, 26 August 1915, TNA, WO 107/43.

76 Memorandum, Ellison [DQMG] to Hamilton, 18 August 1915, Appendix, General Staff War Diary, GHQ MEF, AWM 4, 1/4/5 Part 3; Diary entry, 19 August 1915, DQMG War Diary, GHQ MEF, TNA, WO 95/4266; Letter, Ellison to Cowans, 26 August 1915, TNA, WO 107/43.

77 Summary [August 1915], 40th Depot Unit of Supply War Diary, TNA, WO 95/4358.

78 Corbett, *Naval Operations*, Vol. 3, p. 81.

79 'The Mitchell Report', AWM 124, 3/48, p. 217.

80 Aspinall-Oglander, *Military Operations*, Vol. 2, p. 395.

81 Ellison, 'War Diary Summary for the month of August, 1915', 20 September 1915, Appendix, DQMG War Diary, GHQ MEF, TNA, WO 95/4266; Evidence of Major-General J. Poett to the Dardanelles Commission, 9 March 1917, TNA, CAB 19/33, pp. 1131–32.

82 Memorandum, '1st Australian Division Distribution of Duties – Administrative Branch', Gellibrand Papers, AWM, 3DRL/1472, item 98.

83 R. Lee, 'The Australian Staff: The forgotten men of the First AIF', in P. Dennis and J. Grey (eds.), *1918 Defining Victory*, Army History Unit, Canberra, 1999, p. 117; Evidence of Major-General Sidney S. Long to the Dardanelles Commission, 22 March 1917, TNA, CAB 19/33, p. 1251.

84 Diary entry, 17 July 1915, DST War Diary, GHQ MEF, TNA, WO 95/4269.

85 Letter, Altham to Cowans, 23 July 1915, TNA, WO 107/43.

86 Letter, Altham to Cowans, 23 July 1915, TNA, WO 107/43.

87 Diary entry, 3 August 1915, DST Supply Diary, GHQ MEF, TNA, WO 95/4269.

88 Diary entries, 13–14 August 1915, DST Supply Diary, GHQ MEF, TNA, WO 95/4269.

89 I.S.M. Hamilton, *Gallipoli Diary*, Vol. 2, Edward Arnold, London, 1920, p. 302; Evidence of Major-General J. Poett to the Dardanelles Commission, 9 March 1917, TNA, CAB 19/33, p. 1126.

90 Diary entry, 13 August 1915, DST Supply Diary, GHQ MEF, TNA, WO 95/4269.

91 Memorandum, 'Supply', [n.d.], Appendix, DA& QMG War Diary, IX Corps, TNA, WO 95/4279.

92 H.M. Alexander, *On Two Fronts: Being the adventures of an Indian Mule Corps in France and Gallipoli*, William Heinemann, London, 1917, p. 204.

93 General Staff (War Office), *Field Service Regulations, Part II: Organization and Administration*, His Majesty's Stationery Office, London, 1909 (reprinted, with amendments, 1914), pp. 98–99.

94 Moharir, *History of the Army Service Corps*, p. 108.

95 Evidence of Lieutenant-Colonel L.R. Beadon to the Dardanelles Commission, 31 August 1917, TNA, CAB 19/33, p. 1645.

96 Aspinall, 'Appendix to Force Order No. 25', 2 August 1915, Appendix, General Staff War Diary, GHQ MEF, AWM 4, 1/4/5 Part 2; Stopford, 'Operation Order No. 1', 3 August 1915 Appendix, General Staff War Diary, 11th Division, TNA, WO 95/4297.

97 Telegram, Aspinall to 'Heeltool, London', [n.d.], Aspinall-Oglander Papers, Isle of Wight County Record Office (hereafter IWRO), OG/AO/G/20.

98 H.M. Alexander, *On Two Fronts*, p. 222.

99 Note to Aspinall [origin unknown], 7 November 1915, 'Suvla Transport Scheme', Aspinall-Oglander Papers, IWRO, OG/AO/G/25.

100 Ellison, 'War Diary summary for the month of August, 1915', 20 September 1915, Appendix, DQMG War Diary, GHQ MEF, TNA, WO 95/4266; Note to Aspinall [origin unknown], 7 November 1915, 'Suvla Transport Scheme'.

101 'Operation Order No. 1', 3 August 1915, Appendix, General Staff War Diary, IX Corps, TNA, WO 95/4276.

102 Diary entry, 7 August 1915, DQMG War Diary, GHQ MEF, TNA, WO 95/4266.

103 Moharir, *History of the Army Service Corps*, p. 121;

Memorandum, 'Return of mules and carts, August 1915', [n.d.], Appendix, DA&QMG War Diary, IX Corps, TNA, WO 95/4279.

104 Moharir, *History of the Army Service Corps*, p. 116.

105 Alexander, *On Two Fronts*, p. 168.

106 Alexander, *On Two Fronts*, p. 168; Moharir, *History of the Army Service Corps*, p. 113.

107 Diary entry, 26 August 1915, DDVS War Diary, GHQ MEF, TNA, WO 95/4268.

108 Letter, Altham to Cowans, 22 August 1915, TNA, WO 107/43.

109 For a detailed account of the reasons for the failure of the water supply system at Suvla, and the impact that it had on operations, see T. Travers, *Gallipoli 1915*, Tempus, Stroud, 2003, pp. 153–57.

110 Diary entry, 8 August 1915, Wellington Battalion War Diary, AWM 4, 35/20/5.

111 Quoted in, T. Coates (ed.), *Defeat at Gallipoli: The Dardanelles Commission Part II, 1915–1916*, The Stationery Office, London, 2000, p. 185.

112 Altham in Chapman-Huston and Rutter, *General Sir John Cowans*, p. 107.

113 Telegram, GHQ MEF to War Office, 13 July 1915, Hamilton Papers, LHCMA, HAMILTON 7/4/8; Memorandum, 'Evacuation of Casualties in the August Operations', [n.d.], Hamilton Papers, LHCMA, HAMILTON 8/1/12; Diary entry, 5 August 1915, DQMG War Diary, GHQ MEF, TNA, WO 95/4266.

114 Telegram, Porter (HTO) to 'Natronglas', Medical, London, 22 August 1915, TNA, MT 23/434.

115 L. Markovich, '"Linseed Lancers, Body-snatchers, and other cheery and jovial names": The Role of the Stretcher-Bearer, Gallipoli, 1915', BA Honours thesis, University of Wollongong, 2009, pp. 38–39.

116 Bean, *Official History*, Vol. 2, p. 645.

117 Bean, *Official History*, Vol. 1, pp. 563–64.

118 Diary entry, 13 August 1915, No. 1 Australian Casualty Clearing Station War Diary, AWM 4, 26/62/7 Part 1.

119 Diary entry, 6 August 1915, No. 1 Australian Casualty Clearing Station War Diary, AWM 4, 26/62/7 Part 1.

120 Evidence of Captain H.V. Simpson [Superintendent Transport Officer, Mudros] to the Dardanelles Commission, 2 February 1917, TNA, CAB 19/33, p. 822.

Chapter 13

1 The work of the Australian Historical Mission is comprehensively covered in C.E.W. Bean, *Gallipoli Mission*, Australian War Memorial, Canberra, 1948. See also Janda Gooding, *Gallipoli Revisited: in the footsteps of Charles Bean and the Australian Historical Mission*, Hardie Grant, Sydney, 2009.

2 C.E.W. Bean, 'Australia's records. Preserved as sacred things. Pictures, relics, and writings', *The ANZAC Bulletin*, no. 40, 10 October 1917, p. 14.

3 C.E.W. Bean, 'Australia's records', p. 14.

4 A.W. Bazley, 'Australia's Official History of World War 1', *Stand To*, vol. 6, no. 6, November 1958–January 1959, p. 23.

5 G.W. Lambert, letter to Amy Lambert, 15 January 1918 , 'Lambert Family Papers', Mitchell Library, Sydney, ML MSS 97/10.

6 G.W. Lambert, letter to High Commissioner for Australia, 26 September 1918, AWM93: 18/7/7 PART 1.

7 G.W. Lambert quoted in Andrew Motion, *The Lamberts: George, Constant and Kit*, Farrar, Straus and Giroux, New York, 1987, p. 70.

8 C.E.W. Bean, letter to Defence Secretary T. Trumble, 25 June 1918, AWM16: 4378/1/8.

9 General Birdwood's recommendation of Hubert Wilkins for Military Cross 1917, AWM Honours and Awards pages, http://www.awm.gov.au/cms_images/AWM28/2/404/0003.pdf

10 General Birdwood's recommendation of Hubert Wilkins for Bar to Military Cross, 1918, AWM Honours and Awards pages http://www.awm.gov.au/cms_images/AWM28/2/19/0005.pdf

11 In Lowell Thomas, *Sir Hubert Wilkins: His world of adventure: An autobiography*, Readers Book Club in association with The Companion Book Club, Melbourne, 1963, p. 87.

12 Bean, *Gallipoli Mission*, p. 20.

13 C.E.W. Bean to John Treloar, 4 December 1918, AWM16 4359/1/13 noted: 'Wilkins is able to get away and I should like him to come with me to Gallipoli partly as a reward for his work & partly because he knows his way about very well in Turkey and we shall probably have to camp there for some days.'

14 Lieutenant William James (1st Light Horse Regiment), who was photographing the Anzac area and collecting relics for the Australian War Records Section, noted the name in his diary entries for early 1919; transcript held in AWM Photograph Section archive.

15 C.E.W. Bean, *The All Australian Memorial*, British–Australian Publishing Service, Melbourne, 1919, p. 104.

16 Sergeant W. Cameron, 9th Light Horse, diary entry quoted in Peter Burness, *The Nek: The tragic charge of the Light Horse at Gallipoli*, Kangaroo Press, Kenthurst, NSW, 1996, p. 106.

17 Bean, *Gallipoli Mission*, p. 109.

18 George Lambert, from a letter to his wife, Amy Lambert, *Thirty Years of an Artist's Life*, Society of Artists, Sydney, 1938, quoted in Bean, *Gallipoli Mission*, p. 111.

19 Bean, *Gallipoli Mission*, p. 109.

20 *Lone Pine looking towards the Nek, Walker's Ridge*, 6 March 1919, oil on wood panel, 13.8 x 21.8 cm, AWM ART02826.

21 George Lambert, 6 March 1919, 'War Diary 1919', Mitchell Library ML MSS 97/4.

22 George Lambert, 8 March 1919, 'War Diary 1919', Mitchell Library ML MSS 97/4.

23 George Lambert, 9 March 1919, 'War Diary 1919', Mitchell Library ML MSS 97/4.

24 These albums are held at AWM38: 3DRL
    606/1016.

25 *ANZAC, the landing 1915*, painted 1920–22, oil on
    canvas, 190.5 x 350.5 cm, AWM ART02873.

26 *Study for 'The charge of the 3rd Light Horse Brigade at the
    Nek, 7 August 1915'*, pencil on paper, 25.8 x 36.8 cm,
    AWM ART11391.308.

27 Notes prepared by C.E.W. Bean for George Lambert
    in ML MSS 97/8, Item 9 frame 0543.

28 See Burness, *The Nek*, p. 96; Bean, *Gallipoli Mission*,
    p. 110.

29 *Sydney Guardian*, 26 November 1930, p. 8.

30 George Lambert, letter to C.E.W. Bean, c. 1924,
    AWM38 3DRL 6673 Part 303.

31 Figures from *The Daily Telegraph*, Sydney,
    22 August 1925.

32 This is the steel lifeboat from HMT *Ascot* (A33) used
    in the landings at Gallipoli by the 13th Battalion, AIF,
    RELAWM05086.001.

Chapter 14

A note on sources:

For much of the material on which the section on the
British naval mission and the German military and naval
missions is based, I have drawn on the Oxford doctoral
thesis 'Emulous Missions' by Charles Verner Reed (which
I supervised in the early 1990s). I have also used Jehuda L.
Wallach's *Anatomie einer Militärhilfe: die preussisch-deutschen
Militärmissionen in der Türkei 1835–1919*, Droste Verlag,
1976, in this section.

For the section on the land defence of the Gallipoli
peninsula, I have drawn on Reed and Wallach (cited above),
and *Der Kampf um die Dardanellen 1915* by Major Dr Carl
Mühlmann, vol. 16 in the series *Schlachten des Weltkrieges*,
produced by the Reichsarchiv, Berlin, and published by
Gerhard Stalling, 1927. I have also drawn on Otto Liman
von Sanders *Fünf Jahre in der Türkei*, Berlin 1920, and Hans

Kannengiesser Pascha, *Gallipoli, Bedeutung und Verlauf der
Kämpfe 1915*, Schlieffen Verlag, Berlin, 1927.

For material on Mustafa Kemal Atatürk, I have drawn
on Andrew Mango, *Atatürk*, John Murray, London, 2004.
For other material on the Turkish side of the conflict I have
used Kevin Fewster, Vecihi Başarın and Hatice Hürmüz
Başarın, *A Turkish View of Gallipoli: Çanakkale*, Hodja,
Melbourne, 1985.

And for much else I have drawn on the huge array of
excellent material available on the Dardanelles campaign
and its context, in the report of the Royal Commission on
the Dardanelles, Randolph Churchill's and Martin Gilbert's
biography of Winston Churchill, and the accompanying
volumes of papers, and the works of Charles Bean, Robert
Rhodes James, Ulrich Trumpener, Marian Kent and many
others. It has been a particular pleasure in the course
of preparing this chapter to have studied Robin Prior's
excellent book *Gallipoli: the End of the Myth*, Yale University,
Press, New Haven, CT, 2009, which, I am sure, will become
the standard one-volume work on the campaign.

1 The Turkish vessels were the super-dreadnoughts
   Reshadieh (23,000 tons, armed with ten 13.5-inch
   guns), renamed *Erin* when Churchill requisitioned it
   for the Royal Navy in August 1914; and the *Sultan
   Osman I* (originally ordered by Brazil in 1911 and
   launched unfinished in January 1913 as *Rio de Janeiro*,
   displacing 28,000 tons and armed with fourteen
   12-inch guns), renamed *Agincourt* when it too joined
   the Royal Navy.

2 General Liman von Sanders is incorrectly referred
   to as 'General von Sanders' in most histories; he
   should be properly referred to as General von Liman.
   Robert O'Neill, 'For want of critics . . . the tragedy of
   Gallipoli', Martin Gilbert (introd.), *The Straits of War:
   Gallipoli Remembered*, Sutton Publishing, Stroud, 2000,
   p. 67.

The published literature on the Gallipoli campaign is voluminous. The initial wave of publications began with first-hand accounts by soldiers, diplomats and war correspondents while the war was still underway. It soon expanded into a 'battle of the memoirs' as major political figures and senior military commanders published their own accounts to vindicate their actions and preserve their versions of events for posterity. These emerged in English, German, Turkish and French language publications. The controversies and disputes between key participants were fanned by the publication of the first significant histories of the campaign in the 1920s. For insights into some of the most influential of these, see the following:

Green, Andrew, *Writing the Great War: Sir James Edmonds and the Official Histories 1915–1948*, Frank Cass, London, 2003, especially chs 5, 6

Macleod, Jenny, *Reconsidering Gallipoli*, Manchester University Press, Manchester, 2004

Prior, Robin, *Churchill's 'World Crisis' as History*, Croom Helm, London, 1983, especially chs 6–10

For summaries of the extensive literature on Gallipoli, the following historiographical surveys are useful:

'Gallipoli: Continuing historical controversy', in Robertson, John, *Anzac and Empire: The Tragedy and Glory of Gallipoli*, Hamlyn, Port Melbourne, 1990, appendix, pp. 268–76

Spiers, Edward, 'Gallipoli', in Bond, Brian (ed.), *The First World War and British Military History*, Oxford University Press, Oxford, 1991, pp. 165–88

The following is a selective listing, arranged by subject and nation, of some of the most important and accessible books and articles, as well as some valuable, more recent works.

General histories of the Gallipoli campaign

Broadbent, Harvey, *Gallipoli: The Fatal Shore*, Viking, Melbourne, 2005

Bush, Captain Eric Wheeler, *Gallipoli*, George Allen & Unwin, London, 1975

Carlyon, Les, *Gallipoli*, Pan Macmillan, Sydney, 2001

Hickey, Michael, *Gallipoli*, John Murray, London, 1995

James, Robert Rhodes, *Gallipoli*, Pimlico, Random House, London, 1999 (first published 1965)

Liddle, Peter, *Men of Gallipoli: The Dardanelles and Gallipoli Experience, August 1914 to January 1916*, Allen Lane, London, 1976

Moorehead, Alan, *Gallipoli*, Macmillan, Melbourne, 1989 (first published London, 1956)

North, John, *Gallipoli: The Fading Vision*, Faber & Faber, London, 1966 (first published 1936)

Prior, Robin, *Gallipoli: The End of the Myth*, Yale University Press and University of New South Wales Press, 2009

Robertson, John, *Anzac and Empire: The Tragedy and Glory of Gallipoli*, Hamlyn, Port Melbourne, 1990

Steel, Nigel, and Hart, Peter, *Defeat at Gallipoli*, Macmillan, London, 1994

Travers, Tim, *Gallipoli 1915*, Tempus, Stroud, Gloucestershire, 2001

Studies of particular aspects of the Gallipoli campaign

Çelik, Kenan, and Koç, Cehan (eds), *The Gallipoli Campaign: International Perspectives 85 Years On*, Atatürk and Gallipoli Campaign Research Center, Çanakkale Onsekiz Mart University, Çanakkale, Turkey, 2002

Chasseaud, Peter, and Doyle, Peter, *Grasping Gallipoli: Terrain, maps and failure at the Dardanelles, 1915*, Spellmount, Staplehurst, Kent, 2005

Fewster, Kevin, 'Ellis Ashmead Bartlett and the making of the Anzac legend', *Journal of Australian Studies*, No. 10 (June 1982), pp. 17–30

Hill, J.G., 'The Dardanelles campaign: lost opportunities: an allied perspective', in *Canakkale Savaslari, SebepVe Sonuclari Uluslararasi Sempozyumu* ('International symposium on the 75th anniversary of the Dardanelles campaign, March 1990'), Turk Tari Kurumu Basimevi, Ankara, 1993, pp. 165–76

Liddle, P.H., 'The distinctive nature of the Gallipoli experience', *Journal of the Royal United Service Institute*, Vol. 122, No. 2 (June 1977), pp. 51–6

Macleod, Jenny (ed.), *Gallipoli: Making History*, Frank Cass, London, 2004

O'Neill, Robert, 'For want of critics . . . the tragedy of Gallipoli', in Gilbert, Martin (introd.), *The Straits of War: Gallipoli Remembered*, Stroud, Gloucestershire, 2000, ch 6, pp. 65–81.

Pedersen, P.A., *Images of Gallipoli: Photographs from the collection of Ross J. Bastiaan*, Oxford University Press, 1988

Prior, Robin, 'The Suvla Bay tea-party: a reassessment', *Journal of the Australian War Memorial*, No. 7 (October 1985), pp. 25–34

Roberts, Chris, 'The landing at Anzac: a reassessment', *Journal of the Australian War Memorial*, No. 22 (October 1993), pp. 25–34

Thomson, Alistair, '"The vilest libel of the war"? Imperial politics and the official histories of Gallipoli', *Australian Historical Studies*, Vol. 25, No. 101 (October 1993), pp. 628–36

Travers, T.H.E., 'Command and leadership styles in the British army: The 1915 Gallipoli model', *Journal of Contemporary History*, Vol. 29 (1994), pp. 403–442

Winter, Denis, 'The Anzac landing—the great gamble?', *Journal of the Australian War Memorial*, No. 4 (April 1984), pp. 13–21

Winter, Denis, *25 April 1915: The Inevitable Tragedy*, University of Queensland Press, St Lucia, 1994

Australia

Bean, C.E.W., *The Story of Anzac: From the outbreak of war to the end of the first phase of the Gallipli campaign, May 4, 1915*, Vol. 1, *The Official History of Australia in the War of 1914–1918*, 12 Vols, Angus & Robertson, Sydney, 1921

Bean, C.E.W., *The Story of Anzac: From 4 May, 1915, to the evacuation of the Gallipoli Peninsula*, Vol. 2, *The Official History of Australia in the War of 1914–1918*, Angus & Robertson, Sydney, 1924

Bean, C.E.W., *Anzac to Amiens*, Australian War Memorial, Canberra, 1946. Digitised versions of this volume and the volumes of the official history are available to read online on the Australian War Memorial website at: http://www.awm.gov.au/histories/volume.asp?conflict=1

Bean, C.E.W., *Gallipoli Mission*, Australian War Memorial, Canberra, 1948, reprinted by ABC Enterprises in association with the Australian War Memorial, Sydney, 1990

Burness, Peter, *The Nek: The Tragic Charge of the Light Horse at Gallipoli*, Kangaroo Press, Kenthurst NSW, 1996; second edition by Exisle Publishing, Auckland, 2012

Butler, A.G., *The Gallipoli Campaign*, Vol. 1, Part 1, *The Official History of the Australian Army Medical Services in the War of 1914–1918*, Australian War Memorial, Melbourne, 1938

Denton, Kit, *Gallipoli Illustrated*, Rigby, Adelaide, 1981; reissued as *Gallipoli: One Long Grave*, Time-Life, Sydney, 1986

Fewster, Kevin (ed.), *Gallipoli Correspondent: The frontline diary of C.E.W. Bean*, George Allen & Unwin, Sydney, 1983; reissued as *Frontline Gallipoli: C.E.W. Bean diaries*

from the trenches, Allen & Unwin, Sydney, 1990; reissued with an updated introduction, as *Bean's Gallipoli: The diaries of Australia's official war correspondent*, Allen & Unwin, Sydney, 2007

Gammage, Bill, *The Broken Years: Australian Soldiers in the Great War*, Penguin, Harmondsworth, 1975; reissued as an illustrated edition by Penguin in 1990; large format illustrated edition by Melbourne University Publishing in 2010

Gooding, Janda, *Gallipoli Revisited: In the footsteps of Charles Bean and the Australian Historical Mission*, Hardie Grant, Sydney, 2009

Hill, A.J., *Chauvel of the Light Horse: A Biography of General Sir Harry Chauvel*, Melbourne University Press, 1978, ch 5

Inglis, K.S., 'The Australians at Gallipoli', 2 parts, *Historical Studies*, Vol. 14, No. 54 (April 1970), pp. 219–30; Vol. 14, No. 55 (October 1970), pp. 361–75

Pedersen, P.A., *Monash as Military Commander*, Melbourne University Press, Melbourne, 1985, especially chs 4, 5

Robertson, John, *Anzac and Empire: The Tragedy & Glory of Gallipoli*, Hamlyn, Port Melbourne, 1990

Serle, Geoffrey, *John Monash: A Biography*, Melbourne University Press, Melbourne, 1982, especially ch 8

Britain

Ashmead-Bartlett, Ellis, *The Uncensored Dardanelles*, Hutchinson, London, 1928

Aspinall-Oglander, Brigadier General C.F., *Military Operations: Gallipoli*, 2 vols, *History of the Great War based on official documents by direction of the Historical Section of the Committee of Imperial Defence*, William Heinemann, London, 1929, 1932

Callwell, Major-General Sir C.E., *The Dardanelles*, Constable, London, 1924

Churchill, Winston S., *The World Crisis 1911–1918*, 2 vols, abridged and revised edition, first published in single volume, 1931, reprinted by New English Library, Mentor, London, 1968 (originally published in 3 vols, 1923–1927)

French, David, *British Strategy and War Aims 1914–1916*, Allen & Unwin, 1986

Hamilton, General Sir Ian, *Gallipoli Diary*, 2 vols., Edward Arnold, London, 1920

Lee, John, *A Soldier's Life: General Sir Ian Hamilton 1853–1947*, Macmillan, London, 2000

Penn, Geoffrey, *Fisher, Churchill and The Dardanelles*, Leo Cooper, Barnsley, Yorkshire, 1999

Strachan, Hew, *The First World War*, Vol. I, *To Arms*, Oxford University Press, Oxford, 2001, especially chs 8, 9

France

Andrew, Christopher M., and Kanya-Forstner, A.S., *France Overseas: The Great War and the Climax of French Imperial Expansion*, Thames and Hudson, London, 1981

d'Andurain, J., *Le General Gouraud et la Grande Guerre (1914–1919)*, PhD thesis, Paris IV Sorbonne, 2010

Cassar, George H., *The French and the Dardanelles*, London, George Allen & Unwin, 1971

Chabanier, Colonel J., 'Avec les combattants de 1915 dans la presqu'île de Gallipoli', *Revue Historique de l'Armée*, Vol. 21, No. 2 (1965), pp. 49–56

Charles-Roux, Fr., *L'expédition des Dardanelles au jour le jour*, A. Colin, Paris, 1920

Delage, E., *La Tragédie des Dardanelles*, Grasset, Paris, 1931

Collectif, *Dardanelles, Orient, Levant, 1915–1920: Ce que les combatants on técrit*, ANSDFO, L'Harmattan, Paris, 2005

Desmazes, Commandant, 'Les Débarquementsalliés aux Dardanelles, 1915', *Revue militaire française* Vol. 21 (1926): March, pp. 356–84; April, pp. 57–83; May, pp. 183–207; June, pp. 318–29; July, pp. 5–18

Doughty, Robert A., *Pyrrhic Victory: French Strategy and Operations in the Great War*, Cambridge, MA, The Belknap Press of Harvard University Press, 2005

Facon, P., *Soldats Français de l'Armée d'Orient, 1915–1919: Recherches sur le moral et approche des mentalities*, PhD thesis, 1978

Fogarty, Richard S., *Race and War in France: Colonial Subjects in the French Army, 1914–1918*, Johns Hopkins University Press, Baltimore, 2008

Greenhalgh, Elizabeth, *Victory through Coalition: Britain and France during the First World War*, Cambridge, Cambridge University Press, 2005

Les Armées Françaises dans la Grande Guerre, French official history of the Great War, 103 vols, Paris, Imprimerie Nationale, 1922–38, tome 8, vol. 1

Mordal, Jacques, 'L'Expédition des Dardanelles 5 Novembre 1915–9 Janvier 1916', *Revue Historique de l'Armée*, Vol. 21, No. 2 (1965), pp. 27–48

Saint-Ramond Roussanne, F., *La campagne d'Orient, 1915–1918: Dardanelles, Macédoine*, PhD thesis, 1997, Atelier de reproduction des thèses, 2001

Germany

Der Weltkrieg 1914–1918: Die militärischen Operationen zu Lande, German official history of the Great War, Bearbeitetim Reichsarchiv, 14 vols., Berlin 1925–1944 (Vols. 13–14, new edition, Koblenz 1956), especially Vol. 9, pp. 164–92; Vol. 10, pp. 603–16

Kannengiesser, Hans, *Gallipoli, Bedeutung und Verlauf der Kämpfe 1915*, Schlieffen Verlag, Berlin, 1927; English edition, *The Campaign in Gallipoli*, Hutchinson, London, 1938

Mühlmann, Carl, *Der Kampf um die Dardanellen 1915*, Vol. 16 in the series *Schlachten des Weltkrieges in Einzeldarstellungen*, Reichsarchiv, Berlin, and published by Gerhard Stalling, Berlin, 1927

Mühlmann, Carl, *Oberste Heeresleitung und Balkan im Weltkrieg 1914–1918*, Berlin 1942

Wallach, Jehuda L., *Anatomieeiner Militärhilfe. Die Preußisch-Deutschen Militärmissionen in der Türkei 1835–1919*, Düsseldorf 1976

Wolf, Klaus, *Gallipoli 1915: Das Deutsche-Türkische Militärbündnisim Ersten Weltkrieg*, Sulzbach/Ts. and Bonn, 2008

Von Sanders, Otto Liman, *FünfJahre in der Türkei*, Berlin, 1919; English edition, *Five Years in Turkey*, Baillière, Tindall& Cox, 1927)

India

Anon., *History of the 5th Royal Gurkha Rifles (Frontier Force) 1858 to 1928*, Aldershot, Gale and Polden, n.d.

Ellinwood, De Witt C., and Pradhan, S.D., *India and World War 1*, Manohar, New Delhi, 1978

Farwell, Byron, *The Armies of the Raj: From the Mutiny to Independence, 1858–1947*, Norton, New York, 1989

Government of India, *India's Contribution to the Great War*, Calcutta, 1923

Lucas, Sir Charles (ed.), *The Empire at War. Edited for the Royal Colonial Institute*, 5 vols., Humphrey Milford, Oxford University Press, London, 1921–1926, Vol. 5, Part IV, 'India', by Sir Francis Younghusband, ch VI, pp. 242–60

Mullaly, Colonel B.R., *Bugle and Kukri: The Story of the 10th Princess Mary's Own Gurkha Rifles*, Vol. 1, Naval & Military Press, London, 1993

Talbot, Colonel P.E.G., *The 14th King George's Own Sikhs 1846–1933*, Royal United Service Institution, London, 1937

Naval aspects of the Dardanelles campaign

Corbett, Sir Julian S., *Naval Operations*, Vols. 2, 3, *History of the Great War based on official documents by direction of the Historical Section of the Committee of Imperial Defence*, Longmans, Green and Co., London, 1921, 1923

Denham, H.M., *Dardanelles: A Midshipman's Diary 1915–16*, John Murray, London, 1981

Frame, Tom, *The Shores of Gallipoli: Naval Dimensions of the Anzac Campaign*, Hale & Iremonger, Alexandria, NSW, 2000

Hough, Richard, *The Great War at Sea 1914–1918*, Oxford University Press, Oxford, 1986

Keyes, Sir Roger, *The Naval Memoirs of Admiral of the Fleet Sir Roger Keyes: The Narrow Seas to the Dardanelles 1910–1915*, Thornton Butterworth, London, 1934

Marder, Arthur J., *From the Dreadnought to Scapa Flow: The Royal Navy in the Fisher Era, 1904-1919*, Vol. 2, Oxford University Press, London, 1965

Massie, Robert K., *Castles of Steel: Britain, Germany, and the Winning of the Great War at Sea*, Jonathan Cape, London, 2004, chs 23–26

Penn, Geoffrey, *Fisher, Churchill and The Dardanelles*, Leo Cooper, Barnsley, Yorkshire, 1999

Stevens, D.M., 'Naval Support at Gallipoli', *Australian Defence Force Journal*, No. 117 (March/April 1996), pp. 57–63

New Zealand

Crawford, John (ed.), *No Better Death: The Great War Diaries and Letters of William G. Malone*, Reed, Auckland, 2005

Harper, Glyn (ed.), *Letters from Gallipoli: New Zealand soldiers write home*, Auckland University Press, Auckland, 2011

Malthus, Cecil, *Anzac: A Retrospect*, Whitcombe & Tombs, Christchurch, 1965

Pugsley, Christopher, *Gallipoli: The New Zealand Story*, Hodder and Stoughton, Auckland, 1984

Waite, Major Fred, *The New Zealanders at Gallipoli*, Whitcombe and Tombs, Auckland, 1919

Wilkie, Major A.H., *Official War History of the Wellington Mounted Rifles Regiment, 1914-1919*, Whitcombe and Tombs, Auckland, 1924

Turkey

Anon., 'The Turkish General Staff History of the Campaign in Gallipoli', an analysis in two parts, *The Army Quarterly*, Part I, Vol. XI, No. 2 (January 1926), pp. 343–53; Part II, Vol. XII, No. 1 (April 1926), pp. 88–95

Arda, Ahmet 'Extracts from the Diary of a Turkish Officer' (Colonel Izzettin Calislar, Mustafa Kemal's chief of staff), [Australian] *Defence Force Journal*, No. 81 (March/April, 1990), pp. 83–98.

Atatürk, Mustafa Kemal, *Complete Works*, Vol. 1, Kaynak Yayinlari, Istanbul, 1999

Belen, Fahri, *2 Onci Yüzyılda Osmanlı Devleti Tarihi* ('Ottoman History in the 20th Century'), Remzi Kitapevi, Istanbul, 1973

Belen, Fahri, *Çanakkale Savaşı'ndan Alınan Dersler* ('Lessons learned from the Gallipoli Campaign'), Yeditepe Yayınevi, Istanbul, 2009

Çanakkale Savaslari, SebepVe Socuçlari Uluslararasi Sempozyumu ('The Gallipoli Campaign: Cause and Conclusion, International Symposium'), Çanakkale, 14–17 March 1990, Turkish History Society Printing House, Ankara, 1993

Cemil Conk, *Çanakkale Savaşlari*, Arma Yayinlari, Istanbul, 2002

Danisman, H.B., *Day One Plus . . .* Gallipoli 1915 27th Ottoman Inf. Regt. *vs ANZAC's* (based on the personal account of Lieutenant Colonel Sekif Aker, Commander of the Turkish 27th Infantry Regiment), Denizler Kitabevi, Istanbul, 2007

Erickson, Edward J., *Ordered to Die: A History of the Ottoman Army in the First World War*, Greenwood, Westport, CT, 2001

Erickson, Edward, *Gallipoli, The Ottoman Campaign*, Pen and Sword Books, Barnsley, UK, 2010

Esat Pasha, *Memoirs*, Örgün Yayinevi, Istanbul. 2003

Fahrettin, Altay, *10 Yilve Sonrasi*, Eylem Yayinlari, Ankara, 2008

Fasih, Mehmed Bey (translated from Arabic script and edited by Murat Çulcu), *Kanlisirt Günlügü* ('Bloody Ridge Diary'), Arba Yayinlari, Istanbul, 1997; English edition, *Lone Pine (Bloody Ridge) Diary of Lt. Mehmed Fasih, 5th Imperial Ottoman Army, Gallipoli, 1915*, translated and prepared for publication by Hasan Basri Danisman, Denizler Kitabevi, Istanbul, 2001; second illustrated edition, Istanbul, 2003

Fewster, Kevin, Basarin, Vecihi, and Basarin, Hatice Hürmüz, *A Turkish View of Gallipoli: Çanakkale*, Hodja Educational Resources Co-operative, Richmond Vic, n.d., c.1985; reissued as *Gallipoli: The Turkish Story*, Allen & Unwin, Sydney, 2003

Inönü, Ismet, *Memoirs*, Bilgi Yayınevi, Ankara, 2006

Kinross, Patrick, *Atatürk: The Rebirth of a Nation*, Phoenix, London, 1996 (first published 1964), especially chs 11, 12

Köroğlu, E., *Ottoman Propaganda and Turkish Identity: Literature in Turkey During World War I*, I.B. Tauris, New York, 2007

Mango, Andrew, *Atatürk*, John Murray, London, 1999

Oral, Haluk, *Gallipoli 1915: Through Turkish Eyes*, translated by Amy Spangler, editor, Bill Sellars, Türkiye Is Bankasi Kültür Yayinlari, Istanbul, 2007

Özdemir, Hikmet, *The Ottoman Army 1914–1918: Disease and Death on the Battlefield*, translated by Saban Kardas, University of Utah Press, Salt Lake City, 2008

T.C. Genel Kurmay Baskanligi ('Turkish General Staff official history'), Çanakkale *Cephesi Harekati* ('Gallipoli front operations'), 3 vols, *Birinci Dunya Harbi'nde Turk Harbi* ('Turkish War during the First World War'), *Genelkurmay Basimevi* ('General Staff Printing House'), Ankara, 1978, 1980, 1993

Turkish General Staff, *A Brief History of the Çanakkale Campaign in the First World War (June 1914–January 1916)*, Turkish General Staff Printing House, Ankara, 2004

Index